Praise for *Some Day: Insid*
Fanning's 2007 Championship

Swanton's account bears not the slightest resemblance to the footage of Kerr's wave. But the crucial thing was, for those of us who are not Josh Kerr, Swanton's version was better. It will stick in my mind longer, thanks to the vividness of the hyperbole. Like the fishing story or the war story or the explorer's story, the surfing story grows bigger in the telling. It is a shaggy-dog story. How best to write about surfing? Not in trying to accurately limn the experience, but in lying about it, glossing it, misting it over as epic and legendary, turning Josh Kerr's half-second into a mountaineer's odyssey. – *The Monthly*

Will Swanton isn't just a gun writer for Sydney's *Sun-Herald* (and occasionally this title), he's also a self-confessed surfing nut who spent every spare moment (and more than a few others) following the tour last year. For anyone jealous of the lifestyles of these top pro surfers, travelling from exotic surf break to exotic surf break (only interrupting their busy schedules to travel to other exotic surf breaks to shoot videos), this book won't help. Swanton's produced a jumping, dramatic, insightful account of the year's events, presenting intimate insights into the pros' personalities and pressures. – *Inside Sport*

The author, Will Swanton, is a journalist who is so close to these guys you feel it has been written by them. The language and style of writing are quite extraordinary—almost poetic at times, but also as crude as some of the conversations he relays. This is sports writing at its absolute best: powerful, immediate, unexpected, funny and totally absorbing. – *The Manly Daily*

I've never been interested in surfing. That's what made Will Swanton's book about a world championship surfing tour of 2007 such a surprise. I found myself captivated by the story. It was clearly a story Swanton not only wanted to tell, but one he wanted others to discover. It is a strong and revealing read. Every now and then, it's good to get into a world that you know little, if anything, of and find the blood and muscle that makes it move. Swanton's book does that. If you let yourself into the narrative, Swanton's easy style will bring its reward. His bold and honest journalism brings to life a great Australian sports story. – *The Walkley Magazine*

Will Swanton received the 2008 Australian Sports Commission award for best contribution to the coverage of sport by an individual. He is the author of *Some Day: Inside The Dream Tour and Mick Fanning's 2007 World Championship Win*. This book is written for loved ones.

MURDERBALL

Head to head with Australia's toughest team

WILL SWANTON

First published in 2009

Allen & Unwin
83 Alexander Street
Crows Nest NSW 2065
Australia

Phone:	(61 2) 8425 0100
Fax:	(61 2) 9906 2218
Email:	info@allenandunwin.com
Web:	www.allenandunwin.com

Cataloguing-in-Publication details are available from the National Library of Australia
www.librariesaustralia.nla.gov.au

ISBN 978 1 74175 676 0

Set in 11.5/15 pt Fairfield Light by Bookhouse, Sydney
Printed and bound in Australia by Griffin Press

10 9 8 7 6 5 4 3 2 1

Contents

People tell us we look really happy. I don't always understand why they say that. I kind of know what they mean, but I don't see why people would think we're not going to be happy. What do they expect us to be? What do they expect us to do? Are we supposed to hide away and live our lives in shame and be too embarrassed to do anything? I'm really, really happy with my life. Why wouldn't I be? I've got no legs. Who cares? We're all in wheelchairs. So what? Some of us had problems when we were born. Some of us broke our necks doing the simplest things. Some of us had accidents when it wasn't our fault. They're amazing stories and they're amazing people in our team. I'm lucky to know them. You only get one life and we're living it to the fullest. Why wouldn't anyone want to do that? I look at some people and I'm thinking, What are you waiting for?

Ryley Batt

Part I

IN THE BEGINNING

1

The Rock

SHIT CREEK, 8 AUGUST 1993: The arrival of Brad Dubberley in the least attractive of all the creeks has more to do with him being in it rather than up it, and if we're going to paint a perfectly accurate picture here of the harrowing predicament now facing a previously robust twelve-year-old smart-arse, the kid should be seen as laying face-first in the muddied waters of Shit Creek as a torrent of bloodied water gushes over the severed skin still trying valiantly to remain attached to his battered skull. Dubberley suspects his best course of action at this point is to get the fuck up, quite the idea, but there has been a development: He cannot move a God-forsaken muscle.

'I thought I may as well just lie there,' he says now, dunking you in the impression he was largely unperturbed by the grim reaper shuffling towards him with his ugly blank face, shuffling and whispering with their ugly blank faces and blatant disregard for the imminent tragedy of the death of a child. But with all due respect to a self-described cripple who has just turned up late for your first meeting with the wholly unexpected excuse of 'Sorry, mate, they just had to do some panel-beating on my head', you're here to suggest the whole I-thought-I-may-as-well-just-lie-there routine is a mushroom cloud of bullshit because surely no-one is capable of such overwhelming calm right when they realise they're on their way to whatever comes next. Unless that's when there is nothing but calm.

Dubberley's memories of this day are vivid. Black and white photographs taken without his permission. The raw sting of acidic water spearing through his eyes. *Snap.* The disbelief at being one missed heartbeat away from dying in what amounted to little more than a puddle. *Snap.* Such a piss-weak and unthreatening body of water, teasing him and mocking him in the after-wash of his own lame fall. *Snap.* The incredulity upon realising that no matter how desperately the millions and billions and trillions of interconnected neurones in his distinctly unparalysed brain were howling at his arms and legs to get a wriggle on, they were capable of doing no such thing. *Snap.* He remembers the putrid sickness in the pit of his stomach at being so hopelessly unable to provide his lungs with what they were presently screaming out for—blessed oxygen. And he remembers the thought, just a thought, that Shit Creek would be no place for a boy to die.

Help me.

Please.

They're the most desperate words of all.

There was the harmless walk on a frigid Victorian morning with two mates who saved his life but have since vanished clean off the face of his Earth. The bush track and that's all it is, you know, just an unremarkable bush track, nothing that could ordinarily be described as a killing machine. There was the freedom of it all, being so young and energetic and running wild outside, the football game coming up that afternoon, life, growing up, getting bigger, getting smarter, embracing everything and everyone, the perpetual bliss of living like this. But then came the slip, just one slip in one millisecond of a lifetime, the 50-metre tumble, the silent repeating of the most desperate words of all and then the arrival in his path of the merciless rock; the big old ugly rock that remains in Shit Creek to this day without offering so much as an apology. Brad Dubberley remembers the wailing sirens of the ambulances and the whirring blades of the emergency helicopter and the hurried marching footsteps that stopped at his side and the rat-a-tat-tat machine-gun talk of his frazzled mates and family. He remembers being wrapped in the aluminium foil and the scream of hypothermia and the stretcher that took him into the helicopter and this other life. He remembers thinking, 'Funny, but I can't feel my legs.'

Snap.

Dubberley can still see the looks on the faces of his mother, father and bawling younger brothers because no matter how hard people try to mask their feelings, they never really can. He could read the lines on the faces of his mother, father and bawling younger brothers and when he put them all on the same page they read HEARTACHE. Dubberley remembers these looks because you never forget the things that haunt you as a child. The things harnessing enough power to keep you awake at night before you hide them in the basement with every other fear and loathing; the things that trigger nightmares of enough force to make you sit bolt upright in bed whenever they escape their chains and come out to play in adulthood; the things that forever burn a hole in your brain. Dubberley recalls all this and shakes his head because the day he landed in Shit Creek was the day he should have died. There are few more unflappable, honest and magnificently free-spirited people in this world than Bradley Wayne Dubberley, but right here and now, re-telling and re-living the most horrific moment of his life, the blood drains from his face and he shivers. Someone just stepped on his grave.

2

The Game I

Officially, it's wheelchair rugby. Bullshit to that. In the US, it's Quad Rugby. Bullshit to that, too. It shall be called neither on this watch. This is murderball. This is smash-up man carnage based on the age-old sporting principle of spotting the man with the ball, moving in like a pack of street hoods and killing him. Who cares if he's a quadriplegic? Kill him. Who cares if he's already suffered enough physical and mental torment for one lifetime? Kill him. Who cares if he's an amputee, or was born without legs, or arms, or half an arm, or half a leg, or a claw instead of fingers? Kill the fucker. Who cares if there's an unmistakable sadness in his eyes because away from the 32-minute adrenaline rushes derived from this high-voltage metallic warfare, life is an ordeal. Bee-atch needs to be put on his arse. If he has the ball in his lap, hands or tray, if he's so much as *thinking* about getting it, you need to knock him through the floorboards, wheel over to him, stare at his spinning eyes and squawk like vultures over the maggots of a rotting carcass. *Out of the eater, something to eat; out of the strong, something sweet.*

3

Fallen

'I slipped, skidded, fell over and hit the ground hard,' Dubberley says. 'I kept getting back to my feet but going over again. I was trying to stop but I couldn't. I was going too fast. There's an embankment that goes across the creek. I remember thinking, "I'm going to have to try to jump this." I got to the bottom, tried to jump the embankment and—I just remember smashing my head on this rock and falling into the water. I'm thinking, "I can't move. Why can't I move?" I couldn't breathe. My face was straight down in the water. It was winter in Victoria, and it's such cold water that I was frozen, basically. I remember this kind of gargling. My mates had never done any first aid so I don't know why they did this, but when they got to me they kept my neck and body in a straight line when they turned me over. If they'd twisted my neck or turned my face out of the water, it would have severed my spinal cord. That would have completely done me over. I've thought about this a lot. If I was them, I would have run down, picked me up and thrown me out of the water to get me breathing again. If I was them, I would have grabbed the head and twisted it without even thinking about the neck or the spinal cord or anything like that. If they had done that, it probably would have killed me. But they didn't. I hope they know what they did. They were calm and did the right thing and saved my life. I got lucky in a few ways, with how they reacted and with the water being so cold, it was like putting ice on the injury. I was really pretty lucky.'

Blessed.

Dubberley has lost contact with the friends who did more good than they know. Their names are Nathan Chrystal and Matthew van der Veer. Chrystal's father, John, was the first outsider on the scene, and when he arrived, Dubberley was on his back with his head resting on the rock like it was a pillow, the thing that nearly killed him now trying to cradle him. Altogether too late for that. Chrystal and van der Veer are the ghosts who were there when the bad thing happened, sweeping down the muddied hill and into Shit Creek to rescue their mate before going up in plumes of unwanted smoke. Dubberley regrets their departure from his life. 'I can't work out if it's because they don't want to be reminded of what happened, or if they think it was their fault, which it clearly wasn't,' he says. 'It's not like they pushed me down the hill. They didn't hit me over the head with the rock. I honestly believe they saved my life. Maybe they think I'm in a wheelchair because they did the wrong thing. If they think that, they're wrong. Why didn't they just throw me out of the water? They were so calm. One of them rolled me over really gently, keeping my neck and my body level. I can't even tell you which one stayed and which one went for help. Nathan lived across the road, so he must have gone. His old man came across with a blanket and held me in his arms until the ambulances and fire brigades came. I remember being numb and feeling like the situation was completely out of my control. It felt like nothing was in my hands.'

Dubberley's C5, C6 and C7 vertebrae were dislocated. His spinal cord was cut and bleeding. 'The ambulance got there and they asked me where my parents were,' he says. 'I told them Dad was probably at work. I gave them his number, but he wasn't at work, he was watching my brothers play basketball. The number they called, my uncle answered the phone. They told him there had been an accident. He went to get Dad but he didn't tell him everything because he didn't want to stress him out. I think he might have just told him I had a broken leg, something like that. He told Dad to get up to the creek.'

Phillip Dubberley walked into the black and white photograph to be confronted by the most harrowing scene imaginable—a child, *his* child, immobilised on a stretcher. His child was immobilised on a stretcher. 'Mum and Dad and my brothers came and the foil was getting my temperature up—and that's when I started thinking, "Shouldn't I be able to feel my legs by now?"' Dubberley says. 'I thought it must have been the cold or the shock. You're twelve and you think there has to be a reason that isn't going to be too bad. You're too young to properly understand. You get hurt and you think you just have to wait a while and your body will fix itself pretty quickly. I didn't know what a quadriplegic was. I didn't know anything about the spinal cord. I thought I'd broken a few bones, something like that. They put me in a helicopter and took me to hospital in Melbourne. Dad was in the helicopter with me. Mum had to drive up. I guess they both had an idea what was wrong by then. They didn't say anything but I could kind of see from the way they were looking at me that there might be a pretty big problem.'

Van der Veer was blond with a bowl haircut. Chrystal was taller with neat brown hair. *The Ballarat News* ran stories accompanied by photos in which the haunted van der Veer never smiles. Chrystal manages an unconvincing grin when his father is by his side. The report stated: 'A twelve-year-old Ballarat boy was airlifted to the Austin Hopsital with severe spinal injuries after he fell down a steep hill and creek embankment . . . Brad Dubberley, of Nelson Street, was playing with two friends on a steep hillside behind Progress Park, Brown Hill, about 11.30 a.m. when he slipped on wet ground . . . rolled across a dirt track and then fell down a four metre vertical drop into Yarrowee Creek, landing on a large rock . . . breaking his neck in three places and causing bruising, bleeding and swelling in the spinal area. Unable to move, Bradley had taken his last breath and was choking on the water. One of the injured boy's friends, Matthew van der Veer, twelve, raced for help while the other, Nathan Chrystal, eleven, went to his aid. Chrystal says: "I knew he was hurt so I came flying down. He was sort of talking funny, really slow."'

It was half an hour before the paramedics arrived. By then, John Chrystal also had hypothermia. Dubberley was taken to Ballarat Base Hospital. He was immediately transferred to a terrifyingly confronting place called Austin Hospital, where a single blue door has the words INTENSIVE CARE UNIT plastered across the top of it and untold terrors inside. The waiting room is full of resolve until another stern-faced doctor comes out to deliver another round of life-altering news. It's impossible to sit in the waiting room of the Austin Hospital without growing old. Phillip Dubberley says of van der Veer and Chrystal, 'Bradley owes them his life.'

Dubberley says: 'Those mates, you know, they were the difference between me being an incomplete quadriplegic and a complete quadriplegic. I'd broken my neck. Any little movement when they got to me would have just about killed me off. We were really good mates. We used to do everything together. We played footy together, played cricket together, spent nearly every day together. I'd just always hung out with them. It's a shame we don't see each other any more. Maybe they think if they see me in a chair, they'll feel uncomfortable about it. Maybe it would make them relive the whole thing. I'm not really sure. It was a long time ago and if they do feel bad about any of it, they shouldn't. They did nothing wrong. Things just happen. I'm not religious or anything, but I do think things happen for a reason. You'll hear this a lot from blokes who have had these sorts of accidents—it can be just as hard, or harder, for the other people involved. Especially the families. I don't think it's in anyone's nature to go out celebrating if they avoid getting hurt while their mates are badly injured. It must have been frightening for them. I really wanted to keep in contact with them, but I just ended up thinking there's no point in trying any more if it was going to make everyone feel uncomfortable. I never thought we would lose contact but that's the way it has gone.'

Dubberley was expected to die before dawn. 'The doctors said I wouldn't see the night through,' he says. 'They thought the hypothermia was going to kill me. I just wanted to wake up the next morning to prove them wrong. Then they said I'd be dead by the end of the week and it was the same deal. I just wanted to get through the week because they said I wouldn't. They were like, "You're never going to walk again." What was I going to do? Take their word for it? I was like, "Fuck you guys, I'm going to prove you wrong." Being so young, you just want to do the things you're told not to do. They'd tell me to pick up a block. I'd slide it to the end of the table. "There you go, you pricks, I've got it." I was too young to realise the point of it was to learn how to pick things up, not get it into your hand by sliding it across the table. I thought I was being clever when I wasn't. It was cheating, but cheating is just finding a way to help yourself out. We're always cheating, I reckon, in all our day-to-day stuff, just working out the easiest way to get shit done.'

There are seven virtues, seven deadly sins, seven fires in Hell, seven stages of grief and seven cervical vertebrae in the human neck. The central nervous system comprises the brain and the spinal cord. The C1 to C7 run along the spinal cord, the 45-cm communication super highway of nerves delivering instructions from the brain to the body of a fully functioning human being. Quadriplegia results from the breaking of a vertebra followed by the shattered bone slicing through the spinal cord like Jonah's Spear. The brain can then howl all the orders it likes to the hands, arms, feet and legs, like get the fuck up you're drowning in Shit Creek, but it's pointless because the telephone line has been slashed by the reaper's knife. The dead cells are unable to rebirth so once the spinal cord is severed, it can never be repaired or replaced. 'It's possible to break your neck without becoming a quadriplegic—if the bone doesn't cut the spinal cord,' Dubberley says. If this fate should ever befall you, if you ever get this ridiculously lucky when only *millimetres* separate mild trauma from a full-blown medical Armageddon, get down on your knees and pray in thanks to whoever you think may have been responsible.

Dubberley's saviours were van der Veer and Chrystal.

Quadriplegia is a loss of movement in all four limbs but not, as per the popular misconception, the loss of *all* function. The C1 is at the top of the neck. The C7 is at the bottom. A slashing of the spinal cord at the C4 or above leads to a lifetime of respirators, 24-hour care, electrical wheelchairs, and in all likelihood, an expedited funeral. Complete quadriplegics, and a smattering of incomplete, including a few of the magnificent bastards to be introduced in these pages, will think they're better off dead. Damage the spinal cord at C3 or above and you won't have to wait long. Dubberley's cord was nicked, bruised, swollen—but not severed. He's incomplete, the right side of his body capable of restricted movement, the left remaining so stunned by the happenings in Shit Creek fifteen years ago that it hasn't moved an inch since. 'It's almost as if I've had a stroke,' he says. 'The hard thing is getting your head around being in a wheelchair because of something that is nothing more than rotten luck,' Dubberley says. 'I went for a walk. That's all I did, go for a walk. Where was the risk in that? People do more stupid things and get away with it every day. Before and after my accident, I've taken more risks and nothing has happened to me. People have lucky escapes every day. All I did was go for a walk with my mates. What bloody risk, you know?'

A stunt motorbike rider in Australia called Robbie Maddison has suffered brain haemorrhages, paralysis, fractured vertebrae, punctured lungs, smashed teeth, seizures, a shoulder torn off the bone and a bottom lip ripped clean off his face. He's had broken legs, toes, ankles, forearms, collarbone and 28 fractured fingers. Maddison says the devil may care. There's no accounting for how he avoids landing in a wheelchair while a twelve-year-old boy goes for a bushwalk and becomes a quadriplegic. 'You know when you go and jump on a motorbike that it can go wrong,' Dubberley says. 'You know you might head-butt the ground and not get up, but that's part of the risk you are obviously willing to take. It's part of the kick you get from making it. That doesn't mean anything bad *should* happen, because it's not like a motorbike rider deserves to have anything go wrong. But if things do go pear-shaped, at least he knows it was part of the bargain. Going for a walk, it—you know what, it doesn't matter. You can sit and sook and take forever to get over it, or you can never get over it, or you can try to get going again. You just move on.'

Piss off with *just move on*.

It's crap, *just move on*. Had your heart ripped to shreds by the person you thought was the love of your life? Suck it up, Romeo. Just move on. Lost a parent before you wanted them to go? That's the nonsensical circle of life, my friend. Just move on. Stuck in a hospital bed in the crucifix position for what feels like an eternity? You'll be right, tiger. Just move on. There is more to dealing with quadriplegia than some idealistic resolution to just move on when the bolts have finally been removed from the halo nailed to your skull, the doctors and nurses have washed their hands of you and it's time for your crippled body to be taken home for the really hard part, the rest of your life. Just move on? How? You cannot move at all. The saddest story you hear is of a suicidal quadriplegic being unable to kill himself because he didn't even have enough function to blow his brains out. Imagine that poor man, sitting there wallowing in his loathsome desire to perform one of the saddest acts you can, knowing how desperately hopeless it is, but still being so physically useless that he couldn't even go ahead and do it.

Dubberley spent 117 days in the spinal unit of the Austin Hospital. He denies being suicidal at any stage. Family members were constantly by his side, touching his arm, hoping beyond hope. He was in head tongs for a week before they attached the misnomer of a halo. The black and white photograph in this book shows the excruciating discomfort of Dubberley while trapped in his skeletal straitjacket. 'I was in a kids' ward instead of a spinal unit,' he says. 'It was good because I wasn't around a lot of other spinal victims. A lot of them smoke and get on the piss, and I was kept away from all that. But at the same time, I didn't have the full-on professional care. I had the kids' ward nurses looking after me instead of the spinal professionals and, yeah, it wasn't easy for a long while. I couldn't do anything. Couldn't eat, nothing. I had to eat through this nasal-gastric thing. I couldn't scratch. I'd be like, "Dad, scratch me, quick." I could see how hard it was for the old man, but he was being strong for me. He was sleeping next to me on one of those little stretcher beds in hospital for a couple of weeks. When someone asks me how hard it was, I think of him and Mum, to be honest, and the rest of my family, more than I think about how hard it was for myself. It's not good for anyone to be injured, but I do think it's almost harder for the people around you. The hospital had little apartments across the road. That's where I ended up, and Dad was there with me for another couple of weeks, sleeping in the room with me because I kept having these nightmares, reliving it every night. Every time I went to sleep, every time I closed my eyes I could see it happening again. Mum and my two brothers were living in Ballarat at the time, they were an hour and a half away from Melbourne, so Mum and Dad were virtually separated for the first month or so. Every week, they'd come to visit me and Dad in hospital. It really was harder for them, I think.

'I was living it, so there was always the next step to concentrate on. I had to go to rehab. I had to do all these things I had no choice in. But Mum and Dad and my brothers, they couldn't actually do anything to help. They all wished it was them, and I would be the same, but all they could do was watch. I was busy trying to get over it, but all they could do was stand around and wait. They must have felt pretty helpless. The weird thing is, if they do help, it almost makes it harder for you. I remember one time having to pick up something off a table. Mum and Dad wanted to pick it up for me. I was like, "How is that helping me? If you're going to pick it up and give it to me, how am I going to learn how to do it?" They're trying to do the right thing, but really they're not doing the right thing at all. You have your moments. It's not what you'd call fun in there.'

Dubberley's halo, the confronting metal brace used for patients with spinal injuries when they're tap, tap, tapping on heaven's door, was nailed to his skull approximately one-eighth of an inch above his eyebrows. 'Dad was there when I had the halo put in,' he says. 'That might have been the hardest thing of all for him to watch. I had my halo for two months. The choices they gave me were surgery, or the halo, and we went for the halo. There was a risk that surgery could stuff it up even more. And because I was so young, I still had a fair bit of growing to do. If you do some surgery at that age, it might not fit in a few years when you grow so you have to go through it all again. They put the halo on, and Dad is sitting there watching a drill get put in his son's head. They put screws through your skull, basically. I doubt that was something he enjoyed too much. No parent would want to see that. Anyone would do it for their kid, stay there to watch it all, but that's what I mean—getting the halo put on was harder for him than it was for me. He had to sit there and watch it.'

A Buddhist fable about a woman called Kisagotami. Her only child is dead. She begs Buddha for a miracle cure. He agrees to provide one but only if she returns to him with a supply of mustard seed from a neighbour's house where no child, spouse, parent or servant has ever died. Where there has never been any kind of grieving. It's impossible, of course, and Kisagotami sees she is not alone in hardship. She agrees to let go of her son because others are in the same boat. But Dubberley has to take the diametrically opposed and more difficult road to Kisagotami in his search for elusive acceptance. None of his neighbours has endured this kind of grieving. He's the odd man from the moment he leaves hospital and all hope of miracle cures is gone. 'That's when you start finding out the truth,' Dubberley says. 'You haven't got the nurse there, you haven't got all that help, you haven't got all these other people around in their wheelchairs. You're back home, and it feels really quiet. And then how are you going to pick that cup up? If you fall out of your chair, how are you going to get back in it? There can't always be someone there for you. It felt really quiet, but then I was like, "Right, let's go."

'Before I could walk again, I could ride a bike. My brothers were out in the backyard riding their bikes and I was like, "Get me on there, I want a go." Mum was like, "You're not going to ride a bike." I'm like, "Yeah I am." I got on and had a ride when Mum went inside. I rode down to the shops with my brothers. She had no idea I went. I couldn't go in the shops because I would have just collapsed if I got off the bike, so I had to stay outside when my brothers were in the shop. We all rode home and Mum never knew we were gone. She'd seen me trying to walk, but I couldn't really do it. When I was in hospital, the doctors were all like, "You're not allowed to walk, don't even try." But fuck 'em, I thought. I started trying to walk beside the bed. I'd shut the curtain so no-one could see, and I'd drag myself up, hanging on to the bed, trying to keep standing up and walking along the bed. I started to take a few steps. They weren't real steps, just this weird kind of shuffling, but I was pretty proud of being able to stand up and move at all. I was like, "Check this out, Dad." None of the nurses knew I was doing it.

'I got out of hospital on the second of December. The fourth of December was Mum's birthday. I walked into her bedroom and put my hands along the wall because that's what Mum had seen me trying to do before. She thought that was all I *could* do. I kept walking into her room, took my hands off the wall, started walking at her without holding myself up and said, "Happy birthday, Mum." She was blubbering. They were my first proper steps.'

~

Now we're in Brad Dubberley's garage. Cricket bats are everywhere. 'Bats are broken,' he says, broken. We're inside Dubberley's house and he's giving us the grand tour. The normal kitchen with the linoleum floor and whistling kettle. The lounge and a sofa chair in front of a plasma widescreen TV the width of a credit card. Televisions get skinnier while inside every living room of every house on every street across every town, city and country on earth, the people watching them get fatter. Dubberley shares the house with his brother Ash and his father, who lives on the Central Coast but stays two nights a week while working in Sydney. At Dubberley's feet is a really small dog called Gypsy. 'Bloody princess,' he says. Five dog beds are strewn about. 'Spoiled rotten, aren't you?' He falls to his knees to pat the really small dog. He offers a formal introduction while telling the really small dog with her pink name tag that she has to be good for the visitor. Bowls filled with sausages are outside the fly-screen door. The really small dog is free to jump on the furniture. If it's true you can accurately sketch a person from the way they treat children, animals and especially really small dogs, the man might have a bit going for him.

As a player, he did more ripping and tearing than Beowulf. At the Sydney Paralympics, where Australia lost the final by one goal to the United States, he proved himself to be the best murderballer in the world, retaining that lofty status until his swift and unexpected retirement in the lead-up to the Beijing Games. Drowning in the additional responsibility of being Australia's assistant coach, and after Australia had been spanked pink at the world championships, finishing fifth or sixth or a hundredth or something equally diabolical, Dubberley hobbled into the offices of The Learned Gentlemen Of The Australian Paralympic Committee to quit the coaching role and concentrate on playing. Half an hour later, his head spinning off its surgically enhanced axis, he had quit as a player and become the head coach.

DUBBERLEY: 'I handed over my resignation letter and said, "Here you go, I just want to play from now on." They said, "Hang on to it. We want you to be the coach, but that means you can't play." I was like, "What?! Oh, man. *What*?!" And then they told me, "We want an answer in half an hour." I had to leave the room, make up my mind and go back and tell them. No kidding, they gave me half an hour. I was like, "Shit. What do I do? I loved playing." Our manager, Kim Ellwood, she was there too, for an interview. I said, "Come here now. I need to speak to you." I told her they wanted me to be the coach and said, "I really don't know what to do." They wanted me to throw away my whole playing career. It was a bit too much to take in. I spoke to Mum and Dad. It was a pretty hectic half hour. Kim said the team would support whatever I did. It was the same deal with Mum and Dad: "Whatever you want to do, we're behind you." They said anything you do, just do it properly and you can't go wrong. I spoke to a girl I was hanging out with at the time. She wasn't my girlfriend, but we were pretty close and I said, "What do you reckon?" She didn't know the ins and outs of rugby like Kim, or Mum and Dad, but she said, "I think if you want to do it, you'd do it really well." I was like, "Right. Thanks for that." No-one could really tell me what to do. There was about five minutes to go and I just looked at Kim and said, "I'm going to do it".'

KIM ELLWOOD: 'They'd called me and Brad in for meetings. I said, "You go first, I'll wait outside." He comes out after half an hour, acting all serious, which isn't normally him. We thought we were going in to evaluate our last coach. He'd been quite sick, and we were worried about him being alright to keep going. We actually had a plan to get a new coach if we needed one. We'd started talking to a guy called Marco about coming in. He's Canada's high performance manager now. We'd been emailing him back and forth, saying we really wanted him as the coach. Brad said he was going to put it to them at this meeting. But then he came out and kept saying, "Kim, I've got to talk to you, I've really got to talk to you." I remember my jaw just dropping. I never would have picked that they wanted him to be coach. I had no idea. He was always assistant coach but that was it. He was our best player and he was still so young. I was speechless. We were outside, trying to discuss all the pros and cons, going through everything. It was all so rushed and I was like, "Just think about yourself". I wasn't entirely sure they had made the right decision. I mean, I supported Brad, but I thought he should still be playing. I kept asking him, "Are you really ready to retire?" He was an amazing player. He was so dominant and I knew how much the team was going to miss him. I kept saying, "Are you sure?" The team was going to do so well at Beijing with him playing but without him there, I didn't know what would happen. What was the point of having your best player not playing? I was like, "What the fuck? What have they done?" I wasn't sure it was the right way to go. Brad rang his parents, we kept talking and then he just looks at me and goes, "I'm taking the job." That was it. He took it. I went in for my meeting and it was like, "What the hell have you done? You've taken away our best player for someone who might be a shit coach."

'The other countries found out and they thought it was hilarious. They were like "You guys are so stupid. Could you be making any more mistakes? You've just lost the best player in the world." I told Brad I would be 100 per cent behind him, which was true, and I told the APC I will give him all my support. But I didn't necessarily agree with it. I told Brad to his face that I didn't think he had made the right choice. It wasn't like I was saying it behind his back. I still have no idea why they did it. Maybe they just saw that leadership quality in him.

'I was really worried because he's such a bloke's bloke. He's such a boy. I was like, "I don't know how he's going to go with this." It was just completely out of left field. He used to play up and muck around a lot. But he's been awesome. He's just stepped up in every way. He's a different boy now than what he was. He's talked to a lot of people, he's gotten advice from the people he thinks can give it to him, he's just really stepped up and taken it so seriously. He's separated himself from the boys just a little bit. He can still go and have his fun with them when the time is right, and I try to include him in everything they do, but there's more pressure on him now and he knows that.'

DUBBERLEY: 'I spoke to Steve, our captain, when I left the meeting. He said, "How'd you go, big boy?" I said, "Are you sitting down? I'm the coach now." The players were a bit concerned, I think. Ryley was a good player back then, but nothing like he is now. I was still playing pretty well. Most of the guys in the team, even the ones who don't speak up too much, they were like, "Are you sure about this?" There were a few times in the days afterwards that I thought, "Oh, shit, what have I done?" If I had more time to think about it, I probably would have said no and just kept playing. But I did it because I thought it was the best thing for the team. I thought I might be able to make a difference as coach, given a bit of time to get used to it. But I did question it a lot, to be honest. I hoped I had the respect of the guys. I hoped they would listen to me. We had been playing together so long, but I had to get the confidence in myself to do it. It can be hard to sit there in front of your mates and tell them the way you want things to be done. Just to step up and make the calls. The first camp, I found that pretty hard. A few of the guys were like, "We should be doing this, we should be doing that." I was like, "Please, everyone, just shut the fuck up. I'm the coach now." And then amazingly, they shut the fuck up. I'd never said anything like that to any of them. I told them we'd have a little debrief after training every night, after our games, whenever, so if there was something they wanted to bring up, they could do it then. But we had to get away from wasting our time with everyone talking over the top of each other. I wanted to show them I was serious.

'I didn't plan on going schizo with them, but I guess I did. If I didn't do it, we'd probably still have everyone trying to coach the team. I was meant to be the boss, so I had to try to run the show. The Paralympics were only two years away and we had to get moving. We had to rebuild the whole thing and I thought I knew how to do it. I'd played for five years in America, played at two Paralympics, all the world championships. I felt like I'd been thrown in the deep end a bit, to be honest—but I wanted to take it on. We're all still mates, but I'll come down heavy on them if I have to. We still call each other all the time, still talk the same old shit. We'll still go to the pub and have a few beers but now they know, if we're at training camps or tournaments, I'm the boss and that's the way it has to be. I'm lucky they understand and respect that. A coach couldn't ask for a better bunch of blokes to work with. You're going to like them. If they saw me as nothing but a mate, if they did the wrong thing they'd think, "Ah, he's not going to do anything, it's just Brad." And maybe they thought that at the start. But we've moved on from there and I've moved on from worrying about it all. I've got confidence in what I'm doing and saying now. As a player, I was never nervous in the slightest. I was more worried about getting everyone else to chill out. But then I started coaching and, shit, I just didn't know how it was all going down to start with. Are they listening to me? Am I a bit young for this? But now it just feels like second nature. I don't even second-guess what I'm saying. At the start, I was always wondering if I'd said the right stuff. I'd replay it in my mind for the rest of the day. Did they understand what I meant by this? Did I say that other bit right? But now I trust myself to just go off the top of my head. Ask any coach of any sport at any level. If you finish a talk and can't remember it afterwards, you've probably done it pretty well. You need to be running on instinct.'

Dubberley crawls across the carpet of his cul-de-sac home to point out the nuances of the dastardly Americans on the TV no wider than a credit card. He hits the pause button to explain all sorts of intricacies that will never make any sense and they don't really have to because the ballad of Brad Dubberley is concerned with more than just murderball. He contradicts himself by rattling through a long list of tactical movements—Player A will block Player B, see, then Player C will take the ball off Player D, and here comes Player E because Player E will run the screen down the left—before putting down his conductor's stick and saying, 'I'm not that big on tactics, to be honest. I believe in ripping in.'

~

Dubberley seems resigned to the fact he was going to become a quadriplegic at some stage.

'It was better it happened when I was younger,' he says. 'Not that you get to choose when it happens, but when you're younger you haven't gotten into your life yet. When you're younger you don't worry so much. When you're twelve, if the doctor says you can't do something, you go and try to do it. When you're older, you're probably more likely to just do as you're told. You get a lot more careful. *The doctor says I can't do it, so I won't. I'd better not. I don't want to get into trouble.* But you're so optimistic when you're twelve. You find a way around things. When you're twenty or 30 you've already started living the life. You're into adulthood. You're going out, you're getting girlfriends—but then you hit this blank and you have to think, "Shit. What now?" When you're younger, you look past that a bit faster and try to find a few things to look forward to. I look at my situation now. I look at mine and Ryley's situation. We're travelling the world, we're playing and coaching a pretty great sport, and it's something we love doing. We're not getting paid that much to do it, but that's okay. We're loving it.'

And then he says this: 'I wouldn't change a thing.'

Dubberley has no function in his left hand. 'No toe movement in my left foot,' he says. 'There's no flex in my left ankle. My left knee hyper-extends. I do more a rotation of the hips than an actual walking movement, but I'm not complaining. I really wouldn't change a thing. At home, I don't get my wheelchair out at all. It's always in the car or in the shed. If I'm at home I'm usually on the lounge or the computer. It's only a small place. I walk to the gym because I couldn't be bothered using the wheelchair lifts. Rugby, whenever we go to training, I'll always have my chair with me because it can get pretty tiring if I have to stand too much. I stand up for the actual training then get back in the chair. Besides that, I live in my chair. I can drive an automatic car. I don't have enough movement or strength in my left foot for a clutch, and I can't change gears because of my left hand, but I can drive an automatic, no problem. Nothing about it really pisses me off. When I was young, all I wanted was to get up and go play footy with my brothers. I played all the sports and who knows where that might have taken me. That's the kind of thing that can bug you, just never having found out how far you might have gone with those sports. But my family never let me give up or worry too much. And vice versa, because I didn't want them to give up on me. They'd be feeling sorry for me but I tried to be like, "Don't feel sorry for me, shit, everything's sweet." The family pushed me to make sure I got stuck into sport again so that's what I did. I'd always been a footy fan so I just got into another type of footy. When I was in hospital, there was a guy called Sandy—he's dead now, committed suicide—who played wheelchair basketball for Australia. They took me out to basketball, tennis and rugby. When I saw rugby I was like, "Yep, that's mental, that's what I'm going to get into." You could take people out and that was enough for me.

'The weird part was seeing my family's reaction to me getting smashed around. I was still only a kid and the other players were all bigger than me, and my family kept saying, "Be careful, you don't have to play if you don't want to." But I was loving it. The eyes lit up again. It's the best thing that can happen for anyone after an accident. You get to compete again at sport. It gets you moving in the right direction; gives you something to work towards and be motivated by. The risk after an accident is that there's too much idle time and you're going to just sit around and waste away watching TV. I started playing about a year and a half after I'd gone down. I kept playing and the family stopped getting so worried. I finished school after Year 10 because I had the opportunity to go and play in America. It was like, "I'm sick of all the rehab crap, I just want to go and enjoy myself, I just want to get away from all this." Everything about being at school kind of reminded me about the accident, so I just wanted to get away. That was my opportunity to escape, so I took it. I was playing in San Diego and living it up. Some billionaires paid my way over there, paid for the place I was living in at La Hoya. I was sixteen and living the life in America.'

The Learned Gentlemen Of The Australian Paralympic Committee pay Dubberley \$10 000 a year to coach the team. That's a pitiful financial package but receiving little more than church money for indulging his passion can be placed on a long list of things that Dubberley doesn't particularly give a shit about. He takes the microphone for the official naming of the Australian squad at the Melbourne Sports and Aquatic Centre. Gusts of wind receive more attention. He's wearing his standard attire: shorts and sandshoes.

'We're not doing this, trying to win a gold medal, for the recognition,' Dubberley says and well, old boy, that's just as fucking well because there's no-one fucking here. There's one TV camera and two half-asleep journalists, one of whom has spilled coffee down the front of his shirt. The players are introduced. George What? Scotty Who? Wiley Ratt? What? Ryley Batt? There's no stage. A half-baked microphone is set up on the floor like we're all down at the Avalon Beach RSL Club waiting for the chook raffle to be drawn. People walk straight through the ceremony on their way to their morning swims, games of squash, gym workouts. Whatever the reasons for their presence, none of them is remotely interested in seeing the Australian murderball team receive their tickets to some unremarkable sporting event in the Middle Kingdom.

'Even if we win, we're not going to get any recognition,' Dubberley says. 'We're not doing this to try and get rich. That just isn't going to happen. We're doing this because we love our sport and we want to represent our country. This is serious for us. We're treating it as seriously as any elite athlete in any other sport. The people trying to win the 100 metres at the Olympics, they're deadly serious. We're no different. This is our shot. This is it.'

Dubberley says success isn't what you think it is. He says success is a John Maclean, the Beijing Paralympian cleaned up by a twelve-tonne truck when he was a promising rugby league player in the 1980s. Maclean was left with multiple fractures to his pelvis and back, a fractured sternum, punctured lungs, a broken arm and paraplegia. He spent his four months of rehabilitation setting goals. Topping his list was to finish the toughest multiple-sport event in creation, the Hawaiian Ironman Triathlon. He did it. 'What's a Hawaiian marathon to someone like John Maclean?' Dubberley says. 'A piece of piss, that's what it is. I think there's a pretty warped idea out there on what achieving is. We can't fail with this. We might not win a medal, but we still won't have failed. We're going to have a red-hot go. What more can you do than that? That's a win. You might get unlucky and lose a game of rugby by a point, but does that mean you've failed? Shit no.'

Such a miserably bleak Melbourne morning, so drab and dour and such a depressingly uneventful team launch, but then you look into the eyes of Dubberley's rough and ready crew, all these anonymous men lined up like mischievous schoolboys with their bitter and twisted bodies beneath disarming glints in their eyes, and one cold, hard fact becomes abundantly clear—*they* care. Nothing else matters and you had better fucking believe it. On the outside, yes, they may appear to be nothing more formidable than a group of seriously disadvantaged men in wheelchairs, but on the inside, the only place of any real significance, they can be whatever they want to be. They can be a fucking army.

Bradley Wayne Dubberley didn't find out at the age of twelve if there is a heaven because surely there's never been a twelve-year-old that goes to hell, and if there is a heaven, he never got to find out if there's a wheelchair ramp round the back. If a quadriplegic does go to heaven, is he still a quadriplegic? Dubberley returns to Shit Creek. The rock glares at him. 'It's not a bad memory at all,' he says. 'I always go to where I fell. It's more like, "Well, that's where it happened." I've done my best to keep going. Maybe I'm better off for it happening. Where would I be now if it hadn't happened—I might be worse off, so I don't see it as a bad thing at all. Okay, the first couple of months of recovery were extremely hard—what did I do to deserve this? But I guess I managed to get going again. What else can you do? It doesn't mean everyone can do it, not by any means. I'm not going to sit here and say everyone can overcome it, because not everyone can. It might not be in their makeup. But somewhere along the way I think I got this whole "Tell me I won't do it and I'll do it" attitude and that served me pretty well. I was only twelve so I could probably adapt quicker. I was pretty head-strong. No-one wants to be injured, but I really wouldn't change a thing now. It could have been worse. I could have drowned. I *was* drowning. I could have died when I was a kid, but I'm still here. The things I've done and seen since, the people I've met, the places we're going this year—who knows where anyone would be with a few changes? I can honestly say I don't regret it happening because maybe it wasn't bad luck at all. I didn't die when I could have, so maybe it was the luckiest day I've ever had in my life. It's harder for my relatives. I took my cousin, Kelly, down there a while ago. He started crying when we walked past the rock. He's a big bloke and he started blubbering. I'm like, "Mate, what's wrong? Don't worry about it." He was like, "You know, I just want to get some dynamite and blow the fucking thing up." I just had to keep telling him to forget about it. It's just a rock. Just a big old ugly rock.'

4

The Game II

Murderball became wheelchair rugby because lily-livered, pencil-necked boffins thought the original name was an inappropriate and politically incorrect term. It was thought to be impossible to market because of that word—murder. It has since become impossible to market because of that other word—wheelchair. It should be making a killing, but no. Underappreciated athletes inhabit a secret world.

The monster was created in Winnipeg, the capital of the Canadian state of Manitoba where a man once jumped on a Greyhound bus with a knife and pair of scissors, beheaded and cannibalised another passenger and then walked along the aisle carrying the victim's head like he was cradling a new-born baby before putting the ears, nose and mouth in a plastic bag and stuffing them in his pockets in case he became a little peckish later on. Asked in court if he was guilty, the man replied: 'Kill me. Please.' It's also where Canadian Duncan Campbell hated wheelchair basketball because it was lame and impossible for quadriplegics and so with the help of four wheelchair-imprisoned mates—Jerry Terwin, Randy Dueck, Paul LeJeune and Chris Sargent—half-a-dozen orange witch's hats, too much time on their hands and a burning desire to beat a few people to a pulp if that was alright with everyone, invented a gruelling new sport. Asked if he can believe murderball has since become the fastest growing wheelchair activity on the blue marble planet, Campbell replies: 'Pinch me. Please. It was just two hours of stuffing around in a gym and here we are. It was rough and fun and somebody said "murderball" and we thought, alright, that's it, let's go with that. I honestly cannot remember who said it. All I know is that it wasn't me. It might have been Paul LeJeune. He's not around any more. He was a guy who liked to get ugly. He'd throw his elbows around and come out of games bleeding like a stuck pig. He would go onto the court wearing elbow pads, so you knew what was coming. Nobody did that back then. Now everybody has elbow pads. Everyone is strapped in now. Nobody had straps when we started. We used our day chairs. Now they play in machines. There are more rules, but it's still the same game—rough.'

Matches consist of eight-minute quarters. If a game is tied at the end of regulation play, an infinite number of three-minute periods of overtime can follow. A match cannot end in a draw. We will be here until fucking midnight if that is what it takes. Matches are held on hardwood floors. The courts are the same measurements as a regulation basketball court. If it looks like a basketball court and smells like a basketball court, it is a basketball court. Players score by carrying the ball across the goal line. Modified wheelchairs have front bumpers designed to strike, pick, hold, ram and survive nuclear attack. Each player is graded between 0.5 and 3.5 depending on their level of muscle function. Those with the most bodily function, such as Australia's Ryley Batt, are the 3.5's. Teams have four players on the court at once. Equality among the teams comes from the gradings of the on-court players totalling eight points or less. The Learned Gentlemen Of The Australian Paralympic Committee's official guide to classifications is this:

0.5: *Not a major ball handler. Scoops ball onto lap. Forward head bob is present when pushing/pulling back part of the wheel. Poor balance.*

1.0: *Weak chest pass or forearm pass. Has a longer push on wheel. Forearm or wrist catch. Weak or non-existent chest pass.*

1.5: *Asymmetry is present in arms. Predominantly uses the stronger arm. Good blocker. Good shoulder strength. Limited ball security when passing due to wrist and hand limitations.*

2.0: *Good chest pass. Can hold the ball with wrists firmly, but no finger function.*

3.0: *Can dribble and pass the ball well with one hand. Very good at ball handling. Can begin to grip the push rim in order to manoeuvre the wheelchair.*

3.5: *Has some trunk function, therefore very stable in wheelchair. Usually has very good ball control. Major ball-handler and very fast play-maker.*

Australia's Cameron Carr, an invaluable two-pointer, says: 'It can be a frustrating sport because it's so pre-determined by your level of injury. It's not so much about "this guy really trains hard, he's got this level of skill so he's going to be a great player". It's more like, "Show me your hands. Do you have trunk muscles? Okay, you're going to be a really good player because you broke your neck at this level instead or this other level." It's not quite that simple—you can get two guys with the same injury but one guy will be a better player because he has better sporting ability—but so much of it is about the level of function. It's frustrating because even though you have the different classifications, if someone with more points goes around you, you don't think, "Oh well, that's okay, it doesn't matter because he's a three-pointer and I'm only a two-pointer." You still want to stop him. I've done a few talks at schools and they're like, "Why is Ryley so much better than everyone else? Why does he score all the goals?" You have to tell them it's because he has more function. We're lucky that we have one of those functional guys on our team. Ryley has a lot of sporting ability, but in this sport, you just can't compete against someone who has trunk muscles.'

Neurological disabilities must hamper at least three limbs. Non-neurological disabilities have to affect all four limbs. Wannabe participants are tested for muscle strength and their range of motion. Classifiers then monitor matches to ensure a player hasn't cheated in testing. Players are permitted to protest their classification if they feel they have been improperly evaluated. And if a country disagrees with the classification assigned to a dangerman from another nation, they can and will protest. It can get ugly.

DUBBERLEY: 'The freaks—anyone who isn't a quad is a freak—are taking over. People like Ryley are stronger and they can throw their chairs around better. They're fitter because quadriplegics don't sweat and their blood pressure goes through the roof, but guys like Ryley can sweat it out and keep going. They're taking up nearly half of their team's value so they should dominate. They have to. That's why there's a classification system, and that is why the sport is fair. I think ten years down the track, though, the game will be so different to what it is now. The low-pointers will end up getting out of the game. Instead of having eight points on the court, it will go to ten. It'll be a lot faster with even bigger hits. The freaks are going to start dominating even more. But, honestly, I don't want it to go that way because the game was invented for the quads who couldn't play basketball. It's important for them to play. They add a lot. It's like contact chess; you have your powerful pieces who can wipe everyone out, but then you've got your pawns who have a really important job to do. There's been a lot of talk about the low-pointers having their own tournaments because they're not all that happy about having the Ryleys around. But they don't see the repercussions of that. It'll be like, "Well, if you want to have a low-point tournament, we'll have a high-point tournament." If that happens, it's going to be full mayhem, and who's going to want to see a low-point game after that? It'll be boring compared to watching guys who are flat-out trying to kill each other. The game will just keep getting faster and more physical, but we need to keep the low-pointers. It'll always be a spectacle but at the same time, it would be such a shame to lose those guys. They're really unique players, but they're risking being run out of the game by wanting their own little low-point tournaments. They're starting it and if they keep going with it, they won't win.'

BATT: 'A lot of players like me are coming through. They'll have a couple of fingers missing, something like that. A few people in the game don't like having us around, I know that, and I sometimes feel kind of bad, like, it's supposed to be a quadriplegic's sport. But that was a long time ago. There are different degrees of quadriplegics and different levels of disability. That's why we're all graded by the classifiers. The Australian players in our national league, they don't mind having us here. A couple of countries don't mind it, but a couple of other countries say, "Wait up, these guys can't be playing, they're not quads." But every country is getting them, double amputees and that sort of thing, and once a country gets one, they stop complaining. New Zealand is coming up with one, the US have one now with Joel. Great Britain had one but he got classified out because he was too able. The bottom line is, they're all getting them. If the classifiers didn't think I should be playing, well, I wouldn't be playing.'

Campbell is uneasy about the presence of the freaks. 'Guys have been kicked out before,' he says. 'A guy in Great Britain has been told he cannot play. He had two claws for hands, kind of. He had a thumb so he could hang on to a ball and throw it. He was amputated above the ankle and below the knee, like Joel, so he had that leg stability. They kicked him out, so I don't know what they're going to do with Joel. They seem remarkably similar to me. He should probably be out, too, but—it's not my decision to make. I think if people like Joel are allowed into our sport, there has to be a greater value placed on them because of their advantages. Put four points on them. Four and a half. There's the difference in the abdominal muscles—a lot of quads don't have abdominal muscles. And quads also have a hard time getting their heart rates up. That's a huge advantage right there. The classification committee is going to implement a rule after Beijing that if you're deemed to be misrepresenting your abilities, you get suspended for two years. And if a coach is deemed to be coaching someone to misrepresent their abilities, they get suspended for two years. And if it happens twice, they're out for good. How do you determine someone has been faking it? That is going to be a big call to make. They would want to be sure they get it right. It's a very tough area and I'm not comfortable with a lot of it. We developed the game specifically for people with spinal cord injuries, but now we've got all these quad amps coming in and we don't know what the hell to do with them. They don't really fit the classification system. They've got huge advantages over people with spinal cord injuries and the sport is still trying to work out how to treat them. To be honest, I think they've just decided that everyone is in, any amputee. I honestly don't know if that's the right way to go. My guideline was always that if they can play basketball, or another team sport, then they probably shouldn't have to play quad rugby. It's not here for the guys who just decide to be a superstar in a game where they have huge physical advantages over other people. But you look at some of them and they're exciting to watch and you think, yes, this is pretty darn good. They really do add a lot to the spectacle. We're not letting paraplegics play but some of these people have more advantages than some high-level paraplegics. You've only got to look at this Wilmoth kid. He's got his hands all taped up but he's an able-bodied guy, basically. He's got his arms, trunk, most of his legs, all his upper body—he just doesn't have fingers on his hands, as far as I can tell, and he's missing the lower part of his legs. He can chuck the ball all the way down the court. You know what? He's a guy I don't think should play. But then you've got Ryley Batt. He's a little different again. He's less able because he doesn't have the legs at all and he doesn't have good hands. But I've watched him and he can chuck the ball pretty far, too. I have some issues with how the classification system has gone. Certain players should not be in certain brackets and I cannot understand how the powers of the game can't see that. It's all over the place but at the same time, it's become a great game that a lot of people around the world are getting into. Half the reason is watching a Ryley Batt play. You look at Nick Springer, another American kid, who is an above-the-elbow-and-knee amputee. He can't play basketball. He has no hands or forearms—he's not a quad, but what kind of advantages can you say he has? What the hell do you do with that guy?'

~

Murderball's history is littered with concussions, broken legs, separated shoulders, busted ribs and broken kneecaps. Eight teams will contest the Beijing Paralympics, split into two pools. The pool of death is Australia, New Zealand, Great Britain and Germany. The other is the United States, Canada, Japan and China. The hosts are making up the numbers, a joke, a sham, a farce, and seven other players all rolled into one hopelessly inept and inexperienced squad. The US, Canada and New Zealand are the top three teams in the world. The US and Canada have a seething rivalry while NZ, the mortal enemies and dominators of Australia, are a cold-blooded team of muggers under hoods who bludgeoned their way to the gold medal at the Athens Games. There are two villains of the piece, the American player Mark Zupan and the Great Britain coach Joe Soares, both of whom revealed themselves in a 2005 Oscar-nominated documentary that won the Sundance Film Festival, rave reviews and gave murderball a brief cult following before the cult was killed off.

'You wanna hit me? Fucking hit me. I'll hit you back.'

They're the most famous words in the sport. They should be inscribed on a plaque next to the directive about killing the poor bastard with the ball. Zupan doesn't just say these lines, he *breathes* them in a movie that if you watch once, just once, will make you go outside and howl to the full moon and run through a brick wall with the ease that the chiselled hand of a Tibetan monk can scythe through a slab of stone.

Zupan isn't entirely against the nickname of Zuperman. He is changing his jeans for a pair of shorts. His wheelchair is tarred black. He's wearing a white T-shirt. His red hair is shaved to the bone, his red goatee is thick and so are his sideburns. There's a ruffled doona on his bed. The walls are cream and without decoration. Two beer bottles are loitering with intent. One white lamp is positioned on a small table. A studded black belt is curled on the floor, writhing like the original serpent. Zuperman starts moving. Your stomach tightens. This will take a while. He arches his back and grimaces. His left hand yanks at his jeans without being able to take a grip. The jeans fall towards his fleshy calves. He twists as if electrocuted. The jeans fall to his bare white hopeless feet. Zuperman uses his mildly capable right hand to grab his ignoramus of a right leg. The quiet is only disturbed by the slapping sound of flesh on flesh. Zuperman puts his right leg back in his chair, lifting his leg with the motion of a man pulling up a pair of long socks. The fingers on his left hand are rigid. He lifts his tattooed left leg into the chair. The foot hangs limply. You imagine cutting his foot and no blood coming out. Dark thoughts. Zuperman takes off his shirt. His upper body is lean. Another decorative tattoo on his right shoulder. A large chunk of metal hangs from his pale neck. If Zuperman is trying to look like a bad-arse, he's succeeding in spectacular fashion. Swapping his long pants for a pair of shorts has taken one minute and nine seconds. In blood-red letters on a piece of bandage tape on the side of his wheelchair is the word ZUPAN.

His fate was distorted by alcohol or maybe alcohol was the sole reason or maybe sobriety wouldn't have changed a fucking thing and he was doomed to start with. Zuperman and a friend, Christopher Igoe, played a college soccer game in Florida. Afterwards they went to a bar called Dirty Moe's to get drunk and chase women. Beers cost a nickel. Shots were a dollar. Zuperman had his fill by midnight. He went outside in search of slumber, stumbling across the dimly lit car park, still walking but not for much longer, leaving footsteps for the last time in all his days. He jumped in the back of Igoe's black truck, curled up and descended into a deep sleep. Igoe dozed off in a chair inside Dirty Moe's. He was asked to leave, and agreed to do so. In his thick blanket fog of drunkenness, he decided to drive home. He had done it before without consequence. He turned the ignition, hit the accelerator and found the road. He was unaware that Zuperman was with him. The truck spun out of control on a freeway and Zuperman was thrown into a canal as if he had been shot from a cannon over the fence and trees. His neck broke in the fall. An off-duty policeman, driving with his girlfriend in a car behind Igoe, had noticed the scattergun driving. He saw Igoe hit the tree but did not see Zuperman catapulting over the fence. Igoe was questioned. The scene was cleared and Igoe made it home, still unaware of Zuperman's predicament. Zuperman clung to a branch in the canal for the next thirteen-and-a-half hours. Friends and family thought he had been abducted by the opposition soccer team in some kind of idiotic but harmless prank. Zuperman positively yowled for help.

'All you could hear were the cars going by,' he says. 'I was in a remote place. The way it was situated—I was here, there's the body of water, there are some office buildings over here and then way across the other side are more office buildings and the off-ramp. I was hidden from all of it by the trees. From the off-ramp you couldn't see me. The only way you could see me was from round the back. The guy who found me was a maintenance guy who worked in one of the buildings. He went outside to have lunch and heard the noise, heard my noise. I know nearly fourteen hours sounds like a long time to hang on but, I don't know, I've always been scared to die. I think that has something to do with why I lasted. I just really don't want to die, man. Fear had a lot to do with it. I know I ingested quite a bit of water. I know I had pneumonia. But it's amazing what the human body and the human mind can do when it has to. You can will yourself to do almost anything.'

Zuperman was winched to safety with his dead legs tied together. His father reckons he's a tough kid whom you don't want to mess with. The father appears to be a tough old coot whom you wouldn't want to mess with either. A friend of Zuperman's—a sharp executive type in a crisp white business shirt—says it would be wrong to blame Zuperman's current surliness on the accident because he was a surly bastard to begin with. The Zupan you meet is not surly, nothing like, but he's undoubtedly a formidable, no-nonsense presence in a world No.1 ranked American team that is intense, over-bearing, annoying and dominant. They will beat teams like the LA police beat Rodney King and Zuperman will state coldly: 'That's what we came to fucking do.'

His role in the documentary made him an American hero/celebrity in a country unable to differentiate between the two. There were Hollywood parties, international travel, crowd-surfing at Pearl Jam concerts and a seat at the Oscars in Los Angeles where the real angels are thin on the ground and where, in the wrong place at the wrong time, you can literally feel the devil breathing down your neck. Where, in all the seedy little strip joints and drug dens that punctuate LA, they stopped handing out the real halos long ago. Zuperman continues trying to raise awareness of his murderous little world, but admits, 'People think negatively. "Aw, wheelchairs, I don't want to see that". But shit, man, get them to one game and they'll go back. I guarantee it. There's just this stigma about wheelchairs and it's bullshit. It's a sport like any other. We're athletes. We train our arses off. It's not professional when it comes to the money because we don't get paid, but it's professional in terms of the way we train for it. We bust our arses in every game. Isn't that what people want to see? Isn't that better entertainment than watching some spoilt millionaire going through the fricking motions? I've put my life on hold to play this sport. It's very fucking cool, man. We would do anything to win and when we don't, we're like, shit, we've got to train harder to get the fucking job done next time. The one place we all want to win this time around is Beijing. It's going to be fun over there.'

Fun! Really? Exactly what kind of fun are you anticipating Zuperman? Chinese families used to throw their disabled babies in the river. Australia's Olympic legend Dawn Fraser is boycotting the Paralympics because she's seen the disabled spat on in the streets of the old Peking. The People's Republic has never been especially concerned with the plight of the physically impaired. The services of handicapped children are still sold to businessmen in Beijing. The disfigured children beg for money in Tiananmen Square before the proceeds are handed over to the loathsome individuals profiting from the whole immoral sham. 'China is a different world, but I think they're going to do it right for us,' Zuperman says hopefully. 'It'll be interesting.' Interesting, how? Interesting in that you might be kicked around like the mongrels of the litter? Mocked? Ridiculed? 'It's no secret that in day-to-day life, they kind of keep the disabled people shut away,' he says. 'This is just my take but I've heard they say, "Okay, you're disabled, that doesn't fit into our ideals of the perfect society, we don't want you out here where you can be seen." That's the cultural difference, I guess, but they're going to want to show off their country, aren't they?'

Beijing's Paralympic Committee publishes an offensive handbook for volunteers that says: 'Physically disabled people might have unusual personalities because of disfigurement and disability. For example, some physically disabled people are isolated, unsocial and introspective; they usually do not volunteer to contact people. They can be stubborn and controlling; they may be sensitive and struggle with trust issues. Sometimes they are overly protective of themselves, especially when they are called crippled or paralysed. It is not acceptable for others to hurt their dignity.' Which would seem to raise the following question: Is it acceptable to hurt anyone's dignity? Of all the fucking hide. What are they expecting—trolls? China has 83 million disabled people, nearly quadruple the total number of individuals in Australia of extravagantly rich and varied colours, ages, races, creeds, backgrounds and beliefs. But despite the proliferation of those requiring assistance in China, past prejudices have led to forced sterilisations, the banning of marriages between disabled lovers and abortions of imperfect foetuses. The handbook, not quite the Unabomber Manifesto but appalling nonetheless, continues: 'They show no differences in sensation, reaction, memorisation and thinking mechanism from other people. When you make eye contact with them, do not fuss or show unusual curiosity, and never stare at their disfigurement. A patronising or condescending attitude will be easily sensed by them, even for a brain-damaged patient (though he cannot control his limbs, he is able to see and understand just like other people).' Just like other people! The constant references to 'they' and 'them' is abhorrent. 'Like most, he can read your body language. Show respect when you talk with them. Often the optically disabled are introverted. They seldom show strong emotions. Do not use the word crippled or lame, even if you are joking.' In other words, beware the disabled! Don't touch!

'If they treat us like crap, the rest of the world will hunt them down,' Zuperman says.

Deep lines are carved into his face. He's been through the emotional wringer but burst out of the other side. The bottom line is that Igoe, a close friend, someone who was there for all the good times, ended up wrecking him, cruelling him, consigning him to a wheelchair for life. Mercy sounds like a good idea when you're not the one required to be merciful. Is it really possible? Advisable? Logical? For how long can you let your insides eat at you? When the father of Lauren Huxley stared down the barrels of the nightly news and said of The Bastard Robert Black Farmer, who had tortured and left for dead his daughter, rendering her as pale and lifeless as a mannequin, needing three weeks on life support, a facial reconstruction and brain surgery, he seethed: 'Burn in hell, with petrol, where you belong, you bastard.' Doesn't that deserve a standing ovation? Doesn't Zuperman also have the right to wish for Igoe to be pitchforked into the burning pits of fire? 'Did Chris make a mistake?' Zuperman says. 'Hell yeah. Did I make a mistake? Might have. I got in the back of a pick-up truck when I'd been drinking. But he got in an accident, not me. I could look at him with hate and say man, you know, you did this. Look at me—this is your fault. We went through a bit of a stage, but it didn't last. We are very good friends again now. Think how hard it is for him. Every time he sees me he has to go, Jesus, I did that to him. Once he finally came to terms with it, he was good with it. I don't fault him. My life is better now. I've done more and seen more than I would have. All the people around here, everyone playing wheelchair rugby, we've all done a lot. I wrote a book. Me, write a book? How the hell would I have written a book without this? I had a better education because I went to a better school because I said to myself, "Okay, let's leave Florida and go somewhere else and get your shit together." I played soccer at college, but there's no way in the world I would have gone to the Olympics for soccer. To be able to see Athens for the last Paralympics, and now to be able to see Beijing, to go to New Zealand, travel around Australia—I've only just turned 33. Looking back, man, 33 years, that's not long to have been around. The good news is that there's more to come. Anyone can think that. It doesn't matter where you are or what you're doing, it isn't over yet. I'm lucky. I might not have a full house, but I've still got a pretty good hand. Most of the guys playing this sport, I look at them and I think, "You're a miracle, man. You're a walking fucking miracle. You're alive and you've got this much function and you're living this full life." The human mind and body is very resilient. Look at Dubberley, man, as good as dead. For him to be alive and doing what he's doing, friendships everywhere, you gonna feel sorry for someone like him? The older you get, the more you realise how important friendships are. That's the coolest thing we have. You work out what you really want pretty quickly when you're in our situation. You know what I want to take to my grave? A lot of friends, and Chris is one of them. He walked into the hospital about a day or two after I got hurt. He walked in and thought my dad was going to kick his arse. Dad gave him a hug. But then he had to go off and deal with it all. He's done it, but he still has his demons, for sure. You just have to forgive and forget because what does holding a grudge do? Jack shit. It just makes you more angry and worse off than you were before. Don't get angry. Find something else to look forward to.

I can't wait to have children. That's what I want to do. It's something that just blows me away. Life will be so different. You're responsible for somebody else's life other than your own. You've got to make sure there's food on the table, you've got a whole new set of responsibilities—what a bitch. I want that so bad. It's like my dad wanting to put himself in my body. I cannot think about how my accident affected my parents—I mean how it really affected them when I wasn't around and they could stop putting on an act. They thought it was my brother, you know. The police told them, "One of your sons is hurt." They were like, "What did Jack do?" The police were like, "No, no, it's Mark." They knew something was up. They knew something bad had happened to one of us, either a prank gone wrong or something really serious. I can't imagine. You think about it and your kids are supposed to outlive you. That's just the way it's gotta be. My dad wishes he could will himself into my body and I know that if there was a way for it to happen, he would swap bodies with me right now. That's the parental love. That's unconditional. The neat thing is that I'm a heck of a lot closer to my parents than I used to be. It's fun. Dad and I will go grab a beer. Mum and I will grab a beer. I'm like, what? I'm sitting here having a beer with my mum? That's cool, it's really nice. Dad is like, here, have my body. He would do it in a second. Love, man. What a parent feels for their child—that's just pure love. I think I have the understanding of what it will feel like. I can see how somebody could love something greater than themselves, greater than everything else in their lives. It's something you and your wife have made. No two other people in the world could have made those little people. They're yours and no-one can ever take them away.'

This is not the conversation you expected. *Fucking hit me, I'll hit you back.* Where's that guy? He's asked to define pain. 'How much can you push your body? What's the absolute limit? And is that really the limit, or just what you think is the limit? They might be two different things. I want to find out. What is real pain? Emotional pain? Physical pain? There are different levels of both of them. People have said to me, "Well, you don't really feel pain because you're paralysed." Well, physical pain, there's probably a limit to what anyone can feel. But emotional pain goes way beyond that. I'll tell you about emotional pain—I cannot imagine what it's going to be like when my father dies. You can't put that into words. I understood and coped when my grandparents died, but those were my grandparents, not my actual mother and father, the people who brought me here. They weren't the people who raised me. It's not a fun thought.' Zuperman can hear a tune and think it might be right for the Never-Never of his mother's funeral. 'You think about the times you've had a problem and how you're like, well, I'll just call Mum because she'll know the answer. But what is going to happen when Mum isn't there? You get older and the more you get to see them the better it is because you're all adults now. It's a weird and very hard thought that you're probably going to be here without them. That's just life, I know. Life takes its course and you'll reel from it and you'll figure it out, but it's going to happen and nobody wants it to. You just cross your fingers that it's not going to happen for a while. You want to enjoy your relationship with them while you can. Enjoy them while they're here.'

Zuperman is perceived by many as an arrogant prick. Says one Australian player: 'The only time I've really met him was after a tournament in Wellington. He was drunk, being really loud, just swearing at all the barmaids. They said, "Look mate, can you tone down your swearing?" And he got worse. He was like, "I'm this fucking old and I can swear as much as I like." He's mates with Brad and we were like, Brad, grab your ranga and go home.' A ranga is a red-head. This more hoary stereotype of Zuperman is common among every team trying to knock the US off their perch. Jealousy plays a major role in the compilation of this unflattering image among his peers. Zuperman is not a bad man. He is driven and determined and unwilling to suffer fools, but he is not *bad* in the strictest sense of the most negative term. The easiest thing in the world is to sit back and criticise. It's more difficult and brave to talk someone up. Don't worry about Zuperman. The real villain of the piece is Soares.

He was born into a poor family in Portugal, losing the use of his legs to polio at the age of eleven. His family moved to Providence, Rhode Island, but it was another three years before his family could rake together enough cash to plonk him in a wheelchair. That's no childhood to have, dragging yourself around by the knuckles for three years while a disease crashes your central nervous system as severely as a broken neck. He's stubborn, aggressive and cocksure, pushing his chair like he hates it, snapping his wrists. An exaggerated underbite gives him the appearance of a starved pitt-bull. Soares is a man in constant need of proving himself, which makes him the most painful man of all. Everything is a war and everyone is a potential or proven enemy. Inside Soares' balding head, one of those megastructures you might learn about on the Discovery Channel, every second is a test of his worth and in that same balding head, the battle can never be won. Zuperman says he wouldn't piss on Soares if he was on fire. Given Zuperman needs more than a minute to drop his pants, it's a moot point.

It's been 46 years since Soares' diagnosis. His face is pasty and white with the inactivity of it all. He was called a cripple and gimp at school. To say he developed a thick skin would be to suggest the Pope had merely a passing interest in religion when he visited Australia for World Youth Day and asked 300 000 pilgrims the most challenging question of all: 'What difference will you make?' Soares would get close enough to his childhood antagonisers to rip their bloody throats out. He approaches adulthood with similar fervour. His introduction comes in a brief and illuminating courtside conversation with a polite female member of the American team. She's asking if it might be okay for Soares to move from the sideline while the Americans are training. He says no, that might not be okay. And then when she's given up on the possibility of an adult conversation, even with the documentary cameras homing in, he's concluded their brief dialogue with three choice words: 'Fuck you, bitch.'

When Soares was dropped by the US team because his club, the Tampa Bay Generals, had demoted him from the starting team for a young upstart player—Dubberley—he took them to court. When that failed, seeking the most vindictive form of retribution, he went off to coach the mortal enemy, Canada. The Athens Paralympics became Coach Joe versus America. 'When Joe got cut, and when he couldn't sue the US team, he basically said, "Screw you guys, I'm jumping the fence",' Dubberley says. 'I don't think it's any secret that his motivation wasn't in helping Canada. All he wanted to do was beat America. The American players were like, "You don't go and coach another country. No matter what happens, you just don't do that. Fair enough if you've cracked the shits, but you don't go and coach someone else." I don't know how Joe did that. He was still living in America. How are you supposed to wear the Canadian uniform? How do you sing their national anthem when you're playing against your own country? No thanks. I definitely wouldn't do it for the bitter kind of reason that Joe did it. There are a lot of very intense people in this sport, the Americans and the Canadians especially, and he's the most intense of the lot. He's forever going off at the ref because he believes he's right all the time. He can just never accept that it's possible he could be wrong. He'll just keep saying, "No, no, no, I'm right." He might be good for the sport, but he's a bit of a dickhead.'

Coach Joe has a shrine to himself at home. The Generals once went on a 93-game winning streak and how unbearable he must have been all the way through it. At the 2002 world championships at Gothenburg, Sweden, Coach Joe was celebrating his 22nd wedding anniversary with his dutiful wife, Mrs Coach Joe. Naturally, he invited the documentary cameras along. Romance clearly isn't dead in the Coach Joe household. Mrs Coach Joe looked at her husband through the candlelight and said: 'To you, Joe.' Isn't that a bit weird? Shouldn't she have said 'to us'? Joe clinked her glass: 'To Team Canada, hopefully. To the gold, baby. The golden rainbow.' Come on, who says that? *To the gold, baby? The golden rainbow?* You wish the movie producers had a monitor on Mrs Coach Joe at that moment to provide an accurate reading on precisely how far a human heart can sink. Coach Joe is obsessive, screaming at his players, berating them, belittling them. He screams in the faces of the opposition. He rubs his sweat-soaked head as if all the world's troubles are inside and perhaps they are. Coach Joe worried himself sick before the Athens Paralympics. He started getting chest pains. The chest pains led to shortages of breath and then the shortages of breath led to heart palpitations. The heart palpitations led to a full-blown heart attack. The face of Mrs Coach Joe crumbled as Coach Joe's heart machine flatlined. He was going to die? He recovered but here's the thing, the one staggeringly unbelievable (but all too believable) fact about Coach Joe Soares. When he realised he was in the iron grip of a heart attack, his first telephone call, instead of going to his wife, the beautifully understanding Mrs Coach Joe, went to the cameramen for the documentary. His heart came good, his back stiffened again, his animosity returned to typhoid fever pitch and he guided Canada into a cataclysmic semi-final against the US. Coach Joe prowled the sideline mumbling his opinion of anyone remotely connected to the American team: 'Motherfuckers.' Canada beat America before losing the final to New Zealand. 'I don't even think Joe cared about the final,' Dubberley says. 'He did what he wanted to do—beat America.' Duncan Campbell still has a photo of the Canadians with their silver medals from Athens. Soares is not in it. 'Once a jerk, always a jerk,' Campbell says.

And then Coach Joe was sacked by Canada. And then Great Britain advertised for a new coach in the lead-up to Beijing. And now you can cue the hissing and burn the effigies, because Coach Joe, good old pain-in-the-arse Coach Joe, got the job.

You ask Zuperman if he really would decline to piss on Coach Joe if he was on fire. He replies in the affirmative, ghost rider. 'I couldn't care about him one way or the other, to be honest. If he gets hit by a bus, then he gets hit by a bus. If he doesn't, it has no impact on my life. You won't hear too many good things about him. There are people in life you don't like. The good news is that you don't have to worry about them. I don't give two shits about him. That's just the way it is. He's married, his wife puts up with him so I'm sure he's a good man in some way. But I just don't see it. I know he loves his sport, but there are bigger things than sport. You've got to live your life. It doesn't matter what you're doing, the way you do it is important. I would have thought if you ostracise people, it's going to become a pretty lonely existence. You need friends, and I'm not sure how many friends Joe has. If you're my friend, I'll give you the shirt off my back. That's what friendship is. If you're not my friend, I don't give a shit what happens to you. Certain things are important to certain people and we should probably just leave it at that.' Asked to describe himself, Zuperman says, 'a civil engineer, an author, a friend, an athlete, a rugby player, a mentor, a public speaker, an asshole and an all-round good guy.' He's unable to roll past a bar in his hometown of Austin, Texas, without the owner offering him free drinks. Does Zuperman think about Dirty Moe's and the canal every time he drinks alcohol? Only he knows that. Asked his age, he says: 'I'm a beaming twelve years old. No, I really am 33.' Batt contemplates all the Zuperman hysteria, looks over the trees in his little slice of God's country on the eastern seaboard of Australia, cracks his knuckles and delivers his considered verdict on the most famous murderball player of them all: 'Over-rated.'

We shall see about that. And I deliver this solemn promise: from now to eternity I will rip the head clean off any able-bodied person who starts pissing and moaning about their lot. The disabled can suck up their troubles and do more in one year than most people residing elsewhere on this wondrous planet can manage in an entire lifetime, but everyone else is so spoiled they start crying like little bitches as soon as they become remotely uncomfortable in their surroundings. Suffering is an unavoidable part of life, but some people just don't get that. If you're not suffering right now, you're blessed. And you're the exception to the rule. Want to sit around all day on your fat arse watching television? Fine. Give your legs to someone who would know what to do with them. *Play*. A girl has a house full of dolls. She's bored stupid. Another girl has only one doll with scratched-out eyes and a missing leg. She's having the time of her life. Some people just know how to play. Those of us with all four limbs and a fully functioning central nervous system are the luckiest sons of bitches alive. Watch one game of murderball and you will be hooked. Attend one Paralympics and you will haul your sorry arse to every Paralympics for the remainder of your lifetime. The look of raw determination on the face of a murderballer pumping his arms like the pistons of a freight train cannot be forgotten. The boundless inspiration provided by every disabled athlete about to run, walk, jump, limp, fall, swim, float and ride through the Beijing Paralympic Games will last a lifetime. Disabled athletes and the occasionally trucker-mouthed sub-section of murderballers are a remarkable breed of human being. Bodies irreparably damaged, brains mercifully intact, minds unavoidably bruised, they are taking on the world in more ways than one. This book is unable to do them justice. But it will try its fucking damnedest.

Part II

THE PLAYERS

5

Ties that bind

Name: Ryley Batt
Age: 19
Home: Port Macquarie, NSW
Classification: 3.5

No legs.

Ryley Batt's hands at birth were devoid of the customary deep Vs of webbing. Instead of receiving fingers and thumbs, he was granted only two slabs of mostly unhelpful flesh. An operation sliced down the middle of his left hand, creating two oversized digits of unlimited capabilities. His right hand has three fingers, also of unlimited capabilities. It seems that God was in an awful hurry when he made Ryley Batt, but perhaps at the last minute He realised He had missed a few bits and pieces and so endeavoured to make amends by injecting the kid with an overdose of the two most invaluable traits of all: character and heart. He's using his good hand, the one with all three fingers of unlimited capabilities, to cradle his mobile telephone when you call to ask if it might be alright to fly to Port Macquarie to meet the greatest goddamn murderball player on the planet.

'Sweet,' he says. 'When does your flight get in? I'll come and pick you up.'

You're not entirely sure what to say because Batt appears to have overlooked what would seem to be a rather significant hurdle to his wanting to drive you back to his joint.

Dude, you've got no legs.

The plane is scheduled to arrive at 10 a.m. He says he will be there.

Aeroplane lands in nirvana. No high-rise buildings, no crowds, no security checks and after a morning spent driving around the white-sanded beaches of Port Macquarie with all the fresh air and frolicking open spaces, no desire to ever leave. Sydney can get stuffed. Sydney is stuffing itself. You shuffle across the burning tarmac and there he is, Ryley Batt, grinning like he knows something.

Big black earring. Another piercing above his left eye. Shoulders as broad as the runway. Forearms like tree trunks. You walk by his side. He wheels back to his van. There is friendly banter but you feel uneasy. You don't know why you feel uneasy and that makes you feel even more uneasy. *Need a hand, mate?* Should you ask him that? Shit. How is he normally treated by the mates who go around to his place for beers, barbecues, whatever? You imagine there's nothing more annoying than being disabled and having an endless queue of people asking you a thousand times a day, *Need a hand, mate?* Then again it might be rude not to ask. Maybe right now Batt is thinking, *Any chance I can get a fucking hand here, mate?* You have no idea what to say, so you don't say anything at all. With all the honesty it is possible to muster, seriously, honestly, how are you supposed to treat *no legs*? Bend down so you're at the same eye level? Stand up straight? But isn't that just rubbing his face in it? How do you shake the hand of someone who can't really make a grip?

Batt jumps out of his wheelchair and lifts it above his head like Atlas with the world on his shoulders. He opens the back of his van. Hurls the chair onto the tray. Bounces inside by pushing himself up off his hands and a couple of drastically undersized stumps he has living inside his shorts. You get in. He turns the ignition. The gears are all handles. Of course they're all handles. Stop thinking the obvious. He winds down his window. There's a kick-arse stereo with the requisite thumping, vibrating speakers. 'Love my music,' he says. You put your feet up. You take them down as if they're going to cause offence. That's patently ridiculous. Stop thinking the patently ridiculous. You keep looking at the floor in front of his seat. There's nothing but floor. Stop looking at the fucking floor. 'That's where I went to school . . . here's the main street . . . there's the beach . . . what's this truck driver *doing?* . . . here's my place . . . come and meet Mum . . . sorry about the mess . . . front yard needs a mow.'

Batt didn't start using a wheelchair until the age of twelve because climbing into one of these steel contraptions would have amounted to an admission of defeat. Previously he burned the flesh of his hands because they were his only brakes. A wheelchair would have stamped him as different and it wasn't that Ryley Batt cared about being different so much as he didn't *see* himself as being anything out of the ordinary. His mates, the people still going to his place for beers, barbecues, whatever, were all using skateboards so he wanted to do the same. On a skateboard he was one of them. In a wheelchair, dramatically less so. Why do we do *anything* when we're young? To conform. First game of sport. First teasing. First sleep-over. First party. First pash. First swig of beer. First joint. You're not doing any of it to realise any long-standing childhood ambition. You're doing it because you want to fit in. The first day of school can be the last pure day you ever have because going home after that first day, you realise you are going to have to start modifying your behaviour to satisfy the natural human craving for acceptance.

Schools can be cruel. Playgrounds can be the most terrifying and intimidating places some people go. A girl at primary school is teased because she has a cleft palate. She feels rejected and alone. Her teacher is testing the pupils' hearing by having them sit at the far end of a large table while she whispers questions. If they answer, correctly or incorrectly, doesn't matter, she knows their hearing is good. What colour shoes are you wearing? Is the weather hot or cold? To the lonely girl with the cleft palate, she whispers, 'I wish you were mine.' Which is all fine and dandy but not everyone can have a sensitive new-age teacher so how, exactly, was Ryley Batt supposed to fit in? He was getting around St Agnes Primary School with more than a cleft palate. School can be torturous for anyone cut outside the norm.

'I didn't get any grief,' he says. 'I was pretty much in a group where we used to pick on the other kids. That's nothing to brag about, I know, but you know how in school you have all the different groups? Well, I suppose I used to be with a pretty popular group of blokes, so no-one used to pick on me too much. There was this one time in Year 6. Someone said something to me. It wasn't even that bad—I can't remember exactly what it was, and I don't even know why—but I just reacted. I tackled him and punched him out. He went running to the teacher, crying, and that's still pretty much the only fight I've ever been in. That was the end of it at school—no-one picked on me after that. My mates will make a joke about me now, but it's all fun. I'll give it back to them. Kids are just kids. I probably get more shit now than I did back at school. I go to schools to give talks and one kid said to me, "You look like an alien." It just made me laugh. I was like, "Bloody hell, hey, an alien!" I said, "Thanks, mate, fair enough!" You don't take anything like that to heart. That's just a kid being a kid. I was like that when I was a kid, everyone is, just saying whatever you think without even thinking about it. I was amazed back at school because I thought people *would* say things, but no-one ever did. No-one used to ask anything, no-one used to point at me, it was all good. I had a really good bunch of mates and still do. They've always stood up for me.'

Batt was in Year 6 when Australian player Tom Kennedy arrived with one of his teammates to give an awareness-raising demonstration of wheelchair sports in the build-up to the Sydney Paralympics. Batt says, 'My pop had always said to me, "You're going to be a Paralympian one day." And I was like, "What? What sports are there at the Paralympics?"' The player who visited St Agnes with Kennedy was going out with Kennedy's daughter. He was living with them at Port Macquarie. 'These two guys were getting all the kids into wheelchairs to help them accept and appreciate wheelchair sports,' Christine Batt says. 'But they couldn't get Ryley into a chair because he said they were for disabled people. He thought he wasn't disabled. He thought that not having any legs was different to being disabled. I rang Tom because I was really trying to get Ryley into a wheelchair before he started high school the next year. I'd let him go until then, but high school was going to be the cut-off point. Ryley said to me, "You can go ahead and get me a chair, but I'm not going to use it." He was twelve years old and he was pretty headstrong, but he was my son and finally I just had to say to him, "Ryley, I want you off the ground. I want you off your skateboard NOW".'

Kennedy had never met Batt. Neither had the teammate. The teammate was Dubberley, who says: 'We were doing a schools' program. Tom and I would go and speak, take wheelchairs out and play in them, show them what the rugby was all about and give them a game. We turned up to this one school and there's little Ryles on his skateboard. He was a little bastard. He'd never used a wheelchair and didn't want one to use one. He just said, "I don't want one of those." He just wouldn't get in. He preferred his skateboard and just hanging out with his mates. He kept saying "I don't need one." But we finally chucked him some wheels, he jumped in and he kicked his school mates' arses. He killed them as soon as he started playing. He loved it. I remember him coming up and saying, all excited, "Braddy, do you reckon I could play for a team?" I said, "Dude, give it a year and I reckon you could play for New South Wales." Before we knew it he was playing for Australia. I ended up giving him one of my old day chairs and away he went. He was a really great kid, rough as guts, and he still is now. It sounds weird calling him a kid because he's a mate.

'There was potential straightaway but, to be honest, I was more concerned with getting him off his skateboard. He was a cool kid and it was more about not wanting to see someone getting around on a skateboard all their life. After that, I thought, "Okay, what do we have here?" I wanted to see if he liked a hit. He liked the hitting better than he liked scoring goals. He didn't care if he got hit, which was a big plus. As soon as he started, I was like, "Here we go, we're on here. This boy can play." I'd started playing when I was about fourteen, so I could see how good he was for that age. He just dominated. He loves the aggro. It means we can go in against the US and know we can rough them up. They're not going to like it. They're not going to like playing him. Other countries play the US and they don't have a Ryley and they panic. They don't know how to go about it. He's without doubt becoming the best player in the game. He's ready to bash some blokes. He scores goals when you wouldn't think they're on and then, defensively, he turns around and starts taking blokes out. Two blokes aren't enough to stop him. They're just speed humps. He goes mad. He's got mongrel, Ryles. It might be a nice mongrel, but he's got it.'

BATT: 'I just started—I don't know—loving it. I wanted to keep going. I owe Brad and Tom a lot, more than I ever tell them. My dad had told me about wheelchair rugby because he'd seen it on TV. I just didn't get it. Wheelchairs and rugby didn't make any sense to me. I thought they played it out on a rugby field. I was like, "Wheelchairs and rugby, how funny would that be!" I thought they pushed themselves around out on the grass, through the mud and all that. I was thinking, "Don't they get bogged?" It's strange now to think I went though all the "Nah, I'm not doing that" stuff. I remember thinking, "Go away. This is crap." Actually, the first time, I was thinking, "This is *really* crap." But then they started up a game and I was like, "Right, if everyone else is playing, I'm in. And I'm going to smash everyone." I was really competitive from the start. I liked the physicality of it. It's the most contact you can have in a chair. It's like any footy player. You get that rush from knocking blokes over. You take someone out, and you're looking at them when they've gone down, and that feels awesome. I fall over too, but a lot of the time it's because I've thrown myself over when I'm trying to take someone else out. It's infuriating, being on the floor. You feel like an idiot, laying on your back until someone comes over and lifts you up. I'm trying to lift myself up these days, but it's just part of the sport, going over. I've fallen out of my chair three or four times in some games. You're trying to smash someone and you lose your balance. You go in to hit them, miss them, spin around or go backwards, turn too hard and you end up on the floor. The first time I hit someone, I loved it. The big crash. Even getting hit was fun. You get smashed and you can do some smashing of your own. It's one of the few ways we can get full-on body contact. It's a proper game of footy for us. You can tell when blokes are worried. You see them thinking, "Here he comes, he's gonna get me again." It's intense. It's a full-on sport and we're a full-on team.'

Batt is asked to describe his role.

'Hitter.'

Batt lives in the downstairs granny flat. There are no wheelchair ramps anywhere on the property. You stand on the top step and peer over the edge like you're about to throw yourselves off Niagara. Batt jumps out of his chair. He bounces down the steps, dragging his chair behind him. 'Sometimes my mates say to me, "Nothing bothers you, does it?" They're probably right. Everyone has little things on their mind all the time, but I'm going pretty good. Whatever my mates want to do, I still want to do it with them. They're my mates. I want to hang around with them. If they go swimming, I'll go swimming. If they're going to a party, I'm there. My mates, you know, they don't stare and they don't care. I'll try to work something out for whatever comes up. If I can't, well, too bad. I'll go and do something else. I've got arms and hands so I've got it pretty good. If there's a problem, I just try to get through it. I've got my own life.

'I've got my quad-bike, I've been kneeboarding. I'd love to wake-board but I can't stand up. I've been kneeboarding since I was three. I've got footage of me doing backflips, but I keep spinning out when I land. I've been quad-bike riding since I was three or four. The quad-bike is definitely a passion of mine. It lets me get away. There aren't any idiots like you get on the roads. There aren't any cars around, nothing. You're just out there on your own and you can do whatever you want.'

An eleven-year-old ballerina in China has been buried in rubble for 70 hours after an earthquake. She's lost her left leg. What is fair about that? In what regard is that reaping what you sow? Why is it all such a fluke? What is *fair* in all this? Why isn't Ryley Batt angry about *no legs*? Where's the self-pity? The awkwardness, the frustration, the embarrassment—where's the sadness in this house?

'I've got a great life,' he says. 'I feel lucky in a lot of ways. I'm playing sport for my country and I'm just starting to realise what that means. When I was younger, I didn't quite get it. But it's a pretty cool achievement. You get to travel the world and represent your country and I'm really starting to appreciate that. It all happened so fast when I was younger but now the sport is getting bigger and I think people are really starting to enjoy watching us play. There are times when I think, "Yeah, I wish I could give this a go, I wonder what that's like, I reckon I'd probably enjoy that." Like, I'd love to have a game of full-on footy. I'd love to get on my mate's motorbike. But there's no point worrying about any of it. I'm just really happy with everything I've got. Everything is such a rush.'

Batt punctured a wheel last weekend. He was miles from home but pushed himself back to the granny flat instead of calling for help. It took hours and amounted to the running of a marathon. Try pushing yourself in a wheelchair with a flat tyre. You'll be lucky to get to the end of the block. I believe that when Ryley Batt is hungry, he eats. I believe that when he is tired, he sleeps. I believe it is all so gloriously fucking simple for him.

'Sometimes, I do feel a bit unstoppable,' he says. 'I don't know why that is. I just get that feeling. Not all the time, but it comes up a fair bit. When I was young, the boys used to call me Woofer. I just used to go full throttle into everything like a dog. You have to go at life with everything you've got. That's all I'm trying to do.' He motions towards *no legs*. 'This is just the way I've always been, so it's all I know. I can't miss walking because I've never done it. I don't worry about what it must be like to go for a run because I can't do it, so what's the point? I can paddle a ski, go for a push in my chair to get the blood pumping, play rugby—why think about things that don't matter? Or things you can't change? It's a waste of time.'

You imagine being Doug and Christine when Ryley was young. Above all else, you imagine being obsessed with this question: Will he be okay? That is all you want to know. Okay, or not? You imagine sending him to the most special of special schools where they could place him in so much cottonwool he'd barely be able to see over the top of it. You imagine telling him it's perfectly alright if he wants to spend every day watching *The Bold And The Beautiful* with a blanket on his lap. You imagine suggesting there isn't much point in him going outside because everyone else is so busy and important and running around at breakneck speed that you'll probably just get under their feet, darling, so stay here and have another cucumber sandwich. You imagine the best thing you could give your son would be a room with a view. You imagine there would come a time when it would be explained to him that there's no real expectation on him to do anything exceptional with his life and just getting through it will be enough. You'd be tempted to tell your son that the world is a survival of the fittest and unfortunately, boy, you ain't all that fit. You imagine every decision, every word of befuddled advice, every tentative plan and every interminable sleepless night being firmly based on 'NO LEGS'. But Doug and Christine Batt were more brave, travelling down the opposite route. If their son wanted to bang himself up on a skateboard, he was allowed to go right ahead and do it.

'He's a pretty good kid,' Christine says in the understatement of the millenium. 'Nothing fazes him much. He just goes with the flow. When I watch him play, I'm in awe of him, actually. I don't like to brag and he's always telling me not to, but I really am pretty proud. So many kids his age are bored or angry or depressed, but then I see the way Ryley is, and he's none of those things. He's not sitting around thinking "Poor me". He just never complains. I'm extremely proud of what he's doing in rugby. Who would have thought, eighteen years ago, that he would have achieved so many terrific things? It's incredible to see him doing all this. The rugby has been fantastic for him. All the guys in the team, Brad and everyone, they're all such good guys. They've all had unfortunate accidents, or something has gone wrong, but they all have full lives and that rubs off on Ryley. You could not hope to meet a better bunch of people and I couldn't have hoped for Ryley to be mixing with a better group. I think he can fit in with anyone. I never tried to hide him away when he was younger. We would walk up the main street and people would look at him in a funny way but I was so proud that he was my son. He went everywhere with me. I did everything with him. We got him out there and threw him into everything. My father bought him his first motorbike when he was three years old. It was a four-wheeler. That's how he started riding motorbikes. If you saw him on it now, my gosh, you'd be amazed. I don't know how he hangs on. I don't know how he does a lot of the things he does, actually. He used to race in a club and do really well. Whatever he takes on, he does it to the limit. He's just built that way, I guess. All through school, he had a go at sport. He played soccer as the goalie. He played squash. He can't say no. He's quite remarkable, really. He's just not fazed at all by his disability. It sounds so basic to say, but that's just the way he lives. He's a happy kid. I hear someone whingeing about something that, really, is so trivial, and I think about Ryley and I feel like telling them, "Get over it, darl. You've got it pretty good".'

Batt will spend a large chunk of the year coming and going from the airport he's picked you up from. Training camps in Melbourne and Townsville. A Super Series in Melbourne and then a full-blown Paralympic dress rehearsal under the salmon-pink skies of Vancouver before eight nations with an interest in murderball converge on The Hall Of Overwhelming Glory in Beijing for The Big Dance. Back through the house and the yard still needs a mow. Back in the van and seriously, what are these truck drives *doing*? People are jogging and riding pushbikes and there's a shoe shop, for Christ's sake. Isn't everything just a reminder of what Ryley Batt cannot do? Of what he hasn't got? The back bone is supposed to be connected to the thigh bone. The thigh bone is supposed to be connected to the knee bone. The knee bone is supposed to be connected to the leg bone. The leg bone is supposed to be connected to the foot bone. But what happens when you don't have dem bones?

'I'm better off than a lot of people,' he says. 'People break their necks later in life and they know exactly what they're missing out on. I've lived my whole life like this. Look at Steve, our captain. He was throwing a footy with his mates one night at the beach. Next day, bang, he's a quadriplegic from lifting something light. The way people like him overcome it all is inspirational to me. I look around our team and I just see people who inspire me. I never tell them that, but I think we definitely all feed off each other. Maybe that's why I hope people start watching our sport. You've got quads and people with other forms of disabilities who are really motivated to make the most of their lives. I think that's probably a little bit inspirational for anyone.'

Batt cannot recall the moment as a child when he realised *no legs*. 'I've been thinking about that, when it really hit me,' he says. 'And I don't remember having one day when I realised they weren't there. I remember wishing I had legs, but I don't think that now. I'm just having fun and I couldn't care less about it. It would obviously be great to be running around doing all the things people do, but I don't really care any more. I used to when I was a little kid: "Why can't I just have legs?" But now I don't. It's just who I am and what I am. Like

Zuperman and a few people say, you do more stuff in a chair than you would out of it. I'm glad I was born with my disability, I really am. I've been like this for eighteen years and I know every bit of my body; what I can do and what I can't do. If I can't do something straightaway, I just try to figure out a different way. Or I go and do something else. I don't think it ever got to the stage where Mum or Dad had to sit me down and talk me through it. I just sort of learned how to get around and it was just the way I was. It wasn't like one day I had legs and the next day I didn't. I always had people around who told me I could do anything. They were right. I don't like to see people who have, say, just had their legs amputated, thinking that's it for them. I don't like them thinking they can't do anything, because they can. There's not much difference in your life. You can still do pretty much anything you want. If I wasn't sure, my mates used to say "You can do this" and I could. I never really had to have a talk with my parents about what it all meant. Which was probably a good thing.'

You leave God's country at dusk. Sydney is flattering. Sydney is flattering itself. Thundering traffic rattles the walls of your home until midnight. You wake at 4 a.m. with a thought, just a thought. Back at Port Macquarie airport, both in the morning when you didn't know Ryley Batt and in the afternoon when you were glad you did, he declined to use the disabled parking, the pig-headed mule. You lie there for the rest of the night thinking about Christine Batt and what she says was one of the more difficult moments of her life. According to Christine, *no legs* became real for Ryley the morning of his fourth birthday, when for no rational reason that Christine can think of apart from the unbridled optimism of early childhood when reality and fantasy can all so easily be rolled into one endless possibility, Ryley convinced himself that his legs were going to grow by the time he woke up. This renders her nearly speechless now. Ryley woke and looked under the covers. *No legs*. He looked again. Still *no legs*. He stayed in bed so long that Christine had to go and check on him.

'Mum,' Ryley said to her. 'Where are they?'

'Where are what?' Christine replied.

'My legs, Mum. Where are my legs?'

~

Name: Ryan Scott
Age: 26
Home: Brighton, South Australia
Classification: 0.5

'It was ten years ago. I was sixteen. I probably wasn't the smartest young kid. Like most kids, I could do the wrong thing. I was hanging out with my brother and his friends. My brother is three years older than me, and his friends are three or four years older than him. One of the guys had come back to our school after being away. We were friends with him from when we were really young. He was really arrogant and full of himself, just one of those real cocky wankers. He went out and bought a new car. It was a V8 Commodore, brand new paint job. We were really impressed by it because none of us could afford a car like that. He was always doing burn-outs and drag racing and just being a dickhead, basically. I was young and immature and just really impressed by it. I always wanted to hang out with him. I always encouraged him to go faster because I was a bit the same as him, a bit full of myself.

'We were going out for a mate's 21st birthday. I was sitting in the back seat, behind the front passenger. I lived out of the city, and we were heading to Victor Harbor, down through the back roads. That's more of a country area, more winding roads. He lost control of the car as it was going around the corner. He was doing 120 and it was pouring with rain. We rolled over, went up an embankment and hit a tree. Because the embankment was quite high, we hit the tree about ten to twelve feet up. It crushed me and pinned my head to my stomach. We went down, hit some more trees and a fence. I broke my neck at C5–C6. It was actually broken at C5, C6 and C7, but my spinal injury is at C5–C6.

'I was conscious through the whole thing. My mates jumped into a couple of other cars, went to the pub and rang the emergency services. They came down and cut me out. They rang my house, but my parents weren't there. They were out. It was Dad's birthday. Two of my brothers were home and they came down to the accident scene. It was about 40 minutes from home. I was still trapped. I was pinned in the car for about two hours. They were cutting me out and I was still conscious, and in some pretty heavy pain. Apparently I was screaming, "Get me out of this fucking car!" Once I got cut out, they airlifted me to the hospital and operated on me. The first week, they weren't sure if I was going to live because my spinal injury was that severe. They had me heavily medicated in that first week. All I remember is being in the helicopter and just wanting to go to sleep, but they wouldn't let me. They were like, "No, you *have* to keep your eyes open." I think they felt like I was giving up. They wanted to keep me conscious. All I remember was not wanting to be there, just thinking, "Let me sleep, let me go away." The day after, the helicopter pilot came in to see if I was alive. He couldn't believe I was. They say that after you've been heavily medicated, your body can put things behind you that you don't want to remember. It can get to the point where if you've had major traumas, you can block it out. I can't remember a lot more about it. I'm glad about that. Being trapped in a car for two hours, I don't want to keep reliving that. It's like being buried alive.'

Tragedy #1: The accident. 'We'd played footy that day. I remember being at this guy's house. We were getting in the car. I'm six-feet-two and one of my mates was about six-four or six-five. This other guy was about six foot. The biggest guy was like, "I need the front seat, I'm the biggest, I need more leg room." I thought, "Whatever, you can have it." I didn't think whoever was in the back seat would break their neck that night. "You want the front seat? Take it. What does it matter?" That was the first day I'd ever been in the back seat. I was in the front seat every day, every single time we were in that car, except this time. The guy I sat in the back seat with, we had a carton of beers. We thought we were being pretty tough. That's one of the fucked things about car accidents. I remember before the accident kind of feeling invincible in that car. You've got this big chunk of metal around you and it just feels safe, there's just something about it. You just never think it could go wrong. You see some car crashes and the car is crushed like a tin can—and the people just walk away. You couldn't fit the people back in there, but they get out. And I end up like this.'

Tragedy #2: Those responsible didn't learn a fucking thing. 'After the accident, those guys were still out doing the same stupid shit.

They were like, "It happened to you, not us." I don't know. Something like that, you'd think it would have some impact on them. It's real life. You'd think it would be a shock. Or that it might kick someone into gear. From what I've heard, different people react in different ways. I think some of my mates might have been in denial. One of my mates just wouldn't talk to me, and he was pretty much my best mate. In the ten years since it happened, probably eight and a half of those, I haven't heard from him. The guy who was driving, it was a bit of a weird situation. His old man killed himself when we were at primary school and I was really worried after the accident that he was going to do the same thing. I was like, "Look, it was a mistake, you fucked up, but let's learn from it." He was my mate, you know? I felt sorry for him for what had happened and the way I thought it would make him feel for having done it to his mate. I was trying to get an understanding of how he must be feeling at the same time as dealing with what I was going through. I think he was definitely in denial, but later on he went out and bought another quick car. He just went straight back into the same lifestyle. It was disappointing to see him go that way. The only thing I can really put it down to is the denial. It was like he was thinking, "It didn't happen to me, it's got nothing to do with me, it's no fault of mine, you just got unlucky, I'll just keep going how I am." Maybe he *had* to tell himself it wasn't his fault. I don't know. He was a dickhead, if we're being honest. I regret a lot of things now. I look at the life I was living and I just think, "Why was I hanging around these fuckheads?" I had so much more to live for. The stuff I'm doing now, it's really good fun and I'm travelling the world. I'm getting out there and playing a fantastic sport, but I look at it all and think I'm doing 10 per cent of all the things I could be doing if I had lived my life properly. I take a lot of the blame myself for what happened. I got in the car. I made some pretty poor decisions.'

The driver escaped with a cracked sternum.

'He was downstairs in the same hospital,' Scott says. 'They weren't allowing visitors because, you know, I was pretty fucked up. He was still in hospital a week later. It kind of seems like he could have gone home. A week in hospital with a cracked sternum? I don't know about that. Maybe it's a really serious injury. I remember my mates coming in and they were just so miserable. I think about that now, and I can understand it. I was always trying to laugh and joke and hear about what they did on the weekend. I kept thinking, "If I'm a miserable bastard, who's going to want to come and see me?" It did get to a point, though, where I think I was doing too much to keep everyone else happy. It was all about not wanting people to be too upset by what had happened to me. I wouldn't wish it on anyone. The main thing was that I didn't want my parents to get down if it could be helped. If I had a shit day, my parents were going to have a shit day. I didn't want that. If it was a shit day, I didn't want anyone to know. If I was up, they were going to be up. They were still devastated, of course, but I thought it was up to me how sad everyone got. But you get to the point where, even now, I have to start doing things for myself. If I want to be fucked off, I'll be fucked off. If I want to go and do something, I'll go and do it and stop worrying about what other people think. I started to realise that a bit more as time went on. I'm just glad it wasn't my brother driving. At that time, he was driving very similarly. It was a big deal between all our mates. He had a GT replica with a 351 chev in it. If it had've been him driving, it would have destroyed all of us. It would have made life very hard. It could have ruined our family. I think about the guys in that car and I see now that they are the ones who have failed. They're the ones who haven't succeeded in their lives. They're still doing the same shit. They're still stoners. Or they're still alcoholics. In moderation, the two of those things, there's nothing wrong with doing a bit of that. But if that's what your life revolves around, what a waste.'

The driver has a bit to answer for.

'I can't move my hands,' Scott says. 'My triceps are paralysed. I had to learn how to brush my teeth again. Something as simple as brushing my teeth, dressing and undressing, stuff you just take for granted, takes me a long time. I'm sure you got up this morning and brushed your teeth and didn't even think about it. It's a whole process for me now. When I go to grab a toothbrush, I have to really think about how I'm doing it so I don't drop it. If I drop it, that's a whole other problem. At the time, when all that starts happening in rehab, it's just fucked. You're just unable to do *anything*. I don't even know how to put it in into words. It's just not easy. I was in a rehab centre with 24 other people. The good thing is you've got 24 people going through a very similar thing at the same time. That helps. But then you're in rehab with someone who gets almost all of his function back, and he's walking again, but then he starts complaining about how fucking hard that is for him. They're the kind of people you have to deal with. I go in there now to work out in the gym. There was this guy in the rehab centre the other day. He was sitting there talking about how much his life sucks. He could walk and while he's saying all this, there's a guy sitting across from him on a ventilator. He couldn't even breathe for himself. And this guy still sits there talking about how hard his life is. Give me a break. People who are like that—they suck up a lot of energy from all the people around them. I don't think they even realise. What do they want? Sympathy? Are they trying to drag everyone else down with them? I don't get people like that.

'The guy driving the car I was in, after he went back to the old life, I just thought "I don't have time for you any more. See you later", but good things can come out of it. I remember my brother saying to me, "Look, man, I'm sorry for all the stupid shit." We were typical brothers. We used to fight over nothing. He was just like, "I love you, man." To hear him say that—I think it really shook him up to see how close we came to losing each other. The day before the accident, we'd probably gone toe-to-toe over something pretty pointless. We would have had that could-not-give-a-shit kind of feeling about each other. We've never had that since.

'My parents, the support from them has just been unbelievable. Where we train, it's the old rehab centre, and you see guys who don't get through it, and they're the ones who don't have family. The family can't deal with it, or the family isn't around, and they leave it up to the injured person to deal with it on their own. You can't deal with it on your own. There's no way you can do it alone. The shit I put my family through, you know. While I was at the rehab centre, they were driving over an hour a day to come and see me. My dad had to change jobs. He took a huge wage cut to help out around the house. The house needed to be ripped apart for me to come home to; in the middle of winter there was no roof on the house because it was being modified. They were just continuously being affected by the stupid decisions I had made. I feel really responsible for that kind of stuff. It's hard. I can look back now and go, "Sure, I didn't mean to do it", but I think about the choices I made leading up to the accident. It started when I was fifteen. I was smoking marijuana, going out drinking, writing myself off, that was fun to me. My parents warned me all about it, but I blew it off. You're young and you feel like a man, I guess. That sounds idiotic to me now. You feel like an adult, but you just don't know as much as you think you do.'

Scott's rehabilitation finished with the doctors' confirmation: *You Will Never Walk Again*.

'I don't remember the day they actually told me,' he says. 'I just remember thinking, "Okay, I'm in a wheelchair and I'm never going to be able to walk." But even then you don't understand what that really means. It's like, yes, that's fucked, but does it mean I'm not going to be able to drive? Does it mean I'm not going to be able to have sex? Will I still be able to get a girlfriend? They tell you that you won't be able to walk. But it's not like you take walking out of your life and everything else stays the same. They don't really portray what your life is going to become. It was like, "Okay, I can't walk, but I can go to rehab and I'll get better." I thought you went to rehab and they fixed you up. I thought even if I can't walk again, I'll come out of rehab and life will be so much better because I've been through rehab. That's what I thought. We started getting further into my rehab and I was thinking, "I'm not getting much better here. When is this dramatic change going to happen?" I realised that it wasn't going to happen at all. It was just—fucked. My life just wasn't going to be the same and there was nothing I could do about it. When it finally hits you that you are getting into a whole different life, it's just a very confusing time.

'You have your bizarre moments. Like recently I had an appointment, and I was a bit early, so I was sitting in the car listening to some tunes. I actually thought about that feeling of standing up, just how easy it used to be to get up out of a car and walk away. I could actually feel that again. In ten years, I could count on one hand the amount of times I've thought about walking. I think I've always just gone along and gotten on with it, but I sat there and could really feel what it would be like to stand up and be upright again, just cruising along. Getting my legs out of the car, all that. It's just day-to-day shit but it's impossible for us. It was kind of weird, sitting down, imagining walking. To be honest, I don't think you ever actually *get over* being in this position. You try to get your head around it so you can function and do the day-to-day shit that's required just to get on with your life, but from my experience, I don't think you actually ever get over it. We were all pretty active before it happened, so that gets taken away. That's the hardest part. The people who break their necks are the ones who used to be the most active. You don't see many computer programmers in rehab for a broken neck.'

Scott's favourite sportsman and well of inspiration is Jamie Carragher, who plays for the Liverpool Football Club, where the crest on top of the legendary Shankly Gates details how all those involved with the club will always have someone by their side. On any given Sunday, to coin a phrase, at any one of Liverpool's home games, 45 000 fans sway inside the rousing 120-year-old Anfield Stadium to bellow their anthem about walking on, and you'll never walk alone.

'My old man came from Liverpool so I was born into a soccer culture,' Scott says. 'Jamie Carragher is a born-and-bred football player. He's not the most talented guy but he reminds me of myself in that he's had to work very hard for everything he's got. When it comes to wheelchair rugby, I'm probably one of the lowest functioning point-fives in the world. I have to work my arse off to even compete. All Jamie Carragher ever wanted to do was play for Liverpool. They could pay him nothing and he'd still do it. For him, just to put on that red Liverpool shirt—that's what it's like for me playing for Australia. I hate sitting on the bench. I hate missing out on playing rugby. I'll do anything to be playing. If someone came in and started paying us to play our sport, well, it'd be great, but it would change the sport, to be honest. Guys are doing it now because we love it. We get a part of our old lives back. When you're able to physically compete in a rough and competitive sport—that's what my life was like before. I was competing all the time, always competing, and I've got that back now.'

Scott will rarely appear on a highlights reel. Point-fives are the blue-collar, grossly underpaid workers who allow Batt to score his match-winners on the bell while they're off-screen having done the dirty work by blocking the other team's defenders. 'There's huge satisfaction in that for me,' Scott says. 'From a 0.5 to a 3.5, there's a huge amount of function difference. For me to be able to hold a guy when he has a physical advantage over me, that's huge. That's why I play the sport. There's the tactical battle and if I can hold up someone with more points than me, we've got all the rest of our points against less of theirs and that's going to make a huge difference. I do my best.'

Be open to the possibility of change. You can change your relationships, you can change your finances, you can change your job, you can change your habits, you can *kick* your habits, you can change whatever you want. Try hard enough, and you can change *you*. A woman is in the darkened corridor of a hospital at 2 a.m. She has just given birth. Her child is unwell. A pastor is driving past the hospital. He's convinced someone inside needs his help. He's standing in the corridor. He sees the woman. She does not have a religious bone in her body. The man asks if he can pray for her and the child. She'd normally say no. She says yes. The man stays with her all through the night. When she leaves hospital, he visits her at home to read her scriptures. He invites her to church. Again, she doesn't have a religious bone in her body. But she goes along. Now she is a pastor. That's a drastic change in lifestyle. A more obvious hint at the need for a shift in priorities would be leaving your mate fighting for his life because you were doing 120 in the rain. Apparently he who criticises is in danger of hellfire but we are prepared to cop a little heat for this. To the bloke who was driving when Ryan Scott became a quadriplegic: You weren't a dickhead then. You simply made an error. But for having failed to change your ways, you are a dickhead now.

Ryan Scott has the Liverpool motto permanently stamped across his chest. You Will Never Walk Alone.

Name: Nazim Erdem
Age: 38
Home: Roxburgh Park, Victoria
Classification: 0.5

Nazim Erdem developed a hunch the size of Tiananmen Square as a teenager, suspecting it might be an idea to learn how to hold his breath for as long as humanly possible. *One, two, three . . .* Unsure why he should do this, he nevertheless became convinced it was going to be extremely beneficial at some later stage of his life. Erdem reached the point of being able to deprive himself of oxygen for more than three minutes, a ridiculously large amount of time, really, and even though he was glad to have built his resistance so high, he remained totally, utterly and somewhat blissfully clueless as to why it felt so obsessively necessary.

'I used to love being in the water,' he says. 'I used to go to the pool all the time. I never had much money and you had to pay to go to the pool, but me and my mates, we'd know all the different ways to sneak in. We used to get in for free. If they saw us, they'd kick us out, but we'd be back in there a couple of minutes later. I just had this love of water, and especially being *under* the water. We'd test each other to see how far we could go holding our breath. It was an Olympic-sized pool in Richmond. I think they used it for the Olympic Games in 1956. We used to swim the width of the pool first, underwater, and I could do that easily. Then I used to try to do it lengthwise and see how far I could go. I used to beat my mates all the time. Before I went to bed I used to hold my breath just to—I don't know, I just enjoyed holding my breath. It just excited me and, I don't know why I thought this either, but it felt kind of serious. I could hold my breath for two minutes, no worries. My record was more than three minutes. That was always in my head, I could do three minutes if I had to.'

At the age of twenty, Erdem launched into an extravagant dive into shallow water off a pier near Melbourne in an effort to impress a group of girls. He cracked the top of his skull on the sand, breaking his neck and severing his spinal cord. The girls did not see it happen. He did not see them pack up and leave. His arms and legs were spread, a human starfish. No-one could see him, so no-one was coming to his rescue. Face down, like Dubberley in the least attractive of all the creeks, literally counting down his time on this remorseless coil, there was nothing to do except stare at the sand and his own mortality. He can still see that paper-white sand with its tiny corrugations. He started counting. *One, two, three* . . . Erdem reached two and a half minutes before being rescued. Without his previously nonsensical desire to clamp his mouth shut and gawk at the seconds ticking by on his watch, he's quite certain that today he would be dead rather than making his way towards The Hall Of Overwhelming Glory.

'I jumped off and tried to do a big dive,' he says. 'I thought I was being a bit of a daredevil. I probably wouldn't have done it if I wasn't trying to impress the girls. I just wanted to get their attention, you know? I dived in and was just floating there, watching the sand on the bottom and counting. My mates thought I was kidding around. I used to muck around a fair bit, so they didn't worry about me when they finally did see me. One of them ended up grabbing my foot, but I didn't know he was doing it. I couldn't feel his hands because I was paralysed. I couldn't move or feel anything. He was moving me through the water, but I didn't know he was there so I thought it was the current. I thought no-one had seen me yet and I was just floating away. When I realised he was there, I'm thinking, "Turn me over! Quick!" But I couldn't move my arms or my legs, nothing. I was just looking at the sand and holding my breath. I couldn't move my head left or right to get air. I was lying flat.

'I could hear people splashing and running through the water, things like that. I can still hear those noises, those underwater noises you get. My mates were going, "Look at him, he's just putting on an act, pretending he's drowning!" I knew something was wrong, but I didn't know what. They could have tickled me, punched me, pushed me further under and I wouldn't have known. My mate ended up lifting my head by my hair, still thinking I was being funny. My brother was there too. I said, "Mate, I'm fucked. Get me out of here." Straightaway they knew I wasn't kidding. They reckon my eyeballs were nearly out of their sockets. Funnily enough, I felt alright. I wasn't in pain. But I couldn't move and I knew that wasn't good. I could move my head a little bit and I could just move my left arm. But nothing else was working.

'We had those girls a bit keen on us, but we never saw them again. Surround yourself with the good people and tell the rest to piss off. I got lifted up onto the jetty and tried to move, but I couldn't. I thought it might have been shock. I hadn't heard anything when I hit the sand. I didn't hear any crack. Four of the lifesavers brought the stretcher out and put me onto it and took me into their change rooms. A couple of them stumbled and half my body just flopped off the stretcher. That was weird. I could see my arms flopping around but I couldn't feel them or stop them. They put the stretcher down again, repositioned me, and finally got me into the rooms. They got the pins out and started jabbing me. *Can you feel this*? *Can you feel that*? I'm saying, "Go on, stick the pins in, you can start now." And they said, "We already have." That's when I thought, "Oh no." The ambulance came and they didn't even put their siren on when they were taking me to hospital. Actually, there might have been a siren, but they were just cruising from what I remember. It felt like they were going 10 kilometres an hour. I lost consciousness.

'They took me to the Alfred Hospital in Melbourne. They took the X-rays and tried to figure out what was wrong. The same day, or the next day, they took me to the Austin Hospital, where the spinal unit is. I had to go straight into intensive care. Both my lungs had collapsed. After that I was lying flat in a bed for six weeks. I wasn't allowed to move for six whole weeks. They put a tracheotomy in my throat because of my lungs. My mates and parents were coming in all the time, and I was lucky I had their support. They were all joking with me, and I was trying to have a laugh. They'd ask me questions: "How are you going, mate? What happened, mate?" I'd try to mouth the words back, but it was impossible. I couldn't even write anything down. I'm trying to explain to them what I mean, and they'd start saying something completely different. I'd try to shake my head a little bit and laugh and they'd start cracking up because I couldn't even get a simple message across.'

A gentle man spent eleven months in hospital.

'They put me in a neck brace after six weeks. It meant I was able to get up out of bed. They didn't bolt my neck together or fuse it or anything like that. After two months, when I was up, they decided I wasn't healing fast enough so they did a fusion. They took some bone out of my hip and sort of welded it into my neck. That set me back a little bit. I broke the C5 but the damage, luckily, was done underneath that at the C6. If it was done higher up I'd be in a power chair, for sure. I'm not in the best condition as it is, but if there was C5 damage to the spinal cord, I would have been fucked. And I don't think I would have become as positive as I am now. I would have had to rely on everyone else for everything, to get anywhere, to get out of bed, to have a shower in the morning, the whole lot. I don't know if I could have coped with that. When I was going through rehab I thought, "I don't want to be alive, but I don't want to do anything to myself either." I was never actually suicidal, but there were times when I thought I was already dead. Then I thought, whenever I die, I want my parents to have died first, and then I'll die after them. They were so positive, there was no way I was going to try to do anything to myself. Having my parents there was huge. I had to stay positive and laugh for them. They were going through a really hard time as well. If I looked like I wasn't doing too badly, it was going to help them. If they saw me depressed when they came to see me in the hospital, they'd walk out depressed. I didn't want that.'

Rehab is an attempt by all concerned to find their bravest face. Erdem says: 'A few months afterwards, my mum and dad told me the story how, while I was in intensive care, my dad walked in and fainted. The nurses had to go to him instead of me. Before that, I thought my old man was so super-strong that nothing could ever get to him. That was the first time he saw me in the intensive care unit. I would have had tubes in my arms and throat and up my nose, and it just got to him. It was hard to hear it affected him like that. After that, it was all good. Everyone says I'm really easy-going but my dad tops everyone. He's the most easy-going guy you'll ever see. But it's just really emotional for anyone, you know, when you see people you love in that position. The attitude I tried to have was, "What can I do about it? How can I make everyone feel better?" You just have to try to make the most of it. Feeling down or feeling upset—you can do that, you have to at times, but you have to get over it because it's not going to help you. What will help is getting on with your life. That's why I do the work I do now.'

Erdem is a counsellor to victims of spinal cord damage. He does it because kind-hearted counsellors helped him escape God's Waiting Room back when he needed them most. 'Some had gotten married and had kids, they still worked, they had these really good lives and I thought, "That's alright—if we can still do all that, what's the problem?" They really cheered me up, those blokes. They did a lot for me. That's why I like doing what I do now. Once a week I go into the rehab unit and just try to cheer people up. Tell them what they can do. Set them up with different people that have a similar condition to theirs. It's one thing to have someone go in and tell you to try this or do that. But if they can see someone actually doing it, someone who has had an accident and started this new life, a great life, there's the proof that we're not just talking shit.

'The other thing is, the doctors can be pretty bad. Mine were terrible. When the doctor came in to tell me what was wrong with me, I was in intensive care, still lying flat in bed. All he said was, right, you've broken your neck at this level, whatever, then he talked to other doctors and started walking away. It was like he didn't even care. I said to him, "Hang on, what does all this mean? What is going to happen to me? Am I going to walk again?" He just said, "Nup. You're never going to walk again. Anything else?" I thought, "What a fucking way to find out." I pretty much knew the story at that stage, but I wanted to hear it properly from him. He started walking off and I thought he would stop and come back. He didn't. He just walked out. I thought, "You fucking prick." I took it alright but I thought about other people who he was going off to treat the same way. I thought, these people are down already. You're going to kill them. I would have liked to have heard him say, "Look, this is the way it is. I hate to tell you this but I'm only doing my job and here's the whole story. I'll stay as long as you want and answer all your questions. I really am sorry but I'm here to help." I wanted him to give it to me a bit softly, you know? It was ridiculous.'

Erdem is devoid of bullshit, and being a veteran of the last three Paralympics, he knows exactly what is what and precisely who is who. 'New Zealand are pretty good guys,' he says. 'We hate them and we want to kill them, but they're good guys. One of their players, Dan Buckingham, plays for our state team. We're good mates and he's going to be hard for us to get past. The GB guys, they're fantastic. But they're almost *too* good. You end up thinking, "Enough! You're nice guys, but that's enough, please." You can't get rid of them. Canada have a couple of guys I might say hi to, but there are a couple of guys I wouldn't want to speak to. They're dirty players, Canada. They grab your chair. They grab your wheels. They do anything to stop you from getting to the ball. They spin people, trying to really hurt them, playing really dirty. Some of the players actually grab your hand and your arm. The referee can't see it. They practise that. They do it on a regular basis when the referee isn't looking, so they must practise it. They're the dirtiest team of the lot. It's good to beat them whenever we play them. The Japanese are probably good guys, but I can't understand a word they're saying. You need sign language to have a conversation with them. Sign language doesn't work when you've got a couple of quadriplegics involved.'

Erdem says: 'This is the best team I've been in. The young blokes, they're still kids, and that rubs off. It keeps us all young. Sometimes I think you have to get loose, you know? Lay back. Have fun. Don't take it too seriously until you really have to. There's a serious side to all this, but you've got to have a laugh. Sometimes you can forget you're here to have fun. That's the reason I started playing—for fun. The secondary thing, the bonus, is to win. That's the whole idea of playing sport. One day you're going to stop playing and you're not going to remember the goals you scored. You're going to remember the good times and the fun you had with your mates. If you're not enjoying it, why would you want to do it?'

Erdem is the king of the point-fives.

DUBBERLEY: 'He creeps in like a pick-pocket and hooks them—gotcha. For us, in a pressure situation, we want Naz out there playing. Nothing bothers him. He's a great athlete and absolutely nothing gets to him. We could be winning by twenty, losing by twenty, doesn't matter, he would just play the same way. He's just really clear in his own mind about what needs to be done. He a genius!'

The Genius Erdem attributes his unwavering calm to his Muslim faith and the influence of his father, Muhammed. 'I think about my parents and what it was like for them when they first moved to Australia,' he says. 'My parents come from Turkey. Dad came to Australia in 1967, on his own. He told me he had nothing except a bag with some clothes in it. No money at all, not a cent, no friends, no English. I try to think about that, and how hard it must have been. He came from a farming community, really, where there was no employment. Everyone was going abroad at that stage to get new lives. He wanted to go to Europe. He went there as an illegal immigrant but got caught, and was sent back to Turkey. He put in his papers to go to Australia and they said, "Okay, you can go." He married my mum in Turkey and I was born there before we moved. I was nearly a year old when I came to Australia with my mum. My dad was already here. Ever since then we lived in Richmond. I grew up in housing commission flats. It was pretty rough. I did a lot of stupid things, I thought I was smart. But I had the best childhood, I reckon. My dad came here and got through and he had to be tough to do that. Maybe that kind of thinking helped me get through my accident. Maybe it was some of Dad's strength. It's all happened for a reason. I don't know what that reason is, but I know I'm like this for a reason. Sometimes I think I would have ended up in prison without this happening. A lot of my mates ended up being junkies. A lot of them went to jail. There's only a couple of my old mates who I'm still good friends with now. Maybe the reason it happened is that it saved me from going to jail or being a junkie. Maybe it was a wheelchair or jail. I'm glad I got the wheelchair.'

The Genius Nazim Erdem holds the distinction of being the world's first solo quadriplegic paraglider.

'I like to try anything I can,' he says. 'We went as a group to Oaks Day, this big horse-racing day in Melbourne, with one of the nurses from the hospital. We started talking about how great it is being outdoors. We were saying, "Let's go paragliding, let's go and do it together!" I was pretty happy about that. She was nice, you know? Really nice. We ended up going and it all went well. She went tandem with one of the instructors but I went on a three-day course you do to get a low-grade licence. The first two days, I was tandem with the guy teaching me. He'd always be with me, telling me how the controls worked and everything. The last day, the weather wasn't too good but he said, "Look, we'll try to get you going solo anyway." The weather came good, really good. He had to strap my arms to the controls. It's like a parachute, you pull to go left or right. I nearly crashed when I took off. There are two sets of cords on each side of you. When you take off from the cliff, you have to hold them all in until you get away from land and the wind starts to take you up. They basically push you off a cliff and when you get some speed, you start to take off. The cords came out of my hand and I started turning to the left really sharply. I started going along the cliff and I was struggling to reposition my hands so I could grab the cords again. The instructors were behind me, yelling at me. I don't know how I did it. It was all adrenaline. I didn't care if I crashed. It was all going to be good, whatever happened. I managed to grab the cord and straighten up away from the cliff and I heard them all in the background: YEAH! YEAH! YEAH! That made me realise how lucky I was. They probably thought I was going to kill myself. That was all pretty satisfying. It's like being able to drive again. You can have a spinal injury, but you can still drive. Paragliding was the same, but better. You're in full control of what you want to do. I was flying! I could go up, down, left, right, and it was so easy. I was on a two-way radio but about halfway up, when I was going in to land, the battery died on me and the radio went off. I couldn't hear a thing. I thought it was looking a bit iffy for me. I headed down, zig-zagging slowly towards where I had to land. You have to pull all the cords down slowly when you hit the ground. At that point, you're not going too fast, but you can do some damage. You have to pull the cords down when you're, I don't know, 5 metres from the ground. I surprised myself because I did it right. I landed badly, but it was all okay. They all came running over and were saying, "Beautiful! You've done it!" It's an unbelievable feeling when you're up there. You can go anywhere you want. If you know the wind conditions, you can go in the pockets of air on your way up. I was up there for about twenty minutes, and loved it. I haven't been back since, but I'll do it again. You *have* to do it. Some things you do, you can never get that feeling again. You just feel so proud that you've done it. It was unreal. And I hooked up with the girl, so it was pretty much the perfect day.'

Honestly, ever felt inclined to fly?

'Up there,' Erdem says, 'you're free.'

Erdem no longer practises holding his breath, content to assume three minutes is beyond him because his belly-wacker-gone-horribly-wrong has left him with ten per cent lung capacity. 'I could have been killed,' he says. 'None of my mates had a clue about resuscitation. They had absolutely no idea. They would have just stood there scratching their heads. By the time they called for help, it was another ten minutes before the lifeguards came. When I was younger I thought I was just holding my breath because I was bored, but it's made me think. I'm a Muslim. I believe in God. My faith and what my fate ended up being—I don't know. I think I was getting ready for what was going to happen. Fate and destiny, I reckon those things are real. I think I knew what my fate was going to be. I know it sounds a bit full-on but I really do think I was getting ready to save my own life.'

Name: Steve Porter
Age: 38
Home: Wynn Vale, South Australia
Classification: 2.5

'I'm a bit never say never, but at the end of the day, I am 38,' says the Australian Captain. 'This will be my fourth Paralympics. I know there are older guys in the team than me, but I've got to look at the contribution I can make given the line-ups I don't fit into at the moment. The biggest thing for me is all the daily training, the time away from the family. I've got two boys and I miss out on some family stuff with my wife. That increasingly weighs on my mind. I'm not going to say that I'm retiring after Beijing, but let's see how we go. In all likelihood I probably do need to change the focus of my life to give back to the family a bit more. This is a pretty hectic life. It's fair to say it causes a bit of friction in a relationship from time to time. Particularly this year because the schedule is so heavy. I've had a pretty good run and I might say goodnight after Beijing. But I said similar things back in Sydney and that was eight years ago. If we'd won a gold medal back then, I could have retired on the spot.

We'll see how we go. The thing is, you don't want to die wondering. You see a lot of sports people retire prematurely and then years later they must be having second thoughts. Especially if they know they can still cut it. Right now, I think I can still cut it.'

Steven James Porter can be as silly as a two-year-old or as sensible as a saint. He can be carefree or contemplative. He laughs with those who are laughing and weeps with those who are weeping. There's a serious side tempered by frivolity. There's a worrying side balanced by a who-cares streak that makes him go hunting for karaoke bars when the time and place are right. There may or may not be a cigarette involved. You've heard better renditions of 'Hotel California', but you've heard worse. Some dance to remember, some dance to forget.

DUBBERLEY: 'There are some characters in this team and Steve is one of them. He's such a funny bloke. He works for Westpac as this big professional and then he's the biggest joker around us. He gets everyone feeling loose. He gets us all relaxed. He'll get a magazine and start narrating it. Not reading it, *narrating* it. We'll all be sitting around listening to him, crying it's that funny. He'll just get everyone together to have a laugh but then he knows when we have to get serious. That's where he's so good. It's getting very professional, but you've got to keep it fun, and he's got the right mix. He's such a funny bastard. He says things like, "If you take a long enough run-up, you can get through it." I love that shit. It's true. He tells the team this all the time—If we do everything we have to leading up to Beijing, take the long run-up and do this and this and this, it won't matter what obstacle comes up, we'll get through it. I like that line. We're taking the longest run-up we can. Sport is sport. You still need luck and a few things to go your way, but we're giving ourselves the best chance. We're coming off the long run.'

The Australian Captain is a tetraplegic.

'How long have you got?' he says when asked about his accident. 'When I was seventeen, I got a pretty rare spinal injury. I was carrying a machine at work, a franking machine, in a suitcase. It weighed about 50 pounds, 20 kilograms, whatever you want to call it. The apprentice who was working with me at the time, it was normally his job to do that. He wasn't in that day, so I had to take this bloody thing over to the post office. It was only about 150 metres away. I took it over there and on the way back, I swapped arms as you do with a suitcase when it's a bit heavy. In that motion, I pulled a muscle in front of the shoulder blades in my back. I tore an artery that basically leads into the spinal cord. I somehow denied the blood supply to the front side of my spinal cord. Over the next hour and a half, I progressively lost all movement from the chest down, and my fingers as well. It took them a few days to work out what the hell was the matter with me. I didn't break my back or damage my spine or anything—none of the scans were showing anything, so they kind of had to piece the clinical picture together over a bit of time.

'I had a couple of weeks in Royal Adelaide Hospital and five weeks in rehab, which was very short for this kind of injury, but because I didn't have a bone injury I didn't have to lay in traction and everything else. I could just get straight into the rehab. I was doing an optical technician apprenticeship at the time, learning how to make glasses and all that kind of shit, but I was away from work for about a year. A tetraplegic still has a spinal cord injury, but it's just that it happened in a different way. We're all a little bit different depending on what happened to our spinal cords. I'm incomplete. I've still got some movement all over, but I went from doing everything to doing nothing, like a lot of blokes. I surfed relentlessly every weekend with my mates, played footy and did martial arts, played squash, everything. To go from doing everything to not being able to do anything tends to fuck you over a little bit. I was lucky in that a lot of my family were in the medical fraternity, nurses and things. I had a lot of support around me at the time and that makes a lot of difference. I think I was a reasonably mentally strong person anyway but to have support at the time made a hell of a difference.

'The night before it happened, I was at the beach with my mates. It was in February, it was hot, it was all pretty good. When it happened—bloody hell. To go from throwing around the footy at the beach to being in hospital the next day, I certainly remember thinking that, you know, I might be better off if I'd just died. After the accident, my boss kept paying me the whole time because he felt a bit guilty about it, I guess. I ended up going back there for a short period but it just didn't work out. I couldn't really do what I was doing before, so I ended up leaving. I went through a series of different jobs, worked for the government for a little while, and then before Atlanta in '96 I pretty much focused full-time on rugby. I didn't work at all the year before Atlanta. We had a pretty shitty tournament there. Out of six teams, we came sixth. We had a few close games but wheelchair rugby in Australia was still very much in its infancy. I remember leaving there and thinking, shit, I really need to do something with my life. My wife was pregnant at the time. I came back and went to uni and got a Bachelor of Management degree.

'The sport was only crawling along, but Sydney changed everything. I sort of fell on my feet. I got a job at Westpac only about a month before they announced their massive sponsorship of the Olympics and Paralympics. They ended up approaching me to be a sponsored athlete. Like, there was Ian Thorpe and Susie O'Neill and Grant Hackett—and me. It was surreal, the whole thing. I had my face on buses and buildings and billboards and Christ knows what else. My mug was all over them. It was just an incredibly exciting time. To have all that, and to be playing sport at that level when you just happen to have the Games in your home country, it's an opportunity you probably only get to *see* once in your life, let alone be part of. The sun was shining on me from that perspective. What athlete at a top level gets that kind of opportunity? To compete at home in a Paralympics? The crowds were enormous. We lost the gold medal by a point. That was the greatest and worst time in my sporting career all wrapped into one. But it was probably the first time I felt like we had equity with the able-bodied athletes. It had never really been like that. Even though we're still a fair way apart, because you're always going to have those differences in people's views, it really turned around for the Paralympics in Sydney. The community, sponsors, everybody got behind us. I was doing a lot of public speaking around that time, and it was a really good experience to go through. The Paralympics is getting bigger and bigger, and Sydney started it.'

The Australian Captain was one of the players interviewed extensively for the *Murderball* doco. 'Yeah, we *were* in it,' he says. 'I did a lot of interviews with those guys, and so did others on our team. Brad did a lot. There was one interview in particular in Sweden. George and I were in a bar after the tournament. We'd had a few jars and the guys were in there filming for the movie. They did quite a lengthy interview with us. They were asking what we thought about the US, and, well, we pretty much told them what we thought. I don't think we were totally glowing in our praise of the American team. We'd had a few beers. We started talking about what we think of Swedish chicks and all that sort of stuff. Not much of it was really related to rugby. When it came to signing the release to use the footage, I was a little reluctant. I wasn't quite sure how it was all going to be portrayed. I thought, number one, I don't really want the Australian public seeing any of their athletes being a bit pissed and shit-canning other teams. And I didn't particularly want my wife seeing us commenting on Swedish chicks, even though it was only for a laugh. We couldn't be sure it would be portrayed in the way we meant it to be. So I didn't sign the release, and nor did anybody else. But as it turned out, the sport was actually portrayed, I think, in quite a good light. They did it really well. Even the sex stuff, I think what they were trying to do was just portray the fact that even if these guys are in chairs, they're still leading normal lives in many ways. There was a bit of crap in there they probably didn't need but all in all, a good show. I liked it. The focus was on the rivalries and the US team, but I guess they were also trying to show the human side of it. I do regret in some respects not signing on. It would have been good to have some of us Australian guys in there. All we ended up with was George and Brad in the background here and there. The two ugliest blokes in our team.'

Porter will react to the overbearing Americans carrying on like card-carrying fuckwits with their self-serving yelling and screaming with a first look that suggests he wants to go bare-knuckle. 'FIGJAM,' he says. FIGJAM is the acronym for Fuck I'm Good, Just Ask Me. 'I've always thought there's a bit of FIGJAM with Zuperman and the whole American team', Porter says. 'You've got to put their dominance into perspective. There are more people with disabilities in America than we have in our entire population. That's just people with disabilities. The pool of players they have is significantly larger, their league is significantly larger, they play more often and the quality of personnel is there. But are they the untouchables they used to be? I don't think so. Certainly I think they're beatable, and I think we have the capability of beating them. We have to get a crack first. We have to get on court with them. You can't fault their enthusiasm. The noise and the energy coming off their bench, as much as Australians might find that sort of stuff a bit over the top—it gives me the bloody shits, to be quite honest—but they have their approach and go all-out with it. More is more for them. Historically, Australia doesn't play well against the USA, and I think there's a bit of a hate factor in it because of the way they go about it. We have to learn to ignore that, or use it to rev us up. We've never beaten them but I don't see why it has to stay that way.

'Zuperman has improved as a player over the last couple of years but when you look at him compared to other three-pointers around the world, he doesn't feature as far as I'm concerned. There are plenty of guys in the American team that make much more of a contribution than he does. But you know, he's got the look, he's got the stamp on the shoulders and leg and all that sort of shit. And I suppose, in some respects, a bit of FIGJAM is good for the game. He's an identity now, or the movie made him an identity. But is he a bloke I would choose to go and have a few cans with? Probably not.'

~

Name: Greg Smith
Age: 41
Home: Wedouree, Victoria
Classification: 2.0

'I'll tell you what I thought. I thought, "Shit, this is it." Outwardly it might have looked like I was moving on with my life but in your dark hours, all the times you're just laying there in the middle of the night, I was thinking, "You know, this life sucks. Maybe I'm better off not having it." I loved the beach, but I couldn't go there for a walk any more. I loved kicking the footy with my mates, but I was never going to do that again. It was probably ten years, I reckon, before I really . . .' Smith pauses. Is he thinking about the dark hours? Then he says, 'Look, I still have moments where I'm at the beach and I think, "Fuck, look at that. I'd love to get up and just go for a run up the beach, go and jump in the surf." You know they probably don't think this, but you hope the person you're watching has a real understanding and grasp of how great they've got things at that moment. I don't mean in terms of their whole life. Everyone has their problems to get through. But at that moment, you probably take things like diving into the surf for granted. I know I did. You don't realise it until you don't have it. Just to be able to dive into the surf one more time—I would give anything for that. Then again I probably take for granted what I've got too. There are going to be disabled people in electric chairs who look at me when I go past and think, "I wish I could push a wheelchair like that." There really is always somebody worse off than you, and that's something you learn to keep in your mind. Get on with it, don't worry about it, you've still got people who support you. You're still going to get the chance to meet some good people in your life. How they accept you, whether you're in a wheelchair, or disabled, won't come into it. They might not have liked you anyway. They might think you're a dickhead and it's got nothing to do with the chair. Being in a chair doesn't have a lot to do with anything too important.'

Smith is a behemoth of the Paralympic movement. He won three gold medals in wheelchair racing in Sydney when one of the great colloseums of world sport was full to overflowing with his countrymen. Beijing will be his fourth Games. Having retired from the track and reinvented himself as a murderballer, the unavoidable selfishness connected to individual competition has been replaced by the selflessness required to slot into a team endeavour.

'Sydney was unbelievable, incredible,' he says. 'Barcelona was really good. Huge crowds and fantastic events and the people were brilliant. Atlanta sucked. Just the whole atmosphere of it all, just the way everyone was treated, just the whole "get 'em in and get 'em out" kind of mentality. The Olympics finished and they shut half the village down. It was just really ordinary. We were second-class in their eyes. You knew you weren't really wanted there. That was a real let-down. In Sydney we were welcomed with open arms. It was our home turf and I got to race in front of my family and friends. They'd never really seen very much of my racing at all. I was kind of peaking in my career at that stage. To win three gold medals at home was just incredible because there was never anything less than 60 000 or 70 000 people in the stands. Just amazing. One of the races was the 5000 metres. It was the morning after my first final, the 800 metres. I'd won that so I was just on this massive high. I really struggled to sleep all night. The race was done and won but I just kept running it through my head so many times. Next morning, I had this 5000-metre final. It was the hardest race I did in my whole fifteen- or sixteen-year career. I thought I couldn't top the night before. I'd always had a goal to win a gold medal at a Paralympic Games, which was a pretty high-end goal as it was, but to pick up two world records in that time. Anyway, this next morning, there was something like 30 000 school kids in the stadium. So when I was getting my gold medal at the presentation, all these thousands of kids were singing the national anthem with me. I was standing there and I could hear their voices and it was the most incredible feeling. I thought I'm just really going to soak this up. It was one of those moments where you think it cannot get any better. I'll remember that morning, and singing the anthem with those kids, for the rest of my life.'

He will also remember this.

'I was a physical training instructor in the army,' he says. 'I'd been posted from Sydney to Puckapunyal, where I was from down in Victoria. I was driving back and fell asleep, ran off the road and hit a tree. I was in a paddock for six hours before I was found. It was the middle of the night and I was by myself. It's a bizarre story, really. This paddock I ran off the road into, all the previous day this farmer and his son had been trying to clear the paddock of all the trees. They worked all day at it and there was this one tree they couldn't get rid of. One tree in the whole paddock. They kept coming back to it, then they'd go away and pull a few others down, come back—but they couldn't get it down. At the end of the day, the farmer said stuff this, we'll bring some dynamite back tomorrow and blow the bloody thing up. So they turn up the next morning and the tree has been knocked over for them, clean out of the ground. I'm lying next to the car. I had hypothermia, and probably about 30 to 45 minutes left before it was all over. They turned up, saw me, called the ambulance. I'd been in and out of consciousness during the night.

The car ran off the road and landed on its side. It slid into the tree, knocked it over and rocked the car back onto its four wheels. I remember sitting there thinking, "Fuck, what's happened here?" I was still conscious. I remember thinking, "Jesus, my neck is a bit sore." I started moving my neck around, which was probably the worst thing I could have done. It was like when you wake up in the morning with a stiff neck, you move your head all around, get all the chinks out. I probably didn't help myself much there. I remember sitting there and touching my knees after that and thinking, "Shit, I've done some damage here." Being a physical training instructor, I kind of knew I'd done some serious damage. The tree had crushed the car right on top of my head. That's what snapped my neck forward. But I'd also split my head open. I could taste the blood running down my face. I couldn't register much sensation but I didn't pick up that my legs were paralysed. I didn't even think about that. I opened the car door and undid my seatbelt and thought I'd better get up to the road and wave someone down, get some help.

'It was pitch black, one in the morning. I was kind of out of the car, but my legs were still in it. I hit the ground and I twisted myself out. I didn't know my legs had stayed in the car to start with. I thought I'd fallen out completely. I got out. I thought, "Righto, I can't walk, I'll just bloody crawl up to the road." I was crawling and crawling and crawling for I don't know how long. It felt like ages. I crawled for as long as I could but in the end, I thought, "Stuff it, I don't know where I'm going, it's pitch black, I don't know if I'm going to get to the road." I thought, "This is it, this is where it's going to end for me." I literally said a few goodbyes in my head to family and I just closed my eyes. See you later. It was all over.

'When they found me in the morning, my legs were still in the car. I hadn't crawled anywhere. I'd dug two holes with my hands and I was still in the same spot, just digging holes. I could feel myself crawling—but I wasn't actually doing it. My hands were covered in dirt and my nails were thick with it. That was the start of my life in a wheelchair. My accident was in 1987, and my first race was in 1988, so it was only twelve months after my accident that I got back into competitive sport.'

Atlanta was followed by Sydney, three gold medals, shoulder surgery and a retirement that didn't stick. 'I had a couple of years of not doing anything competitive,' he says. 'I've got a hand-cycle, so I was just doing some stuff on the hand-bike, helping my old athletics coach with training for some of his racers. I'd ride my bike and pace them, they'd sit behind me—that was the sort of exercise I was doing. I'd been asked to have a try of rugby during my whole racing career, and I always thought, "Nah, I don't want to hurt myself. If I bung a hand, there goes my racing." I looked at racing as my job. Rugby had too much chance of an injury. That's what I was doing with my life, racing, and I thought, "If I'm not racing, what's the point?" I kept saying no, well, one day—maybe. But then after I'd finished racing someone came and said to me again, "Do you want to come and try it now?" I said, "Look, alright. If I come and play socially, that's great. I've retired from competitive sport, I've done what I wanted at the elite level, I'll just play socially." I started playing it, and I wanted to get better at doing what I was doing, and I thought, oh shit, here we go again. I wanted to get as good as I could get. I couldn't help it. Social didn't stay social for long. I loved it again. The fire was re-lit.

'That was 2004. It was the year these guys were heading off to Athens. I was on a national squad in 2004, and I was actually in Melbourne when they were getting all their uniforms given to them, and I thought, "I know what that's like. That's a great feeling." Then I thought I wouldn't mind another crack at that. Seeing the guys get their uniforms for Athens, that's when I thought I can do this again if I really apply myself. I knew I could get fit again. All I needed was to learn the game. If I did the little things I needed to do, if I did the things Brad asked me to do, I knew I could always be a contributor to the team and the result. I put my head down again. I knew how to do that from athletics. I thought if I really have a dig, I might just end up going to Beijing. It's my fourth Games and I just want to get down to those last two teams—and for us to be one of them. And then if we win that last game, we're the best team in the world and no-one will be able to take that away from us. I've had that feeling by myself. I want to share it with these blokes.'

Smith's favourite saying: *Old age and treachery will always beat youth and skill.*

'Everything is a battle of your mind,' he says. 'I've been in a chair a while now. I'm the oldest guy in the team. George was born with his disability, so of all the guys who had accidents, I've been the longest in the chair. Steve and I were injured in the same year. We were only a few days apart. Being older, I hope the guys, especially the younger guys, get something out of knowing what I've done in athletics. I've come to rugby late and I hope they get inspired by that. I learn from guys like Ryley and Scotty, who haven't been playing rugby all that long, but they've been playing longer than me. They give me great ideas and inspiration, and I hope I can give them something in return. I hope they can look up to me and think, "Here's a guy who worked hard and got some results." I want them to think, "If anyone knows how to win a gold medal, it's Smithy. I might just go and have a chat with him, talk about what a Paralympics is all about." Any of the new guys who haven't been around that much, or this might only be their second Games, I hope they know I'm here. I'll help anyone who wants to be helped. This is the pinnacle of what we can do in our sport. You can't get any higher than a Paralympic Games. I hope it's something everyone in the team realises. I hope they see what a rare opportunity it is and use it as a motivation for the training. We've got such a good chance. There's not much between half a dozen teams.

'I write a bit of fitness-program stuff for probably half the guys. I've got a strength and conditioning qualification as well. I don't just have the physical experience of it all, but the training side of it through the army course I did. I help out as much as I can because it sounds like the sport used to be pretty haphazard. Even in the four years I've been playing, I can see huge differences in the teams and their approaches to the game. You just have to look at the way teams travel and all the shit they take with them, video cameras and all their support staff. Look at Canada and Great Britain. The same for Japan. They've nearly got more staff than players. It's becoming an elite sport comparable to any able-bodied sport.'

BATT: 'Smithy has won all his medals, he's been around the Paralympics for years, his dedication to the sport is rubbing off on all of us. I remember playing him for the first time. He had the big reputation for everything he'd done on the track. I remember lining him up and absolutely smashing him. He fell out of his chair, I think, but he got up and kept going. That's the way he is. It's just the passion he has for sport. He loves team sport and it's infectious.'

DUBBERLEY: 'He's a God-send.'

Funny how you can be wrong about people. Smith is an upbeat and unfailingly enthusiastic individual and you imagined that after his accident, he found a way to dust himself off, bill the property owners for knocking down their tree and jauntily embark upon the rest of his life. The truth is more harrowing.

'If you didn't get your head around it, you wouldn't be here,' he says. 'There are definitely people who don't handle it and they end up—it's the ultimate cost—taking their own lives. I would be surprised if there's one person who's had a spinal injury who hasn't thought of that at some stage early on. I definitely did. I brought it up with my mother when I was in rehab. I told her I didn't want to do it any more. I just said to her, "What's the point, Mum?" Two weeks before, I was a physical training instructor in the Australian Army. But now I was a physical wreck. What the heck was I going to do with my life? What was going to happen to me? I was nineteen years old. All the stuff I enjoyed doing most, it was gone. More than twenty years later, those days are few and far between but early on, by Christ, it was a thought that was in my head pretty much all the time.

'The one that blows me away the most is a guy who was in hospital the same time I was. This guy was a family man. He had a couple of kids, it was Christmas. He was putting together a trampoline for his kids in the backyard. He put it all together, sat back on the trampoline, just sitting on the edge of it, admiring his handiwork, lost his balance or his footing or something, rolled backwards and his legs came over the top of him. He was just doing a backwards roll on a trampoline—and snapped his neck. He broke it really high and he's in an electric wheelchair, all for putting together a trampoline for his kids. Then you'll see guys trash a car, write the thing off completely, and walk away. I don't know, those extreme-sports blokes, it's great if you can have that attitude of "If I get hurt, I get hurt", but I don't think they quite get what they're dealing with. Look, if you break an arm, it's going to heal up alright and you'll have use of it again. But I don't think people realise that if you bust your neck or your back, then you lose a shitload more than just your neck or your back. I understand that mentality of devil-may-care. I would have been exactly the same. I *was* exactly the same. I thought if I busted my neck, I busted my neck—without knowing the full consequences of what it really means in your life. It's a big call to make, taking those risks. But nineteen-year-olds are just that way. You're young and you're full of balls and you've got no fear. There's a fair bit of luck that comes into it. It cracks me up.'

He ain't laughing.

'I used to play AFL footy when I was a kid. I broke everything I've got, arms and legs, every bloody thing, just from being a boy. And then one day you just do the same thing again, you just break a bone like you've done before, but this time it's a bone in your neck. The variation is incredible. You can bust your neck and not do any damage to the cord. You're right as rain. Or you can bust your neck and smash it to pieces and be absolutely fucked for the rest of your life. I still relive it. If I had stopped and had a rest, if I hadn't driven so long—all I ever get is a whole lot of what ifs. But you have to try not to dwell on it. I look back at what I've done since and it's been a full life. I can honestly say it's been great.'

Greg Smith tries really hard. That's all he does. He just tries really hard and the rest is a stratospheric offshoot. 'When I was a young bloke racing, I used to train with a guy who was probably twenty years older than me,' he says. 'He would have been the age I am now, and I would have been about twenty. We used to go training together and I'd give him that cheeky little sprint at the end and go past him, smiling. He used to always say to me, "Smithy, old age and treachery will always beat youth and skill." I've never forgotten that. It's funny, because that's what I think now with all these young blokes around. I've gone the full circle. I used to be the one with youth and skill. But these days I've got my old age and treachery. That's still enough to take me places.'

It's taking him one place—Beijing.

Name: George Hucks
Age: 40
Home: Klemzig, South Australia
Classification: 3.0

Quiet, please.

George Hucks is speaking.

'There's none of the, how do I say this, there's none of the shit in our team that you get in other sporting teams,' he says. 'You know how you get your little factions and cliques? There's none of that here. No dickheads, mate. Come in here and act like a dickhead and you're not going to last. We've had that in years gone by and it held us back. There was no *team*. There were a few blokes who used to blow around together, away from everyone else. Not any more. We're all in. We stick together. If we do wander off, it can be with a different group of guys to the ones you were with the last time. It's not always the same two or three blokes hanging out together. Everyone is mates with everyone else, and that's changed us. Brad is really focused on that sort of stuff. Having someone like Smithy come in, he's brought in so much professionalism. You see him, and the way he goes about training and everything else, and you just want to follow him. We've got more guys now thinking the same way. They'll just do everything as well as they can. They're the majority now, so they get their way. It changes the whole culture. Everyone else knows that you're not going to get away with being the slacker or the bloke who doesn't always do the right thing. I've been playing this game a long time. It's all changed lately for the better. You don't have guys any more who are partying and shit, drinking and carrying on. Even if we don't get the results we want, we'll be able to look at each other at the end of this and say, "We did everything we could." In this team, the way it has changed the last few years, you do it right or you can piss off.'

George Hucks is a gum-chewing, beard-adorned bull of a man who calls Ryley Batt 'Poofter Hips' during training sessions and keeps knocking Golden Balls on his arse. More strength to his arm. He can giggle like a schoolboy on a sugar-high. Or yowl with animalistic aggression. Hit him across the head with a plank of wood and the plank would snap in half. You would pay good money to watch George Hucks play murderball, you honestly would. Smashed by Hucks, Batt will be rolling around on his slapped back—left, right, shit, can I get a hand here—like his kayak has capsized and he's still strapped in. Hucks will not blink. Batt never wants to show he's hurt, but Hucks is pumped and he knows Golden Balls needs to be toughened up because he's going to be thrown to the sharks in Beijing.

They're of similar appearance. Hucks looks like Batt in twenty years. Same stocky frame, rugged and tough. Here's what they are. The old bull and the young bull. Heard the one about the old bull and the young bull? Two bulls are standing on top of a hill. They look down to the valley and see a field of cows. The young bull gets all excited and says he's going to run down the hill and introduce himself to the first cow he sees. The old bull casts a lazy eye over the field he's going to stroll down the hill and introduce himself to *all* the cows. Hucks wants Batt to sit back and understand the opportunity being thrown his way. The Australian team is on the up but Batt is misguided if he thinks he'll spend the rest of his career winning gold medals and MVP awards. Hucks is living proof that such youthful displays of unbridled optimism can be stupefyingly misguided. Hucks has been playing for twelve years and this is his resumé since Sydney. Paralympic gold medals: Nil. World championships: Nil. Canada Cups: Nil. Gold medals of any description: Nil. This is the last roll of the dice for Hucks and the old bull wants to do it right. He's less interested in The Big Dance than all the small dances preceding it, launching himself into the next training session, having his say at the next team meeting—and then strolling down the hill to introduce himself to one last chance at a Paralympic medal.

Your first sighting of Hucks came at the team announcement when one of The Learned Gentlemen Of The Australian Paralympic Committee says he hopes Dubberley's foray into coaching will be his first step towards becoming a future Learned Gentleman. He says it with sincerity, or a bloody good impression of it, and there was a flickering of surprise on Dubberley's freshly shaven face. An office job? Not fucking likely. Dubberley reads out his players' names and Hucks rolls forward. You know when someone just catches your eye? What is that? Most of the players, including Batt, *especially* Batt, are sheepish when they are formally introduced. Hucks wheels out, glaring around like his eyes are machine guns and he wants to scatter the room, putting up with the formalities rather than being part of them, disappearing as soon as he's allowed to. He then proceeds to belt the living crap out of Batt and anyone else who approaches him during a no-holds-barred training session in front of the peeling paint and another crowd of two-tenths of fuck-all.

Hucks's beard is dark and thick. He resembles King Henry VIII. But then you sit next to him, listen to his words, and realise he's a pussycat. But then he belts Cameron Carr with a sickening thud and you think he's a tyrant. But then he talks about his belief in feng shui. Onto the court again. Batt is on his back again, groaning in frustration, the ball rolling across the floor. He gets up. Hucks hammers him again. Batt flies across the floor, sideways and helpless. Hucks is prowling and now he's wheeling past a splitting-his-sides-with-laughter Dubberley and here's what George Hucks does then. He winks.

Fucking brilliant.

'As of today, this morning, we're all officially in the team,' he says. 'We're going to Beijing and it's real. A lot of people back home in Adelaide say, "You must be really excited, it's coming around so fast." And they're right, I am excited. But I tend to be more caught up in the process than anything else. You're concentrating so hard on training, then another tournament is coming up with the Super Series, and then there's the Canada Cup. They're the things we have to worry about first. Let's see where we are after the Canada Cup. We've all got the end goal of Beijing, but there's a lot of shit we have to get right before then. I've done four of these Paralympics—it's not that the excitement has gone, not at all—but I just know there are things that need to be done in the meantime. We need to get our shit together. You can't take anything for granted. I've been chosen for four Paralympics, but I only got to play in three of them. I broke my knee at Atlanta. I snapped my kneecap in training as soon as we got there. People think, "You're in a chair, you can play anyway." But when you snap your kneecap in half, you're not doing anything for a while. I went to training, got slammed and the next thing I knew, I was on my way home. I was devastated.'

Further opportunities presented themselves. None were grasped. The gold medal in Sydney slipped through Hucks's fingers right when he was about to clench his fists and run for the hills. Beijing could be the end of a decades-old road for Hucks and that is why it means so much. He looks at Batt like a father looks at a talented but mischievous son. So much potential. So much that he doesn't know. Hucks wants Batt to see the bigger picture because Hucks *is* the bigger picture. Forget the future. All that matters is now, now, now, now, now. After Sydney, Australia should have hit the accelerator and started piling up trophies. Instead, they ran out of petrol and went to the pub. Their results from Sydney to this moment read like an obituary of a man who was born with all the potential in the world but never quite got round to realising it before lights out.

'I had a bit of a rough year last year,' Hucks says. 'I had to sit out for a while. I didn't play the Oceanias. I hadn't missed a tournament for twelve years so that was a bit hard to take. It's good to be back in the house. I'm ready to go again. It's all changed and I'm going to change with it. When I started, all the blokes liked to have a shit-storming time and play a bit of rugby on the side. I was probably one of them. It's the opposite now. The blokes here are still the kind of blokes who like a bit of a party, but rugby has gotten serious. We'll go out the last night of a tournament, and that's it. There's more at stake now. Everybody wants to be the best and everybody wants results. If you want the results, you have to do the work. You can't just turn up at the last minute. And you can't live that full-on party lifestyle. That's the biggest change. Even last year when I was out, Brad had a plan for me. I'd hurt my arm so I was gone for about three months. But then they decided to keep me out for the rest of the year, freshen me up for this year. It gave me the shits but it was part of the bigger plan. I've come back in and I've found there's a different culture from even a year ago. There's more of a central focus. Just the little disciplines. Everyone is training together, everyone is warming up together. There are no separate bits and pieces in our team any more. We used to be all over the shop. We've come close before, in Sydney, without ever quite getting there. We've had really good teams before that could've won gold medals but we've always fucked it up. This is our chance to get it right.'

You can picture Hucks eating raw meat for dinner. Catching the screaming fare with his bare hands, skinning it, blood dripping down his chin. But then he orders sushi. 'Feng shui is important to me, mate,' he says. You assume he's be extracting the piss. 'Really, mate, it's my favourite thing. It's okay to have a group of athletes and bring them all together and call them a team, but unless you've got the feng shui right, you're not going to win shit. That little bit of team work can be the difference between winning a medal and not winning one. It's sport, mate. There are no guarantees. If we do everything right, I really do think we can get a medal. To win a gold, we'll need a bit of luck. But this is the first team I've been in where we're going to give ourselves the best possible chance. This is one of those teams that is getting its shit together like the Americans do. The Paralympics, they're so rare. You stuff it up and four years is a long time to wait for another go. Or you might not be playing again by the next one. I know I'm probably not going to be around in 2012 and you just don't know—some of the younger guys might only get one chance, this chance. And even if you play a lot more, you might not always have a strong enough team to really threaten to win it. This is the strongest team we've ever had across the board. All the ingredients are here. We've got that really good blend of players, Brad has turned himself into a really good coach and hopefully we make it all count. We're doing a lot of talking so let's hope we're good enough to back it up.'

Batt has his pride, turning sharply to go full-tilt on Hucks. They swerve past each other, youth and skill up on one wheel, swinging to a stop like an Olympic downhill skier at the end of another cannonball run. You look at the old bull barging around, grinning from ear to ear, a scowl and a *thump* and then another mad grin, sledging Poofter Hips, scoring goals, whooping it up. 'I like being able to hit blokes,' he says with a comical sincerity. 'There's no doubt we all play rugby because of the contact. It's just that sort of game. It's just got that gladiatorial thing about it. There aren't many sports like that, especially when you're stuck in a bloody wheelchair. A lot of these guys were into competitive sports, footy and motocross or whatever, and this gives them the chance to go hard again. Being a bit bigger, I can throw my weight around a bit. It used to be funny until Ryley turned up and started kicking sand in my face. I've started seeing what it's like to be on the receiving end. That's the bonus of the game now, having guys like Ryley involved. Rugby has changed a lot. It's a lot more tactical now with the middle-range guys. You don't always get a big advantage from the domination you might have with those guys because there's still a limit to what they can do. But then you throw someone like Ryley out on the court and what can anyone do to stop him? He can just obliterate you. I'm not going to grow old before my time doing this shit. I'm loving it. I'm 40 and feel like I'm twenty. It's the best fun. I should grow up and get over it but I'm not quite there yet. I'll find the time to live that other life later.'

Hucks has a spinal *disease*.

'I didn't have an accident,' he says. 'I'm a freak of nature, that's about it. Most people have exciting stories to tell but mine is just having a couple of genes that didn't mix together properly. They couldn't find a way to get along. It's a spinal cerebella disease that just breaks down the nervous system and fucks you up a bit. The rugby for me has a bit of a double edge. It keeps me up physically so I can keep going along. It's good for my health but it's a bloody lot of fun at the same time. That's the main thing. You know, there's probably a side to me that could say, "Do I really still need this?" And I could answer no. I have to get leave from work all the time, I have to leave my family at home to go play tournaments and I'm not getting any younger.

'It's not all gloss. After Sydney, I basically quit then. I thought, "That's it for me, I can't do much more than that." We lost the gold medal in Sydney by one goal, but we were sixth in the world before that so getting a silver medal in our home country, we basically pulled a big tournament out of our arses. I had a really good tournament. I got to play big minutes and had a shit-storming time and left everything I had out there. I thought, "Well, it can't get any better than this, so why bother?" That's kind of stupid but I was just thinking, "I should move on now." That was eight years ago, and now I've been to another Paralympics and there's another one coming up. You just keep getting ready for the next one. It's just gotten into my blood. There are times when it gets a bit hard and there's a lot of bloody training in between tournaments but once the career is gone, it will be gone for good, and I've never been able to let it go. I'll decide one day I've had enough, or someone else will come along and take my spot, but until then I'll keep going as hard as I can. It could be worse. I could be working.'

Hucks does work as—wait for it—an accountant.

DUBBERLEY: 'George is one of our top dogs. But last year, I sacked him. He was injured, sort of overweight and not really enjoying it as much. I dropped him. I laid him down for a year. All the other guys were like, "Fuck, he really has cut him." He'd been playing ever since it started in Australia. He's such a good player but I laid him down for being out of shape and it was like, "Shit, the coach is serious." Hopefully it made them all realise they had to keep their end of the bargain. George was stood down, but he took it the right way. We gave him a rest, and he came back better than ever. He's going to be enormous for us.'

HUCKS: 'I had to get back in, I missed it. It comes down to the fact that once you get on the court, you want to go mad. It's just such bloody great fun. If you can do something at the top level, it's natural for you to just want to do it as long as you can. I feel pretty bloody blessed to have been doing what I've been doing over the last twelve years.'

The Old Bull rolls back for one last stab at the training session, gunning and running for Poofter Hips. Hucks rams him like every other high-pointer is going to ram Batt in Beijing. George Hucks is getting himself ready for the Paralympics, do not doubt that for a second, but he's also taking it upon himself to prepare Batt. Hucks unleashes his verbal and physical might on the young bull and then he throws his head back with the howl of a midnight wolf. Raucous and maniacal laughter. You know what George Hucks is? Fucking magnificent.

Name: Grant Boxall
Age: 32
Home: Success, Western Australia
Classification: 2.5

'On the morning of the accident, well, the night before, my girlfriend at the time said to me, as women do, "You've got three days off work, I want you to spend time with me." I was like, "Well, if the surf is good, I wouldn't mind getting out there." She said she didn't want me to. She said, "Promise me you're not going to go." I was like, "Um, okay." The next morning, the boys were all saying the surf was awesome. It can be hard not to listen to the boys, you know? It was a nice summer's day and there was decent quality swell. It wasn't good because of the size, it was just the quality of the waves. It really was one of those awesome surfing days. Supertubes was about two or three feet, it was all pretty good. The guys started twisting my arm and I was like yeah, okay, sounds good. One of my mate's girlfriends came along, so my girlfriend came too, against all her wishes. She was pretty pissed off with me about it.

'We got down to Supertubes and had a look and we were like, "Yeah, it looks alright." But there was a tonne of people out there. Two days before that, I'd borrowed a mate's four-wheel drive and gone solo down to a place called Muffins. It's about halfway between Yalingup and Beaumont Bay. It's just on the south side of Injilup point. It's a weird sort of set-up. It's got this bombie rock out the back. On the big days the wave hits the bombie and then hits this shelf. It's only four feet deep and by the time the wave sucks over it, it can get pretty hairy. We turned up and it was only knee-high. We just kept seeing these waves hit this bombie and jack on the inside. There were all these magic plumes of spray coming out of the barrel. It was an awesome sight. Even before that, my girlfriend was like, "You're not going out, I don't want you going out there, you've been there twice already and I don't like it." I'd told her I'd been bumped on the bottom a couple of times, that I'd hit the rocks on my back and my hips. It's a pretty dangerous spot and she just didn't like it.'

Boxall paddled out with his mates. One of them was Australia's world no. 2 surfer, Taj Burrow.

'Taj's old man, Vance, was there,' Boxall says. 'He was doing some filming for a new video Taj was doing. Vance was set up on the beach with his video camera. The girls were all set up with their gear. It's just normal to see Taj out in the water around here. We'd surfed together at Bears a fair bit, all over the place. That was the first time I'd seen his old man, though. We kitted up and went out there and got three or four waves. Taj kept getting the inside and in the end I just went, "Mate, fair dinkum, you can take off deeper than me any day of the week, go for it." In the end, he took off on one and . . .'

In the end.

Boxall keeps saying *in the end.*

'He went to get this one off the bombie. It didn't quite carry through to the shelf. He came down, tried to ride it through, but it didn't have enough oomph so he pulled off the back. In the end, that's when I took off and . . .'

In the end.

'I was a little bit further in, and it hit the shelf. It was probably three or four feet. It wasn't massive but it was, you know, quite thick. I paddled into it. I sort of pig-dogged it on the take-off. I'd always been pretty strong with that sort of technique. I took off on it and in the end [*in the end*] it wasn't the size of the wave that got me, it was the volume of water. It was like a shore break on rock. I took off, I was under the wall, going along, beautiful. I got shacked off my head but instead of it letting me push straight through it, it started to close out. I thought I'd pull out straight and just ride the flats, get into the channel and paddle back out. But as I pulled out, the slab hit me on the back of the head. That drove me down vertically, just straight down. I was almost standing up dead straight at that stage, so I was quite high, but as the lip hit me I went straight down head-first and then I heard a crunch. I didn't think too much about it at first. The first thing you think about is surviving the wash, just getting back up for some air. But I'd hit the shelf smack-bang on the top of my head.

'I managed to get a few yelps out, because I sort of knew what was going on. I tried to move my legs and nothing was happening. All the pain was in my head. I'd smashed it open. It was a pretty decent crack of my melon. A couple of guys helped out but within about ten seconds, I'd completely lost the use of my legs. A few more yells of help, then about five seconds after that, a total loss of the use of my arms. Apart from the flotation I had from my wetsuit, I had nothing keeping me afloat. Then I went under anyway. I was telling my body to move but nothing was happening. I was going straight down, just sinking. I was panicking, it was all happening so quick. Next thing I knew, this hand grabbed the scruff of my neck, or the back of my wettie, and ripped me back up. I was gulping air. It was Taj. He was saying, "Get on my board! Try to get on my board!" I was like, "I can't! I can't!" It was just mayhem. I don't know how long all this took. I just completely lost track of time. There were three guys around me and they all brought me in through the inside. I don't know how many waves came through us, but I came off my board a couple of times. They eventually got me to the beach. They just lay me down on the sand and one of my mates goes, "Holy fucking shit, what's happened to your head?" Another mate grabbed a towel and he was saying he wanted to stuff it in my head. That's what he said: "I have to stuff this in your head." I'm like, "What? *In* my head? What are you talking about, *in* my head?" There was a crater in my head the size of your fist.

'You've probably had a local anaesthetic before? Well, you know the area where you have the local, how it feels fat and inflamed and kind of swollen? Well, my whole chest area and stomach felt like that. It's weird when you feel the paralysis first coming on. I felt like my whole body was bloating. I was lying there thinking, "Jesus Christ, this is it. I'm dying. This is where it's all going to end." I knew something fairly diabolical had happened. I thought there were internal injuries that were going to kill me. I was lying on the beach and I said, "Look boys, I'm here in front of these waves, just let me go. It's okay."

'They grabbed a surfboard, put me on the board and took me up this rocky goat track to this old jeep. They plonked me on the front seat, not knowing what was wrong with me, and sat me bolt upright. One of my best mates got in the car and just fanged it, absolutely blitzed it. Usually it's about a twenty-minute drive, in a four-wheel drive, to the car park but he nailed it in about six minutes. You can imagine the ride. It was that rough that my headrest snapped off the chair. I don't want to think about what went on with my head and neck on the drive. My whole body was getting thrown around. It probably made my injuries worse, but I don't dwell on that. They were doing what anyone would—trying to get me to hospital straightaway. They eventually got to town at Dunsborough, parked, and bolted into a bakery and asked for someone to ring the ambos. The ambos turned up and knew exactly what was happening. They got the boards out of the car and took me out of the back of the car because that was the safest way.

'They got me to Busselton Hospital. They told me they'd have to X-ray me to find out what was going on. They did the X-rays. My girlfriend came to the hospital at that point. My brother had been informed because he wasn't with us. My girlfriend and my brother were told there was no evidence of any spinal injury. I had no movement and reduced feeling, but they didn't think it was spinal. I thought, "Okay, cool. What a relief."

'I was going on the flying doctor service to Perth. My girlfriend couldn't come because the patient was the only one allowed on the plane. She got on the bus and went straight to Perth. I don't remember the flight—I was on pethidine and in la-la land. I can't even remember getting on the plane. The next thing I remember is having the doctors and my parents talking by my bedside in emergency. My parents lived at Rottnest Island at the time. It was about a two-hour trip by the time they prepped the boat. I can't imagine what was going through their heads in those two hours. At the Perth hospital the doctor said I'd suffered a severe spinal injury. I was like, "What's the story? I was told there was no spinal injury." He told me that there were two bones in my neck that they didn't quite X-ray properly back at Busselton. They didn't lay me on the right angle, or something. I've never understood that. How can you "not quite X-ray properly"? They got the first five bones on the neck, but they didn't X-ray the sixth and seventh, which is what I injured. That's pretty full-on. That blew me away, that they could get that wrong. Anyway, they put the bolts in my head and put on the halo and said they had to operate.

'I was in the intensive care unit for about a week. I came off the painkillers after about five days. The doctor came in and said something like, "Look, the prognosis isn't good. You've suffered a serious spinal injury and you're going to be confined to an electric wheelchair for the rest of your life." At that time I was in what they call the crucifix position—arms and legs out straight and to either side—to prevent a shortening of the muscle groups. At that point, I still couldn't move my arms and legs. I was pretty wild. I said, "Fuck you guys, you've got no idea what you're talking about." Pretty funny, now I think about it. They were spinal surgeons with about 70 years of experience between them. I'm there strung out on my crucifix telling them they didn't know what they were fucking talking about. I was pretty angry. From then on, I was just determined to get out of hospital without being in an electric chair.

'I've been fortunate to get the level of function I have, particularly with my hands. They're quite functional. The muscles behind my thumbs and little fingers are weakened but otherwise I'm okay. I couldn't extend the fingers on my right hand when I got out of hospital. I did lots of cooking when I got home, lots of stir-fries, chopping up all the carrots and potatoes, and my left hand came back pretty good. I'd hold the vegetable in my right hand and chop it up with my left. The vegetable would get smaller and harder to grip, so my right hand had to get better. Cooking was like my own little rehab at home. I never went to out-patient rehab at all. In the end [*in the end*] I was the fastest wheelchair-bound quadriplegic to get through Shenton Park rehab hospital in Perth. That's the fastest in the history of the hospital. That wouldn't matter to most people, but I was pretty proud of that. It was just a shade over three months—three months and three days, something like that. Generally for quads, the rehab period is between six and twelve months. The upper limb movement came back pretty quickly. The usual rule of thumb is that whatever function you get back in two years is all you're ever going to get back. But then five and a half years after my accident, I had the return of my sexual function and bowel control. I got hurt in February. By July, I was working again.

'In early August, I started playing rugby. I'd been playing for about six months when I made my first State team. It was massively quick.

I never went out with the goal to represent Australia or play State or international rugby. For me, because I lost so much weight in those twelve weeks in hospital, just being completely bed-bound, I needed to rebuild my strength and stamina just to get through the everyday things. I thought rugby could do that for me. I thought pushing a wheelchair around would get me fit, and the whole reason I wanted to get fit was to gain greater independence. I wanted to be able to do the everyday things again. In September 2001, I played my first international tournament for Australia. It blew me away, but there were repercussions.

'Being so new, I was still getting used to the way my disabled body worked. I was still trying to work out the signals that I needed to take a piss, or use my bowel, or whatever it was. That was a real interesting time for me. It was all new. I found out that as I ate different foods, my body reacted differently than when I was an able-bodied person. Some foods would just set me off. Back then I didn't have any—how can I say this—control. Imagine going away with the boys, who are all seasoned quads with all their personal stuff worked out, but all these things were going wrong with me. I felt like an outcast because I just had so many issues, a lot of bowel-related problems. No matter what I did, I had a lot of issues that took quite a long time to sort out. And I had to work it all out with the boys around.'

DUBBERLEY: 'Grant has this full-on determination that can get him in trouble. He played up big-time in the first round of the National League. He's not a problem child, as such, but he can go off the rails. Part of the problem is that there's no-one over in Perth pushing him. He goes great, but he can overanalyse a few things and stress out about stuff he doesn't have to worry about. To me, Grant would be an awesome individual athlete. As a team athlete, he's great, but I can imagine him excelling as an individual athlete just because of the drive he has.

'It wasn't good when he played up. He was nearly banned from the whole thing. It was the first time the National League had been played in Perth. They had all their sponsors and juniors and everyone checking out rugby. WA had two brand-new coaches. Grant gets really involved in every game, but this time he started swearing his head off and going ballistic on the sideline in front of all the sponsors and everyone else. Everybody heard everything he said. I went up to the coach and said, "What are you going to do about this? He doesn't do that with the Australian team." He used to, until I cut him. He didn't go to the Chris Handy Cup in New Zealand one year because I cut him for playing up with this kind of stuff. He doesn't pull these stunts any more with us. But he went off in Perth. I said to the coach, "Look, I want to make sure he understands he can't do it with you guys, either. Lay down the law. If I was you guys, I'd suspend him for a game or two, make him sit on the sideline, but he's not allowed to even talk to the players. He has to keep his mouth shut." The coach went off at him, I went off at him, we all went off at him. If I was in Grant's shoes, I would have been pissed off. He would have felt like the world was against him. But they were ready to pull his membership from WA. If they did that, he couldn't play for Australia, and that would have been it for Beijing because you have to be a member of a State team to qualify for the Paralympics. He went off his head. It was lucky I was there, because otherwise they would have just told him, "See ya." We had a big yarn to him. I'm glad he's made it through. The likes of Ryley and Steve, they'll take a quick look at something and just go, "Yep, sweet." Come game time, they're just worried about their own games instead of anyone else's. It's more instinctive to them. It's great that Grant has all this passion, but he can make things more complicated than they have to be. You almost need to protect him from himself.'

Boxall grabs a handful of stomach fat. 'I don't have any abdominal muscle function, like every other quad, which is why we all get the quad gut,' he says. 'That's what we call it—quad gut. Even if I could walk, I'd be standing up and I'd just fold in half because I don't have the stomach muscles that hold you in an upright position. My lats do all the work. I do some full-on gym work and train for rugby six days a week, so I think I'm pretty fit. I get up at five-thirty and go for a 6-kilometre push. I head off to work three days a week. In the afternoon I'll have two hours in the gym. There's another two-hour training session on court with the State team. I'll just keep doing the training and hope it pays off. When I first got out of hospital, my neighbour—a good mate of the family's—had retired after his wife passed away from breast cancer. He used to pack my crappy old hospital day chair into the back of his car. We'd drive down to the Swan River, get into my chair and push on this paved path around the river. That was a 6.5-kilometre loop. At first he would push me all the way around—I just couldn't push, I just didn't have the strength. The muscles in my shoulders weren't built up, my pecs weren't built up. I had nothing, basically. Slowly, over time, the aim was to be able to push the length of one of the bridges across the river. Then it became okay, let's do half the circuit. Then it became let's do half the circuit and one of the bridges. And then eventually it became both the bridges. That was always the aim, the next little step. I didn't set any goal of wanting to get to Athens. It was more like, first I'll try to make the State team then I'll try to make the national team and then I'll try to make the next Oceanias team and after that I'll hopefully get to the world championships. But then all the little things took care of themselves and I wound up in Athens and now I'm going to Beijing and it's my second Paralympics.

'It's a massive commitment time-wise, and it's a massive financial commitment for all of us. Out of my own pocket, I've probably spent \$60 000 over the last seven years. I hadn't received any grants from the APC until this year, so I think we're all pretty skint. They've given us eight grand. It's the first time in seven years I've been paid anything and that's only because the APC think we're a medal chance. It helps, but it's a drop in the ocean. It doesn't even pay for my chair. I've had four chairs in my career. Just the frame is worth about seven grand. Then you need two pairs of wheels. The full set-up is probably \$8000. You need a new set of wheels every three or four years, a new frame every eighteen months to two years. And then I go through twelve-hundred bucks worth of gloves a year. They last one training session, one game. The cost is huge. I've had a few little corporate sponsors here and there. I made a DVD of the sport and sent it to every company I could think of. But I haven't had any backers for this little Paralympic cycle. It's been pretty tough, to be honest. But I think it's going to be worth it. People say, "It must be so good to travel the world and play your sport." It *is* good, but you've got to put it all in proportion. It's not paying the bills.

People ask, "Do you get paid to play?" They've got to be joking. We pay to play. It would be bloody nice to just get our chairs paid for but generally you have to rely on your sponsors or your family to help you raise funds.'

DUBBERLEY: 'GB and Canada, they're all paid, and all their staff get full-time wages. The GB players are on about 35 000 pounds a year each. And they get scholarships and their pensions on top of it. Some of them are on big coin. Canada is pretty similar. Same with all their staff—even their video people, the people taking their footage, that's their full-time job. Their coach is on about 150 grand a year. We don't rate when it comes to money or resources.'

An email crossing the oceans is entitled *What Cancer Cannot Do.* It cannot cripple love. It cannot shatter hope. It cannot corrode faith. It cannot destroy peace. It cannot kill friendship. It cannot suppress memories. It cannot silence courage. It cannot invade the soul. It cannot steal eternal life, and it cannot conquer the spirit. Is all this applicable to quadriplegia? Boxall does hope for medical science to make a miracle discovery. Find a cure. Christopher Reeve raised hundreds of millions dollars in the same vain hope. Reeve severed his spinal cord at the C1 and C2. His horse, Buck, spooked by a rabbit or a shadow, stopped in its tracks and sent him crashing head-first to the turf. Reeve stopped breathing for three minutes. Drifting in and out of consciousness, he told his wife, Dana, 'Get the gun, they're coming after us.' Severed at the C1, his head and spinal cord were no longer attached. Weeks later, in hospital, he told his wife: 'Maybe we should just let me go.' But he clung like grim death to the hope of walking again. The Dana and Christopher Reeve Foundation poured their millions into stem cell research but nine years after his accident, Reeve died of cardiac arrest. He succeeded in taking one step before he died. Having cared for him throughout, two years later, Dana Reeve was diagnosed with lung cancer. She was not a smoker. She died, too. Their son, Will, had lost both his parents in gruesome circumstances by the age of eleven. Cannot corrode faith? Cannot conquer the spirit? You sure about that? How's Will Reeve travelling?

Only full-blown surfers, those unfailingly restless souls who live and breathe for the early morning baptism of the first wash of saltwater over their faces, can possibly hope to fathom the endless frustration at having their otherworldly invigoration taken away.

'The mental side of rehab was pretty quick for me,' Boxall says. 'I dealt with it because I had to. When they told me I was going to be in a chair, I was like, "So what? My legs aren't going to work. It's not a big deal." But I had no idea about all the other stuff that went along with it. I cannot tell you how much I miss being able to get out in the ocean. As for everything else, I was so naive at the time. The physical issues are nothing, really. The lack of muscle function—it's not a big issue to me. I think you'll find with all the guys that it's the whole pissing and shitting thing. That's the soul-destroying part of it. It's only supposed to be babies and really old people who have those sorts of issues. I was a 25-year-old guy in the prime of life, you know. But I've been gifted the return of that bowel function. To know when I need to go, and to be able to go when I want, and all that sort of stuff, that is just amazing to me. I know it sounds pretty basic, but that is life-changing. Even learning how to walk, I think it's a mental thing. I haven't given up. Every now and then, and I've done this today, I'll sit in my chair and try to move my legs and toes. I'll start with my toes and my feet. Every joint and muscle I've got that I would use to walk, I try to move, to make sure my brain stays trained to using those things in case it ever comes back. I'll always hold on to the hope. You just never know. If something happens and I'm able to walk again, my brain will still know how to send those signals to my muscles. I kind of talk to my legs in case something happens and it all comes back.' There is a heroism to Grant Boxall clinging to hope like that.

~

Name: Shane Brand
Age: 35
Home: Preston, Victoria
Classification: 1.5

One of nature's true gentlemen had an extensive background in martial arts before his neck cracked and grew a jagged edge that cut his most important cord. He held black belts in karate, kick boxing and doce-pares. He still holds them, of course, but a fat load of good they do him now. Brand is polite, decent, quiet, calm and good. He ran a martial arts school for three years, teaching that when you fall, you must protect the neck for dear nonsensical life. If you're falling backwards, slam your hands either side of your torso so the head *has* to stay up. Under no circumstances can the neck be allowed to take any of the jarring impact. That's all fine and dandy but it can be a little difficult to consult the text book when your car is cartwheeling through the dead of night somewhere unannounced in the Australian dust.

'It happened in 2001,' he says. 'I've got family in Adelaide, and I was heading back to my parents' place to go over to my grandfather's for his 80th birthday, which was the next day. It was a very foggy night in Victoria. Rural Victoria, I guess you would call it. There was a really thick pea-soup fog. I had a tyre blow-out in my car. The car just went out of control, I couldn't see anything. I ended up nearly in a swamp. I was stuck in my car for the whole bloody night. It was a really deserted road—those country back roads, a couple of shortcuts—but even if it was busy, because the fog was so thick, no-one could have seen me anyway. I was in a terrible way. I was pretty stressed. Quite a few things go through your head when you sit there for hours on end, like all the people you might not see again. The car had flipped, rolled, hit a fence, rolled again. I'd done a defensive driving course, so I got it to stop rolling and ended up just getting in a spin, which I couldn't stop. All I wanted to do was get out of the car, but it was the same old story, I guess. My legs wouldn't move. I went to open the door, but I'd broken my right arm. I was stuck in there. I tried tooting the horn to raise some kind of awareness if anyone did come by.'

The horn sounded for hours; a long siren cry for assistance falling on thousands of miles of deaf ears. 'I could turn the ignition off,' Brand says. 'I took the keys out and basically just sat there and did the long wait. It was pretty cold, the whole roof was caved in—that's how I broke my neck, the roof basically just caved in on me. It was ridiculous. I had glass cuts on my head, I could feel the blood dripping down all over my face. It was like a horror movie. It was probably five or six hours, but it felt like forever to me. Probably the worst thing was that I remained conscious the whole time.

'I was found the next morning by a policewoman who was on her way to work. When she first saw me, she radioed in to see if anyone had reported an accident or an abandoned car. No-one had. And then she saw I was in the car. She ran back, made her calls, and the State Emergency Services came. They were the first ones to grab me. They were trying to get me out—and I don't remember what happened after that. It was one of my relatives who was actually the first on the scene because he works for the SES. My dad is a police officer. Mum and Dad knew I hadn't been home and hadn't gotten to my grandfather's place, so when the police turned up on their doorstep, they thought I was dead. Dad knew what it normally meant when there's a knock on the door like that. Mum knew something was up. She was telling Dad something was wrong, that she thought something had happened, but he didn't want to believe it. And then when the police rocked up, he went to water.'

Pitch black. Cold. Alone. Broken arm. Blood on the tongue. The hell of it. 'I knew my legs weren't working, but I couldn't work out why,' Brand says. 'I knew my arm was broken, but it didn't occur to me why my fingers weren't working. In that situation, you just think you're pretty banged up but you don't necessarily think, "Am I a quadriplegic? Am I paralysed?" I tried undoing my seatbelt to get out but luckily enough, my seat had actually broken on the seat rail. I couldn't undo it, which was good because I would have only done more damage to myself if I wasn't strapped in. I tried reaching for my phone but because the car had rolled, nothing was where it had been. Everything was upside down.' Including, effective immediately, Brand's life.

'When the policewoman got to me,' he says, 'I blacked out and didn't wake up till after my surgery. They took me to Alderton Base Hospital. Apparently I was communicating with them there, but I can't remember it. They discovered the extent of my injuries and flew me back down to Melbourne to the spinal unit. They did the actual surgery on me there. I just remember waking up and getting the news about what I'd done to myself, and how things were going to be for the rest of my life. It was devastating, like it is for all of us when we're told the definite story. The bottom line is we've all had something similar happen in our lives. We hang shit on each other, there's a lot of crap that goes on. I'll fall out of my chair and everyone starts laughing, but it's all good. We're all just getting on with it. We don't pussy-foot around anything. It is what it is, and we are what we are. My dad, when we talk about it, reckons it took me all of about two weeks to get going again. I was devastated but I figured I would try to make the most of it. Just do the best I could and get back to what I used to be as much as possible.

'You can still be the same person, you can still have the same personality. All the same stuff is going to make you laugh. You can see the same people if they want to see you. I just concentrated on trying to do that, keeping things as normal as I could. I went back to work to keep me focused on things other than myself. Just to keep busy. You can't think about it too much. If you've got too much time, that's what does your head in. There were twenty-five of us going through rehab, and about six of us who were positive about it. All the rest were negative. One of the guys has only just started to turn himself around now, from what I hear. That's understandable. You've probably got to be pretty mentally strong because the rehab can be tough, really tough, just trying to relearn everything. I was in hospital for about fourteen months and because I'd broken my arm, I had to wait a few months for that to heal before we moved on to anything else. My rehab didn't even start until about four months down the track. The body is an amazing thing. It healed the neck first, and then started healing the arm. The arm wouldn't heal until the neck had finished healing. It was like my body was prioritising it all. The neck was the most important, so that came first. That's incredible, don't you think?'

Yes.

'With any surgery for a spinal injury, they scrape part of the bone off your hip and stick it in your neck,' he says. 'I don't know how the hell they did it. I had a neurosurgeon put me back together. I've got a bunch of metal plates in my neck. I can't turn my head too far.' Brand can turn about one inch, maximum, either way. His shoulders swivel either side of an unmoving head as if a steel rod is holding him together from his coccyx to the skull. 'That's about as far as I can go,' he says. 'The head doesn't move without the shoulders. I'm a C5–C6. I actually damaged the C4 and C7 as well, but I've got a C6–C7 break. I've pretty much completely severed my spinal cord. I've got no hand function. I've got no movement below my injury line. Some of these guys are incomplete quadriplegics, which means they can still move their legs. I'm complete.'

Brand's court time in Beijing will be limited. There will be no complaints. He's the best kind of person, low maintenance. Regardless of his own input or the result, he will roll out at full-time, shake everybody's hand, tell them how great they were and then quietly pack up his gear in case he's needed next time.

'Having the outlet of playing this sport, such an aggressive sport, helps me a lot,' he says. 'The martial arts background helps, too. It's a controlled aggro in this sport. You can let a few frustrations out, get a bit angry if you want. Funnily enough, when I first saw it, I wasn't game to try it. It was actually Bryce Alman who convinced me to give it a go. I was a bit gun-shy and hesitant because of the injury and everything else, but once I got over that and discovered it wasn't *always* as brutal as it looked, I was okay. All the banging and crashing in the chairs was a shock to me, but actual injuries have been pretty rare in my short experience. Once I got my head around that, I thought this isn't too bad, I might keep going. It's worked out brilliantly.

'My parents and my sister are going across to Beijing and they're rapt. Not that I'll probably see them much. I've had to tell them I won't get to catch up with them too often. They're disappointed about that. But we'll be in lockdown. We'll be in camp. It's not like you get to have breakfast with Mum and Dad every morning. We're serious about it now, and it feels like the sport might start taking off. One of my friends turned up to a game a while ago. She'd never seen the sport before. I talked her into coming. She loved it so much she kept coming back, and she's bought tickets now to go and watch us in Beijing. Once someone gets a taste, they're in.

'I really appreciate the chance to go over there with the team. I'm just lucky we've got someone like Ryley and that I can sometimes fit into the line-up when the time is right. I know I might not play much and that's okay. I know there might be games when I don't play at all. We have a big squad and if I miss out, that's fine by me. It means someone else gets a lot of minutes and I'll be happy for them. Hopefully, as a low-pointer, I can get out there and make Ryley look good. When I'm on court with him, I'm basically a seagull. I want one of their players to come with me so there's one less guy marking Ryley. Another one of our guys can cover someone else, so there's probably only two players left to go after Ryley. If we can all give Ryley the right help, we can win a medal. That would be absolutely awesome. As a new guy coming in, it would be fantastic. It's taken me a while to get here so it feels like a dream to me, just to be going over there. I started playing for a local team down in Melbourne and it sort of took me a couple of years to get the swing of it. I started playing the nationals in 2005 for Victoria, then got called up to start representing Australia just last year, so there was three years of missing out. It's been a bit mind-blowing lately, a bit of a whirlwind, and I'm just really thankful.'

DUBBERLEY: 'Shane is the most inexperienced player in our team. His biggest weakness is catching the ball, so we're trying to make him a defensive weapon. If he's working well with Ryley or whoever he's on the floor with, it means Ryley or Steve or whoever else is out there can tear shit up. Because his catching isn't always the best, I've told him I want to see him with a ball in his lap all the time. Even when he goes down to the shops, I want him doing it with a ball. If he's with the other guys, he can throw it around—we need his catching to be better. It doesn't matter if he's in a shopping mall or whatever, if he's got a ball there, catching it without his gloves and just getting used to the feel of it, it's going to help him get used to catching. It might sound stupid, but then you start seeing results because he's started doing what you've asked him to. He's probably thinking it's a dumb idea with the ball but hopefully it works and he ends up thinking, "Yeah, you're right".'

BRAND: 'I had no self-confidence at the start of last year. But that's gone now. I didn't believe I should be here, playing for Australia, but all the guys have helped me out so much. They're a really good bunch of blokes. It's nice to be a part of it. Rob, our assistant coach, is Victorian, and during state training last year, he came up to me one day and said, "You're going to be getting a phone call from Brad." I thought he was pulling my leg. I really did not believe him. But then Brad rang and said, "I've heard Rob has already told you." I said, "Yep." He said, "Well now it's official. You're in." He's been a terrific coach, he's helped me a lot. He's definitely a switched-on guy. I couldn't have asked for anything more from anyone in this team. There's so much potential and I reckon we're about to start showing it.'

Brand's cheque from The Learned Gentlemen Of The Australian Paralympic Committee has gone towards a new chair. His old unsteady chair sent him arse over tit if someone so much as looked at it. His replacement is a veritable Rock Of Gibraltar. He taps it proudly; the rev-head with his new wheels.

'We know the US are the big guns,' he says. 'Because it's such a huge country, they've got that many people with disabilities to pool into their national team, they've got reason to be number one. It's going to be good to knock them off—but it'll be bizarre to play them. I can't believe I'm stepping up to play against them. That's weird to me. We know how overbearing the American players can be, and how full-on their rivalry is with Canada. We've seen how annoying the Americans can be, but the Canadians, they've got a lot of dirty players. They grab your arms, which is actually a big no-no. They go in as if they're trying to grab the ball, but it's all an act. They're not actually laying punches, but it's that kind of thing. They try to rough you up. That's their whole plan. That's what makes it fun to beat them. They cheat, and we still beat them. It's alright if they want to be like that. It all adds to the drama. One thing I'm really looking forward to is having Joe Soares at all the tournaments. He's a funny bloke, Joe.'

A funny bloke?

How the fuck is Joe Soares funny?

'He's just funny.'

~

Name: Scott Vitale
AGE: 23
Home: Kurwongbah, Queensland
Classification: 2

'We've got all this acreage at my parents' place and I was riding the motorbike in the backyard,' Vitale says. 'Me and my mates were doing some jumps on our bikes. I'd done it a heap of times and there were no dramas. My mates reckoned the ramp was stuffed, but I don't remember that. I just hit it too fast and took it all too lightly and went too far. I went straight over the handlebars, got upside down and landed on the top of my head. I remember the whole thing happening, but then I got knocked out for about fifteen or twenty minutes. My mates thought I was dead. I came to, and I wasn't even that worried about it. I thought I was sweet—they'd take me to hospital and fix me up and everything would be alright. But it was just me and my mates there and they were freaking out a bit. One of them took my helmet off, which you're not supposed to do, but he was panicking so he just whipped it off. My eyes were open but I wasn't breathing. He thought I was dead—no breathing, big bug eyes, I'd think the same thing if I saw someone like that. Another mate rode up to the house. He was yelling, "There's been an accident!" Mum was like, "Is it bad?" He didn't answer her. He was just looking at her. I woke up when the ambulance got there. The first thing I said was, "How's my bike?" That was all I was worried about. I didn't think I was too bad. You figure that if you're awake, you're okay. They were cutting my gear off and I'm like, "Don't cut it!" I was pissed off because my gear was going to be ruined. I didn't want to have to buy new gear. I don't remember a lot else.

'There were the bolts in the head and laying in traction. I got operated on five days later. What I do remember is my poor parents. Poor Mum. I was sixteen when it happened. She'd always said to me "You're going to break your bloody neck out there", but I'd never really thought about what that meant. I didn't know anything when I was sixteen. I suppose nobody does. I thought if you broke your leg it got healed and I thought it was the same for all your bones, or something like that. The whole spinal cord thing, the way your nerves work, I knew nothing about it. I don't even think Mum and Dad knew too much about it. Does anyone? *You'll break your bloody neck out there*. That's what she said. I think it was just a saying for Mum, I doubt she even really expected it would come true. But it did.

'I can't ride a motorbike any more, but I've got an off-road buggy I can still ride. It's a four-wheeler, this go-kart sort of thing with a road bike engine in it. Me and Ryley still get into it, but rugby's where I get my fun now. When you're in a rugby chair, it's not like being in your normal day chair—you can move around so much better, turn them on five-cent pieces—I feel really alive when I get in it. You get into a game, you've got all the adrenaline going, you can't hear anything and it makes you feel good. I've been in a chair for so long now, but I always look back to before. Whenever something I do now feels like it was before, it's awesome to get those same feelings again. I used to play a lot of rugby league and I used to get nervous before games, all the butterflies in my stomach. When I first came to rugby I didn't get nervous at all but now, just the last year, I've been getting really nervous again. It's great getting those old feelings back. That's why you play sport—the nerves and the adrenaline. It's not just about a medal for me. It's about the whole experience and doing all this with my teammates.'

Someone around here must be pissed off about their fate. Vitale used to be hostile, just *really* pissed off, getting around with his dreadlocks, tattoos, pointed jaw and searing eyes, objecting to team rules regardless of their merit. He's the rebel who has mellowed, more a team man now because if he wasn't he wouldn't be here, but still confrontational enough to watch the Americans' tiresome histrionics and give them a five-star stop-being-such-a-bunch-of-fuckwits scowl. 'I don't want to talk them up,' he says. 'I don't think we have to. When I first saw them, I expected a lot more, actually. We were watching them train and I really thought they were going to blow us away with what they were doing. But they're just another team. They're a bloody good team, but they don't look to me like a team we can't beat. They're just another group of guys like us. And they don't have a Ryley. It's exciting to know we're a chance. I think in the past we've doubted ourselves too much and thought we didn't really deserve to win anything. But now everyone knows that if we put in the work, we do deserve to win. We've got a good shot if we believe we've got a good shot. We've got the Ryley factor and the George factor. I love being in a team with big guys like them, the big hitters. I love it. It's classic.

'I'm always telling Ryley that he needs to harden up. I tell him he needs to get some mongrel into him. "Hit 'em hard, mate! Get into 'em!" He's a nice guy, Ryles, and he doesn't want to hurt them if he doesn't have to. I tell him, "Come on mate, they're trying to hurt you, pound them mate, you're not going to kill anyone. It's just rugby. You've got to hit 'em! We *need* you to hit 'em." When he saw that it was for the whole team he started doing it, and it was great to see. I was like, "Yeah, Ryles, smash 'em, mate!" I think he's started to enjoy it. He gets sledged all the time but it's just started to fire him up even more. He's always copped it from when he was younger. They've always tried to put pressure on him. Canada and the Kiwis, especially. They tell him he's a baby. They want to know if he's teething, that sort of shit—but he's used to it now. He's grown up and now he's starting to dish it out on everyone who used to give it to him. He doesn't sledge anyone, he just canes them. He doesn't take any crap from anyone. I love it. He's starting to hammer the people who hammered him when he was too young to be able to fight back. The bottom line is, he can lay them out and he's starting to do it. They're getting what they deserve.'

Batt and Vitale are tight.

'He doesn't like to think about stuff too much, Ryles,' Vitale says. 'He's good that way. I tend to worry too much. He always tells me, "You think too much." I tell him he doesn't think enough.' What a tiff. Till death do us part. 'I know the Americans are thinking about him already,' Vitale says. 'We'll be having lunch and they'll all be looking at him, sussing him out. They're worried. He's the big threat to every other team, including America. He's that good he could be the difference between America getting a gold or us getting it. I don't think they really know how good he has become.'

Vitale started playing murderball in the hope it would alleviate the boredom derived from being unable to throw himself into the next galaxy off a motorbike ramp. 'When I was in hospital, guys were coming in and giving demos of sports,' he says. 'I never got in a rugby chair then, I just didn't want to. They coaxed me into it. I still had my neck brace on but one day I took it off to play and they're like, "No, no, you can't do that!" It felt alright to me. It was probably a stupid thing to do, but I guess I got away with it. I jumped in. It was fun, but I wasn't in the right chair, I was kind of unstable. My blood pressure was low and I thought, "Nah, I'm not doing that again." I got home after rehab and thought I'd walk again one day anyway, so there was no point worrying about any wheelchair sports. But then you get to the stage where you realise you're not going to walk.

'I went back to hospital for a yearly check-up and the wheelchair rugby guys just happened to be down there again. I couldn't get away from them. I went in and had another look. They coaxed me into a rugby chair. I was starting to get bored at home so I got into the rugby, and I'm glad I did. It was good to find a great sport and, really, making the Queensland team wasn't that hard. We don't have many players. If you play, you're probably going to get in your State team. A lot of disabled guys might not come from a sporting background, so you're ahead from the start if you've already played a lot of sport. I played basketball, rugby league, all sorts of sports, so I suppose I could pick it up pretty quickly.

'But now I've gone up a class, now my classification has gone up to a 2.5, the competition to make the team is a lot stiffer. For me, and Ryley, making the Australian team probably wasn't that hard to start with. That's probably why I took a while to appreciate it. I probably didn't have a great attitude for a while there. But I train hard now. I'm so keen. I just cannot wait for the Games. It's all a lot more meaningful. I've really started getting into the feeling there is between the teams, the aggro. It's like there's more intensity than some able-bodied sports. You'd think everybody would be all friendly because we're all in chairs, and we've all had our accidents or whatever, but you watch a couple of games and you could swear everyone really does hate each other.'

Vitale's only previous stoush against the US was in the smoking ruins of Athens. 'I only had a few minutes on court. That game was a dud. Me and Ryley had our classifications changed, our whole line-ups had to change, and that whole game was a waste of time. The tournament hadn't even started and we were like, shit, what are we going to do? It was a disaster. I only had a few minutes against them just for the classifiers to see me. It's a bit of a blur. It'd be good to play them properly again. Athens, it just all came and went so fast. I'd only been playing for a couple of years. I started at the end of 2002 so it wasn't much experience to have going into a Paralympics.

And then to have all the drama on top of it. I can see now how unprepared I was. I got there and went up with my classification and everything went out the window. But it can't happen again. Ryley and I have just been permanently tested, so our classifications can't change again unless we get protested. I'm a 2 now and it should stay there—unless I get my function back. I'd probably take that if it came along.'

A beggar in the feral Sydney suburb of Kings Cross has the opportunity to move into a hostel and receive the dole from the government. On the surface, that would seem to be a drastic improvement in lifestyle, but he elects to stay where he is. In the gutter, on the street, he has an identity. Passers-by know his name and say hello every morning. Begging makes him who he is. Does murderball make these blokes who they are? Of course not. Given the chance to change their circumstance, of course they would. But might there also be times when they would miss their existence as disabled athletes? All this camaraderie of high intensity? You've been to black-tie functions in large rooms filled with a mixture of disabled and able-bodied people and the most fun to be had, the most enthralling conversations, the most genuine eyeball-to-eyeball connections, were on the tables with the disabled—by a country mile. The beggar doesn't want to become another faceless passer-by. He wants to stay *different*. Different is good, great, the best. There have been times this year when you have felt an absurd desire to be in a wheelchair with Dubberley and the rest. So you could be like them.

'It all feels more optimistic this time around,' Vitale says. 'I'm more experienced, so is Ryley, so is everyone. Having been to a Games, I feel like I know what to expect. I look back and think, "Shit, we were at a Paralympics?" It was meaningful but because I hadn't been around that long, I didn't really have the same kind of drive as the other guys had. They'd been there and knew what it meant to have a Paralympics come and go without taking that chance to get a medal. I look back and regret it a bit. I didn't realise what a big deal it was. But now I can see making the team isn't the important part. That's just the start. Making the team just gives you the chance to take on the rest of the world. In a way, this feels like my first Paralympics because I'm more prepared. We got over there in Athens and it was like, "What's going on here? Why aren't we winning?" We probably just weren't good enough then. Or we didn't think we were after the classifiers got us. Now the top five teams are all pretty close. We know everyone is getting worried about us. America have been going all over the world with their video cameras to get footage. They go back home and pick the footage to pieces. The American coach has been at some of our tournaments, taping every game. They're getting a bit obsessed about Ryley. He takes a drink and they're still filming him. They'd be checking on his function, seeing if they can protest. I wouldn't put it past them.'

Back in Vitale's everyone-can-go-and-get-nicked days, if he thought an idea was dumb, he would scoff, mock and brush it off. Nobody could tell him what to do.

Team manager Kim Ellwood can't quite believe all this happened now, but she recalls: 'I swear, after the Canada Cup two years ago, I refused to talk to him. I'd never had an argument with anyone, really. But he had a go at me in Canada. We were all in this nightclub on the last night. We'd had a bit of an altercation during the week, me and Scotty. We had a team rule that there were no hats to a formal dinner. You can't wear a baseball cap to a formal dinner. He just disagreed with that completely. He goes, "Well, my parents never taught me that, I'm not doing it." I'm trying to tell him we're all dressing up in suits and dresses, and that you don't wear a baseball cap to those functions, it's just rude. You don't eat with a baseball cap on. He was like, "No, I don't believe in that", and refused to take his hat off. I said, "Well, you can go back to your room. I don't care. We've got rules we all go by." He said, "No, I'm wearing my hat." He was having a go at all of us. He wouldn't listen to any of the staff. He got the shits and went back to his room.

'Eventually he decided to come out. I thought, "Sweet, he's come out to the club with us." I'm like, "So, you're talking to me again now?" I was a little bit drunk by this stage, I suppose. He was like, "You're a fucking shit." I said, "Sorry?" He said, "You're a fucking shit." That was the first time anyone in the team had ever sworn at me. I mean, they swear at me all the time, as a joke, it's never meant hurtfully. But this was hurtful. I was like, "Fuck you." I turned around and walked away. That was it. That night, we all got taxis home. He needed help to get out of his taxi and I was like, "Nope, I'm not helping you." I refused to go near him. I was thinking, "You don't realise how much time I spend doing shit for you guys. All the organising, everything. I do so much for you guys and I want to do it for you. But I don't want to have a bar of you if you're going to treat me like that. If you don't appreciate it, if you can't draw the line between what I try to do with my job and just me as a person, there's no point." I was so angry.

'Scotty dropped out of the sport for a while after that. When he came back, I said to Brad that I was really nervous about having him back in the team. I said I didn't want him in. I really took quite personally what he had said to me. But after he came back in, something had really changed in him. I was like, "This is not the same guy!" Scotty is the one who has changed the most over the years. He's done it all himself. He's just the coolest guy. I'm so glad he's come back the way he has. Otherwise I might have left and my last impression of him would have been of a little shit. I love him to bits now. He's just such a different guy. He's quality.'

The schedule for the Beijing Paralympics has been released. If Australia negotiate the seven landmines positioned around The Hall Of Overwhelming Glory to reach the final, *imagine*; if they leave those seven other teams behind to step into the lion's den for the only game that will matter for the next four years, the apocalyptic decider that will be staged at eight o'clock on the evening of 17 September 2008, Vitale's right arm will be adorned with a tattoo that says one word, one of the few words more powerful than the most desperate words of all, and the one word that makes you realise that behind Vitale's tough exterior are more layers than *Evie Parts I, II* and *III*. The tattoo on his right arm is a picture of a man on a motorbike skyrocketing towards the clouds and the word stamped on his arm is REGRETS.

~

Name: Bryce Alman
Age: 28
Home: Hughesdale, Victoria
Classification: 2.0

Bryce Alman's voice creaks like an old wooden ship. He's slim with thinning hair. You are guilty upon your first sighting of thinking the day-to-day requirements of quadriplegic living are wearing him down. Wrong, wrong, wrong. He's merely a laidback and dependable individual whom Dubberley will whisk onto the court whenever the whips are cracking in an important fixture. Alman is reminiscent of the hardy salt-encrusted surfers on the dawn patrol at Bells Beach in the middle of winter when the crests are like avalanches and the water temperature is subzero and the boardriders' lips are blue-purple with cold. Their teeth chatter and they're frozen solid and it looks painful but when you ask them at first light how they're going, all they say is, 'Bit chilly.'

Alman is playing video trivia inside a Melbourne watering hole. Jugs of bourbon are being consumed elsewhere, spilling on the table and floor. The room is filled with animated discussion. Canada's captain David Willsie is handcuffed by the police because he wants to be. He's laughing like a giddy aunt and the whole joint is getting rowdy and Batt is laughing too, laughing himself stupid because he's trying to engage a Japanese player in conversation without being able to understand a single fucking word being said. Batt speaks in English, eyes like firecrackers. Shinichi replies in Japanese, eyes like firecrackers. They stare at each other, giggle, and try again. For hours on end. The barman wants to kick a few people out, but condescendingly says he won't because they're all in wheelchairs. Hucks tells the barman he doesn't need anyone's sympathy and threatens to throw himself out to prove his point. Alman is the quietest and most sensible person in the room.

'This whole year is flying past,' he says. 'I'm actually looking forward to post-Beijing and getting a rest. Ah, I shouldn't say that! But it's a busy year and Beijing is coming around quick. At the moment we're doing between six and eight training sessions a week, so it's really full-on. The problem this year is that there are so many trips that it's hard to get into a consistent flow with your training and get a consistent block of training at one time. You're home for five days then you're away for ten days, then you're back home for maybe two weeks, then you're away again—it's hard to get a routine going.'

The false first impression mistook Alman's casual air for a kind of despairing, as if he'd never quite come to grips with his accident. Again: wrong, wrong, wrong. You could have sworn that Old Age and Treachery has never had a sorrowful day in his life. You could have sworn Alman's journey through the seven stages of grief is never-ending. Asked how long it took, dreading the answer, Alman shrugs and replies: 'Not long, maybe a couple of weeks. A few people have said that I was pretty quick to cope. I think it depends on the people around you, and where you're at in your life when it happens. I don't ever remember making a conscious decision, "Shit, I've got to get on with my life." It just sort of happened. I don't ever remember being depressed. I guess, for the first few years, the only negative thing I used to do was regret having to go back to uni. I was working when I had my accident, and then I couldn't keep doing that so I went back to uni and I was always thinking, "I would have been earning X amount of dollars by now, I could be owning this and that." That's probably the only time I used to think negatively about what happened.'

Alman admits to initial fears about D's coaching. 'He's been great for us, but I had my doubts to start with,' he says. 'I was worried about whether, having been a player so recently, whether he'd get the respect of everyone. And I wasn't sure if he had the experience needed to do that job properly. To his credit, he's gotten the right people around him to give him support in the areas he lacks. He'll go to senior players and ask their opinions. He's done an amazing job, really, in a very short space of time, because eighteen months ago I wouldn't have thought we'd be where we are at the moment. Full credit to Brad, you know? We don't really have that many coaching options in Australia. It basically has to be an ex-player, or we have to get someone from overseas and they probably cost too much money. In a way, I think we lost a chunk of time with our old coach. Really, he had no idea. Looking back now, I think Brad was basically trying to coach us anyway, even in the last days of when he was playing. That was like his apprenticeship, really. He's still doing what he did back then, but he's just got the title to go with it now. There are positives and negatives. Because he was such a dominant player—his height was such a big advantage, and we don't have anyone with that height now—he was really good at holding the ball up and being patient. He was never the quickest player, but just his height and his mobility made him a handful. And he did have one of the best passes in the game. He was really strong for us in Sydney and I just couldn't imagine him not playing. Athens was no good for us. Everyone is mates now whereas at Athens, there were a couple of different groups. It wasn't that noticeable at the time but when you look at how everyone is now compared to then, it's pretty clear what was happening back then. I didn't think at Athens that anyone had any issues with anyone, but this is just a closer group. Brad has helped make that happen. We all just get on really well anyway. People used to go off and do their own thing with the same people all the time. That doesn't happen any more. We've lost out a little bit with Brad not playing but now we've got a coach with playing experience, which a lot of countries don't have. Most of the other coaches are able-bods who have never played the game. Brad can see things differently, see the game for what it really is. He can see it through a player's eyes.'

The accident, through Alman's eyes: 'I went to Phillip Island with a group of friends for the day. There wasn't any surf so we were just stuffing around on the beach. I just took off and ran flat-out down the beach and dived into a breaking wave. I smashed my head on the sand bar. I don't even know which part I hit. It just happened that quickly. I just remember smashing my head on the bottom and feeling this wave of warmth go down my body. I was struggling around and I couldn't get any air. If my mate wasn't there I would have died, pure and simple.

'The rehabilitation starts, and you don't realise at the time how hard it is. But it wasn't like the worst thing I've been through. I said this to my parents—the worst thing I've been through is Mum having a brain tumour about two years after my accident. Emotionally and physically, I found that a lot harder to get through than anything I had to do in rehab, or any of the inconveniences I've had since. It's actually happening to you, so I think you just tend to get on with it. You don't really have any choice, do you? You either keep going or—what? You just have to keep going. Every day there are little things you get through, and the days keep going by and you end up kind of getting used to all these new things. Every day, you go into physio, and there's a date they write up when you're leaving, so you're always moving towards that date. I don't really know how, but you just sort of get through it. I didn't really have too many bad days at rehab. Because there were so many guys in there of the same age going through the same thing, I actually had times in there where I have never laughed so hard in my life. Honestly, it wasn't all bad.'

Perhaps it *would* have been through someone else's eyes. 'To be honest, I think it's harder for quads to get through rehab these days,' he says. 'I might be wrong here, but they don't seem to have the experienced staff they had when I went through. It sounds like there's a lot of staff on rotation, so they're learning as they go as much as the patients are. The patient probably doesn't come out as developed or as far down the track as I felt I did. I had really good nurses and really good care given to me. I left there fully independent. There are people with my injuries now who are leaving that still need a lot of care after they go home. That's not good. The biggest thing is that you're getting to the age where you should be leaving home and then, bang, all of a sudden you're back to needing your mum and dad's help all over again. You need to find direction in your life and I got lucky there too.

'While I was in rehab, the Victorian team used to train in the gym there, on the basketball court. I saw training, and went and watched a few rugby games while I was in hospital. They tell you that you can't play for twelve months after you've broken your neck. I started twelve months to the day. I loved it straightaway, never looked back. I've been playing ever since. Within two years I was in the national squad. Back when I made the squad, I was only training twice a week, just with the Victorian team. That was all I did. It just happened that I was pretty fast around the court and that got me into the squad. Now you have to train five and six days a week to get to the level you need to reach to make the team. It's semi-professional now, really, without the pay cheque. This is the first year where we've had a couple of grants. It makes a massive difference but financially, a lot of the guys here struggle. Just not having to find seven grand for a chair makes a huge difference. We've always had a pretty good travelling budget but as far as the equipment goes, that's always been left up to us. Nowadays a chair only lasts two years. They take such a hammering and with our National League, it's gone from being one weekend a year to three times a year. You can easily spend nine grand on a new chair and a new set of wheels. And that doesn't include all your gloves and straps and stuff. It's quite easy to spend ten grand a year on your equipment. But you pay and play because you want to be involved. It's going to be a pretty competitive year.'

Alman on the worst thing he's ever been through: 'Mum recovered. She's as good as gold now. She completely got over it. The tumour wasn't cancerous, luckily. She has to have a check every so often to make sure it hasn't grown back, but she's fine now. I found that whole thing really difficult. The operation itself could have killed her. She had a thirteen-hour operation. That's a big deal. Like I say, those couple of weeks with her in hospital were far worse to deal with than anything I had to endure after my accident. My life was never really under threat. You know what I mean? Like, after the two seconds where I felt like I probably could have drowned, you know you're going to get through it. I mean, you know you're going to be able to keep going with your life. You might not know how good or bad that life is going to be, but at least you know you're not going to die. Whereas with Mum, she was sort of the opposite. We didn't know what might happen. It's not good seeing family in hospital. I don't even want to think about that any more.'

The Austin Hospital has produced a murderballer or five: Alman, Dubberley, The Genius Nazim Erdem, Never Walk Alone, and Old Age and Treachery. Come for a galling peek. Down Bell Street. Past Coburg Cemetery. Bell Funeral Services is on the right, the middle men. A sign offers legal services to those in trouble for speeding, drink-driving, stealing or fighting. A dishevelled man is stumbling through the front gate as if he's in serious strife on all four counts. Austin Hospital is a white multistoreyed building. Flowers on the window panes. It's neat and symmetrical in the fashion of a Lego building. A concrete slab says it was opened in 1881. All that curing since, all that carnage.

The foyer is a heavenly bright-white. There is pastoral care. A multi-faith chapel. Not a speck of dust on the *blindingly* bright floors. In a gift shop, ashen-faced ghosts buy teddy bears for their favourite invalids. The Food Emporium seems an unnecessarily extravagant name for what appears to be a cafeteria. A quadriplegic woman, early twenties, is eating a toasted sandwich. Does a day go by without someone becoming a quadriplegic? The Food Emporium has a happy hour from 7.30 a.m. to 8.30 a.m. when small Styrofoam cups of coffee cost $2.20. A green banner arched across the foyer boasts, AUSTIN HEALTH—PREMIER'S AWARD FOR MOST OUTSTANDING METROPOLITAN HEALTH SERVICE. Hurrah. Two female receptionists have big hair. They wear headsets and talk non-stop. *Intensive care, just putting you through.* There's an Austin Commemorative Circle filled with names of the deceased on bricks. *In Loving Memory of Olive 'Popsy' Perrin. A wonderful friend to Michael and Pat.* That's the way to be remembered: loving and wonderful friend. A shop called Barbello serves stiff drinks for those in need. The queue is long and agitated. Flowers by Lisette is busy. There's another shop called Soul Tonic, offering nothing more insightful than sandwiches and juice.

On shimmering blue reflective glass panels under the headline of COMPASSION is the following description of that most difficult emotion to embrace: 'A thread of connection. A bridge between humanity, the essence of morality, an awakening of the heart where spirit and nature meet. Or a moon shining in the sky, its image reflected in a hundred bowls of water.'

Outside, a taxi has its motor running. You imagine an incomplete quadriplegic speeding through the foyer in some turbo-charged wheelchair and telling the cab driver, *Get me the hell out of here.* Up to the intensive care unit which Dubberley, Alman, Scott, Erdem and Smith used to call home. The lift opens at level two. *Ding.* There is one single blue door next to the waiting room with three heart-rending words above it: INTENSIVE CARE UNIT.

Nine paintings on a white wall, in brackets of three. A mother and daughter in a field of flowers; the flowers every colour of the rainbow. A blue sky. A picnic. A traditional house with the picketed fence. Families together in the sun. A loving couple sharing a blanket. All of them have bright flowers and blue skies in the background, and they're all so idyllic and wonderful and perfect and unattainable. Nine reminders of the good things waiting outside. And nine reasons to go and top yourself. God's Waiting Room has a colour television with a screen that stays on 24/7. Think you've got worries? DO YOU HONESTLY BELIEVE YOU HAVE WORRIES? They are light and temporary. Go and sit in the waiting room of the intensive care unit at Austin Hospital for half an hour and see what's on your mind after that.

A doctor tells a family of three—mother, daughter and son, or perhaps the daughter's boyfriend—'I'm sorry but I can't tell you anything more until we do some more x-rays.' The same doctor tells a father of Italian heritage that he's too early for visiting hours. He must wait till the end of the hour. The Italian man takes it in good grace. He walks around the room greeting everyone, upbeat but a bit *too* upbeat, taking it upon himself to inject cheer into this sorrowful place. There are more paintings, infantile in their simplicity. The mother tells her children, 'He'll be right, right as rain.' None of them look convinced, and the mother bawls.

Through the blue door (want to paint it black), past the Gideon's bible on the desk at reception, three arrows point to the three wards of the unit. ICU A and B are to the left. ICU C is to the right. A trio of grim-faced posters on the wall behind the Italian man unsuccessfully try to cheer everyone up. 'A PLEDGE TO OUR PATIENTS: At Austin Health, we are committed to upholding the following values. Respecting the inherent dignity of every human being. Respecting the autonomy of the individual. Exercising care and compassion. Striving for excellence. Practising justice, fairness, honesty and integrity.' Then an admission. 'SOMETIMES WE GET IT WRONG: If you have concerns about your treatment, please tell one of our staff.' And then fair warning. 'VIOLENT AND THREATENING BEHAVIOUR IS NOT ACCEPTABLE HERE: We understand that you may feel upset and anxious during your stay or visit in hospital. We understand that you want the best care possible for your loved one. But please understand that physically or verbally threatening our staff will not help. Please try to stay calm.'

Leaving, or more accurately needing to escape, you stumble back to the B1 level of the car park, punch-drunk after hearing a procession of families hit the buzzer to the blue door and asking in uncertain voices (unsure if they can go in, unsure if they really want to) for permission to visit. They brace themselves before walking through that blue door. Their faces harden. There really is no place quite as depressing as a hospital bed, let alone three wards filled with them, all the beds home to motionless flesh and bone. Down in the car park, you see the too-upbeat Italian father near the glass panels of the lifts. He's slumped over the bonnet of his car, and he is weeping. *We understand that you may feel upset and anxious during your stay or visit in hospital.* It might not always be the people you think.

Name: Cameron Carr
Age: 32
Home: Springfield, Queensland
Classification: 2.0

It took six years to come to terms with an accident so unfair it makes you want to scream and seek retribution. Initial plans twice promised to take Cameron Carr out of harm's way but two unscripted diversions cruelled him. One of them was an order to delay his arrival at the famous football club he was about to join. The other was a decision that amounted to nothing more foolhardy than an attempt to do the right thing. There are strong arguments for the existence of karma in this life and the notion of good things happening to good people but Cameron Carr's story makes you fear there's also the distinct possibility that spiritualism is crap and we're all just playing Russian roulette.

How the fuck can this happen? If Cameron Carr's life had stayed on its original course he would have become a professional footballer for the Sydney Roosters in the National Rugby League. His currently soft body would have been sculpted into that of a rock-hard Caucasian

Adonis, he would have made a fortune, he would have been allowed to immerse himself in the heady and exhilarating lifestyle of pro sport, he would have been following in the footsteps of his famous footballing father, Norm. But at the most cruel and inopportune moment, Carr was stopped in his tracks by an automobile accident less than 100 metres from his destination. Didn't Jesus die on the cross to take away our pain? Why, then, all the pain? There was nothing risky with anything that Cameron Carr did. He got into a car. That's it. He got into a car so he could get some sleep before attending a christening the next morning. He decided against the less dignified act of slaughtering himself with alcohol and what did he get for his troubles? Quadriplegia, that's what he got.

'It was all, I don't know, fate,' he says. 'Pain in the arse that it is.'

Cameron Carr is a resolute and sharp-witted man. He's played for Victoria with plastic bum cheeks on the back of his chair and an expression of *What's the problem* worthy of the Edinburgh Comedy Festival. He wants nobody's sympathy but gets some here. This makes you so fucking angry. He was living in Brisbane when the plot sickened. The morning Carr was supposed to drive to the big smoke for the beginning of the rest of his life, the Roosters telephoned and told him to hold fire for a fortnight. In the meantime, he attended a 21st birthday party. Nothing wrong with that. Afterwards, he jumped in a taxi with his mates to continue the revelry past the witching hour. Nothing wrong with that, either. But at the very last minute, he decided to get out of the taxi and take a lift to a mate's place in order to get some shut-eye. Most definitely nothing wrong with that. You imagine this being a movie and you're cowering in the back row for the second viewing of the main scene and when Carr is getting out of the taxi you're screaming at him no, no, don't get in the other car. The driver fell asleep and crashed. He can't have crashed, he can't have, but he really did fall asleep and crash.

'The Roosters rang up the morning I was supposed to leave home,' Carr says. 'They said, "Look, how about you wait and we'll fly you down in two weeks. Just hang on a bit longer, can you hold it off for a couple of weeks? We'll fly you down then." There was a problem with the accommodation, something like that. Something minor. I said, "Yeah, no worries. Flying down beats driving." I'd been out the night before as a going away thing and I was a bit hungover anyway. I thought it was perfect. I went to the 21st the next weekend and next thing I know, I'm waking up on all these machines in intensive care. I woke up thinking I had dreamed it. I was going, "Geez, I had a really weird dream last night, it was just so real, I was in this car accident." But then I looked at the bed head and thought, *This isn't what I'm used to seeing.* And then I'm like, "What are all these things beeping in here, what are all these machines?" And then I've got the doctors and family leaning over me and looking right in my face. What a nightmare. The doctors ran me through it all and I was still like, "Am I going to be right for training next week? What's happening? I've got to go to Sydney next week."

'It probably wasn't until the guy who I was going to Sydney with [pause] . . . it probably wasn't until a week later, when I was supposed to go down [pause] . . . that it really hit me. My mate came to the hospital to visit me and that was the day I thought, shit, I'm actually not going to get the chance to go down there to play. He had his Roosters shirt on and he was going down and [final pause] . . . well, yeah, that knocked me around a bit. That's when I really started thinking, "This is a little bit serious." His story is probably worse than mine. He had already gone down to Sydney for a year before me. First game in the Under 19s, he did one of his cruciate ligaments and had the whole season off. He went back down the year that I was supposed to go with him—he started sitting on the bench for first grade, and did his other knee. It completely wiped him out. He had a two-year contract and that was it for him.'

That guy's story might be worse than Cameron Carr's.

And it might not be.

Another driver fled.

'I haven't seen him since about a month after the accident,' Carr says. 'That was twelve years ago. He just took off to Western Australia and I never heard from him again. One of my good mates is his step-cousin, and he's starting to see him a little bit now, but I haven't seen him since he took off. He just went away and there was no more contact from him. I was pretty angry after the accident, but it's probably more upsetting now that—Look, I understand it was an accident, but you can sort of judge your friends, and what sort of person someone is, by how they respond. For him just to take off and to have not heard a word from him in all those years—I can understand it would be a hard thing to deal with. I know for myself, I wasn't the most pleasant person to be around for a long while there. But twelve years without a word?'

You used to agree wholeheartedly with the notion of people not growing up, not really, until their parents die. But now you think growing up is the first moment of genuine tragedy. A violent crime, financial rack-and-ruin, serious illness, a mate falling asleep when he's driving you home then pissing off to Western Australia without so much as a how-are-you-these-days or you-will-never-know-how-sorry-I-am phone call. Perhaps it's such a God-awful thing to have done, such a demoralising accident to have unintentionally been a part of, that you cannot bear to make contact because the guilt (real or imagined) is debilitating.

Seven deadly sins, seven fires of hell, seven vertebra in the human neck and seven stages of grief: shock, denial, bargaining, guilt, anger, depression and acceptance. Carr took six years to reach acceptance, Does it really exist? The terror of all this is that it's irreversible. You cannot repent and be cleansed of quadriplegia; you cannot apologise and make amends; you cannot re-evaluate and start over; you cannot do a fucking thing to wipe the slate clean. That is not fair. Nothing can be done, no matter how good and strong the intentions. A rapist can go to church and be born again, telling himself his sin no longer matters, but a quadriplegic can do nothing to improve his lot except squint and toughen up. An Australian stood in the flames of the Bali bombings and told herself, 'I am not going to die like this.' That is a brave and noble stance, but let's get fucking real: it was out of her control. That woman could rustle up all the mule-headed resolve in the world but if Amrozi's flames were going to melt her flesh, they were going to do so regardless. Why all the flukes? Carr's fate might have been different had the Roosters let him travel to Sydney as originally planned.

'The physical side, you get used to,' he says. 'You can adapt. The mental side is the hardest. That's what has taken the longest for me. It's really hard. I just never wanted to live my life with what-ifs but all of a sudden I woke up and thought, "Shit, I've got this massive what-if in front of me and I can't do anything about it." When you're in hospital, it's all fine because you're in this closed little community and everyone is getting around in wheelchairs and everyone is living in similar circumstances. But then you go home, and your mates and your family want you to fit straight back into the lifestyle you were leading before. I was like, "Hold on, it's not that easy. I've got to get used to my body again." They meant well. Everyone wanted to pick me up and take me down to the footy but I was like, "Leave me alone. I don't want to watch the footy. That's the last thing I want to do." The family was great. Even some of my mates' parents, I seemed to develop a whole new relationship with them. It can bring out the good in a lot of people. But you find out a few things, too. You're lying in your hospital bed and people will say, "We'll have to come up and see you." But you never see them again.

'And then rehab was a little disappointing. You have your injury and you think you'll go to rehab and they will try to get you to walk. I'm expecting massages and this miracle physio. I'm expecting *something*. Just someone to say, "This is what's going to happen when you get home." Someone to show me how to do everything. You have to learn how to dress yourself again, sit up, all that type of thing. But that's it—you're out of rehab, they send you on your way and wish you good luck. It's almost like you get a certificate: "Congratulations, you've passed Spinal Cord Injury 101, see you later."

'Going back home, it's overwhelming. I found it really hard for a good six years. You're sort of sheltered in that spinal injury unit. Everyone is in the same position as you, everyone is getting around, wow, you've got a new shiny chair, well done! It hasn't really sunk in and little things keep pissing you off, but a few things can make you laugh. When I first had my accident, I was doing some swimming. They had me in this plastic chair to put me in the pool. This little kid came up to me: "You can't bring that in here, mister." I was like, "Okay, mate." Every day he had something to say to me. Then one day I just wasn't in a great mood and he's come up again: "What happened to you, anyway?" I said, "I ate too many lollies. If you eat too many lollies, you'll get like this." His face was like, "What?" Sometimes it's better with kids. They just spit it out. But you go home and your mates ring and say, "We're going down to the pub, want to come?" And you're like, "Nah, piss off, leave me alone." They wanted to continue with how things had been six months prior. Some people can do that, but I just couldn't. I just struggled big time. I look back now and of all the regrets, especially now, going to my first Paralympics, I think there were another two Paralympics I might have been able to go to if I'd sorted myself out earlier. I missed out on those, and I've probably only got one more in me after this.'

A compass-changing night. A car. A cab. A what-if, a what-if, a what-if. 'I thought about the what-ifs all the time in rehab, and I still do now,' he says. 'Just when you see little things. With me, before my accident, I always wanted to be someone who got out there and had a go. I never wanted to be the guy down at the pub watching someone playing first grade saying, "He's shit, I remember him, I'm way better than him." Well, you're not better than him. You're not playing and he is. Then I rocked up at the pub and that was me. I didn't want to stay like that. I guess the worst thing is that I'm not going to get the opportunity to see if I really was good enough to make it. That was probably the hardest thing for me, and it still is. I'll never really know what was possible.'

Six years.

'Yeah, it's longer than it takes most people,' he says. 'All those years, I just wasn't doing anything. There was nothing I could do, nothing at all. It probably just crept up on me and then one morning, it was like, "Okay, if I don't start doing stuff soon I'm going to wake up and I'll be 50 and my life is going to be nearly over. And I'm going to have all these regrets." That's when I thought, well, I might go back and try a bit of hand-cycling to generally get fit. When I was training for that, I thought I might go down to rugby again and see how that was going. It had been the last thing I wanted to even think about during rehab. I'd be lying there with tubes coming out of me in hospital and they'd be all enthusiastic: "Hi! How are you going?! Want to play wheelchair rugby?! It'll be terrific!" It was mainly the nurses trying to get me into it. I just thought, "Do what you have to do while you're in here, but I don't really want to hear anything else you have to say." They were like door-to-door salesmen: "Such a shame you're a quad but the good news is, that makes you eligible for our wheelchair rugby program! Congratulations!"

'Rugby back then was in a different phase in Queensland. There might have been two point-fives and a paraplegic at training. Myself and two other guys from hospital went down. The physio took us. I was like, yeah, this is okay but I didn't really want to get into it. It was still the last thing I felt like doing. I went down another two times and over the next couple of years I had people ringing me up: "When are you going to play for us?" I was like, "Nah, that's okay, I'd rather go to the pub on a Tuesday night than go to footy training. I started doing a little bit of coaching. I coached my brother's rugby league team. Did that for three years, but I got to the stage of thinking, I want to do something for myself. So I went back down for another look at the rugby, and started playing in 2003. It gave me something to get stuck into. My first year playing for Australia was 2005.'

Carr can see the similarities between his accident and Zuperman's. They both had a mate driving the car and they both became quadriplegics through no fault of their own. The difference in the aftermath is that Zuperman would never have played sport for his country without becoming disabled. Hence Zuperman's near-thankfulness for being catapulted from Igoe's truck. It's given him a chance to make a name for himself. Full credit for seeing it in such a positive and opportunistic light, but Carr's accident stopped cold a legitimate sporting career. He was on his way (in one more week) in one form of rugby and while it may have taken as long as it took for Amrozi to face the firing squad for the tempest of Bali flames, he eventually ended up finding another.

'One of the better things being around these blokes is that if you have any problems, everyone here is so good at adjusting, you can ask someone for advice and you know it will be the right advice,' Carr says. 'Even if it's not rugby-related, someone on the team will be able to help you out because we're all in the same boat and we've been through similar situations. We're all mates. A couple of us are going to Vegas after the Canada Cup for a week. That's not going down too well on the home front, but we get on well enough that we want to do trips together outside of rugby. The bottom line is, we're representing Australia and we want to do it well. We're not just some guys out here having fun—well, we're having fun—but we take this seriously. We're playing for our country. We do a lot of training and there's some light at the end of the tunnel now. The tournaments are coming up fast. Training and getting up in the mornings is that much easier because we're about to start playing. It's the same with any team sport—part of the appeal is that you're in it together. We all come from different backgrounds but we're all here because we've been through the same sort of trauma.

'I think there's a belief that we can actually go into Beijing and be really competitive and give this a shake. Just talking to the guys, it sounds like teams in the past haven't really been fully committed. It was still lagging in that style from the start of rugby where it was just guys getting around for a laugh and throwing together anyone who was available. You put everyone in a chair and sent them out to play and no-one really put in that much of an effort, apart from one or two countries and players. But now, with the Kiwis winning in Athens, and the US and Canada always being up for it, they're all training hard and putting in so everyone else has to if they want to compete. In the past you heard a lot of stories about the Australian guys being the ones to go to if you wanted to have some fun. If the other blokes were looking for someone to drink with, they'd go to the Australians. We're shaking off that tag. We're going to let everyone know we're coming and we mean business. To have come from where we've all come from, a gold medal would be a massive achievement. But it's such a quick opportunity—you have to grab it. I know the guys who won the silver in Sydney were expecting huge things in Athens. But as a whole they probably weren't quite putting in and had a few things go against them. We're aiming up now.

'Ryley has come on a lot. He's just this big ball of energy bouncing around all over the place. We've got to follow him and support him. If you don't get pumped up and excited watching Ryley putting people on their backs, there's something wrong. Especially when you're lucky enough to be on the same team as him. I've seen the American coach filming him and he must be sitting there thinking, "Shit, we're going to have to do something to contain this little germ." We'll take Ryley over any other player in the game. He does a great job for us. He's just a typical nineteen-year-old. He thinks he's out there getting every woman he can, drinking with his mates. How fast he wants to go depends on what girls are in the crowd. It's bad enough that we have to play him in our national league. I keep turning around and thinking, Thank God he's on my team.

'It's getting serious, and it's getting closer. It just sort of creeps up on you, this sport, and you get really involved and it almost starts taking over your life. It's the same with any sport once you get the bug for it, especially if you've still got that competitive streak in you. Wheelchair or not, I still have that streak. I hate losing as much as I ever did.'

Time to play ball.

Part III

THE SMALL DANCES

6 So what?

'Don't give a shit,' Dubberley says. 'Don't give a shit about the Super Series, don't give a shit about the Canada Cup, don't give a shit about what happened in Athens, don't give a shit about any of it. The only thing I give a shit about is the Paralympics. It's all about Beijing. It's all about the big dance.'

The tournaments preceding the Beijing Paralympics are the Athens Games, the Oceania Championships in Sydney, the Super Series in Melbourne and the Canada Cup under the salmon-pink skies of Vancouver before everyone holds their breath, blocks their ears, works up a throat full of phlegm and strides into the polluted, spit-covered hub of the oldest continuous civilisation in existence.

For all his protestations to the contrary, Dubberley will manage a very decent impression of someone giving a shit when Batt detonates the final of the Oceanias by crunching a Canadian nemesis who has been taunting him for years with a hit so frightening his rival will never dare sledge him again. Whistle while you work. Dubberley will also appear to give a shit when his hands go to his head during a couple of excruciatingly tense battles at the Super Series as two prime Paralympic contenders, Great Britain and Canada, attack Australia with the force of the Red Army. Dubberley will kick a chair and cuss as his team implodes at the Canada Cup in a dog-ugly dress rehearsal for the Games, and even if these are merely the small dances leading to the big raucous midnight dance, and even if Dubberley says till he's Bells Beach-blue in the face that he couldn't give a shit about any of the events proceeding Athens and preceding Beijing, at every one of these tournaments, here's your take on the mindset of a man who is more of an open book than he realises: He most definitely gives a shit.

Paralympic Games, Athens

A holocaust of demons. Dubberley nearly quit the sport for good. Australia's Plans A, B, C, D and E revolved around Dubberley and Batt playing together with Batt carrying puppy fat fake ID, rough edges and a bargain basement classification of 2.5. He was upgraded to a 3.5 before the first match as The Rebel Scott Vitale went from a 1.5 to a 2. Every aspect of the team's planning disappeared up the chute with those altered numbers. In truth, the team didn't have Plans B, C, D and E. No Plan A meant no more plans at all. Matches were virtually thrown in a misguided attempt to prove the classifiers wrong. A hollow loss to the US came and went without a fight. Let's not swamp ourselves in technicalities. Nothing is more boring. Is this too technical? Dubberley and Batt were planning to scamper around like Butch Cassidy and The Sundance Kid but when the classifiers decided the auto cannon that is Ryley Batt had to be graded alongside all the other big guns, the 3.5s, the Australians, instead of vowing to soldier on regardless, reacted by throwing toys, bibs, dummies, dolls, plastic trains and every other toy out of the cot. They reacted immaturely and ruinously.

BATT: 'I wasn't allowed to talk about my classification in Athens. It turned into this really big deal. I'd be about to go out on the court and these people would just appear and start asking questions: "How does it feel for this and that?" I thought they were volunteers, or people just asking out of their own interest, but they were sneaky little journos trying to get me to talk. That probably didn't give me the best first impression of journos. I'd been feeling nervous as soon as the plane landed because I knew I was going to have my classification looked at. I thought I was probably going to go up to being a three-pointer. I was really scared about it because the line-up we had at that time, before they changed the classifications, had beaten New Zealand two weeks before the Games. We beat them pretty easily, and they ended up winning the gold, so we would have gone close with that original line-up. It was scary going in there to see the classifiers, thinking I was going to go up to a three—and then when I got my classification, hearing them say "You're a 3.5", I was just like, "What?!" All this stuff happened so fast. Scotty went up to a two-pointer, I was a 3.5—it stuffed us up 'cos we had trained with myself in the main four players with Brad as the 3.5. The whole thing was a disaster, but that's old news. We learned a lot. We've made sure we've run every line-up in training. We've made sure our players are permanently classified. We can't get stuffed around again.'

One of the Learned Gentleman Of The Australian Paralympic Committee believes Batt was so shaken by the Athens debacle that he nearly retired at the ripe old age of fifteen. Batt denies this: 'No way. I was pretty new to the team, I hadn't played in Sydney, so I was never going to quit. But I could feel the pain of the older guys. We thought we were a good team with a great chance but everything just went haywire and I could see how much it frustrated them. They had silver from Sydney and it was all systems go—but then the classification thing knocked us over. Me and Scotty were in the middle of it and that wasn't the best feeling. We hadn't done anything wrong, but we kind of felt like we had, like we'd been cheating or something. With our old classifications, most of the same players have stayed with the team and fought back, so we're getting another chance.'

Australia finished fifth.

NEVER WALK ALONE: 'You tell people you've been to a Paralympics and they say, "That must have been so great!" It should have been but for me, it was one of the worst times I've had. I went there and I was just so excited. We had a fantastic chance with Ryley and Scotty being so young and so good, but then their classifications changed and it was just devastating. Everything we had practised meant nothing because we couldn't run the same players on the court. Our coach at the time wasn't a great people person. That was his downfall. Things just went from bad to worse with the way he dealt with it all. As a team, it was horrible. We were concentrating on the classifications instead of thinking, "Fuck this, let's just win it with the people and classifications we've got." A lot of the time we were trying to get Ryley's classification sorted out, it probably wasn't worth all the time and effort. We just wasted so much energy on that instead of moving on. I thought it was going to be the best time of my life. Up until then, I'd only been around tournaments that were exclusively wheelchair rugby, so to go to the Paralympics and have all these other athletes—they're all the elite of the elite for what they do, they're all in their different situations—it's mind-blowing in the athletes' village. This time, in Beijing, I think if we can compete, just compete every minute we're out there, without any bullshit technical stuff going around, we're going to leave with a whole different feeling and a lot different result.'

BOXALL: 'Athens was insane. Everyone other than the coach knew Ryley wasn't going to stay a 2.5. He was far more functional than that. He was a 3 or a 3.5. He was made a 3.5, Scotty got classed up and it changed everything. There weren't enough other guys prepped properly to be able to perform at that level. We could see it coming, but the coach couldn't. The other eight guys in the squad were trying to get in, trying to get some court time in case we ended up being needed—we'd go to training camps and say, "Come on, get us on board, teach us some stuff." It didn't happen and when the Paralympics came around and the shit hit the fan, we were well pissed off. Everybody knew what was going to happen, and we tried to tell the coach, but he wouldn't listen.'

ELLWOOD: 'Athens was shit. Every day, all I did was have fighting matches on my phone with the classifiers. It was just hell. I was so upset or angry the whole time. It was a horrible experience and a really negative team. It wasn't much fun to be around. For a while, people were ostracised. I remember that I didn't really feel like part of the team. It wasn't good. Without the classification issues, it's so much better already. Just a different team. Ryley's classification became a big thing with the media. He was only young and he had all these journos hounding him. With Scotty's change we'd gone up 1.5 points with just two players. When we lost Scotty as our 1.5, that's what really wrecked it. The fact we played him in the first game just to get him looked at again by the classifiers, that was infuriating. We played him to prove his classification, but we lost the game. And then the classifiers said they didn't really see him anyway. A lot of things went wrong. Classifications are much better now. Nothing can change for Beijing. We're set, sorted. We know going in what we've got. You look at Ryley now and you'd have to say he's in the right class. The real drama was over Scotty but all the attention was on Ryley. He was only a boy.'

DUBBERLEY: 'I still think Ryley's classification is wrong. There were a few protests about Ryley from the other countries, just because of how good he was. They thought he had too much function. It all depends on how much mobility and hand function you've got. He's got trunk muscles, but his fingers aren't great—he's got two fingers on one hand and three on the other, and they don't really move anyway. He's got no legs so even though he's got a trunk, he's got no stability to help him stay up. One arm is longer than the other, which affects his pushing. He should be a 3. He dominates because he's such a good athlete, but if we're talking about pure function levels, he's only a 3. Joel Wilmoth is a 3.5. He's virtually got full legs so how does Ryley, without legs, have the same classification? Their hands are basically the same. Another athlete with Ryley's body wouldn't be half as good. He's basically a three-pointer who plays better than that. I think they're classifying him on how well he plays, not on what function he has. But 3 or 3.5—it doesn't matter now. He's got permanent classification and no-one is going to protest. We still think we're being hard done by, by half a point, but we know the whole Athens thing can't come up and bite us on the arse again.

'It was a massive distraction. God, it pissed me off. I'd been saying to the coach, "We can't revolve everything around Ryley, we can't revolve it all around the kid. We've got other players here who can help us win. We need to get them ready in case something happens to him, in case he gets stage fright or hurt or his classification changes." But the coach was like, "Nah, we'll be right." Of course, we weren't right. And once the classification issues happened, it just affected the whole team big-time. We could've still done really well, we could've still made the final, but it probably wasn't handled the right way. We lost to Canada in the game that would have put us in the semi-finals. We still could have been playing for the medals if we beat Canada, but we lost. We ended up beating Belgium for fifth instead of sixth. That sucked. Playing Belgium for fifth, it was such a rotten game to be in. You go out there and the best you can do is fifth. It's completely demoralising. We should have been in the top four but we blew it. The whole thing was a bit of a joke. If I didn't go to the US and play after that, I probably wouldn't be around rugby at all now. I would have quit. I was just so pissed off and over it. It was all so avoidable.

'I remember being in Athens and just wanting to get on a plane and come home. There was all the political crap and having games thrown when we could have done better. It was like, "Why did we even bother the last four years?" Ryley was playing in line-ups he wasn't used to, so basically the game was getting thrown when we could have had other combinations out there good enough to win. I remember sitting on the bench against Japan, sitting there with George and Steve watching the game, watching us lose, and we're looking at each other like, "What are we doing here? Why aren't we on the court?" I was probably one of the better players, but I was on the sideline all bloody day because we were trying to prove a point to the classifiers. The coach walks on by and says, "So, what do you think? Reckon you can get us out of this?" I'm like, "Why have you got us sitting here watching?" I went out and we got it to overtime, and we won it in overtime. But it was like, why did we have to cut it so close? If you wanted to win it from the get-go, why did you let us get so far behind? It was more of an insult than anything. It was the Paralympics but all we were worried about was all the other shit we should have just moved on from. Nothing worse can happen than what happened in Athens. Say something does happen to one or two players with classifications or injuries or whatever else, we still have the team to recover. Even if Ryley goes down and can't play, we know we'll still have a good shot. The other teams don't see that. They see Ryley as the be-all and end-all for us. They see us as no Ryley, no chance. Tell George that. We don't have a chance without Ryley? Go and tell George Hucks that.'

Let's not and say we did.

7

Oceania Championships, Sydney

Australia reach the final to qualify for the Paralympics. Two weeks later, Dubberley is still exhausted. That's okay. He's been through longer and more arduous recoveries. The Australian Captain organises the biggest rally since the Eureka Rebellion. A players-only meeting vows to turn this into a full-blown assault on the Games rather than some bumbling half-arsed attempt that might *hopefully* succeed if everything miraculously falls into place. They want to *make* it happen. They set the bar of expectation high. They promise to do everything within their considerable powers to get their hands on a medal. An optimist will say this increases their chances of success. A pessimist will roll his eyes and harrumph and say it sets them up for an even heavier fall. Dreams are desperate and flukey. They sound fucking terrific but sometimes they fall apart. Clowns can be petrifying and carousel music can be gut-wrenchingly sad. A mother can lose her eleven-month-old son on Christmas Eve. Not everything is always what it's cracked up to be. Australia could protect themselves from disappointment by pretending they don't care. But, go on, swallow your pride and admit it—deep down, everyone wants to try their hardest. Anything else is crap. Dubberley's team make a commitment more permanent, risky and heartfelt than a tattoo. The fear is that it might all end up in tears with eleven quadriplegics and their coach slumped in their chairs wondering where it all went wrong and why the fuck did they bother in the first place.

OLD AGE AND TREACHERY: 'Ten thousand people at the Oceanias, stomping their feet, clapping their hands, screaming themselves hoarse, it's so motivational. Atmosphere—that's a great drive. We've come to play.'

American coach James Gumbert rolls into town like the garrulous Texan he is. All swagger, tipped hat and a wheelchair. He has a video camera to record every second of every Australian game. 'He's a good guy,' Dubberley says. 'I've known Gumby a long time. He wanted me to play for Texas. Whenever I see him, I know what he's going to say: "Gimmee some sugar." He's an older guy, but he's a dude. He's loaded, absolutely loaded. When he had his accident, he had something wrong with his neck, went to hospital, got operated on, walked out of there. A couple of days later, one of the doctors checked out his X-ray and said, "Where is he? Where is this patient?" They told him, "He's gone home." The doc said, "Get him back here right now." His neck was still stuffed but they had let him go home. He came back for more surgery—and they dropped him off the operating table. He sued the fuck out of them. He's probably got about 20 or 30 million dollars in the bank. He basically owns the hospital now. It's kinda funny. They just dropped him clean off the operating table, bung neck and all. They fucked up twice and he cashed in.'

Would you break your neck for 30 million? *Would you?*

Gumbert's state-of-the-art camera becomes increasingly interested in Batt's impersonation of Janis Joplin and The Full Tilt Boogie Band midway through a show when the vodka has kicked in and she's found both her wings. Gumbert films Ryley Batt in slow mo, fast mo; Larry, Curly and Mo. Gumbert believes the gold medal to be America's barring any unexpected foreign raids. He leaves Australia with two concerns. His first is Batt, and the apparent transformation of the gun-shy boy from Athens into a gung-ho young man ripping the head off anyone not wearing a green and yellow singlet. His second concern upon trying to leave Australia is that airline staff have lifted him into his seat for his flight home, dropped him cold and broken his leg.

Spectators are frog-marched to the stadium with guns to their heads. The guns are taken away and they . . . stay? *Just one taste.* Ten thousand bums on seats is ten thousand bums on seats, regardless of who owns them. The announcer clears his throat moments before the final and declares, 'Ladies and gentlemen, one more thing to do before we get play underway. Please stand for the national anthems of Canada and Australia.' No offence, pal, but are you taking the piss? Please stand? 'Go Number Three!' scream the school kids. Ellwood tells them that number three's name is Ryley Batt. 'Go Ryley Batt!' One of Batt's chief antagonisers has been Canada's Fabien Lavoie, a mirthless but dangerous three-pointer who has harassed Batt since his international debut in the proverbial pair of nappies. Batt was too young to fight back and Lavoie was all over him, *all over him*, but every one of the catty and condescending comments was being added to the ledger. It's time to get square. The players not-stand for the national anthems and the joint is humming and this is murderball?

BATT: 'There can be a bit of niggle. Normally you're getting around so fast you don't have time to worry about it. If something does get said, afterwards it's like, "Ah, don't worry about it, mate. I didn't mean it".'

Lavoie and another Canadian, the curmudgeonly Mike Whitehead, have always meant it. Their treatment of Batt has been a systematic and prolonged attempt to intimidate him. 'Everyone from Canada has talked shit to me for years,' Batt says. 'I started young and they always tried to take advantage of that. Fabien says shit like, "I am going to beat you." I'm like, "Yeah, whatever." I just want to smoke him in all our games. Playing a lot of court time, it takes it out of you, and then he tries to race you when you're tired—and you still beat him. That feels good. He always comes at me and tries to spin me, yelling and whatever—I think it takes away a bit of their power if we shut him down like we do. He's always yelling in my face and talking it up.'

Doug Batt is a cool and happy man. His son's last words have been, 'K*eep an eye on number eleven for Canada*.' Batt takes a deep breath. Rolls his shoulders. Cracks his knuckles? Did we imagine that? The Canadians tear onto the court. The Australians are in a huddle. Now Batt is charging around like a heat-seeking missile. Wherever Lavoie goes, Batt goes. When Lavoie reverses, Batt reverses. Lavoie puts his head down and sprints; Batt puts his head down and sprints faster. Lavoie could go to Bondi Beach, take off his shirt, put on his sunscreen—and Batt would be next to him, grinning like a fool. Lavoie gets the ball, goes forward five pushes, just in front of the halfway line, jams on the brakes. Batt is closing in like a thunderstorm. The ball is in Lavoie's lap. He takes off wide and to the right, on the outside of Old Age and Treachery. Batt swings left and takes the shortcut. When Lavoie swings towards the goal line, he meets Batt at the intersection of I Might Score Here or I Might Get Killed. Lavoie bounces the ball, looks left and sees the truck coming. He blinks. Batt is leaning heavily into his turn, all shoulders, eyes locked on his target: number eleven for Canada. It's like the school nerd becoming a hit man in adulthood and knocking on the door of his bully with a steel pipe in his hand: *Remember me*? Lavoie turns white. He throws the ball away as if getting rid of the ball might be enough to get rid of Batt, too, but Batt is *flying* at him with only limited interest in the whereabouts of the ball. The full force of Batt's tearaway chair hits Lavoie on a 45-degree angle. At the moment of collision, Batt coils like a venomous snake. He snaps forward as Lavoie is forced onto his left wheel. Batt's chair keeps ploughing ahead. He's perfectly balanced, arms spreading into a condor as Lavoie falls face-first onto the hardwood floor. Right next to him is an advertisement with the address www.arrivealive.com.au. More extraction of the piss? A large portion of these players are quadriplegics because of motor accidents. What are the sponsors trying to say here? Drive safely or you'll end up like this? Right when Lavoie's teeth split the floor, Batt's chair ploughs into him one more time, shovelling him sideways. Lavoie is lifted again before another thumping into the wood. He's on his right side and when he looks up, Batt is right there, haunting him, peering at him one last time before speeding away. Childhood is over. Lavoie will never again sledge Ryley Batt if he knows what's good for him.

In the stands, 10 000 people without guns to their heads get to their feet and yowl. It's 52AD at the animal hunt. Lavoie drags himself onto his back before the officials come to his aid. Two strong men lift him into position. He's lost all the colour in his face. There's a restart and when Lavoie has stopped shaking enough to take his position, in those few quiet seconds before the hunt restarts, that moment of calm that always descends just before the breakout of bedlam, Batt gives his chair a nudge. Just a tiny little tap. *Clink. I'm still here*. Classic. Lavoie scores and Batt is displeased. Lavoie keeps scoring and Batt is ropeable. His attention shifts to the entire Canadian team. He has too much speed and manoeuvrability. No matter how much a 0.5 extends himself, he's a 0.5 and a 3.5 will always eat him alive. Lavoie is caught with the ball. Turnover. Nothing in murderball is more valuable than a turnover. Batt scores. The pot-bellied Canadian coach Benoit Labrecque paces the sideline. This man is a bulldog, a verbal rocket ship, a Benoit Jett. Canada's Ian Chan swipes the ball away as Australia wrestle their way to the lead. Benoit Jett fills with rage every time Batt scores.

Batt is fouled for making contact with Chan. He spends the next minute in purgatory. A small painted square past the sideline is the destination for those committing fouls. It's purgatory, the naughty corner, the sin-bin, Sin City. Batt has reached out to take the ball off Chan, but he's brushed his arm. Off you go. You can crack a player's kneecap with your chair, but you cannot touch him with so much as a fingernail without being sin-binned. Batt takes his foul and apologises to the ref, Chan and Dubberley, too nice for his own good.

Lavoie pummels Old Age and Treachery. Batt waves for help. Old Age and Treachery is put the right way up and a sign on the floor says, 'Don't Dis My Ability'. Batt leaves jail, scoots free to score—but gives the ball to Alman so he can do the honours. Lavoie's turn for the naughty corner, giving Australia the power play, four against three. He sits there like an admonished schoolboy, hands in his lap. Batt is sending Lavoie right where he wants him—up the fucking wall.

The Canadians scrape together goals, wiping their brows in a mixture of relief and exhaustion. Australia breeze through their one-point replies like they're dancing across the face of the moon. Batt chases Chan's red wheels. Chan throws the ball over the sideline and hides. Alman delivers a long pass, four bounces. Batt catches it between his elbows and waist and scores like he's the only player on the court. Stacks on the mill. Batt finds space doing his alternate left-right pushes, the fastest of all his pushes. He adds another point to Australia's rapidly rising tally and goes to the sideline and guzzles water like he's spent the last month stranded in the Bogdo Khanate (water is life). Australia gather around Dubberley in a half-moon shape as if they're listening to a priest in his pulpit.

Travis Mauro is wearing spectacles. Australia bash him. The Canadians keep triple-teaming Batt, who keeps throwing the ball to Alman for goals best described as pieces of piss. Old Age and Treachery is a workhorse. An old wives' tale suggests that babies who never crawl are unable to draw figure-eights in adulthood. Batt never crawled, not really, but there's nothing wrong with the high-speed figure-eights he's punching out here. He puts the ball in his tray like eggs going into Grandma's basket. There's a chase for a stray ball. Whenever the ball bounces or rolls free, away-away-away, there's the instantaneous cry of, 'Ball!' If it's the last quarter, 'Fucking ball!'

Batt needs a break. He's breathing hard while parked on the far end of the wooden interchange bench. For all their man-handling of Lavoie and Whitehead, Australia only lead by two goals. With Batt off the court, Canada score more swiftly. Batt gets out of his chair and slumps on the bench, like he's abandoning his car on the side of a deserted road. Carr comes out with the best handlebar moustache since Federation. There's a dispute over possession. Boxall lets the referee know what he thinks of the decision, not fucking much. Batt is back in his car, turning the ignition again, giving it one more try, still beside the road, idling the engine now, foot down, revving it up, dirt and sand everywhere, accelerating from the bench. Lavoie keeps looking at him, flinching as if they're in a dark alley and he fears being king-hit and left for dead.

Australia hold their lead without Batt and Boxall keeps nodding his head: *Yes, yes.* Dubberley keeps rubbing his chin: *Not bad, not bad.* The Australians gather and this time it's a poker circle, Dubberley cutting the pack. The Canadians spend the break watching the Australians wheeling and dealing and that is when they are defeated. U2 sing about the beautiful day and the importance of not letting it slip away.

Batt jinks, the sidestep you do when you're not doing a sidestep. Whitehead is a good, albeit dirty, player. He's telling his compadres what to do, running his mouth. Batt thumps the ball over the line. Goal. The Canadians are fatigued. They're shells of the team that burst onto the court for the start; heroin addicts when the heroin is all gone and the sun is coming up on Sunday morning and the city looks dirty and empty. Three goals is a massive lead in the final quarter because three turnovers take some doing. And they take a lot of time. Alman is clobbered, slinging back and forth like a crash test dummy.

Dubberley stands tall. Arms akimbo. Then he chews his nails. Batt charges at three Canadians and they turn their flags upside down, the international signal of distress, and Australia finish in a mad swarming rush. Their world ranking of number six is about to get a bullet from a Tommy gun and rise to number three behind the US and Canada. Canada cannot get out of their own half in the allotted fifteen seconds and there's a late turnover for Carr to grab a goal. Batt keeps going at warp speed. Puts the ball in his tray. Pushes. Gets the ball out of his tray to bounce it within ten seconds. Puts it back in his tray, a metal U-shaped contraption welded to his wheelchair where his lap would be if he had one. Pushes again. Scores again. Jared Funk scores while in possession of the coolest name since Don Quixote de la Mancha. Batt slaps the side of his chair. For the second straight tournament, he will be named MVP.

Batt gives Lavoie one last caning. Every whip of the cane may (or may not) be accompanied by an instruction. Do (cane) not (cane) ever (cane) sledge (cane) me (cane) again (cane). Batt has been ruthless. He has to be. A 3.5 must earn his keep. He can't just poonce around looking pretty. When Lavoie swerved, Batt sent sparks flying off the rim. He's just been *better.* Dubberley is still goading him, still pushing him, to the final whistle. One of Australia's last passes is a gem from Batt to the Australian Captain and then, right at the death, on his way to the line, Batt sends Lavoie tumbling over, one for the road and the long flight back to Canada and everybody's going to the moon.

Satisfaction seeps from each of Batt's thirsty pores. Lavoie rubs his head. 'There's only one guy, in the US, who wears a helmet,' Batt says. 'He's been knocked out a few times, but I think he gets a bit of grief for wearing it. Everyone asks about why we don't wear helmets, but you don't need one. If you hit your head, you hit your head. You just cop it. There's always the chance you'll get in some serious trouble if you hit your head that hard on the floor, but there's probably a bit of a macho-man thing that comes into it. You just don't wear a helmet. I'm never going to wear one.' Easy for him to say. Being Ryley Batt, he never has to play against Ryley Batt.

'Some hits don't hurt, some do,' he says. 'Some of them jar your whole spine. You lean back, get smashed and your whole spine compacts. It sucks the wind out of you but hopefully you've hurt them more than they've hurt you. It doesn't bother me. Whoever we play, we just try to pound them. You hit someone and you can tell it's taken the gas out of them. They don't like it. Ourselves and the US are probably the biggest hitters. We can hurt teams, game after game. We keep hitting them, and it's going to wear them down. They start getting a bit hesitant. They start worrying. You can tell what they're thinking: "Here he comes again, he's going to wipe me out again." They panic and pull out or throw a ball to no-one because they're worried about getting smashed. Look at the chairs. That'll show you how hard the hits are. The chairs get cracked and you have to weld them up. After two or three years, your chair has just had it because it's been hammered so many times. I've got this one chair I used to use, it looks like a tin can after you've crushed it.'

Or a car after it's been wrapped around a tree.

The clock keeps ticking and then it stops. Australia win, the masses say hell yes and Batt high-fives Porter. He back-slaps Alman: *Beijing!* Lavoie puts his hand out and initially you think he's only offered the cold fish but to be fair, the cold fish is the only kind of handshake he has. Batt has beaten him to a pulp but Lavoie has kept coming back for more and that alone deserves a large stack of respect. Dubberley walks off with a flushed face, his right leg striding, his left hanging around like the harmless friend you can never get rid of and, come on, be honest, you don't really want to. Australia have annihilated the number two team in the world. They have sent their message to the USA via Gumbert's DVD recorder and thrown the pot-bellied Canadian coach into fits of apoplectic rage.

DUBBERLEY: 'Canada have gotten a taste of what we can do. We gave Ryley a few rests and we still beat them. I gave every player a start. That will mess with their heads: *they rested their best player and they still beat us*. There's a lot of experimenting going on. We'll get ourselves sorted then go to Beijing and destroy them.'

BATT: 'That's the best experience I've had since I started playing. I'm older, for starters. It's the first time I played for Australia when I was over eighteen so I can celebrate properly with the boys. I got MVP and it all feels pretty good. We beat Canada and New Zealand and it's qualified us for Beijing. We're going in the right direction.'

The Sydney media jump on the bandwagon and Batt is front and centre, swinging a lasso. 'I don't really like the attention,' he says. 'A lot of people come up and say, "Are you Ryley Batt? You played awesome!" I don't really enjoy that side of it too much. It's nice of them to say but it's a team sport. I might play alright but the whole team is awesome and I don't ever want to take anything away from the rest of our guys. Kim, our manager, will ring and say, "Ryley, there's a radio station that wants to talk to you." And I'm like, "What do they want to talk to me for? Put them on to one of the other guys. Put them on to one of the new players. They don't need to talk to me." I used to hate that stuff, sitting there being interviewed by someone I don't even know. It used to make me feel really uncomfortable. When I was younger it was like, "Ryley, the *Today Show* want . . ." and I was like, "No." But I'm trying to get used to it all now. It's good for the sport. Anything that's good for the sport, I'll try to say yes to.'

Batt is offered a contract to play for the South Florida Rattlers in the US. 'There's actually some money in it,' he says. 'But I told the bloke, "Mate, I'm only eighteen, I think I should stay home for a bit. Maybe next time".'

~

Gumbert goes home. *Snap*.

'Poor prick,' Dubberley says. 'The day he was flying home, they dropped him on the plane and smashed his knee, smashed his whole leg up. They had to take him back off the plane and take him to hospital. He had to wait a day before they could find a bed for him. His missus had to fly out from the US because they wouldn't let him fly home alone, but her flights got delayed and cancelled. He was stuck here for two weeks. A doctor from the Prince of Wales ended up flying to the US with him. He'll probably sue United. Get himself another twenty mill.'

The Americans remain far-off mythical creatures whose demonic faces ruin premature visions of Beijing glory, but Dubberley says, 'I know those players and I know their coach, and I am not scared of any of them. I keep telling our boys I *know* we can beat them if we get the chance to play them. There is nothing to be scared of. When you play the US, you just need to withstand their first five minutes. They throw everything at you from the start. But if you get through that, you're right. They try to steamroll you. But if you're still with them into the third and fourth quarters, if the game is close, they start shitting themselves because they're not used to having to fight. They're like most Americans, really. They think their shit doesn't stink. They think they're the greatest but if people start pushing them around, they don't like it. They can get rattled. They're a good team, but I still think they're very wary of us. They've seen all the videos. Me and Andy Cohn don't play games. He knows I don't fall for all their shit. They've seen footage of Ryley at one of their US camps and Andy was telling me straight-up that they all had their mouths open, jaws on the floor, thinking "Oh shit". We don't want to get too cocky but if we keep playing like we have here, I honestly believe the only team that can beat us at the Paralympics is us. I think this is the best team we've ever had. Andy was saying, "How does Ryley do that?" I told him, "Don't worry about how he does it. That's our boy. See you in Beijing".'

Murderball is prominent in the newspapers for precisely one day before the publicity dies and the public interest goes back to being nil, nada, nought. Everyone forgets about murderball again except for the only people in all this who really and truly matter. The murderballers.

8

Super Series, Melbourne

A 6.05 a.m. Virgin Blue flight from Sydney. You're sitting next to a man reading a document entitled 'Root Cause Analysis'. Breathtaking stuff. The man reading Root Cause Analysis is bald and unwelcoming. A tongue of fire. He is wearing a suit. He sits stiff and angry, pouting and pissing and moaning about everything from the breakfast menu to the sun coming through his window and hurting his precious bloodshot eyes. *Mate, don't eat, then. And shut your fucking blind if that will fucking help.* Root Cause Analysis appears to be falling short of the requirement to live every day as if it's his last. You think of him, and you think of Brad Dubberley, and you know who you'd rather be. One of your own eyes hurts like hell. You have a sty. It's sore, watery and pussy. You are about to do some A-grade whingeing of your own but suspect there are worse physical conditions to have. Root Cause Analysis decides it will be in everyone's best interests if we spend breakfast hearing his complaints about the lack of leg room. Mate, *please*. Piping hot coffee at the crack of dawn is a nectar of the gods, but Root Cause Analysis says his is too strong. In Melbourne, waiting for a taxi, you hear: 'Charlotte, you've got to look up when you're walking, darling. You nearly got run over. You don't want to have an accident, Charlotte.' No, Charlotte, you don't ever want that. You tell the taxi driver you want to go to AquaLink. He says Aqua-*what*?

There's the sprawling Melbourne Cricket Ground with its 100 000 seats. Telstra Dome with half as many, *so* many. Rod Laver Arena and Olympic Park and all these endless stadiums with their Friday, Saturday and Sunday night lights attracting people like moths to the great sporting flame. You drive past all the sporting and heavenly cathedrals early on a Sunday morning and end up in the nondescript Melbourne suburb of Box Hill. In the middle of Box Hill is Aqua-*what*? The tall sign at the entrance off Surrey Drive promotes tennis lessons, the availability of an Olympic-sized swimming pool for morning laps, the possibility of hiring courts for badminton, basketball or volleyball, and the presence of the curiously named, all things considered, 'Sit Down Café'. There is no mention anywhere—not even on the cork noticeboard inside—that this is also the venue for the Super Series. You walk into Aqua-*what*? and fight your way past the three people inside to receive another caffeine injection. There were more people (four) in the lift at the airport. There were more people (a dozen) in the 7-Eleven you visited on the way here. There were as many people in your row when you all had the pleasure of spending one hour and twenty minutes with Root Cause Analysis. You could squeeze more into a phonebox if you felt so inclined. The taxi driver parks at the back door of Aqua-*what*?. You're tempted to tell him to keep the motor running because maybe the Oceanias was a one-off eruption and this is going to be a dud. Low-key has never been like this, not even the last key on the piano going doink. One of the staff workers declares, 'Too early for this shit. I need to go home.' You've been to parent–teacher classes with more hoopla. Outside, there's a dog. Why does every lonely scene have a dog in it? Standing at the Sit Down Café with a guy who reckons it's too early for this shit, at a tournament the Australian coach still reckons he doesn't give a shit about, you have no idea that unfolding before your eyes this afternoon will be the single most engrossing, entertaining and emotional sporting contest you have ever been blessed enough to witness.

It's building, you know. This whole thing is building.

Assembled are the team Coach Joe used to coach (Canada), the team Coach Joe now coaches (Great Britain), a team Coach Joe would give his eye teeth to coach (Australia), and just about the only team Coach Joe-san hasn't yet coached but give him time (Japan). Eight months have passed since the Oceanias and Australia haven't played one match since, their lack of match play bordering on organisational criminality, murderball suffering its infuriating absence of exposure and public awareness partly because the Australian Rugby Union has made it clear they want nothing to do with their physically fucked friends. Their overriding fear has been that parents will link wheelchair rugby to injuries sustained while playing traditional rugby, making mothers and fathers haul Little Johnnie out of the sport because there's a recognised risk they might break their growing necks. The other cause of the Australian murderball team having a lack of profile is that they never have any fucking tournaments to play.

'This is annoying me,' Dubberley says. 'Two of the boys, Grant and Shane, are late with getting their reports in. It's supposed to be about helping the team. We all do written reports on the other teams, then I put them together for one big report. We want to know all their strengths and we want to know all their weaknesses so we can go to China and pounce on them. But Grant and Shane haven't done it. We don't know what the punishment should be. They have to do something for us. I'm not going to fine them. It's not like any of us are loaded and anyway it's almost too easy just to hand over your cash. They've let everyone down, so they can help everyone out. Get our breakfasts. And if they don't get our breakfasts, they can get up and sing the national anthem. It's the principle. Singing the national anthem—you know they're going to hate it. No music in the background, you know they can't sing, they'll really hate it. Steve is like, "Maybe we should make it worse for them. Maybe we should make 'em pash." Steve trains the house down and he works full-time but his reports are the most detailed out of everyone. He says, "Well, if I can get mine done on time, why can't these blokes?" He's furious with them. He's going to blow up. I hope he does.'

No TV feeds from Aqua-*what*?. No live radio broadcasts, hell no. The Moustachioed Taxi Driver has followed you inside, sparking a

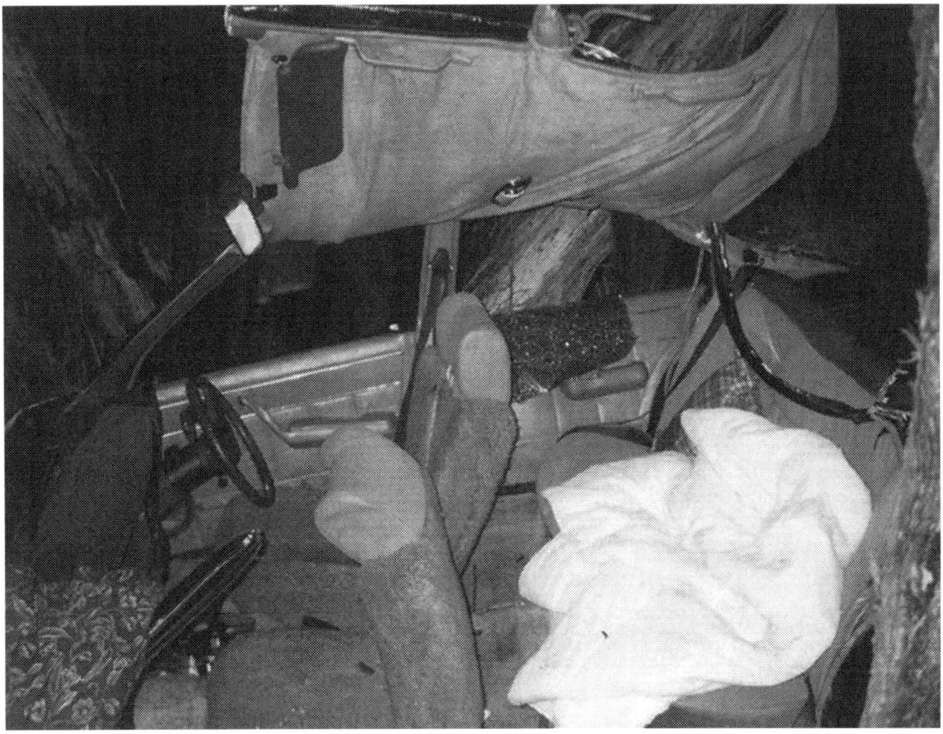

A consequence of speeding. Ryan Scott's car.

The rescue of Brad Dubberley from Shit Creek. Years later, his mother looked at the blanket on the embankment and thought . . . angel's wings.

Dubberley's family about the time he's wondering why he can't feel his legs.

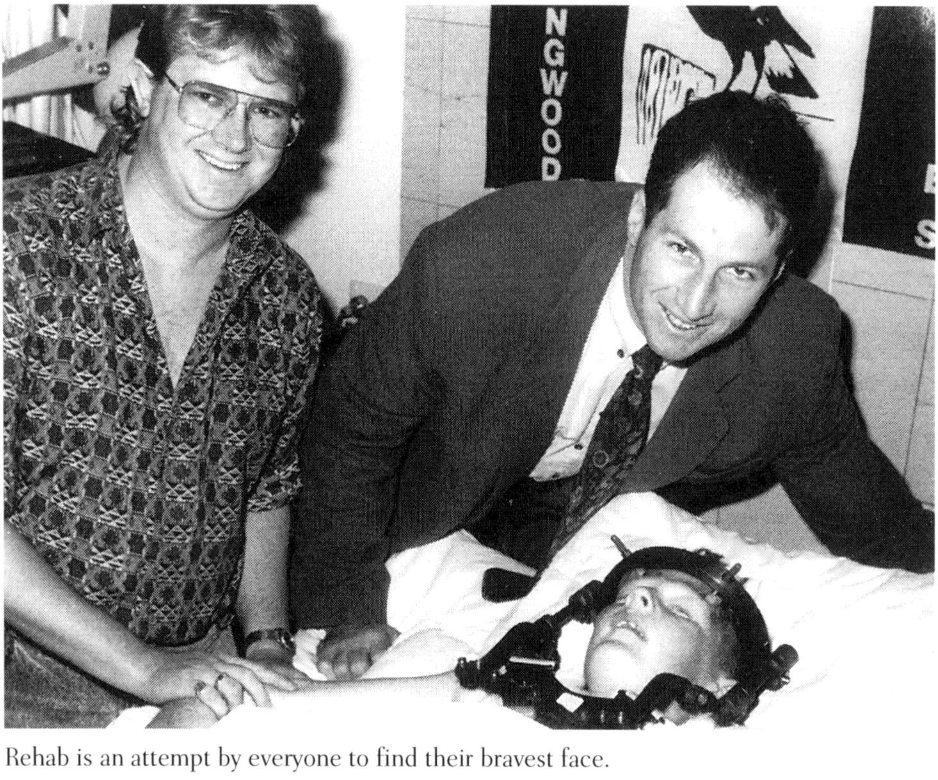

Rehab is an attempt by everyone to find their bravest face.

Brand. Off-land.

Nazim Erdem. Counsellor, murderballer, genius, paraglider, quadriplegic. In that order.

Erdem. Free.

There are times when Ryley Batt bends his knees. Unless you imagine it.

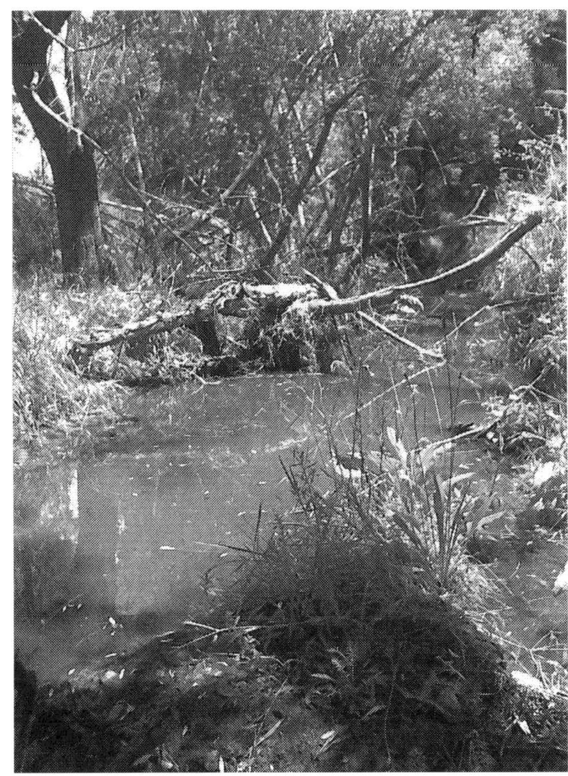

Shit Creek, 1 December 2008.

Batt and buggy.

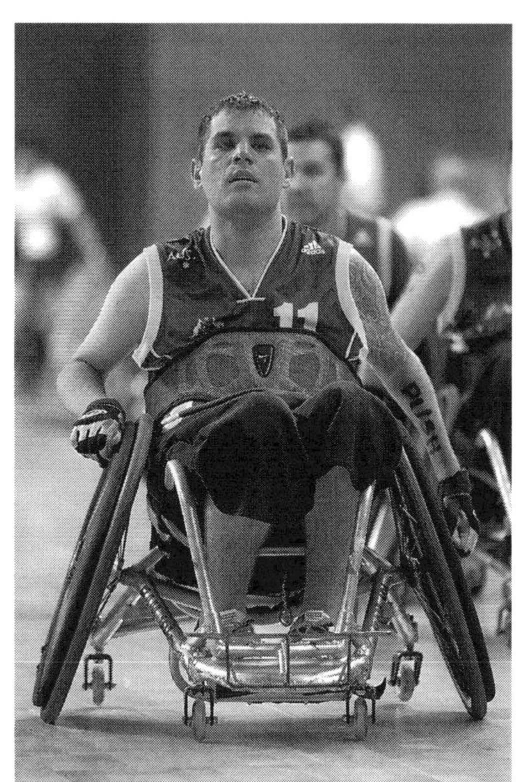

Never. Ever. Walk. Alone.
PHOTOGRAPHER: SERENA OVENS

Clink. Erdem and Springer. PHOTOGRAPHER: SERENA OVENS

Smash-up man carnage. Vitale and Kirkland. PHOTOGRAPHER: TOM GRIFFITH

Bradley Wayne Dubberley. PHOTOGRAPHER: SERENA OVENS

Beijing poker circle. PHOTOGRAPHER: SERENA OVENS

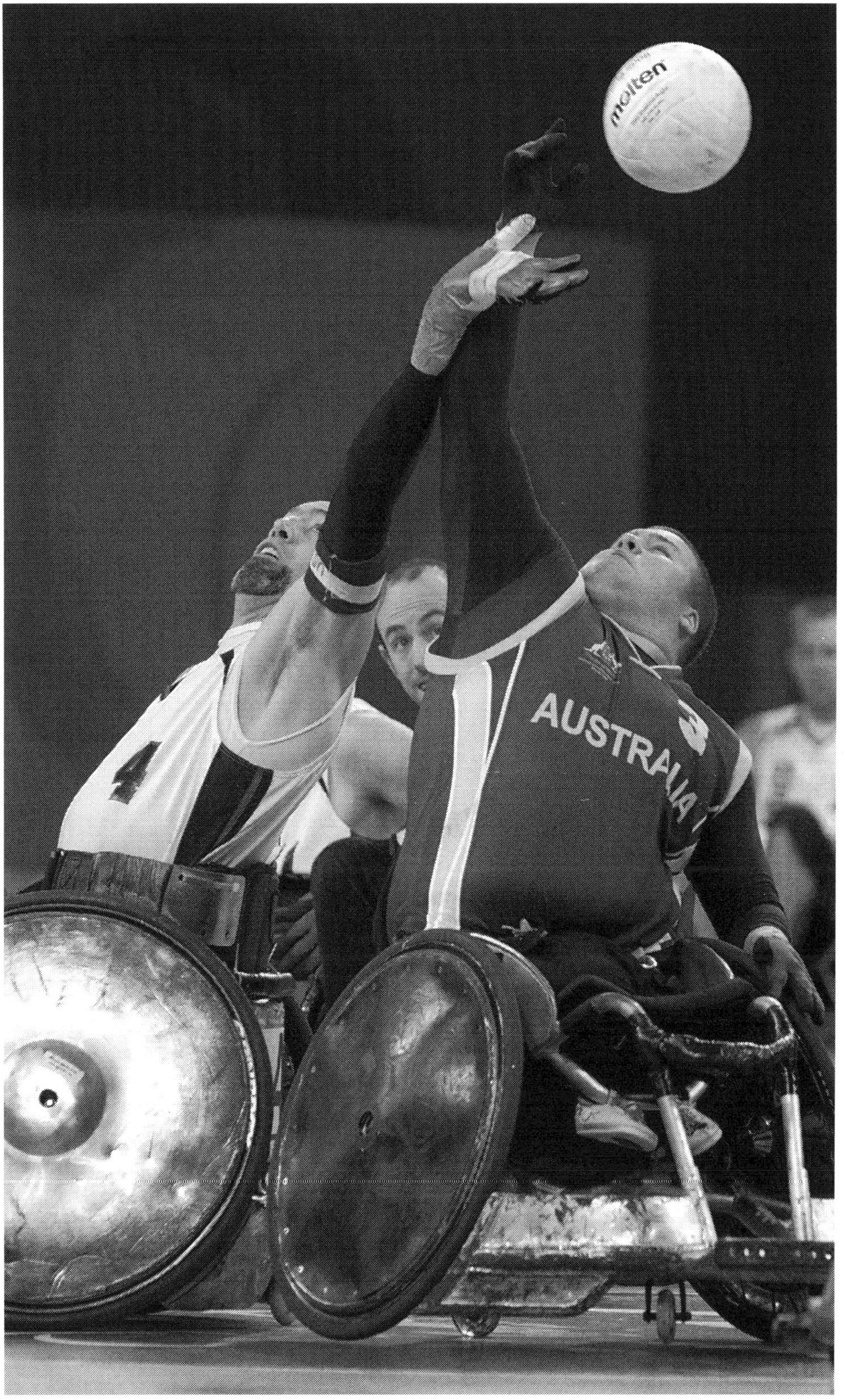

Tip-off. Batt and Kirkland. PHOTOGRAPHER: TOM GRIFFITH

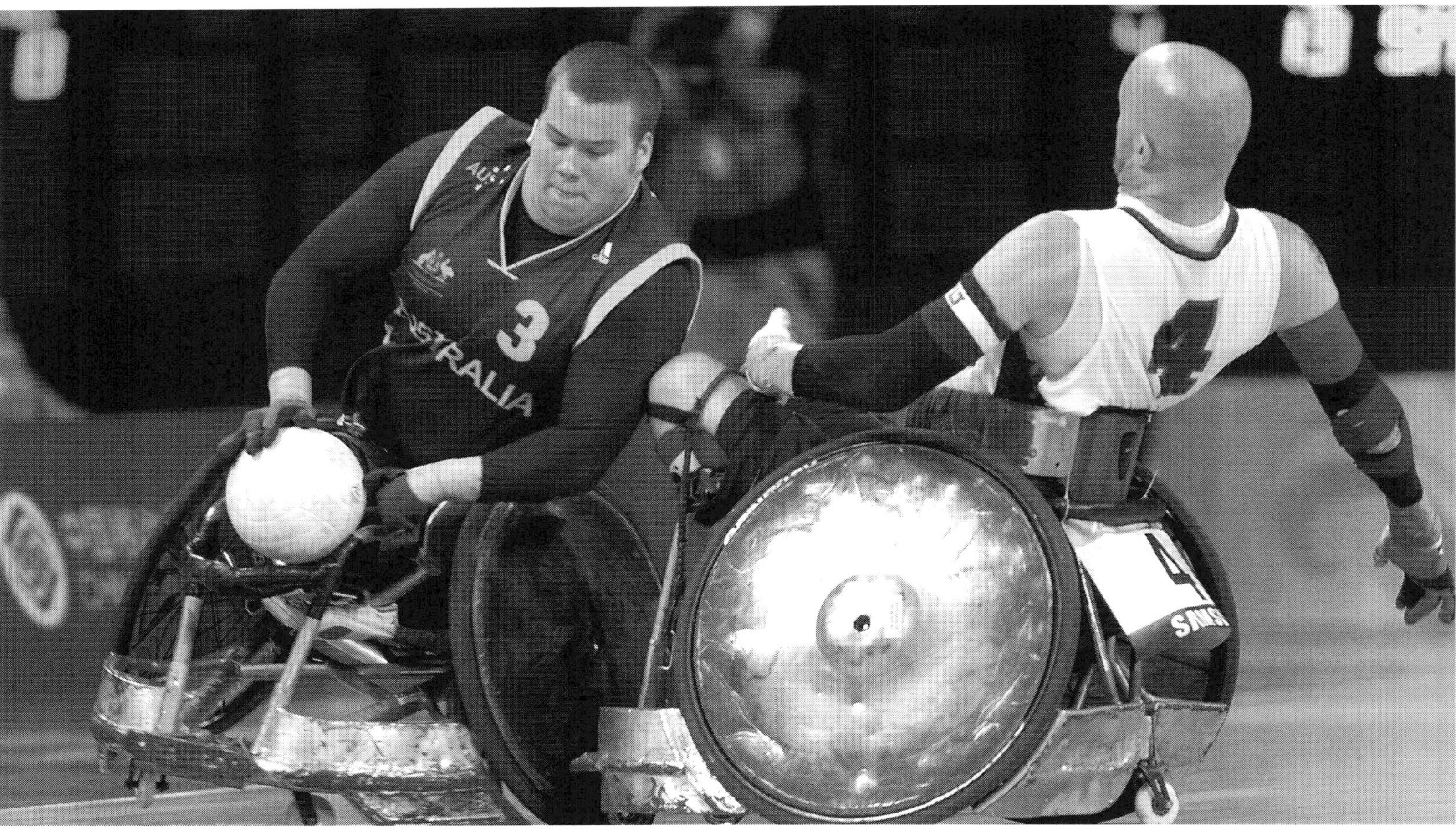

Batt, full tilt. PHOTOGRAPHER: SERENA OVENS

Hucks and Springer. PHOTOGRAPHER: TOM GRIFFITH

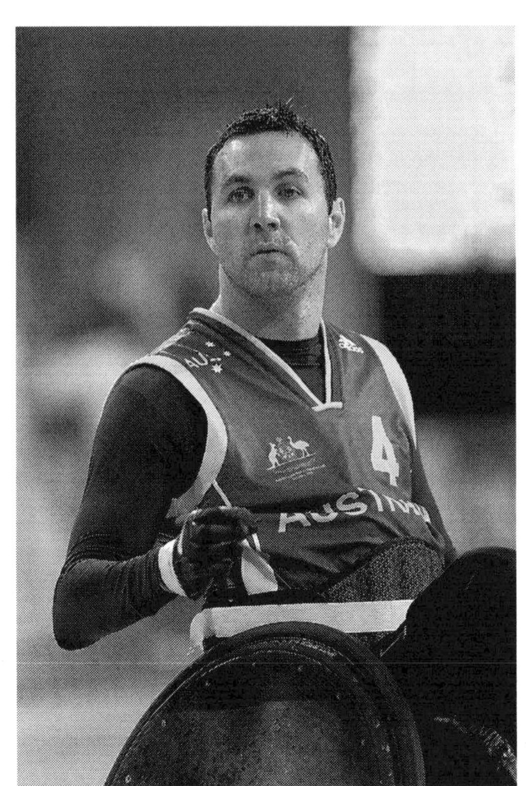

Cameron Carr.
PHOTOGRAPHER: SERENA OVENS

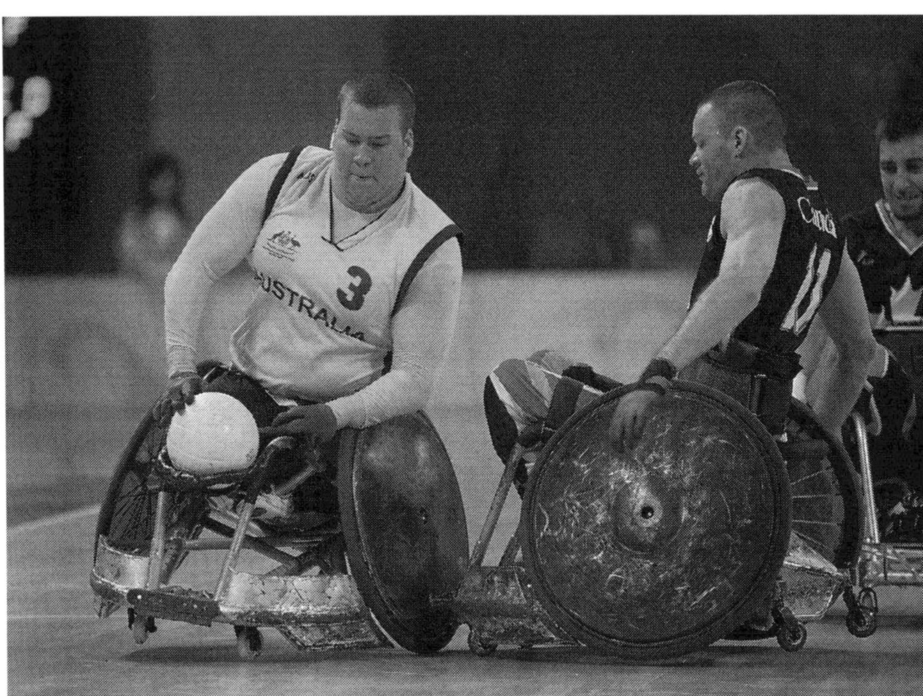

Batt and Lavoie. PHOTOGRAPHER: ROGER BOOL

One left hand, and individual, of unlimited capabilities.
PHOTOGRAPHER: SERENA OVENS

Rebel. PHOTOGRAPHER: ROGER BOOL

Grant Boxall.
PHOTOGRAPHER: SERENA OVENS

The Australian Captain. PHOTOGRAPHER: SERENA OVENS

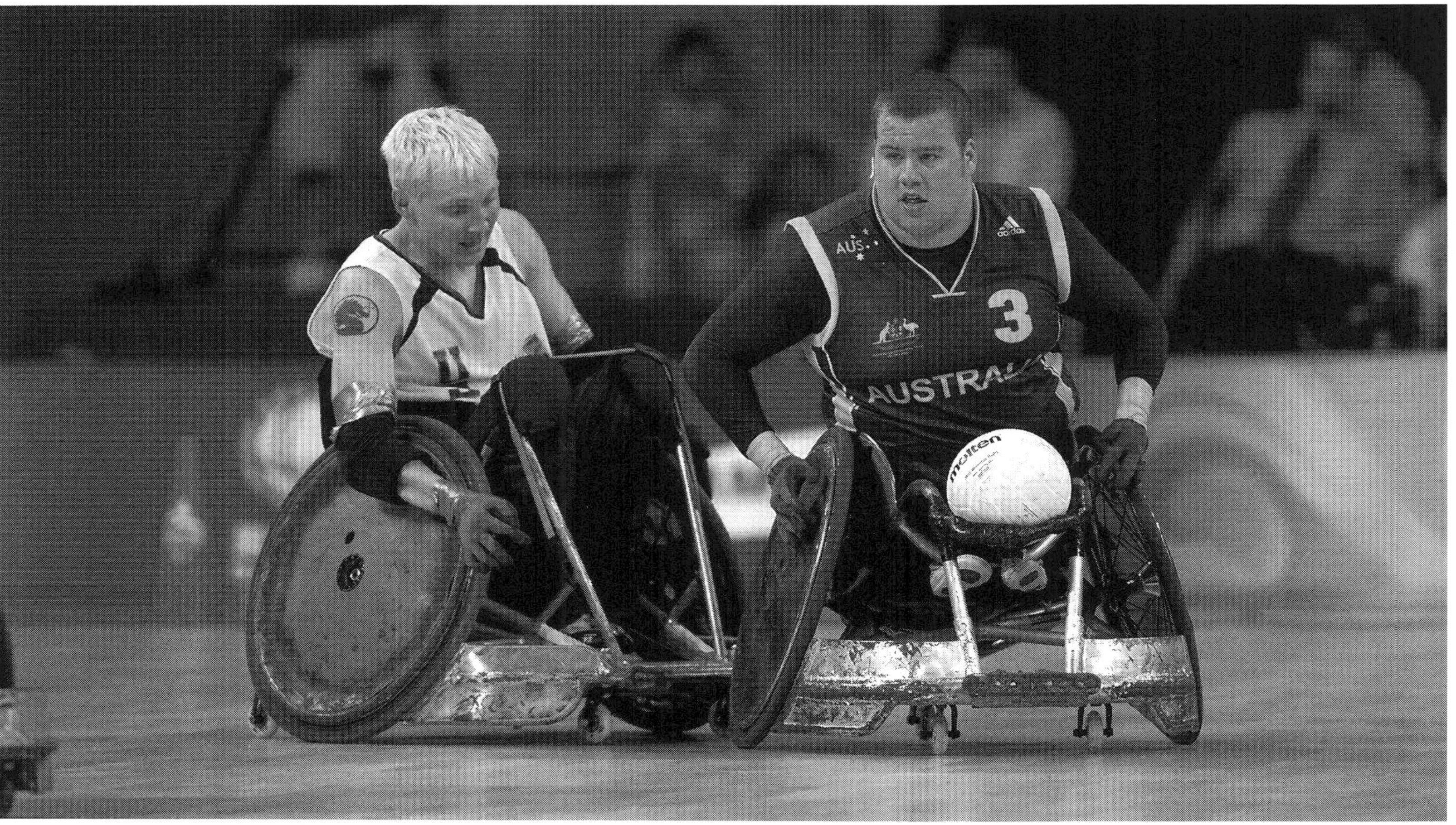

Batt and Slim Shady. PHOTOGRAPHER: SERENA OVENS

Smith, Porter, Scott, medals. PHOTOGRAPHER: SERENA OVENS

Silver lining. Beijing medal presentation.

20 per cent jump in the crowd figure. He's been an early morning revelation. A silver cross has hung from his rear-view mirror. 'Have a good day this whole day!' he said. *This whole day!* No pressure. Volleyball games commence down the far end of The Hall Of Underwhelming Glory. No-one is going out of their way to taste the delights of murderball. The world just keeps rolling along. Australian Rules Football games are held outside. An older man in a green jumper receives a golf lesson on the adjoining Surrey Park. *Put your feet here, bend your knees like this, keep your head still, swing your arms around your torso like this, curl your fingers around the grip like that you lucky bastard, keep your back steady and swing around your spine if you can.* Young mothers walk babies in prams. They look so perfect and so do their children, but the child bawls and the mother gets angry and you imagine how she would react if the little mite had no legs or meningococcal or a slashed C6. Who would be bawling then? The fire alarm in the gymnasium goes off but there's hardly a rush to get outside. Two of the five people, including The Moustachioed Taxi Driver, finish their coffees first.

Dubberley walks in, tall and straight, like he's taking the New York Giants into Superbowl XLII. More foot-tapping. It's all so quiet. A Quakers meeting? Quakers are devoted to silence. Their meetings amount to everyone sitting around in quiet contemplation before racking off home without a word being said. The birds are saying give-us-a-break. That can't be right. But they've just said it again.

The combatants arrive. Hucks is first through the door. On the main court, where the stand (not so grand) can fit literally *dozens* of people, Australia will play Japan in the first semi-final. On the second court, where there are no stands of any description, on the other side of a mesh net that appears to have been flogged from the nearest prawn trawler, Canada will be facing Great Britain. Someone should tell Coach Joe where his allegiances lie because we'd really hate for there to be any confusion. We'd hate him to put his hand over his heart and start belting out *O Canada* instead of *God Save The Queen*. Is that sarcastic enough?

The Australians are doing their warm-ups. The crowd has skyrocketed to seventeen. That's not a rough estimate. It's an exact count. The Australians are throwing quick passes to each other.

Hucks is reminding Ryley Batt that he's in possession of poofter hips. They catch and pass, catch and pass in perfect time with Hucks saying poofter hips, poofter hips, you've got poofter hips. Batt is laughing so hard he keeps dropping the ball. Poofter hips, poofter hips. Batt needs an oxygen canister. Both the young and old bulls have slices of white tape covering their earrings. Heaven forbid they ever take the earrings out. The Australians are loud like a playground. The Japanese are quiet like an assassin in that single breathless moment before he gently squeezes the trigger. You cannot hear them. They wear navy singlets with rising suns large on their chests. Dubberley is wearing Dunlop Volleys with scribble on them. He describes the scribble as art work. Art work is a stretch. Everyone in the team did it except The Rebel Scott Vitale. 'They might look stupid, but we all did it, it's just something we did together,' Dubberley says. No socks. His feet must stink.

The Japanese warm up. Their hits look soft and unthreatening but they *feel* dangerous. The Assassin's Bullets. They are fast and light and you cannot hurt the things you cannot touch. Shinichi Shimakawa is wearing slick wraparound sunglasses. His hair is tinted red and he's bullet-thin, slick like a martial arts movie. He will pierce the skin smoothly and quietly. He has a stare of Vitale-like ferocity. He can grip the ball one-handed to throw a strong overhead pass.

Coach Joe! You old sandbagging son of a bitch! He's on the next court, slouched forward as if knitting. He's alone. He's wearing a red and white cap. GB's players are doing anxious laps of the court as if anyone slackening off will be shot. They appear scared. 'STEELERS!' The Australians yell their nickname, a reference to the material both the wheelchairs and the players are constructed from. Coach Joe hears the Australian chant and waves his hands around like he's pretending he's seen a ghost: Wooo, Steelers, I'm scared. The Australians do their laps in a conga line behind Batt. He turns left and they all do, the last three players the sting in the tail. Coach Joe sits sullenly and shakes his head. You get the impression he could hold a newborn baby and find fault with it. Come up with a reason why *his* newborn was better. He doesn't talk to anyone, Coach Joe. In every jungle on Earth, every forest and shrubbery and every overgrown stretch of bushland, snakes travel alone.

One of the Great Britain players, the willing Jason Roberts, approaches his erstwhile mentor and pants, 'Coach Joe, I think . . . Coach Joe, can we . . .' Coach Joe ignores him. More pressing matters are at hand. He's sending a text message. 'GB RUGBY' is emblazoned on Coach Joe's tracksuit. You know, there's nothing wrong with Coach Joe working for Great Britain after he's played for the US and been a mentor to Canada. A man needs to make a quid. Shrines to one's self do not come cheap. Coach Joe is entitled to an income whether he's paid in American dollars, Canadian dollars, yen, rupees, pounds sterling, baht or sticks. A man can work for whoever he damn well pleases. Coach Joe rolls away for some quiet time. Some Coach Joe time. His favourite time. You get the side-on profile: groper. There must be a hundred teeth in that mouth. He's in earnest discussion with his assistant coach near the coffee machine. You ask if it might be okay to grab an interview. 'Yeth,' he says. Coach Joe has a lisp! 'I'll look after you.' It's like having a cold hand placed on your shoulder by The Godfather just before he nods at an underling to put a bullet through your head. Coach Joe comes over to look after you. Words come from the side of his mouth. He always seems to be whistling. It's not a joyful whistle, but an urgent, moody whistle as if there's some place else he wants to be. Interview or not, he just always appears to be a bit fucked off.

Coach Joe keeps licking his lips. GB's semi-final begins. He's more quiet than anticipated. We're a good fifteen seconds into the first quarter and he hasn't abused anyone. Not so much as a dirty look. He says that's because this isn't The Big Dance. Coach Joe is caked in sweat. His trademark pose is leaning back, defiant chin pointing skywards, arms folded, plotting something. You don't know what he's plotting, but he's plotting *something*. Roberts is playing with a Herculean amount of effort, grappling with the Curmudgeonly Whitehead and saying, 'A little love-in, ref, we're just having a little love-in.' Roberts keeps looking at Coach Joe for words of wisdom. He receives none. 'I've got the eight,' Roberts screams. 'I've got the ball, I've got the four.' The four scores. 'I thought I had the four.' Inked on the right shoulder of The Herculean Jason Roberts is a triangle inside a circle representing the union of body, mind and spirit, the divine encircling of protection and power. Or Alcoholics

Anonymous. Coach Joe takes off his jumper, the snake shedding its scaly skin. He's being disarmingly friendly, too friendly, hissing. The red mist will inevitably descend. You feel uneasy like the time you saw a pastor in snakeskin shoes telling a thousand devotees in his parish that he would change their lives before pointing out the ATM at reception so they could make their donations and while we're at it, saints, here's my new book and DVD that you can buy from the cash you can get from my ATM. Now, where were we? Changing your lives. Funnily enough, he did and you have been going back ever since. You sit and listen to Coach Joe. Dubberley has to write one of his report cards on all the teams and individuals involved in the Super Series and here's your own personal appraisal of the Great Britain coach: lunatic.

Australia have had one loss during the preliminary rounds, to Canada. And they have survived a game against GB by the barest margin since Coach Joe's humility, one point in triple overtime.

OLD AGE AND TREACHERY: 'My family haven't seen me play for Australia before. They've only heard bits about it but they've been here this week and they're like, "This is unbelievable!" Up until now they probably thought, "Oh yeah, he plays wheelchair rugby, that's nice, good on him." They didn't understand the game, they didn't understand the physicality of it. They came and saw it here during the week and it's just blown them away. They love it, they want to know when the next comp is on so they can come and see it.'

HUCKS: 'We need more of these international tournaments. We really stuffed up after Sydney. All the hype went away. We let it go. Everybody was wanking on, you know, "This is the new coming of everything, this is when our sport is going to take off", but then we didn't play again. Can you believe that? It's all been forgotten about. There was all this publicity, there were 10 000 bloody people watching us and for most of us it was like, "Jesus Christ, look at this, people want to watch us!" It was exciting. Most of us were used to playing in front of Mum and Dad and a few cousins but all of a sudden we had people coming along to watch. The sport should have really capitalised on that but we wasted it and have to start all over again. We blew a really big chance there, but here we go again.'

THE INVALUABLE CAMERON CARR: 'People are getting interested. An older woman came down here to do some swimming and she watched one of our games. She's ended up coming back every day instead of doing her classes. She was pretty funny. We were having lunch and I could hear her explaining rugby to her friend. She was like, "Look at these guys, aren't they great! I can't believe they're out here!" It was like we were at the zoo, and we were the animals. She was nudging her friend and pointing at us and saying, "Look, look!" She was pointing at Naz, or Ryan, and she was telling her friend, "Look, look, he's using his teeth to open the sandwich! Look, look, now he's eating the sandwich!" It was pretty funny. I can understand it from the older generation, but that's kind of the biggest message we have to get out there about people in wheelchairs. There's nothing different about any of us. We're not playing the sport because we've got nothing else to do. We need people to see that instead of having guys coming up to you saying, "Good on you boys, great to see you outside." I've heard that so many times and I'm like, "Good to see us outside?" One guy said it to me—"Great to see you out, mate"—when I'd just gotten back from a safari in Africa. I was like, "Mate, I've just come down for a roast dinner. Is that okay?" Hopefully with our younger guys coming through it will show a bigger section of the public what life in a wheelchair is about.'

The crowd has swelled to nearly 200. 'They're so close you can almost touch them,' says Never Walk Alone. 'You go off the court and you're about to crash into them. The kind of atmosphere this game produces, under a roof in an enclosed gym, with the crowd on top of you like that, it can be pretty unbelievable. It's a pretty intimate and full-on atmosphere. Most of the people in the crowd have a personal interest in the players. They're not just passing through. There's a reason why they're here. They *really* want us to do well.'

Great Britain has a female player. Her name is Josie Pearson. Cream skin, pink cheeks, white hair, an English Rose. She became a quadriplegic when her boyfriend totalled their car when they were love-struck teenagers. The boyfriend died. Canada also has a female player, Erika Schmutz, another Lady Bump destined to play only a token role this year.

People keep giving Coach Joe a wide berth. 'We all know he gives a bit of lip,' Erdem says. 'He'll tell people to fuck off, he's done things behind people's backs. He's just a bit of a dickhead. One of those people a lot of people hate. He can be good to talk to, though. If you're talking about him, or his team, man, he can talk on and on. But you ask him about the Americans and he's like, "Who? I don't want to talk about them. Let's talk about my team. Let's talk about me." You won't get that much out of him. Unless you let him talk about himself—me, me, me, me, me.'

The Gentleman Shane Brand bumps into Coach Joe. 'It's the first time I've met him,' Brand laughs. 'He comes up to me and goes, "Oh, so you're Shane Brand." I go, "Yeah, I am." He says, "I'm Joe Soares." I go, "I know who you are." Joe says to me, "I've been watching you. And I'm gonna keep watching you." He probably liked that I knew who he was. He's a bit of a character.' You can say that again, Shane-o. 'He's a bit of a character.'

Then comes a surprise. The gong for the greatest loud-mouth pain-in-the-arse of the tournament goes to someone other than Coach Joe. It goes to the overbearing and antagonistic Benoit Jett.

~

'Here we go!' Dubberley shouts. The three-tiered wooden stand (still not grand) is smack-bang on the sideline and you can hear every grunt, every breath, every word coming from the combatants. Doug Batt is to your right. 'Big D!' yells Dubberley. He's not welcoming Ryley's father. 'Big D! Big Defence! Naz, go long! NAZ! GO LONG!' Erdem goes long. The instructions from the coach all sound pretty fucking enthusiastic for someone who doesn't give a shit. Erdem is still going long, but it might take a while. Batt knocks The Bullet Train Shinichi Shimakawa over the Himalayan cliff and smiles at Dubberley. He scores a couple of early goals, but congratulations are directed towards Carr and Erdem for their ground work. The Bullet Train takes another tumble. A trickle of blood escapes from his bent nose. Batt hits him again; takes the ball like he's wearing a balaclava and pinching jewellery from behind a glass counter. He puts the loot in his tray. The tray is right where he wants it to be—fingertips. He can feel for it without needing to look. He pushes off like he's leaving the dinner table in a huff, finds space, adjusts his skin-tight yellow shirt, scores and then absent-mindedly tosses the ball to the referee. He could do it in his sleep.

And then everyone congratulates Erdem. He's hooked his chair onto The Bullet Train's and for all the pushing and shoving and frustration building with enough pressure to make The Train's head explode clean off his shoulders, he's been unable to break free. Batt has scored but Erdem has allowed him to. Erdem attaches himself like a fishing hook getting jagged on a rock. You can push and pull and twist all you like—he isn't coming free. The Bullet Train wants to set off after Batt but he can't move because the world's first quadriplegic paraglider is attached to him. The best analogy is of a dog trying to run while he's chained to a fence. Get back here.

The Bullet Train looks at The Genius Nazim Erdem with an oh-for-the-love-of-god-can-someone-get-this-fucking-guy-off-me (or Japanese equivalent) expression and by the time he's extricated himself, Batt has racked up another goal. 'Yeah, it is pretty funny,' Erdem says. 'If I've got a good pick on them, they're going to struggle. If they do end up getting away, they're exhausted anyway. How good is that pick?!' Rhetorical question. He answers with boyish enthusiasm. 'It's a top pick!' Then he says, 'If they have to fight me off three or four times, they're fucked for the rest of the game. I'm sucking the life out of them. It does makes me laugh. You've got to have a laugh on the court.' For the entire year, not once will you see Nazim Erdem have a laugh on the court.

DUBBERLEY: 'Naz is a freak. In the point-five class, he's the crème de la crème. He's got more function than any of them and uses it. If you could put Ryan's head on Naz's body, you'd have an unbelievable point-five. Ryan is a great point-five, but unfortunately for him, when it comes to making the starting team, Naz cannot be beaten.'

Dubberley is prowling the sideline. He's wearing a black trucker's cap, pointing at areas of a court he views as a chessboard. 'You know the drill,' he shouts. 'YOU KNOW THE DRILL.' He says everything twice, the second time with capital urgency. Batt is the focal point of the attack. When he's scored, he becomes the focal point of the defence. He keeps pounding The Bullet Train. He's like a one-man swarm of bees. Japan are pressured into turnovers. Australia's lead increases. Shingo Fujishima offers a panic-strewn pass to no-one in particular and screws up his face. *I cannot believe I just did that* (or Japanese equivalent). Dubberley is chewing gum. Arms crossed, the master of his domain, or at least Aqua-*what*?, he has the words 'Well done, Ryles' on auto-loop. Everything Batt is doing is on auto-loop because on the top deck of the small stand (nearly grand) are spies from Canada, Great Britain, Japan—and New Zealand, who aren't even playing. Gumbert has given up on travelling to Australia and expecting to leave in one piece. The spies record Australia's games, but one extra camera of unknown origin is ignoring the match altogether to focus solely on Batt. Every move he makes. If Batt rubs his chin, it's recorded. You suspect the breakaway camera aligned to Great Britain and that Coach Joe will use the footage to have the classifiers take another look at Batt's involvement in the sport. In the best indication of how close the crowd and competitors are, when Erdem is replaced and slowly rolls over the sideline, the sister of The Rebel Scott Vitale whispers, almost to herself, 'Well done, Naz.' Erdem looks over his right shoulder and says, 'Thanks.'

Batt begins his you-cannot-break-me routine, Japan stumble, riddled with soft-tailed bullets. Erdem annoys the crap out of The Bullet Train while Hucks produces a roar from the bench that could wake the dead. Or turn Aqua-*what*? to rubble. Which might not be a bad idea. What a dump. Boxall needs a new tyre. He's going ballistic. The sound of the tyre bursting is the high-pitched popping of a pistol. Boxall throws his head left, dances right, better than a real jink. Whatever real is. On the Japanese side of the grandstand (a properly pulsating grandstand by now), half a dozen assistant coaches are scribbling like mad in notebooks.

It's 25–24 at half-time. Dubberley crouches in the middle of the ring of No-Limit Texas Hold 'Em and talks about 'playing smart with maximum intensity'. Don't give a shit? Play smart? Maximum intensity? Take your pick. Dubberley is calm, but emotional. Take another pick. He shakes his head (to the right), rolls his eyes, yahoos, kicks the floor (with his right foot) and scratches his head (with his right hand). 'No, Ryley, no!' Dubberley gives Batt a don't-you-dare look. Batt argues: 'But shouldn't we . . .' Dubberley responds: 'NO.'

That's the end of that and we're into the second half, the Bullet Train cannoning into Alman, who is less than impressed. The shot has come from his blind side. Next chance he gets, Batt clobbers The Bullet Train and nods at Alman. Batt's gloves have five fingers each. The spare slots are flapping in the breeze, just like that, flap-flap-flap.

Batt rarely yells for the ball. In a moment of extreme urgency, he might raise his right hand and say 'Oy'. Otherwise he's quietly destructive. Any talk is a controlled discussion. Japan are back to 31–30—when did that happen? Dubberley is telling Carr, 'No rush, mate. No rush.' But it feels as though there should be a rush. The Japanese players don't talk to each other. Their captain, Koichi Ogino, complete with a hole in his throat and one-point classification, is about to score even if it will take him an eternity to travel from the front to the back of the eternal black line. Batt waltzes in and takes the ball off him like a parent snatching a sharp object from a toddler just before he or she is going to swallow it and choke half to death. Or all the way. Dark thoughts. Australia's hits are Krakatoa. Japan's are a sand hill about to be washed away by the rising tide, taking the buckets and spades with it. Australia spit, but the Japanese expectorate. That's the difference. This is not the place for politeness. Batt's conscience is clean about pummelling the 0.5s because their 3.5s try to pummel *his* low-pointers. Batt is the enforcer, guardian, protector, bag-snatcher. He's wedged between two Japanese pickers and cannot break free, but Carr is on his lonesome to receive the ball and score. Easy, so fucking easy, and Australia lead by three goals with five minutes left. Batt scores at such a frantic pace he nearly goes through a glass panel behind the goal line. Goals are rarely celebrated as lustily as the success of the BIG D that allowed it. Hucks screams hard. 'No risky shit, you blokes' is Dubberley's command and you wonder what kind of risky shit he's talking about. The most simple passes can require indepth concentration and effort because nobody on the court has fully functioning hands so risky shit? What risky shit? It's all relative. The Bullet Train tries to knock over The Invaluable Cameron Carr but he hasn't counted on an interjection from Hucks, who stares at The Bullet Train with an incredulous expression of: *What did you think you were doing*? The Bullet Train is afraid: *Nothing* (or Japanese equivalent).

Australia reach the final, where Batt has secured the win by scoring just inside the orange witch's hat in the final few seconds. We can provide no greater proof that this whole thing is on a gloriously small scale than the presence of orange witches' hats.

The Canadians are waiting for another skirmish. Men need their skirmishes. The Japanese do the most thorough and complicated warm-down in modern sports history. Australia are halfway through lunch—'Look, Doris, he's using his teeth!'—and the Japanese are still making little circles with their arms. Video cameras are still whirring and notes are still being taken. Batt will be lucky if he can go to the disabled toilet without being caught on film.

Coach Joe's new team has gone down the gurgler to Coach Joe's old team and Coach Joe remains as motionless as a statue. Perhaps he's had another heart attack but in the absence of anyone making a documentary, he'll keep it to himself. He does not appear to have moved a muscle or said a single expletive-laden word for the last 32 minutes.

~

THE FINAL: Canada are fist-pumping in the warm-up. Oh, gawd. Some people are just a lot of hard work. Do they even know? Patience is a virtue but you are feeling less than virtuous. The fucking warm-up! You've heard 'Thunderstruck' enough times to know a ball-tearing introduction when you see and hear one. Fabien Lavoie has returned. Dubberley tells the Australians that everybody needs to be cool. Are we cool? Lavoie's lips are sealed, his back teeth still swimming in the Oceanias. One thing about Lavoie—he can play. He has a shaved head and broad shoulders. The appearance of a young man in his first year of military service. The Canadians are *still* fist-pumping when the game begins at breakneck speed. Three of the Canadians clot around Batt but he swats them away. Benoit Jett lets out the first of his blood-curdling screams.

'That's just the way Benoit is,' Dubberley says. 'He learned off Joe, so he's just doing the same as Joe did. He was Joe's assistant for a long time. They punted Joe and put Benoit on. He's just learned the traits of old man Joe. I've played for coaches that go schizo like him. It doesn't really worry me because I never listened to them when I was playing, so I'm not going to start listening to their crap now that I'm coaching against them. I don't think they do their teams much good. They're panicking, basically, lashing out, and I think that's going to make their players panic. I think the way you act as a coach definitely rubs off on the players. They need to see you're in control, even when you might not feel like you are. If we start losing and I'm screaming at our guys, what's that going to do for their confidence? It's only going to cause more panic and put us in a worse spot. That's what Canada always start doing. They end up panicking, throwing the ball away and losing. The whole team starts acting like Benoit.'

'Good stuff, boys,' Dubberley hollers. Benoit Jett is sitting but he won't stay there for long. There are so many blue, yellow and white lines on the court, the markings for badminton, volleyball, basketball and murderball, that you don't know which is for what. The first two goals are Batt's. Lavoie looks more wary than he did before Batt knocked him to a place called RESPECT.

This game is faster and more desperate than the Oceanias' decider. The Canadian bench keeps yelling, 'D! D!' Then, 'Nice set-up! Nice set-up!' The set-up must well be just fucking wonderful, but the execution stinks. Benoit Jett is impeccably dressed. And deplorably mannered. Dubberley is in casual shorts. He'd wear them to a wedding if he could. Maybe even his own. Chan is back on his red wheels. See a red wheel, you want to paint it black.

The Invaluable Cameron Carr scores a couple of clandestine goals; Canada's main hope against the battalion of Australian defenders is to throw a Hail Mary pass and hope like hell someone catches it. Batt gives a turnover, shock, horror, and the Canadian reaction is YAAR! Chan tries to put Batt in traction but it's a futile attempt. Benoit Jett scrubs up alright in his red (the most dominant of colours) polo shirt, creaseless blue (still the coolest of colours) jeans and a brown belt to match his brown shoes. Pity the attitude isn't so pretty, so brown. Brown doesn't have a whole lot going for it. Whitehead appears to have taken more than the recommended daily intake of angry pills. Hundreds by mouth. They're not playing aggressive, Canada, they're playing angry. Benoit Jett springs to his feet and it might be an idea for everyone to run for their lives! 'ON RYLEY, ON RYLEY, ON RYLEY!' he shrieks. Batt scores and Benoit Jett swears and then he shakes his head and then he complains: 'I thought I told you to get on Ryley.' Welcome to Whine Country. Batt has scored because Old Age and Treachery has upended something called a Trevor Hirschfield. There's a loose ball—jump on it! Batt escapes a traffic jam to get his mitts on the white orb—keep hold of it! The orange witches' hats are nudged and must be put back in place. Witches' hats! Benoit Jett has moved to the edge of his seat, hands on his knees, Vesuvius about to erupt, a spew of lava moving up his throat as another turnover goes to Australia and Doug Batt—resplendent in blue (still the most cool of colours) jeans, slick black collared shirt and purple pork-pie hat—applauds. Yes, Doug Batt is wearing a purple pork-pie hat. He's explaining the game to Porter's father. He's an upbeat and likable character, Doug Batt. His son burns off all four Canadians to score. He beats the same four to score again.

A quick chain of Canadian passes equals goal. They're competitive. Dubberley has gone quiet, shooting sideways glances at a clock he isn't supposed to be giving a shit about. Chan crosses the stripe. Benoit Jett hollers 'Get The Ball!' six successive times without taking a breath, his face turning heart-attack purple. The Canadians go 'WOO!' whenever a play goes their way. 'Why don't you shut up,' Dubberley finally says. His words are lost in the wind. Hucks pulls off a great one-handed pass. With all the time-outs and roadside assistance for upturned vehicles, an eight-minute quarter takes closer to 23 minutes. Chan breaks free for a goal. Dubberley and The Australian Captain are applauding because the D was set up right. It can still be right even if it doesn't work, just like anything and everything you can think of. Benoit Jett keeps trembling with rage. His face grows increasingly angry every time Batt breaks free, all that heat and bile in his swelling mouth and then comes the biggest single eruption since the Shaanxi earthquake killed four million Chinese in 1556.

'GET RYLEY! GET RYLEY! GET RYLEY! GET RYLEY!'

Batt goes for a rest. The spies turn their cameras off. Hucks is back on. 'Come on, baby,' Whitehead says. Hucks obliges like a Hell's Angel agreeing to take it outside while throwing his chair at one of the Pissed Off Bastards Of Bloomington. You want some? You can have some. The Curmudgeonly Whitehead is the dirtiest Canadian of the lot. Australia lead by three. 'Your fault, coach,' Doug Batt says in the direction of Benoit Jett as Batt goes back on. 'GET RYLEY! GET RYLEY!' Restraining orders are issued for statements delivered with such blatently malicious intent. Let's just make this perfectly clear. Ryley Batt is a disabled athlete getting around in a wheelchair while some able-bodied Canadian porker is hurling abuse at him? Benoit Jett keeps screaming 'GET RYLEY' and in this intimate atmosphere, everyone can see and hear him. They can see the frighteningly real hostility in his eyes—and one of those people is Ryley Batt's father. If Doug Batt loses his cool and gets it on with Benoit Jett, you will follow him in and get it on like the Rum Rebellion. Most likely, so will 200 others. Let's swap their roles. Put Benoit Jett in a wheelchair. Insert him into a game of murderball even if all this is slather and whack, would he really think it's okay for someone to stand there hurling invective? No. It's as if Benoit Jett *hates* Batt. He keeps looking at Dubberley for a reaction. As if he wants them to engage in their own private verbal warfare. Erdem is cruising around like De Niro in *Taxi Driver*. The two-goal lead has been maintained in Batt's absence and no more need be said about the capabilities of George Hucks. 'GET THE BALL! GET THE BALL!' They're Benoit Jett's favourite words. He has a silver bracelet and when Doug Batt snots him you must remember to look at that bracelet in case it says he's allergic to penicillin or warns of any other medical precautions that will need to be taken when we wheel him into emergency. Benoit Jett is talking incessantly to his assistant coach and now he is yelling again at Batt. You honestly wouldn't like him any less if he was delivering racial slurs. 'Sit down,' Doug Batt says.

Old Age and Treachery is everywhere. He rarely scores and rarely sends anyone base over apex so hard that they land on their base and need to be lifted back to their apex, but he's everywhere Dubberley wants and needs him to be. Be great. That's what Old Age and

Treachery makes you think. Just try to be great. May as well. Digging ditches for a living? Be the greatest ditch digger who ever lived. He has a tattoo that reads, 'Carpe Diem', but so does every other quadriplegic man and his quadriplegic dog around here.

Boxall bangs his chair in disgust. It must be extraordinarily frustrating to see where you want to go, and where you *need* to go, and where everyone is willing you to go, and where you used to be able to go so effortlessly, but now you cannot get there so quickly. It's a game of patience for the low-pointers. They just keep grinding away. Hares and tortoises. Carr is head-butted. Hucks is puffing hard. Boxall slaps Whitehead, who shakes his wrist to let everyone know it hurt. Boxall taps him on the back with a hint of *diddums* attached. Boxall's elbows start flailing as he makes his way down the court and what a shit fight this is. Canadian roadblocks are everywhere. All eight players are in gridlock like the scene from *Falling Down* where Michael Douglas gets out of his car, leaves it in the middle of a traffic jam in Los Angeles and shoots up half the city. Benoit Jett is screaming, 'PRESSURE! PRESSURE!' Hucks is the first to escape. For a moment you imagine him going over to Benoit Jett and cracking him across the skull with an iron bar. More dark thoughts. Boxall rams Chan in the most impressive sight of the day since Doug Batt's purple pork-pie hat. Chan slingshots over the sideline and lands at Dubberley's feet. Batt is forced to throw a long ball that comes to nothing. The Canadians let out a deafening, 'WOO!' Benoit Jett goes through his 'GET THE BALL' routine every time Australia have it. 'PRESSURE! PRESSURE! PRESSURE!' We'll give you pressure, Benoit Jett. Blood pressure. You know what that dude oughta do? Dude oughta ease on up.

Doug Batt is beginning to shift in his seat. His son rolls over for a breather. 'How uncoordinated am I?' he says. The truth, big man? You're not uncoordinated at all. Australian sportsmen inducted as Bradman Honourees receive a framed certificate with the selection criteria from Australia's most legendary sportsman on it: 'When considering the stature of an athlete, I place great store on certain qualities which I believe to be essential in addition to skill. They are that the person conducts his life with dignity, with courage and perhaps most of all, modesty.' Ryley Batt should be a Bradman inductee.

It's unclear why Benoit Jett is continuing to waste his breath. Does he expect his players to listen? Does he think Batt is going to break down and sob into Dubberley's shoulder that he cannot play any more because that mean man over there is yelling at him? Doesn't he understand his players already have enough on their plates without listening to his incessant ramblings? Now he's not even bothering with instructions to get the ball. He's just yelling, 'RYLEY! RYLEY! RYLEY!' And he's doing it when Batt is just centimetres away. For an instant you honestly think Doug Batt is going to get involved. You assume that people who wear purple pork-pie hats are the coolest of all the cats and most unlikely to start a melee, but you are also here to suggest that Benoit Jett deserves a fat lip. It's unlikely he realises that Doug Batt is in the front row because if he did, he would have shut his cake hole by now. He's acting more like a teenager than the teenager. There is a genuinely stunning intensity to Benoit Jett's eagerness for Ryley Batt to fail. Batt keeps playing as if he doesn't care but listen carefully enough and you will hear the ticking of a bomb.

'Too easy,' The Curmudgeonly Whitehead says after one of Canada's goals. It can't be that easy, champ. You're losing by two. Vitale hits Lavoie hard enough for the Canadian to end on all fours. Batt skirts the sideline. Now Lavoie is chasing him as quickly as you can without a siren. Another loose ball creates another frenzy of activity, some players trying to grab the ball, others attempting to belt the players trying to grab the ball, the ball turning white with fear and doing its best to evade everyone. The players are torn between catching and belting, most opting for a bit of belting while Benoit Jett shrieks, 'GET IT! GET IT!' Batt is pushed over the sideline, becoming entangled in the mesh netting. Benoit Jett goes skidding across the floor like Sinatra at the end of 'My Way' and the result is the only thing that matters now. Succeeding in a gentlemanly manner can go hang.

Australia defeat the Canadians with another goal to Batt in the final seconds. If this was the 1950s, Doug Batt would be throwing his purple pork-pie hat into the air right now because after the torrent of intimidation from Benoit Jett, it has been Doug Batt's son who has finished the game with a primal scream. In one of those spine-tingling moments you get in the great unscripted land of athletic endeavour, enough to make a man start shadow-boxing on the spot, the final has ended with Batt pulling off a thud of a hit on Whitehead before roaring louder than Benoit Jett has at any stage. The sight of Batt finally venting is enough to send the stand, so grand, into delirium and you never thought it could be possible for 200 people to make this much noise and why is there a tear in your eye? Benoit Jett has to realise that antagonising Batt from the safety of the sideline has done his players no favours. Batt has taken in all the cheating of the Canadian players, all the WOOs and the YEAHs and GET RYLEYs and his reply has been to lop the head off Whitehead and leave it pulsating on the floor for Benoit Jett and all the squawking Canadians to see. Batt is celebrating as if he's the last man standing in a bar room brawl, which he is. Benoit Jett staggers backwards like he's receiving jab-jab-jab, uppercut. For a fleeting moment, even if Batt hasn't considered this at all, you imagine him attacking the Canadian coach. All these dark thoughts.

Batt has sucked up every piece of harassment Canada can find, and he has prevailed. Right at this moment, when the referee in his black-and-white shirt is blowing full-time, and Batt is howling at Whitehead, and 200 people are falling out of this poxy little makeshift stand (really, so grand!), and the Australian players are celebrating as if it's the greatest single thing that has ever happened in their lives, you are quite certain you have never experienced a more emotional sporting scene, and it's all come at some low joint in Melbourne called Aqua-*what*?. Is this as good as it gets? You squint and look out to sea. Beijing on the horizon and the gospel truth is you ain't seen nothing yet.

BATT: 'Benoit reminds me of The Grinch. You look at him, and he just looks like The Grinch. He's a loud bloke but I reckon he's a pretty good coach. He does yell at the players a lot and it might look embarrassing for them but he's just a very loud coach and it's not a bad thing for the game. It makes it interesting, right? He's always yelling about pressure but he probably doesn't know that psychs us up as much as it psychs up his own blokes. If you hear someone yelling pressure, you almost feel like he's yelling it at you too. I can't even hear most of what he says. I know he's yelling but I don't even really hear it. When I'm playing, I can't even hear Brad talking unless I look at him. You're just in the game and in that moment, all I can really hear is my own players. I wouldn't be able to block out all those voices if I actually tried to, but it just happens. You get so caught up in the game that everything else disappears. When we go back and watch the replays on video, when we're doing our video analysis, I hear Benoit and I'm like, "Turn the volume down, this guy is annoying me!" But I'd rather belt his players than belt him.'

DUBBERLEY: 'Ryley did well to keep calm. That was pretty full-on, but he didn't flinch. Not bad for a nineteen-year-old. He's not that calm all the time. He can have his moments when he's ready to go schizo. Don't worry, he was ready to bash some people then. It's funny. He gets this rage on, but it's like a polite rage. Whitehead or someone will be bugging him and he'll say, "Braddy, I'm really sorry, but I'm just going to have to punch this guy out." I tell him, "Dude, that's what they want you to do. If you do that, you're out of here. Keep it calm. They want you to blow up. I know you want to hit him. I want to come out and help you but it's more trouble than it's worth." If they're carrying on like that, it's a dead giveaway to us that they're worried. We were sixth in the world not long ago. None of these other countries would have cared enough to act like that. But they're worried about us now. They can't beat us fair and square, so they've got to carry on. I don't think we need to do that. If we play well, do our own thing, I reckon we win anyway. We want to be amped up enough, but not too much. If you're too amped up, if you just snap and get pissed off by whatever they're doing, you end up looking for hits that aren't there, you throw passes that aren't on and you end up just punishing yourself. But if you're too mellow, you're not motivated enough to look for hits or throw the passes that might be on. It's all about keeping that balance—get stirred up but not too much. Ryles is good at that. The funniest thing is, Canada thought they had Ryley all worked out. They told one of our mates, "We know which way he turns, everything." I just straight-up laughed. I'm like, "Yeah, whatever. As if." I told Ryley and he's like, "They said what?" He said *he* doesn't even know what he's going to do. I said, "Ryles, mate"—I was geeing him up a bit—I said mate, "Canada reckon they've figured you out. And they also reckon you can't hit for shit." He goes, "Aw what? I can't hit?" He was more worried about that than if they'd work out how he plays when he's got the ball. They said I can't hit? He kept saying we'll see about that, we'll see. They came at us in the final, but we shut them down. We've figured *them* out. Benoit was freaking: "How do we beat you guys?"

'Canada lose their composure pretty quickly. They're trying so hard to prove they're dominant, but I don't buy it. You can be all show and pumping each other up but if it's 30–all with ten seconds to go in a semi-final or a final, a game you have to win, talking shit isn't going to do you much good. If you've got a team pulling together the tighter it gets, and they're not trying to win because they're terrified of getting their arses kicked by their coach. You don't want anyone worried about the coach saying, "We lost because you fucked up." Leave me out of that. Everyone makes mistakes. Someone stuffs up for us and I'll try to be like, "No worries, let's go back and make up for it." Especially in this sport. I've played this game—I reckon I know what a player wants to hear from his coach. The odds of you making a turnover, but then getting a turnover back, are quite high. The more you hang your head when it gets tense, or when a few little things go against you, the less likely you are to get the ball back. We're going to give up turnovers. It's unavoidable in any game. We're going to have goals scored against us. But we just want to keep hanging in and wait for them to come our way. I don't think Canada are so good at that.'

~

The Australians pile onto their bus. An electric ramp goes *brrrr.* They return to their hotel for a meeting in Dubberley's room. Downstairs, Coach Joe is having a beer with his Great Britain players. 'I reckon his players are scared of him,' Dubberley says. 'You don't want to be in the situation where players feel like that. You need respect, but not fear. He really is a weird individual. On the first day we were here, I'm not shitting you, he's just rocked up down one end of the court when we're training. He starts sprinting from one end of the court to the other. We're like, "Joe, what the fuck are you doing?"

It was so strange. It was like he had to get on the court with us and do *something*. He always needs to prove himself. Good on him. He can do what he likes. But coaching shouldn't be about the coach. Coaching has to be about the players. I think for Joe, it becomes about him. The players aren't stupid. I think they know where he stands. I'm not sure that he's coaching Great Britain because he's passionate about Great Britain becoming successful as a rugby nation. But I do think he's still pretty keen on seeing himself succeed—they *are* improving. They gave us a pretty good game here on the first night, triple overtime. It was such a slow game. We like to play flat-out and I knew Joe would do it slow, try to annoy us. It's good to know we can grind out a win if we have to. We didn't get too impatient even if it was the kind of game we hate. They slow you down, we want to speed it up. It's as boring as batshit, really, but we still got there. For all Joe's aggro, they're getting a pretty good team together. The biggest threat is Jason Roberts. He's a big guy and he's in your face the whole time. He's a maniac.'

And then we have the pleasure of the company of Joe Soares. *What would you like to talk to me about?* You, Coach Joe. Let's talk about you! Coach Joe gets comfortable in his chair. Me, me, me, me, me. He says he has absolutely no problem with his portrayal in the movie. He does not think his life has been especially tough. He says the biggest wars and most serious dilemmas and greatest conflicts and most intense explosions of joy—all the passions and pleasures that get us out of bed in the morning—are all in our heads anyway so who cares if we can't walk. The conversation is all very cordial until the suggestion is made that coming stone-motherless-last in the Super Series has been a less than impressive Paralympic warm-up for Her Majesty's finest.

'Oh, do I look worried?' he snaps.

No, Coach Joe. You do not look worried.

'Because I'll tell you, pal, I'm not worried.'

Okay, Joe, you're not worried.

'We had three players not available to come here. They'll be back and we'll be back. Australia had all their players and needed triple overtime to beat us. You go off and join the dots, pal.'

Coach Joe, we've gone off and joined the dots and here's what we've come up with—you're a bit of hard work.

'I've quietened down,' he says. 'My doctor told me to. He said, "Joe, another heart attack and that'll be it for you." Coach Joe is asked to expand on *that'll be it for you* and he does the most comical throat-slitting gesture of all time. And then he looks up—*up there*—to erase any doubt about where the slit throat will take him.

'In Beijing,' he says, 'I might not be so calm.'

Promise?

'It's going to be some tournament, boy,' he says. 'If I could choose one player to have, it would be your kid Batt. Damn kid. But the US have three Ryley Batts. They're all six-feet-ten with wing spans like . . .'

'Wing spans like vultures, Joe?'

'That's it, like vultures.'

'I'll tell you this, pal,' he hisses. 'When we get to Beijing, everyone is going to be playing for second. Believe me. It will be America first, someone else second.'

Dubberley is peeved to the eyeballs.

'So Joe's sitting there saying America have already won it?' he says. 'That's fine. The only team that might be playing for second is GB. I guarantee that we're not. I guarantee that Canada aren't. I guarantee that New Zealand aren't. I guarantee that Japan aren't. If Joe is saying that about everyone playing for second, maybe he doesn't think his own team can win it. That's great if he thinks that. One less team for us to worry about. He's just a smart arse, Joe. He said to me, "Wait till we get our other players back." I was like, "Do it, Joe, I'd prefer you to for the Canada Cup." Let's see how everyone goes there. When they get their other players back it means Jason Roberts is off the floor more often, and that's what we want. He's a threat, Roberts, so we don't want him playing so much. If Joe gets all these other players—sweet. Makes it easier for us. That's such a Joe thing to say. "Wait till we get our other players back." Shut up, Joe. For me, why is he even talking about America? He's the coach of GB. America are a good team, without question. They're number one for a reason. But at the same time, if you put anyone on a pedestal like that, you'll never beat them. Fuck that. If you're a coach or a captain or a player or a team, why are you talking up any other team besides your own? Why do that?'

~

Canada's captain David Willsie shouts across the bar close to midnight, 'You boys sure are quiet for a team that just won.' Carr shoots back, 'We haven't won anything yet.'

You watch Coach Joe and his Great Britain players from the far end of the bar in the foyer of the hotel. The GB scene feels tense and inhibited. As if the players are talking to the school principal after being given Ds in their exams. The Herculean Jason Roberts is still saying, 'Excuse me, Coach Joe . . . Coach Joe, what do you think about . . .' The Japanese are in another corner, villains in a James Bond movie, quietly preparing to blow a miniature dart through Dubberley's heart. Coach Joe's table falls even more quiet. When he goes to the bar, he does not see the looks of disdain being hurled his way. Coach Joe's players have begun regarding him with withering contempt as if the family has finally made up its mind about the bastard son. He does not feel the knives in his back.

You go up the lift and prepare to knock on the door of Room 322, hesitating because you feel like a complete impostor. Your fist is raised again, ready to knock on wood again, but you freeze again because you honestly believe you have no right to intrude on these people. You just stare at the door a while and afterwards, that corridor will be remembered as being eerily long and unusually quiet. You decide to leave them to their own devices. But then, fuck it, you knock. Stepping into Room 332 is like a scene from a science fiction movie where someone walks through a small door and on the other side is a whole other world he or she had never previously contemplated and momma, that's where the fun is. The corridor was so quiet. The room is so full of *life*. Australia's murderballers are carrying on like they've just heard Obama banging on about 'Yes we can' in Nashua, New Hampshire. The Australian Captain has thrown the door so wide open it could fly off its hinges and go somersaulting down the hall. Old Age and Treachery is to his left, hooting and hollering like he's at a twenty-year high school reunion with all the people he liked the most. The Invaluable Cameron Carr is to his right, crying because something you have missed is so funny. You could not have been more intimidated and downright impressed if the three of them had been The Father, The Son and The Holy Ghost.

9

Canada Cup, Vancouver

The sky is purple perfume. The clouds are salmon-pink or pink salmon swimming upstream to where the yellow-bellied marmots are giving the mountains their whistle, and then Coach Joe, good old polio-ravaged pain-in-the-arse Coach Joe, is sacked by Great Britain and you feel nothing but sympathy for the poor delusional bastard. The people with the greatest bravado are those making the biggest cover-ups, you are sure of it, and Coach Joe would be hurting as much as the next paranoid overachiever. It's all an act. If he really is as on-top and fuck-you-all as he wants us to believe, why does he exude such an obsessive desperation? Why, despite his advanced years, is he still trying so hard to prove himself? Why bother? When does it end? Coach Joe has proved beyond any reasonable doubt that he can coach. He has gained a degree of Hollywood notoriety, okay a stuff-all degree but a degree of it nonetheless. He's made enough money to buy a pretty spiffing house, he's achieved professional success and no matter what anyone says there is satisfaction in that, where assuming he has spent the vast amount of his adult life in the arms of the woman he loves, he has at least one kiddie we can think of—and still the fight continues. He has to be the first and the best and the most noticed. You are willing to suggest going through life as one Joseph Soares has occasionally been more than a little torturous. That may be just another example of stating the bleeding obvious. But nothing kills in this world like rejection and Coach Joe, thrown out with the garbage for a third time, is no better equipped to handle it than anyone else. The fact that he was still around, still hanging in there, still coaching, had been worn like a badge of honour. He had been unbreakable. When the US locked the door and told him to scram, he went to Canada. When Canada gave him the old heave-ho—it's not you Coach Joe, it's us, no hang on it really is you—he moved on to Great Britain. But now he's passed the point of no return. It's too late for him to get another job before Beijing. All staff rosters have been filled. You're also willing to punt on the fact Coach Joe is no idiot, and therefore fully aware of most everyone hating him. For the first time in decades, from when the murderball addiction first kicked and infiltrated places he could never scrub clean, Coach Joe does not have a job as a murderball coach or player. The Paralympic Games will come and go without his involvement, his opinions are no longer sought, his staggering degree of self-importance is no longer based on merit.

A bright-eyed kid called Kevin is doing the transport to and from Vancouver Airport. Kevin has received a telephone call from the Great Britain Paralympic Association saying, 'Take Joe Soares off the list. He's not coming.' The receptionist at The Hilton has received the same blunt message: 'Joe Soares will not be coming.' Kevin seems to know a thing or two about murderball. His mate plays for some team in the US and another mate is playing in Europe and Kevin is dropping so many names we may have to pull over and pick them all up. 'I'll tell you what happens with Joe,' Kevin says and then he's good enough to tell us what happens with Joe. 'Countries hire him to pick his brain about tactics and a lot of technical stuff. He's good at that. And then when they feel like he's told them everything he can, they fire his arse.'

Dubberley sends a text: 'They've sacked Joe!' Exclamation mark! Coach Joe no longer exists in this murderous little world. Says The Gentleman Shane Brand: 'I don't know why they would chop him just before the Paralympics. The players just couldn't cop him, probably. He told Brad to go back to playing and to let him coach us.' Ah, Coach Joe. You were so close to getting to Beijing. All you had to do was keep your nose clean in Melbourne and then come to Vancouver and keep your nose clean all over again. Rack up a few wins and you would have been driving down Beijing's Fourth Ring Road in no time flat. But you've blown it, Coach Joe, you've really blown it. Dim the lights, you're gone.

Dubberley's room is littered with clothes, scribbled-on bits of paper and his assistant coach all spread out on the lounge. This is a week of utmost importance notwithstanding the reluctance of the head coach to admit he gives a shit the size of Uluru. The Canada Cup is the most prestigious prize outside the Paralympics and world championships. It's a full-blown Paralympic dress rehearsal. The same eight teams are competing in the same four-team pools over the same five-day schedule. Australia, Germany, New Zealand and Great Britain are in the pool of death. The US, Canada, Japan and China are in the soft side of the draw with the top two from each pool going hurtling into the semi-finals while the rest are provided with the opportunity to piss off and please themselves.

The first person you see outside The Hilton, the sharp-edged Vancouver Spear, is Benoit Jett. He looks immeasurably pleased with himself. A takeaway coffee is in his right paw. Last seen bursting a blood vessel courtside in Melbourne unaware that Doug Batt was in striking distance, Benoit Jett now carries the pompous air of an individual whose portly body has become bloated, blown-up like a five-feet-eight hydrogen balloon, with a Coach Joe-esque degree of self-satisfaction and approval. No doubt there are those walking among us who are prepared to carry themselves in this regal fashion regardless of the realities of their existence and good on them, hey, because you can live in a grotto believing God gave you style, God gave you grace, God puts a smile on your face. But Benoit Jett is strutting around like an Indian Blue Peacock and there's something decidedly aggravating about it. He's working the room, or in this case the marble foyer of The Hilton. 'How are you? And what about *you!* Great to see you!' He's pointing and slapping backs and having a fine old time.

The reason for Benoit Jett's delirium: Canada has flown to Vancouver having beaten the US in the final of the North America Cup. It means Benoit Jett gets to walk around all pot-bellied and smug but it also means Coach Joe got it horribly wrong when he claimed Beijing would be a race for second behind the three blokes with big wing spans. 'We have proved to ourselves that we can beat them,' Canada's captain David Willsie says. 'And we have proved it to every other team. It's a big result. We're the only nation who has ever beaten the US, but it doesn't have to be like that. I've got a lot of mates in the Kiwi squad and I'm always telling them, "You know, it wouldn't piss us off if you beat them once in a while." They are definitely the powerhouse but the way we have beaten them, they are clearly not the powerhouse they used to be.'

Dubberley says, 'The US are not untouchable.'

You watch a few training drills. The US seem less than massively confident. They look like a team trying to be massively confident again. The Genius Nazim Erdem sits quietly, almost holy in his peaceful contemplation. Where do people get their faith? The woman in church who gives $200 every Sunday in tithes and offerings: What makes a person do that? Such *cheerful* giving? The Americans are the glammed-up superstars of the *Rocky Horror Picture Show* even if Andy Cohn, one of Dubberley's better mates, is more of a dead spit for Slim Shady than Frank N. Furter. His mate crashed their car into a tree on the way home from school at the age of sixteen. The car flipped and the roof crushed him. He cannot walk or close his hands. In fact, Cohn's right hand seems to have a permanently raised middle digit so unless you are sorely mistaken, he's getting around giving everyone the bird. Get fucked, the lot of you. Cohn hates it when he drives to the grocery store and people ask if he needs help getting home again. How the fuck do they think he got there? But he shouldn't get too down on them because in one of the great universal injustices, the people who care can be the most aggravating people of all. Cohn was initially too ashamed of his condition to go outside and grab the newspaper off the front lawn. There were times when he plummeted into tenfold depression but now he's just rolling around giving everyone the bird. Maybe his hands *can* move. Maybe this is his defiant choice: you can all go and get. Brilliant. His teammate Scott Hogsett says of becoming a quadriplegic, 'It's a mind-fuck in the beginning. And then you either make it or you don't.'

A great shame is the absence of Bob Lujano, the most compelling support character in the documentary. Lujano is a quadruple amputee. Thin air past his elbows, not a leg to stand on, and a pony-tailed girl asks him in the movie: 'How did you lose your arms?' Lujano tells her and he does so sweetly. A boy wants to know how he can possibly hope to eat pizza. Lujano tells him and again he does so sweetly. He's filmed playing cards, his arms flapping like the flippers of a seal, just like that, flap-flap-flap. He looks at the inquisitive children with a slightly pained expression: 'I got sick when I was nine years old and contracted a blood disease,' he says. He's on the floor. He isn't standing. He's just on the floor. The pony-tailed girl is towering above him. 'But I'm alright,' he says. 'That's all that matters. I'm alive and I use everything I do have to get through life.' Lujano was nine when he contracted a form of meningitis called meningococcosemia. A priest was called to read him his last rites. His last memory of having legs was looking at them while being wheeled into emergency surgery. When he woke from his drug-induced haze they were gone. A plant needs only the scent of water to revive itself but the only soaring regrowth for Lujano has come in his vast expanses of imagination. 'There's a dream I have where I'm flying,' he says. 'I've actually had this dream a couple of times. It's very much the same dream. I'm at my grandmother's house. I sort of have a dream where I'm just flying up. I'm flying over the roof of the house, flying among the trees. I have limbs as I'm flying. It's a very liberating feeling and I don't want it to end.'

The American captain is Bryan Kirkland. He has a huge head. You have a near-irresistible urge to measure its circumference. The woman at the first-aid desk is reading *Eat, Pray, Love*. Zuperman struts out. Yes, it is entirely impossible to strut in a wheelchair. He reminds you of the gambler with the shirt off his back. It's been no easy run. For some reason, you imagine him shooting a loaded revolver. The most enthralling life stories are the most complicated and difficult. Falls and resurrections, all the come-boldly-at-your-worst-moments. Chance Sumner grabs the ball one-handed and throws it with the most extravagant wind-up and grunt since Roger Clemens was throwing seven different kinds of smoke for the Boston Red Sox. Cohn comes closer and he doesn't just look like Slim

Shady—he *is* Slim Shady. Must be, has to be. Gumbert has his fingers across his mouth: 'Well, just get there, Scott,' he barks at Hogsett. The most subdued player in the US camp is Tropical Cyclone Joel Wilmoth. His moment of truth is coming because tonight he discovers if his classification has kept teetering on 3.5 or plunged into go-find-a-new-sport. 'There's been talk that he's gone,' Dubberley says.

Wilmoth has disfigured hands. He needs prosthetic legs to get from A to B. He sits behind the goal line of the Bonsor Recreation Complex—'HOME OF THE BURNABY EAGLES! SOUTH BURNABY METRO CLUB YOUTH BASKETBALL!' He's ordered to sit out training. There's a US team meeting and again Wilmoth is almost cruelly excluded. He looks morose and uncomfortable. Earlier you have seen him taking money from an ATM. What an ordeal. Wilmoth puts on his prosthetic legs, untapes his hands and walks out, he *walks* out and that is the cause of the unrest. It's doubtful anyone should be playing murderball if they can walk briskly in and out the front doors. Yes, Dubberley can walk—but only just. Remaining vertical is not his forte. What he would give to be in Tropical Cyclone Joel Wilmoth's comparatively spectacular condition.

Australia have a poor session. When Batt goes down hard and cracks his elbow, there's a frightful split second when he's writhing in pain and clutching at his elbow and Dubberley's face crinkles up into a shape that says this: 'No.' Batt is fine. The American Captain Bryan Kirkland says to Zuperman, 'It goes without saying . . .' If it goes without saying, don't fucking say it. With the Americans glaring at the training session—*we're watching you*—Australia's handling becomes sloppy enough to be thrown to the pigs.

ERDEM: 'I know America are trying to intimidate us. I know they're trying to mess with us. I was like, why are we training like this? Why are we throwing these stupid passes? Just because they're watching? Let's not embarrass ourselves here. Fuck 'em. If we get to play them, and I really hope we do, I'm going to go out there and do my job. Really, mate, fuck 'em. I don't even want to say hello to them. We're here to do a job on them.'

DUBBERLEY: 'The US have a few superstars. Zuperman is one of their better players but he's not an absolute standout like some people think. He's a three. George is a three but they're different players. Zuperman is a hyped dude but he's still kind of mellow. He's nowhere near as intense as George. I'll tell you who is a good player for them—Nick Springer. He's only a two-pointer, but he's a fucking awesome player. He's a quad amp, looks like he's been through a meat mixer.'

Another thing about Nick Springer.

His mother is dying. Soon, and very soon, she will be going to meet the King.

Dinner is a burger and fries. Welcome to Little America. Newspapers contain calls for Americans and Canadians to start driving smaller cars but judging by the clientele at A&Ws, Americans and Canadians cannot start driving smaller cars because their big fat kids will be unable to fit in the suspension-boosted cars with all their big fat parents. A big fat waitress serves dinner and here's the reason why they're all so big and fat: the big fat burger sitting on your plate. It's polished off and the big fat waitress says, 'Well, now, I hope you left room for dessert!' And you think, yes, let's hope for that! More dessert for everyone! More cream! More sugar! More big fat food for our big fat American friends! In the bible, Man is told he will live an average of 120 years. Maybe that's how long we're supposed to be living. Maybe it's how long we WOULD be living if we weren't eating all this crap.

The English Rose does some late-night shopping. In a mall, some nondescript mall, just another unremarkable Canadian/American shopping mall, and now you are imagining her gentle and angelic demeanour as a ruse and that she's secretly plotting to take advantage of historically helpless men in the presence of real beauty. She's Anne Boleyn in the middle of all these King Henrys. Forget Zuperman and The Herculean Jason Roberts and Nick Springer and The Assassin's Bullets and the whole of them because there's only one person here who can get the better of Ryley Batt and that's the English Rose. She sits where The Blind Boys Of Alabama can see the mountains and quietly peers at the dusk clouds and beyond and she looks up to where the mountains reach infinity and a pale-faced blue. She applies lip gloss that goes back into the bright pink backpack slung over the back of her chair and she does not seem to notice that three out of four of her teammates are taking a peek down her shirt. More power to the fourth guy who, from this particular vantage point, appears to be clearly smitten by her.

The German team are blind drunk, filing out of a smoke-filled bar called The Station. They're so intoxicated they nearly fall out of their chairs. Eyes are glazed. Cigarettes hang limply from slits of mouths. Their narrow tongues are dry. Halfway back to The Hilton, just a two-minute push across flat terrain, The German Pissheads stop as if cryogenically frozen. They regain their blurred senses and roll away. 'They're a better team than you think,' Dubberley says of the German Pissheads.

~

A sharp left off Central Boulevard. Formalities begin with a speech from one of the organisers as players from all eight nations circle behind their national flags like gangs. Wilmoth looks ten years younger having escaped the hangman's noose when the classifiers, those understanding and completely unpredictable souls, gave him a big fat green light to play both here and at Beijing. 'You're looking at some of the most intense athletes in the world, and they're about to get it on for your pleasure,' says the man at the microphone. 'I'm a little bit confused, though, because I don't know if the mayor has turned up. I guess it's my duty to declare open the Canada Cup.' And he looks more than a little pissed off to be doing it. Nice job, Mr Mayor. The microphone collapses, folding in half like it's got quad gut, and then about 500 people make the walls shake. You can have your half-empty Olympic Stadium in Sydney with 80 000 seats and 5000 people. Give us a claustrophobic Canadian high school gymnasium any day.

Canada gets the volleyball rolling by dispatching of Japan. Shin Nakazato goes skidding across the floor like a ten-cent piece and disappears straight under the scorers' table, heads and tails all rolling into one. He can only break free when the table is lifted and shifted like we're on loan as furniture removalists. Shin! You're under the table? Get out of there! The trumped-up little Canadian coach Benoit Jett screams 'Li! Li!' with all the urgency of 'Batt! Batt!'. The US beat China while a toolbox sits alone on a wooden bench by the court. Inside are three things holding most of these blokes together: spanner, screwdriver, surgical tape.

Australia play The German Pissheads. You try to resist this, you really do, but you find it extraordinarily difficult to look at any of The German Pissheads without wondering how all the intaking of piss has affected them. They have black Adidas uniforms with Deutschland written on them. They are a battling team without monster plays, gasping at Batt's power in the way reporters gasped at the press conference that announced John Lennon was dead. Batt and Hucks are The Blues Brothers. Hucks is Jake. Batt can be Elwood. They may (or may not) require four fried chickens and a Coke. They may (or may not) be on their way to ordering eleven orange whips when all this is said and done, they may (or may not) be eyeing off a couple of cheese whizzes, boy, Bryce Alman may (or may not) look like the Penguin and they may (or may not) be on a mission from God.

Batt thumps his chariot. 'Let's get 'em, boys!' Fist fights start from such combative proclamations. Alman sidles up to Batt and tells him, 'Heaps of talk, woofer. Let me know what you're thinking. I want to know what you're thinking.' The German Pissheads have tall timber in the form of their captain Oliver Picht. But there's a problem with Oliver Picht. He has grey hair. No professional athlete with grey hair can ever be taken seriously. Dubberley's brow furrows. 'Too flat,' he tells Hucks. 'Everyone is too flat.' No cause for alarm, not yet, but soon enough it'll be an air-raid siren in wartime.

Again the Americans are watching Australia, huddled together like street hoods. 'Everyone is too quiet,' Hucks repeats. Everyone except Hucks. Batt pushes The Grey-Haired Oliver Picht over the sideline and Hucks creates his own sonic boom: 'Yeah Ryley Batt, yeah!' The team representing the United States of Goddamn America go sauntering past. Yes, it is entirely possible to saunter in a wheelchair. You just kind of get out there and saunter. Now they resemble the hot chicks at school pretending they don't want to be noticed when really they're desperate to be seen and commented on. They really do think they're better than everyone else, but given the scarcely believable fact that Canada beat the US last week, and Australia have beaten Canada in their last two finals, they might not be quite as shit-hot as they think.

For now Australia just have to beat The German Pissheads. One of them has arms the width of twigs. He has no involvement in the game whatsoever. He doesn't get the ball, he doesn't defend, it's as if he's a lost tourist who took a wrong turn at Kincaid Street that landed him on a murderball court in the middle of the Canada Cup. The Australians do not hesitate to shit on him from a great height. Batt receives an elbow to the face. 'Right in the eye,' he says. Few sports are intimate enough to have players coming off injured and then talking you through it. 'Weakest part of the body, eh? I thought it was split.' A German Pisshead is wearing goggles. Not beer goggles, just your regular everyday plastic protective goggles. Hucks is hit, but refuses to budge. He scoops up the rolling ball with one hand and that is no mean feat. Vitale needs help with his chair. Calling on all her years of experience and expertise, Noni Shelton, the team's mechanic and wife of the assistant coach, Rob Doige, goes out and gives it a good kicking. Problem solved. Australia win in unimpressive fashion and the court smells like a brewery. The real test is yet to come: New Zealand.

Canada line up against China. Let's see if Benoit Jett feels any sympathy for the worst team in history. 'China shouldn't be playing in Beijing,' Erdem says. 'But they have to play there. They live there.' See? Genius. It's one thing to scream about pressuring Ryley Batt in the final of the Super Series but another thing altogether to explode when your team is taking on four pot plants placed strategically around the court. 'Pressure Tao Zhenfeng! PRESSURE HIM!' No sympathy then, and Canada cruise into the semi-finals.

Before the stoush with NZ, Dubberley says, 'They won gold in Athens so they're good, but they might be in a bit of a decline.' Thirty-two minutes later, Dubberley no longer thinks New Zealand are in a decline. When you think you know something, you don't.

BATT: 'I get really nervous before a big game. It can feel like there's a lot of pressure to do well. Our biggest rivalry is with New Zealand, just because that's the way it is in sport with our countries. That US–Canada rivalry, it's the same between us and New Zealand.

They're good blokes. We're friends off the court, but we're not friends on it.'

Australia are belted in a horrible performance. It's the most agitated Dubberley has been all year. It's more of a *beating* than a loss, without any shadow of a doubt their worst performance since Dubberley took the reins. The first half has gone blow for blow across the Great Southern Ocean, more or less, but the thousand-mile monsoonal winds have kicked in and the Kiwis, starting fast and finishing faster, have inflicted a comprehensive and shocking defeat. Australia, and Dubberley, are shattered. Where'd they go? Where did those irrepressible souls from the Oceanias and the Super Series go? Now Dubberley is aghast. 'Why are we so flat?' At first it's a rhetorical question. It will end up needing to be answered because serious problems have arisen.

Batt has been strong on this global stage without dominating. The Kiwis have manhandled Australia, illegally sideswiping Old Age and Treachery twice before their captain Sholto Taylor, a physically imposing specimen, is hauled off the court to have ice packs placed on his body so he doesn't overheat. If he does overheat, he'll have a life expectancy of about two o'clock. This is a formidable group of men: Taylor, Dan Buckingham, Curtis Palmer—they're former able-bodied rugby players with a continuing affection for the brutal act and the ferocious word. There's a lot to be said for imaginative tactics in murderball but there is also a raging argument to be mounted for belting the crap out of people. The Kiwis do a bit of both, grunting like wild boars, all immovable. Buckingham has Vitale-style dreadlocks, a bursting black eye and a white strap wrapped tightly around his left bicep as if it's a tourniquet and he's about to inject himself with crack cocaine. They are raw and fearless. They call a time-out and they're all putting in their five cents worth and the coach tells them, 'Can everyone just shut up a minute?'

Errant Australian passes limp over the sideline. Full-time comes as a perverse relief. A convincing win over Great Britain will sneak Australia into the semi-finals on aggregate, but they need to win by six goals or more. And the way they're leaking oil right now, coughing, jackknifing, spluttering and stalling right where and when they need to get going, they'll be lucky to win at all. Dubberley is not himself.

He spits his chewing gum into his hand and hurls it into a bin like he's had enough of the whole thing, it's all too hard and he just wants to get away before he says something he will always regret. 'Heads up, eh?' he says. 'We don't want them to see us with our heads down.' But his own head is down. The Australian Captain mumbles 'shit' under his breath. What a disaster. Earlier this week, Hucks had said, 'We're going pretty well and we're talking it up, but let's see how we're travelling after the Canada Cup. That's when we'll know if we're kidding ourselves.' The answer isn't funny.

~

The opportunity cannot be missed to witness World War III: the US versus Canada. Last night, flicking TV channels in the hotel really early, kind of 5 a.m. when the day and everything else feels impossible for about fifteen seconds, 101 channels have combined to produce the greatest load of brain-dead crap you have ever seen passed off as alleged entertainment. People spend their lives watching this shit? For fuck's sake, wake up. Watching these 101 channels, all these puerile reality shows filled with tragically unfulfilled people trying to be the things they never will be, forfeiting their human nature for something less beautiful and so depressingly fake, celebrity, the stream of advertisements make one thing crystal clear. If you are a Canadian or American male of the species, you have an obligation to your nation to man up and make yourself larger than life. You have to be bigger, louder and stronger because bigger, louder and stronger makes you superior to the poor schmuck you're competing with down the road. An advertisement for Budweiser says, 'Rule 73: Go Big Or Go Home.' Americans have all this drummed into them from childhood and the reason to bring it up now is that two large men in the US murderball camp are straight out of a Budweiser commercial. They give the impression of also knowing their way to a couch and a remote control. These two able-bodied individuals on the US team's staff wear red shirts the size of circus tents and I hate them already.

WWIII begins with a Red Shirt slamming the ball into the court so hard that it bounces 30 metres to the roof. There's the drum-busting war cry of U-S-A . . . RUGBY! Who are we? U-S-A! WHO ARE WE? U-S-A! One of The Red Shirts starts stomping his feet and flexing his muscles, as if he's preparing for WWE Smackdown. He slaps the American players—the kind of excessive slap that makes false teeth fly out in cartoon strips. First thought: Pal, what has all this got to do with you? Good on you for being on the staff but now the games are on, how about you take a step back? Do not try to steal the show like this. It's about the players, see? You're an embarrassment. IT IS NOT ABOUT YOU. One of The Red Shirts is that aggravatingly upbeat gigantic American who only ever says YEAH! He wants to high-five everyone. YEAH! HIGH FIVE! Lord, oh Lord, above all, give me strength.

Benoit Jett is happy-crazy, crazy-happy. Split the difference and give the other half to Gumbert, who is more in control of his emotions. The following program contains coarse language, violent themes and may offend some viewers. Zuperman cruises out, cooler than kung-fu. He can play an entire tournament without acknowledging the presence of any of his opponents, rarely even looking at his own bench. He knows precisely what he has to do at every turn of a game and he does it with barely a shift in facial expression. Just a single release of breath when the arrow of momentum bends the American way. Once the US take the lead, they usually run away with it. They expect to lead and so it doesn't scare them. The US and Canada hate each other like the Greeks and everybody else hated the Romans. They have eaten breakfast in the same room at The Hilton this morning. Cereals were consumed in silence.

The Red Shirts scream when Canada have the ball, placing their hands on their knees, putting their buffalo-sized backsides in the air, spreading their feet, squatting and hollering. Sportsmanship goes to pot in murderball. Yes, it's four-fifths of the attraction, but The Red Shirts are genuinely cretinous in their way, blithering and vacuous and up to no good. If they were less than six-feet-six and three thousand pounds each, you'd go and shut them up yourself. When the Americans score, The Cretinous Red Shirts are chest-bumping. When Canada score, the rest of the stadium erupts but The Cretinous Red Shirts sit on their hands like big fat spoiled children. They are rude in the extreme. Benoit Jett reclines with his legs crossed, one arm resting behind his head like he's waiting for Mrs Benoit Jett on a park bench in autumn. Zuperman, Hogsett and Cohn come on at 8–6 up in the largest collection of Oscar nominees since Vivien Leigh, Clark Gable and Leslie Howard. Their arrival gets Benoit Jett to his feet. Here we go, we're on here. All he needs is a sniff. You imagine him running onto the court and biting into the Americans like a real-life Chuckie Doll with the slash marks down his forehead and the one bleeding eye. The Cretinous Red Shirts go very, very quiet, very, very quickly, when Canada gain any kind of ascendancy. Their behaviour would be less nauseating if they at least tried to acknowledge the Canadian goals, but they don't. They are either screeching their high-pitched disapproval or turning their backs and that is no place to be. Benoit Jett ruefully claps the American goals, but at least he does clap. The Canadians score two on the trot and the US only lead by one at quarter time. Every other team is watching—except Australia. You assume it has something to do with Erdem's preference for looking the other way and fuck 'em.

America's strength is their smothering defence bolstered by the verbal hand grenades launched by The Red Shirts. Try concentrating on your attacking combinations and calls with a couple of Chrysler Air Raid Sirens going off in your ear. Cohn looks angelically white with his bleached hair and pale skin, the little devil. You pick him to be wise as a serpent, harmless as a dove, depending on circumstances. Pencil-thin moustaches are less mischievous. On his right shoulder is a tattoo of a fire-breathing dragon. He plays quietly against the Canadians. That places him in the minority.

Tropical Cyclone Wilmoth remains a person of interest to authorities. You've watched him walking around. He's a strapping lad when his legs are on. He does not have the rolling gait of Dubberley but a full-length stride. Wilmoth is a three-quarter leg amputee; a Ryley Batt with legs, basically. Watching him get around the streets of Vancouver on his own steam is to see a person more hampered than disabled. Maybe he deserves credit rather than suspicion. He's letting it all hang out. He places his blue prosthetic legs beside the court with all the drink bottles. His legs stand there with no-one in them. What an unusual sight it is. Wilmoth is legs with no body on top of them, even more unusual than a body without any of Ryley

Batt's legs underneath them. He's not as single-handedly dominant as Batt. He expends a lot of energy on pointless loop-the-loops but when he does land a hit, the victim stays hit. WOO! The Red Shirts and their ever-present YEAH! Your reputations are poor, universal and well-deserved. Just go away. At half-time, Cohn and Lavoie fire up like a couple of stumbling drunks who have taken a comically intense and hopeless dislike to each other over a packet of stale cigarettes.

The US edge ahead and Captain Red Shirt starts jumping up and down like an angered gorilla. He's punching the air and then he clutches at his heart. Benoit Jett gives the referees a pizzling 'Oh good job' that he says in the most sarcastic and condescending manner he can find in the deep reservoirs of his intellect. At the height of the mayhem, Zuperman calmly takes a one-handed pass and rolls into the promised land for a goal. This entire year will pass without Mark Zuperman making an error. Benoit Jett starts grinding his teeth. The US win and Captain Red Shirt jumps around with his stomach belching and clearly you don't need to be a quad to develop quad gut.

NEVER WALK ALONE: 'The US and Canada hype themselves up, but we're not really like that. We're more laidback. If someone came up to me, screaming in my face like those US guys do to their players, I'd probably want to punch them out—even if they are on the staff. I guess it's just not something we'd do. We're just not like that.'

THE GENIUS NAZIM ERDEM: 'They're so arrogant. They scream for the sake of screaming. They're like that all the time. There are times in a game when it's super-exciting when you can understand it, but they just do it constantly. They must plan it. They're annoying. They're too loud. I reckon their own players get embarrassed by them. I've been watching their players, to see if that's true, and I'm sure it is. That's alright. It's all part of it. Everyone has their different personality. I reckon it's more embarrassing for them than annoying for us.'

Dubberley wants GB players sprawled on the floor. He wants turbo-shock aggression, he wants fire-alarm-nutso-bongo enthusiasm for the task at hand and most of all, more than any of that, he wants a legitimate reason to dismiss Australia's last insipid display as an aberration rather than lore. 'Doesn't matter who it is, just knock them over,' he barks. The Australians are more talkative than during their mime act against the Kiwis—but the words feel forced. It's like telling someone everything is okay when, really, it's not okay at all. 'I'll take Roberts by myself,' Batt tells Dubberley before he goes and takes The Herculean Jason Roberts by himself. Australia lead 28–24 at the break. The Australian Captain grabs a drink and tells his players 'do or die'. It's all relative.

An appalling refereeing decision robs Australia of a goal. GB score instead—a two-goal swing. The English Rose is coming on. Don't hurt her, you bastards. The English Paralympic Association have thrown vast sums of money at their murderballers in the belief they are near-certain medallists. They have a staff of approximately one million and a professional edge to all they do, with the possible exception of holding their pre-match team talk out in the car park with all the gravel and dirt. Their warm-up is performed with military precision but Australia have forged a five-goal lead and that's more like it. The margin swings between four and five. It needs to start swinging like a New Orleans cafe between five and six and then it needs to fly across to where the difference is six and seven, and then it needs to stay at seven until the cafe closes and the referee rings his bell to clean up the last drinks. The English Rose isn't coming on after all, which is a good and timely thing because this is no place for a lady anyway. The lead hits the six–seven roundabout and Dubberley says, 'So close.'

GB crawl back. Batt keeps shaking his head. *What is going wrong*? Something is amiss again and Australia start leaking goals again and the lead goes from six to five (oh no) to four (*oh no*) to three (OH NO) to two (OH NO!) to one and then to none. Forget about the finals. Forget about a dream semi against the US. The Australian Captain is gritting his teeth. Boxall is telling everyone, 'It's okay, it's okay.' But it's not okay. It's fairly fucking horrible. The English Rose claps politely. The game settles back into a flow but an Australia win by seven becomes an impossibility while the Canada Cup simultaneously slips away like a snake from fire. Put a little heat on a snake, human or reptile, Joe Soares or squamate, and it will vanish.

Australia lead 41–40 at the start of the last quarter. Six unmatched turnovers in eight minutes will require a miracle to compare with the conversion of water to wine. GB are trapped in their own half but a spectacular overhead pass from Ross Morrison sticks. The scores are level with six minutes left. You keep looking at the clock in the hope it will slow down or stop or rewind, but nothing of the sort can ever happen. Batt is upbeat despite the ship going down like the *Titanic* in the two hours and 40 minutes it took to snuff out 1500 lives. The Kiwis are watching, furrow-browed and serious, one of them rather optimistically and prematurely stating that Batt is being easily contained. A teammate tells him to shoosh.

Australia sneak home by one goal in overtime. It's a hollow victory. Not even another match-winner from Batt on the final whistle can generate feelings of genuine excitement. Australia have failed to reach the top four in a tournament they wanted to win. Batt is downcast. Old Age and Treachery tells him, 'You played well, mate, real well.' Batt takes losses hard though. When Australia win, he heaps praise on everyone else. When they lose, he thinks it's his fault. They sing happy birthday to Dubberley. He's turned 27 and all things considered, done well to make it. Celebrations are muted.

Australia versus China brings on all the clinically recognised symptoms of melancholic depression: physical agitation, insomnia, loss of appetite. Dubberley tells his players that from this moment they are climbing the 29 000 feet left between them and the Paralympics. 'Get heavy,' he commands. 'Play fast, knock 'em down.' By quarter time, he wants twenty goals. They give him seventeen. Australia beat China blindfolded in a game most memorable for Ryley Batt nearly killing Zhenfeng Tao. Batt tells Dubberley: 'Mate, I know what you said before but, bloody hell, I didn't want to put him in hospital.' Tao is *crushed* by Batt. The paramedics revive him and get back to *Eat, Pray, Love*.

In the most detailed possible illustration of Australia's struggles, providing the most damning evidence that Australia's Paralympic dress rehearsal has been an unmitigated disaster, they need *overtime* to get past The Assassin's Bullets just to finish rotten, stinking fifth. The US ease away from GB to reach another final. Batt leaves before the end. He doesn't want to watch them. He wants to play them. Canada lose a heartbreaker to NZ courtesy of a turnover with 45 seconds to go. Benoit Jett turns white, but he doesn't blow his stack. He claps his players off the court, repeating 'good job, good job'. Why does everyone say everything twice? Why, exactly, does everyone say everything twice? The US beat New Zealand in the decider. Nick Springer is lively and outstanding. Zuperman is the consummate professional. Australia's world ranking falls back to number five. They've retreated instead of surging. The Canadians have a first and a third from the last fortnight, the US have a second and a first, and the Kiwis have a third and a second. China's most significant contribution has been unveiling a player with one backwards foot. This is some foot.

~

For all the shaken heads and mumbled disbelief, the most appropriate mid-game comment has come from Alman during the befuddled performance against Japan. He's looked around the court, and across at Dubberley, and to all corners of the gymnasium as if the answers must be in here *somewhere*, and said, 'What the hell is going on?' That just about sums it up. It's during the Japan game that Dubberley finally loses it. He's exhausted and his team is playing like crap. He kicks a chair and swears. While those two misdemeanours do not exactly make him the Zodiac Killer, it's as out of control as he gets. There's a difference between swearing to emphasise a point and swearing in full-blown exasperation. This is full-blown exasperation.

'We're just not playing well and I don't know why,' he says. 'We really struggle when we go overseas. The way we play at home, somehow we've got to take that to the rest of the world. It shouldn't be any different. We fly in, we stay in the same hotel, we eat together—all the same as the Super Series. It's gone on for as long as Australia has been playing. When I think back, any trip overseas, we've always badly underachieved. Then we go home and play awesome. I can't work it out. It's not being in a hotel because we stayed in a hotel in

Melbourne. It's not the travel because we're used to that. We got here early to recover from the flight, we had our trainings, we did some sightseeing—I just don't know what it is. Look at the difference between this and the Super Series. There just wasn't the same intensity. If we produce what we've got, we can do some damage against these teams. But we've got a shitload of work to do. Ryles knows he has to get fitter, and he will. Ryles is going to go back home and work his arse off before Beijing. For us to come here and finish fifth—that's a real kick in the teeth. We had the chance to get a semi with the US, but we fucked it up. We shouldn't have lost by as much as we did to New Zealand. And we should have beaten GB by more. But it's pointless even talking about it. We didn't do it. The Paralympics are going to be about what we do, not what we should have done.'

DUBBERLEY ON BLOWING HIS STACK: 'Yeah, I've been more pissed off than normal. I was just off all week. I don't know what it was, whether it was a lack of sleep or what. I was just angry and uptight the whole time. It's a lesson for me to learn for Beijing. I've got as much to work on as the players. I need to make sure I get plenty of sleep, for starters. If I'm not thinking clearly and I'm angry, that's going to rub off on the players and I don't want to do that to them. It hasn't been what we wanted. I wanted us to lose a game here—or I didn't want us to lose so much as I wanted us to be beaten. There's a difference. We all know we're much better than we showed. It wasn't my best time coaching-wise. I did some stuff I probably shouldn't have. I'm still new at it. I think I go alright, but I'm still new. We go back home now and Beijing is basically another five-game tournament that we have to get ready for. Years of work have gone into it, a lot of time and money and effort, all the training sessions the players do on their own, all the tournaments, camps, everything. It will all come down to a few games—half an hour here, half an hour there. That game against NZ could be the defining match. The good news is that six teams can win it, and we're one of them. No-one else might think it now, but we do. We've just got to sort our gear out. Come Beijing, we've got to be on.'

THE AUSTRALIAN CAPTAIN: 'It hurts to come over here and not even make the semis. The way these tournaments and the Paralympics are structured, you lose one game and it can be all over. You can't slacken off for a second. The momentum went against us and we couldn't get it back. The real killer is that we wanted us to play the US. They're the benchmark and we wanted to test ourselves against the benchmark. We won't get that opportunity before Beijing now, and it's our own fault. We didn't play well enough. There are things that happened in this tournament that we can't let happen again. Mainly the energy we need to take to the court. We just didn't have it here. But it's all about Beijing and when we get there, no-one is going to care about what happened at the Canada Cup. A bit of short-term pain for long-term gain, hopefully.'

NEVER WALK ALONE: 'The Oceanias and Super Series, we dominated with our offence. This tournament, it was our weakness. We struggled to get out of our back court. We didn't get the turnovers we usually do. The whole week, we just didn't, I don't know, we just didn't *feel* it. It's like we either do or we don't, and there's no in-between. The Americans pump themselves up in their own way and you have to say it works for them. Look at all the sports they play—gridiron, ice hockey and the sports really ingrained in their culture. Getting themselves all kind of frenzied is part of it. That's their normal behaviour. They're running up and they're head-butting each other, that kind of thing, fighting is condoned, they play aggressive sports. We play physical contact sports in Australia but it's not in our nature to go over the top. Everyone has a different approach. We have to admit the US were unbelievable here. Every player in the US team is world-class. Not putting anyone down in our team, because I'm including myself in this, but not all of us are at the top of our classification. We're all fairly solid but we need our teamwork. We have our standout guys who are at the top of their classifications, but then we have guys who are quite below it. That's where we have to work hard. I just want to play America. If we can shut them up early, turn the tables on them and get a lead, I'd love to see how quiet they go. If they're up, they're right up. But when they're having trouble, if there's a risk they could lose a game, they're just not used to it and they freak out. The last two years, they've only lost that one game to Canada. The pressure on them in Beijing is going to be pretty immense and that's going to work against them. They're not used to being hassled and I still think we can do that if we get the chance.

'Still, it's been a bad tournament for us. I'm a bit gutted, but the good thing is that Beijing is next. I've been focused on this for two years. Up until now we've had all these smaller tournaments to think about. There was the Super Series, so it was hard to look too far past that. The same with the Canada Cup. Now the next stop is Beijing. That's it. No other tournaments, nothing, just Beijing. I'm going to train my head off.'

Why? Why bother? 'Because when you're fucked, and you know you're fucked, you've got to have one more push left in you. Your teammates are relying on you. It might only take one more push to win a game, and I want to be able to make that push. I really think Beijing is going to bring out the best in us, all the desire we've got. I've just got this good feeling about playing America, like Ryley and the rest of us can push them around a bit. You watch them this week, and they're awesome. But when we're out there on the court with them, we might just be one of those teams who can make them look ordinary.'

THE INVALUABLE CAMERON CARR: 'I know that for myself, personally, it just felt flat, sitting around all day, not doing much, then being expected to go out there and play. The good teams, they turn up anywhere in the world and play well. They're consistent. We'll play really well in a game but then have a shocker. We just need that balance and consistency where we start creating that aura and fear about us. We don't want teams to think, "Shit. We've got to play Ryley." We want them to think, "Shit, we've got to play Australia." That's the difference between us and the US. They don't have a standout star, just a lot of really good players. Ryley is so dominant, and it's fortunate that he's playing for us, but I think everyone under him has to lift again.'

BATT: 'Most Canada Cups I've been to, we haven't played our best. That game against New Zealand, we were down a few, we put on a few of the new line-ups to give them practice—not even thinking about the for and against. But I really think losing that game will help us in the long term. Who cares about Canada Cup? Beijing is the one. Coming fifth might give us a wake-up call. After Oceanias and the Super Series, we were still on such a high—maybe we needed to be brought back down. We've still got a lot to do. Who cares if America has won this? It's all good. The way I feel now, coming fifth, I just want to get to Beijing and make amends.'

HUCKS: 'We were crap. We were just really down. Melbourne, there was a lot of fire. We would have beaten any team down there. But we came here and it was just a bummer. It's all momentum. You're striving so hard to get it. You're trying to force it but you can't. It's an amazing thing, that zip you get some days, but other days you just can't find it. It's the feng shui, mate. When the feng shui's on, everyone clicks, everything is fine and we're all smiles and we do our shit easily. We don't even worry about it, everything just happens. But we didn't have everything going well here. We weren't on top of it all. We still nutted out a few wins and if we get to Beijing and get the feng shui right, we'll be as competitive as anyone. America might blow a few people away on their day but basically, there's not much in it. One day every four years—that's what it comes down to. I'm going to quit work completely for a month. I just really want to train and stay on top of it, finish on a high and feel good about it. We've just got to make the gap as small as we can between our worst and our best. Every now and again you have a blinder, but most times you don't. When you have a bad day, it's still got to be pretty good. You have to grind out a win. We did that here a bit against GB and Japan but still, fifth—that's crap. We're better than that. It's not just that we weren't at our best. It's that we fell so far. It's really important we get less of a gap between our good and bad games. That's been my problem over the years. I've been either on fire or I've completely fallen over.'

THE GENIUS NAZIM ERDEM: 'That game against New Zealand is going to be massive in Beijing. It was a really bad loss to them here but if we beat them in Beijing, I reckon we're definitely in the finals. GB, we shouldn't be in overtime against them. Even our wins were ordinary. It will bring us back down to earth and I think it's a good time for that to happen. We know how the system works. We know what can happen. If we lose to New Zealand on that second night, we could be in trouble. Even if we're losing, we have to keep going because every goal could count against GB. New Zealand really beat us up here. We haven't lost an important game for a while but it might not be as bad as it sounds. It might be a blessing. I reckon those other teams will underestimate us now. Everyone has been watching everyone here, even if no-one has wanted anyone to know they're watching. No-one has wanted to be caught.'

If The Red Shirts sit at one end of the behavioural spectrum, Erdem resides at the other. 'Those able-bodied guys?' he says. 'You're a helper. You're a backroom boy. You're not the coach. You're not the assistant coach. You're not a player. But that's their way of getting into other teams' heads. They want to psych people out that way. I've seen it work on so many teams, because they're so arrogant and loud and it can fluster people. But so what? Some people react to it. Some people get overawed, but I look at the US and just see another bunch of people we can beat. I think we might be able to shut up those two guys. Gotta bring them back down to earth, too, you know? They're so arrogant they won't even play a practice game against us. I know what they're saying: "We're too good for you. We're not going to share a court with you unless we have to." There's only a few weeks left, and there's plenty of motivation there now. We've got to do our own homework, we've got to do our jobs. But what happened here, you know? I think everyone is feeling the pressure. I can see it in my teammates and coach and the staff. When America are sitting there watching us, is that fucking with our minds? When we go to the northern hemisphere, why aren't we the same team? What's going wrong? Does coming to the northern hemisphere do something to our bodies? Everyone realises there is something psychological going on with us when we travel. But what goes on? I'm pretty laidback, so I'm not going to worry about it. A lot of things, I don't give a fuck about. I try my hardest and do my job out there but nothing else is going to get to me. Not other players or anything else. That's the way I handle pressure. I'll just keep doing my own thing.'

Dubberley can barely speak. His eyes are bloodshot and his laptop is broken. 'Yeah, rough week,' he says. 'Even the wins were pretty sketchy. The game against Japan, we had no right in the world to win that game, but we came back and won. There's a positive in that. I guess a year ago, we wouldn't have had the fight in us.

Fifth—we got what we deserved. If we come fifth again in Beijing, that won't sit too well with any of us. We lost that spark that gets us going. I need to work out what that spark is.

'I made some errors here, the same as any player did. It's not the coach's fault when an athlete at this level goes out and goes ten seconds, no dribble. I can't go out there and take the ball off them and bounce it for them. Silly mistakes are in their hands—but the coach has to take responsibility for it. I should have them prepared so well they don't make those mistakes. I feel like it's on my head. As I said, I'm making errors as much as anyone. We didn't have the intensity, and it's my job to make sure they have it. We made some very uncharacteristic mistakes, and it's my job to make sure there are none. We know now how tough the competition is. We have to come out of that Kiwi game with a win. Right now, the way I feel, I know how bad a fifth feels. I don't want it again and hopefully the rest of the boys feel the same way. We need the . . .' Dubberley clicks his fingers three times. 'Spark. We weren't edgy here. It's an aggressive sport but there was no energy, no fire, none of that spark. We've got a lot of heart and passion, as much as anyone else, but it's just our curse, the curse of our team. What happens to us when we travel? We can't put our finger on it. It's up to me to work it out. What we normally bring to the table is a physicality the other teams can't handle. But against NZ we didn't have much at all. The US would have put twenty on us here and a few teams were a lot more dangerous.

'GB are the big improvers. They're a different team without Joe. He didn't support his players, Joe. They hated his coaching. Bagging the shit out of his players, basically, for making mistakes. They're better off without him. I still can't believe he said everyone is fighting for silver. He really didn't have much faith in his team. I've got more faith in my blokes than that. GB looked pretty good to me—but they still finished fourth. That shows how tight Beijing will be. Just a couple of goals here and there. We should have been in the finals. That's where I feel like we belong at these tournaments, the finals. But we weren't there. Unforced errors cost us. Everyone is to blame. Players messed up, I messed up, we got ourselves into trouble as a team, we got ourselves out of trouble as a team. Or we tried to. We dug in and won a few games but we'd already made it too hard for ourselves.'

Dubberley wants to get out of here by the count of ten but this is what he says on the behaviour of The Red Shirts: 'Yeah, those blokes. I reckon it's just ingrained in them. It's such an American thing. Aussies are so laidback. We don't get into that carrying on. In any sport, we're generally awesome athletes but we're not loud and arrogant and in your face. Then again, I don't mind it. I'm happy they do it, and the same goes for Canada. It adds to the whole package. I'm all for it, the cockiness and confidence, and part of that is seeing how awesome it will be when they get knocked down a level and start crying their eyes out because they've had a loss. To us.'

Zuperman holds his gold medal and says, 'This doesn't mean jack shit, man. It doesn't matter. We want Beijing. That's all it is. Go to Beijing and get five more wins. That's what all this is for.' Wilmoth is surrounded by well-wishers. There have been times when he thought professional sport was beyond him, or about to be taken away.

He is a quiet interviewee, reading from the gospel according to Ryley Batt: 'The way I am is the only thing I've known. I don't know what it's like to have hands or to be able to walk on normal feet. I have never known it, so I can never miss it.' He's six-feet-two and 220 pounds. 'If the other person has a real solid chair like mine, and I hit him straight on, it can actually hurt my insides,' he says. 'But when I put a hard hit on someone and the hit goes through them and their chair, that's the best—when they get the pain and I get all the glory. I'm completely stoked about the whole weekend. We know what we have to do from here, and I believe this is the team that will bring the gold back to the United States. We have aspirations of greatness in Beijing.'

DUBBERLEY: 'I know America are less worried about us, but I don't really care what they think. I'm more concerned about us and the way we want to play. I'm sure they're still pretty cautious. We haven't played each other yet and they've seen what we can do. We definitely weren't that impressive here but we could come back in Beijing and give a few teams a shock. It's not over yet. In four years, we still haven't played America. We've tried everything, but they just don't want to play us. They still know who we are and what we can do.

We're not nervous about them. We're ready to hook right into them if we get the chance. We just need to get on the same court. Teams were sussing us out here because we'd been making a lot of noise by beating teams that make a lot of noise themselves. We were a bit of a target and that should have made us even more pumped. But that X-factor we have just wasn't there. We still don't really know where we sit, but we're not going to stress about it. You don't want to peak a month before a fight. You want to leave it until the last minute. The Americans used to have this intimidating aura but to be honest, we don't care because we still think we'll be right at Beijing. It still feels to me like they're running scared of us. Why else would they have avoided us for so long? We invited them to play in the Super Series and they said, um, no, we can't afford to come down. Then I said let's play a few matches before Beijing and they said, um, no, we don't have the time. They just don't want to play us. We don't care. Don't play us. You'll have to in Beijing. Fingers crossed.'

DUBBERLEY ON BATT: 'He was very flat here. He said he felt fine, I'd ask him and he was fine, but he was just very flat. There wasn't the zippiness we're used to seeing. I think it's been good for him, to be honest. It's been a bit of a kick in the guts for Ryles, as it has been for all of us. I've heard him talking about how hard he's going to train. That's a good thing to hear—the best player in the world getting hungry and wanting some revenge. It's a reality check. Things had been going so well for us. I don't think we'd gotten too cocky, we were very humble, but there might have been a part of us that lost our edge after the Super Series. Every single player is committed to making amends for this.'

The after-party is held in a swish function room of The Hilton, everyone swollen with alcohol and unwinding, and the more the able-bodied coaches and officials drink, the more humungous becomes their desire to lift the disabled out of their chairs. Benoit Jett persists in raising Lavoie rather than his glass for toasts, trying to get him head high as if the giggling Lavoie is a trophy, but here's what all the able-bodied lushes should do: piss off and leave the players alone. Not all the coaches are here but Dubberley has bells on. You can see him now in his past life as a carefree player, the chief troublemaker, the one the others hang off, the ringleader for a bit of mischief. He looks happy again and that's brilliant. 'When a tournament is over I'm still going out with the boys—they're my mates,' he says. The MVP award goes to American two-pointer Will Groulx. 'That'll hurt Ryles,' Dubberley says. 'He's used to getting them.' Groulx's award is a mystery. He hasn't been the best player in the tournament; he hasn't even been the best player for America. That honour goes to Nick Springer. His mother is hanging in there. There's a lot to be said for hanging in there. Wilmoth watches Batt drink a can of beer as if he's seen neither Batt nor a can before. Wilmoth has one hooked finger on each hand. In the outside world he is disadvantaged but in this world, he is blessed. No wonder he wants to play. The Australians started the evening downcast and dispirited. Now they become uproarious. They are representing their country in a foreign land and that can never be bad. Porter, Carr, Smith and Alman will wake in the morning and do what any grown man should do when the walls start caving in: pack up and go to Vegas. Near the end of the night, a referee starts hassling Batt in the back courtyard by grabbing his chair and tilting it backwards as if he wants to tip him over. The entire Australian team move in like sheriffs around a rundown ranch. The referee is embarrassingly drunk and starts blabbering about it all being in good fun. There is a saying about the truth always coming out when you are drunk, but that is such bullshit. The real truth hits when you're sober. 'No,' Batt tells him. 'I'm not going to shake on it. I'm not going to say it's all in good fun. You shouldn't do that to people.' Gumbert wears cream slacks, an impeccable white oxford shirt and purple suspenders. The American flag is printed on his tie. He downplays his slick attire by suggesting you can put lipstick on a pig but when all is said and done, it remains a pig. Gumbert is a driven individual but for a brief moment straight after the medal ceremony, he's seen kicking back and laughing so hard his well-rounded body reverberates with every chortle. 'We won't be celebrating for long,' he says. 'We have to get back to work. This is a very nice win at a very nice tournament, but ultimately, there is someplace else we need to be.'

Part IV

THE BIG DANCE

10

And on the first day

Four thousand athletes. A worldwide television audience of 1.5 billion. The second most watched sports event of the year behind the Olympics. The humanity, oh! 'It's an area of sport that is so fresh and so unaffected by some of the negative elements that affect able-bodied sport,' says The Most Learned Gentleman Of The Australian Paralympic Committee, president Greg Hartung. 'The Olympics is so big it denies you that feeling you had about sport when you were growing up. That was about the participation, about winning, yes, but about working in a team environment. There are so many areas we have lost over the years in sport. We have gained as well, but we've lost some of the unique elements that attracted us to sport when we were children. I see that in the Paralympic Games, the athletics, the swimming, the rugby. It has a real appeal for people who see that inspirational endeavour; that triumph of the human spirit, if you like. The triumph, not adversity, but the triumph of having a goal and meeting an objective. Inspiration is one of the most overworked words in the English language, but this really is inspirational. These athletes, their endeavours and the entire Paralympic movement has the subliminal benefit of influencing community attitudes and civilising the joint.' For joint, read WORLD.

'We're infinitely more powerful in getting that message across because we don't ram it down people's throats,' he says. 'We don't deliberately go out of our way to do it, so we do it better. That's not to downplay the immense human side to disabilities. But we are about sport. Our main concern is building high-performance athletes. If we tried specifically to affect public opinion, we wouldn't be successful. We have an uncompromising approach to sporting excellence. The growth of the Paralympic movement internationally has been staggering and Australia has played a significant role in that because there's a very ambitious dynamic where we can change preconceived ideas and stereotypes of what a disabled person actually is. We're breaking that stereotype down. You can see it happening as each Games goes on. Believe me, anyone who has exposure to these Paralympics will be blown away by it.

'Our research has shown that 87 per cent of the Australian population believe Paralympic athletes should get the same level of financial support as Olympic athletes. There's an increasing appetite for exposure to Paralympic sport and I don't think the cynics really get it, to be honest. Sometimes it's too easy for people to look at sport with disabilities and say it's social welfare, just an extension of the rehab area. It's not. This is to do with high performance. This is to do with excellence. This is results-driven and this is to do with Australia's role, reputation and prestige in the world. We have to be very frank and say there's nothing wrong with excellence. There's nothing wrong with winning. There's nothing wrong with striving to be your best. We shouldn't have to apologise for that. In some areas of Australian culture it might not be desirable to be too outwardly ambitious. Well, I'll tell you what, it's not part of the Paralympic culture. We want to be the best. Our athletes want to be the best. We want to introduce every Australian with a disability to sport if they're interested but at the top end, at the sharp end, these people want to win and they can be bloody ruthless about it. There's no reason to be coy about that. I detect there's a little bit of cynicism out there, the tall poppy syndrome in sections of the Australian public, who don't think trying to achieve is necessarily a good thing. I have a message for them—get over it.'

Hartung's shirt and hair are ruffled. He's one of the best men of authority of all.

'I'll tell you a story about the Paralympics,' he says. 'There's this guy from New Guinea. He was in the New Guinea defence force. He was ambushed one night in Bougainville and left in a ditch for dead. His fellow soldier was killed. His colleagues came back along the track next day and found Benj still alive—with his eyes shot out. They sent him to hospital in Adelaide for a year or so to be mended. He came to Beijing for an IPC meeting. He's totally blind, obviously, but found his way down to Moresby, got an international flight from Moresby to Burma and hop-scotched it all the way across. He got all that way himself. We take a lot of things for granted, you know. These Games will be remarkable. If you haven't seen a Paralympics yet, you have no idea how good it is going to be.

'Just prior to Sydney—and I think this will tell you a lot about the kind of people you are dealing with here—we had two or three days away with our athletes, many of whom were amputees. They put on a movie on the bus, *Monty Python and the Holy Grail*, the one where all John Cleese's limbs are chopped off and he stands there saying let's call it a draw. The amputees were absolutely pissing themselves laughing. There would be people who think, "Oh no, you can't show them that", but it was one of their favourite movies.

'You can't underestimate these athletes. There are some amazing people at the Paralympics, stunning and extraordinary stories from properly incredible people. The Paralympic movement is genuine, the sport is ruthless, and of course they've all jumped some significant personal hurdles to get to the point where they want to show their skills and talent and expertise on the world stage. A fair chunk of that world is affected by disabilities. It seems most people have a negative mental picture about what a disability is, and what disability sport is, and we are going to change that. The people with the wrong idea, they lose, in my mind. These are some of the most optimistic, full-of-life people you can come across. There's an infectious spontaneity in them; there's no pretension and no assumptions. Without a doubt, sport with a lot of people with disabilities can be quite confronting. People get shocked when they first see a Paralympics, but that's only the initial impact. When people come back for the second and third times, they look beyond and around the disability and they see the athleticism, the sport and the competition. The disability becomes almost invisible. We don't want anyone to feel sorry for them. These are high-performance athletes across all sports. The rugby blokes—I hope they get a medal. They *should* medal. I hope they bloody well clean up.'

11

And on the second day

Prime Minister Kevin Rudd has better things to do than farewell the Australian Paralympic team at Sydney Airport so his wife is sent to cut the metaphorical ribbon. More than a hundred disabled athletes can organise themselves sufficiently to get to Sydney Airport on time but Therese Rein arrives 45 minutes late because of a traffic jam on the Harbour Bridge that doesn't seem to have delayed anyone else. The departure turns chaotic while everyone accommodates her tardiness, but it doesn't seem to do her reputation any harm because three days later, she's made an honorary member of the International Paralympic Committee.

The plane heads for The Middle Kingdom with the entire Australian Paralympic team on board. What a crew this is. Sarah Stewart is a divine female basketball player with a university degree in philosophy and an interest in *Mao's Last Dancer*. A single-legged amputee hops down the aisle. Airline staff push a mini-wheelchair along the same aisle to ferry the most needy, the paraplegics and the quadriplegics, to the toilet. Double-leg amputees, or those *no legs* who didn't have anything that could be amputated in the first place, scurry along the floor. A men's basketballer was a deckhand on a high-speed ferry before this: 'We were preparing to leave the pier when the skipper thought he heard me calling "All clear",' he says. 'But the rope I had was still attached to the quayside. When the ferry moved out, the rope tightened and sliced off my right foot as neatly as a chef chopping through a carrot.' A 66-year-old shooter is the woman responsible for disabled people hogging all the good car parking spots. Acres of grin and makeup are smeared across her gorgeous face. In 1976 she became so fed up with receiving fines for exceeding 30-minute parking limits—it took her an age to get to and from the car—that she took it to court in a precursor to the establishment of disabled parking permits. The Paralympic flame awaits, do you see? Another female basketballer throws money into a UNICEF envelope marked CHANGE FOR GOOD. 'I don't feel excited—yet,' Batt says. 'I just want to get over there.'

He's getting over there courtesy of a prime piece of real estate in business class. He looks fitter than he did in Canada. More lean than the big bopper waiting by the gate at Port Macquarie.

'It's here,' Dubberley says. 'We're going to Beijing. We're pumped. It's already sold out over there. Massive crowds, awesome, just what we want. It'll be Sydney all over again. Ryley is really calm. He's been around the block a few times and he knows the game inside out. Most nineteen-year-olds are cocky bastards but Ryley is different. He's got his shit sorted. I know one thing about Ryley—he just hates to lose. The Canada Cup stung him and I don't think he's going to let that happen again. Big game, a few seconds to go, he'll just refuse to lose.' Remember those words.

It's 1 a.m. by the time the players arrive at the Paralympic village, this place of every conceivable physical disability that ever was, sport's edition of The Valley Of The Blind where a one-eyed man really would be king. Dubberley and his drained players have a collective case of the screaming shits when they arrive but it's a mood that never lasts too long.

Dubberley's pre-Games vanishing act has been a psychologist's dream: 'I wanted to go north, somewhere near Newcastle, relax and get away from rugby altogether,' he says. 'Before every tournament, I just like to get in the car and vanish, clear my head. I went up to Newcastle but everywhere I went was either booked out or completely dead. I kept driving and ended up in Port Macquarie. I had no intention of going to Port but yeah, I did end up seeing Ryles. I don't know if it was a subconscious thing, or what. I guess I used to live there. I really thought I was going somewhere south of there, somewhere closer to Newcastle, anywhere I could be alone, but there I was in Port giving Ryles a call. It was a bit weird. We didn't really talk about Beijing. It was more about just hanging out and bullshitting on like we do. Afterwards, to a point, I did think, "That's a bit strange." I wanted to get away alone but I ended up with Ryley. It wasn't planned at all.'

12

And on the third day

China banned seven-year-old Yang Pei from singing at the Olympic opening ceremony with her chubby face and crooked teeth. She was deemed too ugly. If Yang is scorned for her slight physical imperfections, what will be made of Ryley Batt when he turns up? Joel Wilmoth? Have these people seen a Nick Springer? Are they aware that thousands of athletes are about to invade Beijing *because* they're physically imperfect?

Tiananmen Square is lined with disabled children sold by their families to the shameful businessmen using them as beggars to make money. One of these disabled slaves is in The Forbidden City right now, a ghastly and sickening sight. A woman waves a black fan in the face of the boy resting in her lap. His age is about ten. They are in the front courtyard of The Forbidden City and he is either asleep, or dead. Near his left ribcage is a tumour the size of a house brick. His skin is stretched to breaking point. There's an identical tumour protruding from his left shoulder. He has no hair. The skin of his scalp has turned a grotesque brown-green, but more green, and the skin of his left arm is disfigured as if he's being burned or eaten alive. Chinese people walk straight past him. Tourists stop and stare in horror. The woman keeps fanning his face. This boy should not be here. He should be in hospital or else he is on his way to a graveyard. The woman cannot understand your words. The boy is barely breathing. She moves him under a tree to guard his face from the sun. You throw coins in her bucket and go. The truly horrified look on that woman's face, is that the real China? Back at the Yayuncun Hotel, your pen runs out of ink. You ask for a replacement in the bustling foyer filled with over-eager Paralympic volunteers. Three of them at the desk marked 'Inquiries' take you all of five paces to another three people at 'Technical Assistance'. They confer and send you to 'Support Control' and fair fucking dinkum, any danger of someone just handing over a pen?

The hotel room has a warning about 'No the Smoking', but there's an ashtray on the desk. The volunteers are all throwing themselves into the 'Smiling Beijing!' campaign. Five colours of 'smiling wrist bands' are being worn to promote the rampantly fake friendliness for the course of the Paralympics. Each of the five colours represents a commitment from that particular volunteer. Red represents the willingness to help others, black is for the honesty and trust, green is for the environmental considerations, yellow is the civility and manners and blue is the learning and the enterprised, whatever that means. Two days after the launch of the 'Smiling Beijing!' campaign, here's what you would like everyone to do. You would like everyone to stop fucking smiling.

13

And on the fourth day

The Opening Ceremony

BEIJING, THE PEOPLE'S REPUBLIC OF CHINA, 6 SEPTEMBER 2008: Ballerinas, fireballs, meteorites, deep blue oceans, stardust, the flame-throwing stardust lights, 90 000 people illuminating the sky with sabres of purple, blue and red. Helicopters roar through the smog-like medieval buzzards. Sea breezes, haunting autumn mists, gentle snow upon the steep embankments of a space-age gladiator's pit. The heaving cauldron is inflamed by the Paralympic torch and burn, baby, burn. Chinese flags are waved to the beat of drums. Grand opera, giant paper butterflies the size of skyscrapers and the stern command to China's servants that 'when the national anthem is played, we must wave our flags with pride'. Artificial wind so the national flag is never lame. A blind man sits at a white piano. His mother watches quietly from her white wooden bench. No-one takes a breath while he plays something beautiful. The air is choking on so much smog and radioactivity that a lit match would make the old Peking flare then solar explode. 'Come here,' the security woman outside The Bird's Nest Stadium has said with a forced grin. 'Go over there. Thank you for your cooperation.' Her mouth is filled with blood, unless you imagine it.

The President of the Beijing Paralympic Organising Committee lays it on thick. 'The theme of the Games is Transcendence, Integration and Equality,' he says. 'The athletes will demonstrate perseverance, fortitude and their love for life by transcending themselves. The Paralympic Games educates people to the power of love, and encourages people to devote more understanding, respect and support to people with a disability. Through the Paralympic Games, the humanitarian spirit is raised to new heights, and the cause for people with a disability is promoted far and wide. Persons with a disability are important members of human society.' Did anyone suggest they weren't? China protests too much. What about that kid at The Forbidden City? Anyone care about him?

A man from the Czech Republic reverses his electric chair so sharply that the front wheels are raised like the legs of a rearing horse. A Norwegian tries a handstand but crumbles to the ground in a tangled mess of walking sticks and prosthetic limbs. From the team representing Guinea, one athlete—arriving tomorrow. Look at all these banged-up people, happy as pigs in shit, bloody unreal the lot of it. Great Britain wear spiffing white jackets and navy caps. The English Rose glows. She's May Day in *A View To A Kill: Get Zorin for me!* The United States of Goddamn America are resplendent in their navy goddamn blazers and white goddamn caps like they've walked straight off the pages of The Great Goddamn Gatsby. Wilmoth is walking next to Zuperman and once more we suspect that anyone possessing the energy to march around The Bird's Nest and then stand out here for another three hours watching the entertainment has a distinct physical advantage over the rest of his murderballing colleagues from other parts of the blue marble planet. The German Pissheads are admonished for running off the track and hitting pingpong balls into the crowd. Damn Pissheads. *Ich bin kunst.* The German Pissheads are in possession of a banner saying 'RUGBY' in case they all get tanked at the Soho Bar and forget which sport to go to. On and on the parade goes. Australia wait their turn to march. They're in sensible suits. China look the best of the lot in purple coats. The stadium erupts at the sight of them, the Chinese stomping in a one-two beat and waving their red flags on cue as if they're all signed up to become foot soldiers in the most formidable army in the world. Maybe they are. Dubberley pulls up his wheelchair next to the centre stage. A message flashes on the big screen: The celebration of life! The celebration of life!

A single spotlight. Thousands of flashbulbs fall on eleven-year-old Li Yue. She dances. There's no rhyme, reason or understanding of the earthquake that ripped China, and Li, in two earlier this year. No reconciling how a school at Dujiangyan collapsed, killing 50 children. Or how a man from Mianyang was buried under rubble and only survived by eating toilet paper and drinking his own urine for a week. Or how another man had to tie his dead wife to his back with a rope and ride his scooter across Sichuan to find a respectable place to bury her. How more than 70 000 people were killed and 375 000 were injured. How five million Chinese became homeless and 5000 children were orphaned. How up to 25 000 aftershocks have since hit the area, little warnings, *Clink*. How a hospital in an almost post-apocalyptic town still stands barren. There are no windows or doors and every room is gutted and the floors are still covered in rubble and trash. All around the hospital, homes have been replaced by tents. Dead grandchildren. The tents are filled with insects and swarms of mosquitoes and flickering lights and what happens if another earthquake comes and maybe it's better for the grandparents to be swallowed by the ground with the rats. The third floor of one building is gone and that's a crying shame because the third floor is where the children were sleeping when the floor creaked and fell from under them. There was nothing the grandparents could do because no-one could move the concrete beams and they could see a hand here and a leg there and they could hear all the crying because the grandchildren were still alive but they could not make it stop and poor old Mrs Wei lost her grandchildren while seeing the hearts of her own children being cut to bloodless ribbons. Mrs Wei had two bottles of drinking water because of the heat. She used the water to wash the dust from her dead grandson's face.

Li Yue lived and now she is dancing in her chair with a red shoe on her only foot. She is ungainly. Not everything can be sunsets and lollipops. This is not a free-flowing ballerina. That is the reality but Li Yue has an audience of 1.5 billion people. She would never have experienced this with two legs and no earthquake. Her chair is lifted.

A smile fills her pretty face. The singing sounds like velvet. There's swooning classical music. Floating planets and moons and the stadium feels like the centre of God's own universe—the oceans and the lands and let there be light. There is the grand chorus of *Ode To Joy*: *Be embraced, millions! This kiss for the entire world! Endure courageously, millions! Endure for the better world!* The perpetual hazes of pink and purple. The cosmic chant: The stars are bright tonight! This is a gathering of life in the universe! This is a carnival of life in the universe! The athlete's oath is spoken. Confucius says they will try their best. The officials' oath is also spoken. Confucius says they will try not to stuff it up. The Paralympic flag is raised next to the Chinese flag followed by a forgettable rendition of the Paralympic anthem and then comes the lighting of the flame, do you see?

Drums are rolled and lights are dimmed and bells are rung as the torch is taken through a lap of the sprawling stadium. The helicopter-buzzards stall their engines, while Wu Hongping sits below the flame in his wheelchair.

'A once-in-a-lifetime thing,' Batt says. 'My head is spinning.'

Hongping places his trembling hands on a rope. You think he's going to be lifted to the flame. But he starts climbing. The message is not lost. If you want to get somewhere in this life, bloody well get there yourself, wheelchair or not. The din is immeasurable. Hongping lights the wick of the torch. The most powerful man in China declares the Games open. The singing is how the angels must sound in heaven. That's lovely. Let's rumble.

14

And on the fifth day

Eighty consecutive green, purple and red posters along Tiantan Lu promote ONE WORLD, ONE DREAM. We get the one world. But what's the dream? Blaring car horns fill the most immovable obstruction on Earth: a Beijing traffic jam. Stiff-armed guards and stiff-backed police. The accumulation of soot on teeth and grime on skin. Somewhere along the way, the sight of a loaded gun has ceased to be confronting. There is constant talk, just this never-ending mass of jumbled languages and hand gestures and raised voices and dozens of broken conversations you will never be part of. The bring-bring of the bells on bikes. The Hall Of Overwhelming Glory is a two-storey brick building at No. 30 Xue Yuan Road, which others might call the gymnasium at the University of Science and Technology but one more round of bullshit to that. The fresh-faced security officer has a revolver in his holster. His finger twitches and he grins like a lizard. More green signs say Beijing 2008. There are no green trees, just green signs. Black coffee is thick like molasses.

The loathsome Red Shirts stride out for the opening game between the US and China. You're developing an almost pathological dislike to them. To be fair, one of them appears to have toned down his act. The other has upped the ante and dyed his beard red, white and blue. Springer politely tells US-based reporters, 'Glad you could come along.' The court sparkles, translucent. The polished timber floorboards have been painted blue. Every night, 30 workers get down on their hands and knees to re-polish every last inch of hardwood. The witches' hats are red. In the apparent belief his histrionics are a highlight of the show, a Red Shirt starts stomping and waving his arms to the crowd as if he's the sole reason we're all here. Keep it up and he'll be a good enough reason to leave. He's greeted by nothing more friendly than silence. Out comes China's hard-as-nails female coach with her military background, tasered eyes and a ponytail. Zuperman wears black sleeves. He sits in the centre circle for the opening whistle. Springer is hurtling around the court, possessed. His mother is dying of cancer and he's trying to fulfil one of the bigger promises he made her. The glazed look on Nick Springer's face will remain unbroken for the next five days, and then it will shatter.

China's female coach is joined by a female player, Zhang Wenli, who says she hit rock bottom during and after her accident in 1994. Zhang dived into shallow water and broke her neck and for the next twelve years she felt trapped in her home in eastern China because she'd always believed the disabled were useless and unworthy—and now she was one of them. The documentary ended her funk. 'I doubted I could play,' says the 40-year-old in Mandarin through an interpreter who gives the impression she's making it all up. 'The game seemed so fierce. I watched the movie dozens of times. I don't understand what they are saying, as my English is poor, but I can feel the atmosphere and I understood the lead athlete's situation. He was saying, "We are not patients or victims, we are independent athletes." And now I am representing my country against those same athletes. Many of our athletes did not think they could ever be independent and so strong in their bodies, but wheelchair rugby rebuilt their spirits. In just a few seconds, these people became disabled by serious accidents. Afterwards, they felt depressed. They often underestimated themselves and felt inferior. But now, after training, they have recovered and wear a bright smile. We expect to come last of the eight teams at this tournament, but we will show our spirit and enjoy the experience.' Smiling Beijing! You swear the interpreter has invented every last sentence.

Another Chinese player, Cui Maoshan, had China's Federation For Disabled People knocking on his door looking for murderballers after he broke his neck in a fall at a building site. Cui is on the national team after just one year of training. 'I am not depressed now, but feel great and proud,' he says through the same poetic interpreter. Cui has spoken for about a minute and a half and the translation has amounted to ten words. His wife and two children have never seen him play, and they never will. They cannot afford the travel.

Zuperman is told of the impact of *'fucking hit me, I'll hit you back'* on Zhang's life and replies, 'I think it bridges so many gaps that it doesn't matter what language you speak. The film brings disability to the forefront. Ten minutes into the film, you don't see the wheelchairs, you just see athletes.' Zhang chases Zuperman for a photo. 'I worship him,' she says. Zuperman agrees to the photo but that's the end of the niceties. 'Girl or guy, if you're in my way, get out of it—or I'll move you out of the way,' he says. Zhang is none the wiser. 'I won't understand if any foreign player insults me,' she says. 'On the court, no-one considers me a woman. The intensity and excitement is the charm of rugby.' The charm of rugby! This interpreter is becoming the best show in town. 'It will shock people that quadriplegics can play such an exciting game. That is what I hope the Paralympics will bring to my country.'

The Chinese players are introduced to their clueless home crowd. Springer and Bryan Kirkland applaud. Zuperman does not. It takes fourteen seconds for the world champions to score their first goal. Then China score. Arise all those who refuse to be slaves! Benoit Jett is watching closely. His arms are wrapped tightly around his bulbous stomach. The US play poorly. Wilmoth is only a mild force. Springer, Kirkland and Cohn are the dominant forces. Springer has the spunk to go looking for a fight and enough mongrel to win it. He is hurting and so he wants collisions and he wants to lash out. Kirkland puts Guifei Han in a humidicrib and then points at him and winks. There's an arrogance to Kirkland. He looks like a sleepy-eyed man whose favourite song might be 'Honky Tonk Bakonkadonk'. He speaks with a slow southern drawl and has an ink job of barbed wire around a skinny bicep, the kind that pissed Pommy tourists leave Bali with. Gumbert watches the US's routine victory with little animation. His head and body are tilted to the right in the manner of a deranged scientist undertaking an experiment that cannot be allowed to fail. Gumbert is an intriguing soul. Instead of stomping on an ant to kill it, you imagine him leaning over to study it. How does it live? What is it doing? And then he would kill it. A private schoolboy's haircut parts with precision down the left. A few grey hairs for authority. Gumbert's lips are pursed as if he's preparing to peck his wife on the cheek after arriving home having sued the pants off United Airlines. 'I believe the most important thing is not to win the gold or the silver medal,' says China's hard-faced coach. Which is just as well. The US win 65–30.

Zuperman talks incessantly about this match being one down and four to go. He rolls past Ed Suhr, the assistant coach of the American team. Suhr's brother Daniel was a New York firefighter who died in the 9/11 terrorist attacks. He wasn't killed by fire or smoke inhalation. Standing on the street outside the World Trade Center, preparing to run inside, Daniel Suhr was killed when a jumper landed on him. Unbelievable, no? Former New York Mayor Rudy Giuliani says his recurring nightmare from the day the world changed is the sound of the jumpers splattering on the concrete outside the Twin Towers. Daniel Suhr unintentionally broke a jumper's fall and lost his life because of it. Zuperman says Ed Suhr is having a difficult day. This is September 11: the seventh anniversary of 9/11. You do not interview Ed Suhr because you do not have the heart.

Zuperman is bailed up by British and American journalists salivating from their first taste of murderball.

Salivating Journalist #1: 'Mark, is it true they made a movie about the sport?'

Zuperman: 'Yeah dude, they made a movie.'

Salivating Journalist #2: 'What's the movie about, Mark?'

Zuperman: 'Go rent it out, we'll talk then.'

Salivating Journalist #1: 'And you're the star of that movie, Mark?'

Zuperman: 'I'm one of the people in the movie, dude.'

Salivating Chinese journalist: 'Do you think China will get a medal here, Mark?'

Zuperman: 'We'll see, dude, we'll see.'

We'll see China not get a medal here.

Salivating Journalist #2: 'What's the biggest attraction of this sport, Mark? The speed, the physicality?'

Zuperman: 'You hit 'em both, dude. The tactical side, it combines a lot of aspects of a lot of sports.'

Salivating Journalist #1: 'How much do you train?'

Zuperman: 'I just push, miles upon miles upon miles, two and a half hours a day. It's a balancing act between my career, my sport, my relationship and staying sane.'

Salivating Journalist #1: 'What's the hardest part?'

Zuperman: 'Staying sane.'

Salivating Journalist #2: 'You think you're going to get the gold medal, Mark?'

Zuperman: 'That's why we came, dude.'

Later, with more time on his hands, Zuperman says: 'We've really been itching to play. We just wanted to get this thing going. It's good to be able to play against somebody else instead of beating up on each other at training. We've got four more games to win. Gold is what we want, that's where we want to be. The atmosphere here is a blast. It's a cool stadium—you can't hear yourself think. The communication gets dicey. You can't understand what people are saying. Go here, go left? Where am I supposed to be going? You can't hear anyone.' No thanks to The Red Shirts. 'China were better than we thought,' he says. 'Since the last time we saw them, they've improved 110 thousand per cent.' Quite the jump.

Gumbert and Kirkland piss as much as possible in Chinese pockets. 'We played an incredible opponent here today,' Gumbert says. 'They've just started the game and we can see the progress they have made. It was a spirited, fair and competitive match. It was a great day for rugby, to have a country like China debuting in our sport at the Paralympics. The thing with this sport is that most of the players were athletes before they were injured. That part of the person is still there. We enjoy getting new fans to our sport, and now the Chinese have seen it. There's shock and awe in those people because they're not used to seeing athletes in wheelchairs running into each other. It goes against everything people are taught, that as a disabled person we're frail, we can break easily. But these guys are slamming into one another like there's no tomorrow. Hopefully one of the things that happens along the way is that the people understand these are genuine athletes. This sport, I think, helps transcend the stereotypes better than any other wheelchair sport.'

Asked if the snubbing of murderball by US television networks is discrimination against the disabled, Gumbert replies: 'It's not so much about discrimination as it is about exposure. If you take this back to your audience and tell whoever reads your words about this game, then that is exposure. That is what will sell our sport. Once you see it you're like, "I want more of that." Once you get past the running into one another and the novelty of that, you see the athleticism as opposed to the disability. That is very important for us. I firmly believe we're just one small piece of exposure away from being the kind of sport that will achieve widespread appeal. You need exposure to get exposure—people have to be interested in it before it makes the networks. And then there's even more interest because there's a new audience. We work very hard to show ourselves as being professionals, and to treat this as a professional sport, even though it is only amateur in terms of the money on offer. We try to make it professional by the way we prepare and play. I firmly believe there is a place for us alongside mainstream sports. For every good sport currently on air, there's another good sport out there that could be. Hopefully ours is one of them. If you go back and tell everybody you know about it, people will want to know more and it's started snowballing. Our sport has grown this far purely from word of mouth. You go to somewhere like Australia, where their ideas about sport are more pure, and I can see it properly catching on there. You go to the US and it's all about Budweiser making an ad and the money that can generate. So whoever Budweiser wants to be shown on TV, that's who gets shown on TV. In terms of sport in the United States, you don't ever see a wheelchair sport, but in fifteen years we've made a lot of steps towards getting there. Sometimes it's who you know, and we don't know anyone yet.'

China's hard-faced brunette says: 'The Chinese team has played the ultimate opponent. We played them here today to study. We are weak in terms of physical strength, but we have learned much from

Team USA. This is the first time we are playing at the highest level, the Paralympic Games, and we are very young. We are very proud to show the sport of wheelchair rugby to China.' Gumbert takes a photo of the packed press conference—'Nobody will believe this'—and Kirkland mumbles, 'We won't be here long, hopefully.' Then he perks up and says, 'China played with heart, they never gave up. As Team USA, we're very appreciative of China.' Of course they're appreciative of China. Everyone appreciates their punching bags. 'Just because you have a disability, it doesn't change the fire and desire you have to compete at this level,' he says. All the while, Ed Suhr is ghost-like in appearance, frail, gaunt.

Canada dispose of Japan. The sport needs a shot clock NOW because Canada's ploy of playing down Father Time during a slow hand-clap is no way to sell a sport to a billion people. Former Australian cricketer Ian Chappell once told his captain Bill Lawry during a go-slow, 'If that's Test cricket, you can stick it up your arse.' Victory secured, Lawry replied, 'We did what we had to do.' If taking two minutes to score a goal is murderball, you can stick *that* up your arse. Fortunately, it is not—but Canada do what they have to do to defeat Japan. Willsie, Lavoie and Whitehead are all nodding their heads like circus clowns. Confidence is sky-high, and when Whitehead belts Shin Nakazato, the Chinese crowd slap their thighs and point at the court and laugh uproariously: *They're in wheelchairs, and they're hitting each other!* Willsie wants a drink of water but cannot open the bottle. Benoit Jett does it for him. A soft spot is developing for The Grinch. The victory guarantees Canada a semi-final berth. If and when they defeat China. 'That game was a worry for us,' Willsie says. 'Japan took us to overtime back in Melbourne, we only beat them by one, and they've had really tight games with the Kiwis and the Aussies. We knew they'd come to play. That should get us through to the medal round and that's an accomplishment. It was a huge win for us and nobody in our team is overlooking that. We've been studying for that one game since January. I would say 80 per cent of our plans coming here were about beating Japan today and getting into the play-offs.'

Australian supporters file into the far side of the grandstand, diamonds on display, an assortment of wives, girlfriends, mothers, aunts, uncles and mates who at one stage or another must have feared their loved one was a goner. They're all so excited and nervous and you look at them and wonder what it was like the moment they first heard about the accident. When they were struck dumb by the knowledge they were powerless to change it. Perhaps we don't know how tough we really are until we're backed into a corner and have to start fighting for our lives. At Palm Beach in Sydney one Tuesday afternoon, a quadriplegic man rides his electric wheelchair through the sky-blue arches of the ferry wharf, pushing the go button so that instead of slowing near the end of the pier, he goes faster. His plan is to kill himself by driving off the end and drowning, his wheelchair a dead weight pinning him to the bottom, and you wonder if he had any second thoughts when the water started filling his lungs, the blackout began and it was all too late. Even just for a moment. All these families and rock-solid friends on the far side of the grandstand are attached to players blessed enough to be without electric wheelchairs. It's such a heartbreakingly beautiful sight, this assortment of wives, girlfriends, mothers, aunts, uncles and mates. You wonder about their interminable sleepless nights before the moment they first allowed themselves to think *it's going to be okay*. Not brilliant, perhaps, but okay. Christine Batt sits in the middle deck of The Hall of Overwhelming Glory.

Australia v. the German Pissheads

Ryley Batt. You're a volcano, man. Rumble. Don't just rumble. *Fucking explode*. You don't know how formidable you are. Australia's first test of mettle/metal is against Die Deutsche Pisseführt. The perfect chain of events over the next 48 hours would be for Australia to wipe the floor with The German Pissheads and then sit back blowing bubbles while Great Britain beat New Zealand. And then if Australia beat the Kiwis in their trans-Tasman war tomorrow evening, easier written down than done, the defending champions will be eliminated and they can rack off back to their harbourside bars in Auckland while Australia go gallivanting into the semi-finals like Jesse James and the James-Younger Gang arriving in Richmond before they robbed the bank and killed the Lord Mayor. Is that too much to ask? Hucks unexpectedly admits to a degree of apprehension about playing The German Pissheads. He swears they are more formidable than what they appear to be, nothing but a bunch of German Pissheads. The Paralympic mascots run around the court waving their cute little hands, but they're a sham because none of them carry a broken C6 or interrupted central nervous system or spina bifida or cerebral palsy and none of them are in a wheelchair or have prosthetic legs or talk to their feet and toes in case they miraculously remember how to walk and go surfing again. There is heroism in Grant Boxall clinging to hope like that. Dubberley strides into The Hall of Overwhelming Glory and says five words: 'We are ready to unleash.'

THE AUSTRALIAN CAPTAIN: 'Nothing is insurmountable. There is one thing we are focused on—making the final. Then taking the gold. We firmly believe we are capable of doing that. A US–Australia final would be a magnificent thing.'

Number 10 for The German Pissheads is a man called Salih Koeseoglu. He has a skunk mohawk and one missing leg. He has another miniature leg with a baby-sized foot slotted inside a baby-sized shoe. He is full of pep. Batt powers out and slaps Hucks's hand. Hucks looks fearsome with a shaved head. He is not smiling and he is not laughing. Comedy routines are over. He is the gnarled old bull again. 'George has been switched on since the day we got here,' Dubberley says. 'He's just had this *look*.'

The Australian coach is on his knees again, imploring his players to deploy controlled aggression. The grey-haired Oliver Johannes Picht wins the tip-off. Scars from the Canada Cup remain. You're anxious more than excited. Are the players feeling up? Down? Hyper? They lost the tip-off—Batt *never* loses the tip-off. They're going to lose to Germany and oh shit, what happens when they lose to Germany? Picht scores first. Batt scores second, determined and resolute. An important tournament has begun that will make or break his reputation. It's all well and good to run riot at the Oceanias and the Super Series at Aqua-*what*? but the Canada Cup placed a question mark beside his tag of world's greatest player. These five days are all anyone will remember on New Year's Eve when it's time to reflect and tell the biggest lies.

Old Age and Treachery secures a turnover. Batt throws a wild and hurried pass to Alman. The ball clunks across the floor like Quasimodo's bell. Australia settle. Old Age and Treachery combines with Batt for a stream of one-pointers. Dubberley stands quietly with his right hand in his pocket as if he's having a smoke while leaning against a pole in a Drysdale. Batt scores, you ripper. Alman puts Wolfgang Mayer on the floor and Hucks screams so hard he coughs, splutters and chokes. Boxall and Hucks yowl with teeth bared and spit on their chins, and before your very eyes, they're turning into a couple of wolves wanting in, scratching the dirt, looking for an opening. Dubberley is up and down the sideline. Smoko is over. Time to get some work done. The Kiwis and Great Britain watch from the VIP Lounge, leaning forward in their chairs like you do when mild interest turns to fascination.

Batt steals the ball from Picht, flees; the German giving up the chase like a shop owner too slow to run down a thief. Hucks thumps his chair like an overexcited toddler banging the side of his cot. The music is WE WILL ROCK YOU, Bump-bump-BUMP, and Batt does a right-to-left swerve for another goal as Dubberley gets animated for the first (but not the last) time this week. Temperatures are rising. Batt scores just before the first buzzer and goes whoooa! He swings his arms by his side, running, running, running free. Australia lead 13–8. Hucks is lovin' it. He's as bald as a coot, the bird variety of coot, not the old Chinese coots in the crowd.

The Grey-Haired Oliver Picht is angry. *Wie Grob!* Carr enters the fray. Go you good thing. His father swings his video camera in the direction of his son, who believes it will be a miracle if the lens cap is off. Defence. Hucks is let out of his cage. Defence. His big block of skull shines under the blinding lights of The Hall Of Overwhelming Glory. Dubberley is raising his voice for the first (but not the last) time this week. Batt is off and the lead is only four. That's a worry. To lead the intoxicated Germanics by only four is enough to make Dubberley fret for the first (but not the last) time this week. Australia cannot quite put The German Pissheads away. Perhaps they're cheating.

Boosting is the Paralympic equivalent to doping. Past Paralympians have pegged catheters to keep their bladders full, creating a backflow to the kidneys and enough stress on the body to summon an injection of power they would otherwise be incapable of. Thumbtacks or nails have been inserted into private parts, bones have been broken on purpose. Athletes have strapped themselves into their chairs too tightly to create the same effect—a shock to the system and dramatic surge in strength. The body feels the pain and reacts violently, but the brain cannot receive the message so the player feels no discomfort. Boosting can increase your performance by an estimated 25 per cent. Or it can kill you through a stroke.

Let's assume The German Pissheads haven't hammered nails into their knobs and are simply playing well because they've risen to the occasion. Koeseoglu is small, nimble and fast. He's an angry little ant who keeps finding open space and trying to match Batt while his little left shoe points to the sky.

Australia lead 24–20. Dubberley gets in his pulpit and preaches once more, Batt lifts. He beats all four German Pissheads to score. The Pissheads become frazzled and disoriented. The Grey-Haired Oliver Picht is yelling at Dirk Wieschendorf, who is yelling at Christian Goetze, who is yelling at the coach Pierre Sahm, who cannot find anyone to yell at so he's yelling at the assistant coach Bert Metzger. Poor old Bert Metzger. That's why you're the assistant, dude.

Dubberley develops that lazy grin he gets when things are cool, mate, sweet as. Those words should end up on his tombstone: 'Here Lies Brad Dubberley. Sweet As.' His nerves will be jangling soon enough. From tomorrow night there will be four consecutive games harnessing the otherworldly ferocity of an electrical thunderstorm over The Great Wall of China, the wall weaving its way through the endless hills and mountains like a fang-baring snake, plummeting into valleys and arrowing to the tops of the dense mountains and disappearing into the rivers with an imperishable noble spirit, a monument to a nation that has become the greatest marching band in the world. Hup two-three-four. Or as Dubberley says after traversing the only wheelchair accessible area of one of the seven wonders of the modern world, 'It's just a wall. I was like, is that it?' Brad Dubberley doesn't concern himself with false sentimentalities.

Batt is having more fun than a kid with a bugle, scoring at will. Dubberley starts issuing his instructions for the next play even before

Batt is back on the court after steamrolling his way to another goal. Turnover to Australia. Batt shouts, 'Nice!' Again Dubberley stands before his troops. The man can hold a room. Ellwood is offering drinks but nobody wants one. Batt is on the sideline, laughing with Never Walk Alone. Stage one is nearly complete. It's 34–26 at three-quarter time. Benoit Jett is in the front row, shaking his head every time Batt scores. You know who is the more impressive physical specimen out of Benoit Jett and Ryley Batt? Ryley Batt. Benoit Jett's eyes follow *no legs* around the court. There must be a chink and he's hell-bent on finding it. Maik Baumann gives Batt the stink eye. Stink eyes are less effective when you're being pummelled on the scoreboard. Baumann shrinks and disappears back into the weeds.

More quiet, please. The Gentleman Shane Brand is on. He picks up a bouncing ball in one smooth motion and holy crap, what about that! He punches a stray ball away. He cannot see where the ball has gone, fuck knows, but he has done well. There is more of the perfectionist in Batt than previously recognised. There have been times when he's appeared to be nothing more than a freewheeling kid who has a lash but now he looks like a wised-up and ambitious professional. The Gentleman grins broadly. Few things compare to seeing a good man succeeding in what the Dalai Lama believes to be the only worthwhile objective—the pursuit of happiness.

Batt hits Koeseoglu hard enough for his little German *feind* to dent the wooden floor. Dubberley gives Batt a rest with 40 seconds to go. He has bigger fish to fry than The German Pissheads. 'Fantastic, boys,' Batt says while undoing his straps. Nods all round. Bloody unreal. Batt grabs a drink and *consumes* it as Australia street away 47–36. Batt swings his arms, warming up more than down. The US have again videoed every second. They started filming from the sideline until the Australians told them to piss off upstairs. In Vancouver, behind his back, the Americans took to giving Batt a nickname—Cheeseburger. They believed the hype was unwarranted and that he was too unfit to dominate a major tournament. Cheeseburger, huh? You want fries with that? You want your arses kicked with that? Take your video camera and fuck off upstairs.

HUCKS: 'Awesome game. The first game, I tell you, it makes my guts churn. You just don't know if it's all going to come together until you actually get out there. The wait has been hard. Just a lot of down time in the village, sitting around waiting and mucking around, just stuck in the village looking at the clock. You say to yourself you're going to get going as soon as the games start, but you can't know that. You can never be sure. Losing to a team like Germany—it can happen. The amount of times we've had shit first games at tournaments, we just couldn't afford to do that here. I was by no means dismissing Germany. I thought they were a danger game. We struggled a bit to beat them in Canada even if it might have looked easy. It can take your best effort to get on top of them. Some of those guys have been playing as long as I have. They're no mugs, but we've just got that little bit extra in us with the dog and a few other things. We played good, but we need to step up a shitload tomorrow night. We still had a few lapses tonight but I reckon come the Kiwis tomorrow night, we are going to be massive. It's a great draw for us and not so good for GB and New Zealand. We've had one game to really get our shit together before we play the Kiwis and GB. I wouldn't have liked to play the Kiwis first off, or GB, because I know we can be a bit slow out of the blocks. It's pretty harsh for your first game to be the one that could decide if you make the play-offs. That's what GB and New Zealand have tonight. No warm-up games, no nothing—they know that if they lose, they could be gone. Germany was a proper contest for us without being too stressful in the end. They could have gotten us in a hole if we weren't on. That's the shit you don't want to deal with on the first night. I'm a very relieved man. We're in the thick of it, that's how it feels to me. At our best, we can win the bloody thing.'

HUCKS ON BATT: 'Dog did good. I reckon this tournament will be the making of him. At Athens, everything before then had come a little bit easily for him and Scotty. They cruised along. They're freaks in their fields, they're both such talented guys so it had come really fast for them but they know now that you have to work at it. Ryley—he's a bit older. Mentally, he's a lot stronger. There's just a different vibe about him. I can see it in his face. He's learned the game and the peripheral shit doesn't get to him like it used to. It's nice to be an old guy watching him. He comes off and I get my couple of minutes and then he can go back on and hopefully I've done my job. I want to be out there, don't worry about that. I want my minutes but I know he has to be out there for as long as possible. He was good tonight, very good, too good for them. He was bloody awesome. But now we've got a ball tearer—Australia and New Zealand, it doesn't get bigger for us anywhere, ever. It's a huge game whenever and wherever we play them—in one of our backyards, any tournament anywhere in the world, we want to kill each other. This is the Paralympics so it goes to a whole different scale again. We need to beat the bastards. That's the bottom line. They want what we want, a place in that top four. That's where we've got to get to, the top four, and then we're a chance. We'll try to give the people back home something to celebrate. I just think that, like it is every time we play against New Zealand, we are walking into an absolute shitfight.'

The Australians sit in the stands for the start of GB and the Kiwis, mingling with their own, all these people who love them and cannot look at them without wanting to wrap their arms around them. Dubberley's own are back in Australia, bombarding him with text messages. 'Got to step up against New Zealand,' he says. 'We have to get more physical. Put them on the floor. Ryles was a freight train tonight and for a team like us, a team that likes a bit of atmosphere, this is a great place to play. The feng shui is all us, mate. It's all us.'

~

There's a visit to Tiananmen Square, the large concrete block worn by China as the national badge of honour. There's The National Museum of China and The Chairman Mao Memorial Hall and The Monument To The People's Heroes where Mao's inscription reads 'Eternal Glory To The People's Heroes'. Across town to The Temple of Heaven. The Temple of Heaven! It's raining when you arrive but bathed in sunshine when you leave. Just a coincidence. During and after your visit, you're overwhelmed by this blissful sense of calm and happiness you cannot get rid of, no matter how hard you try. The gardens are as quiet as when they believed heaven was round and the earth was square. Lush grass is knee-high and the birds are singing. Red lanterns line the paths, decorated with bright white flowers. The Long Corridor is 350 metres by five. Seventy-two rooms shrink down the creepy hall. The walls are closing in. What is in those rooms? Perhaps it is better not to know. Choirs of serene old women. They throw red and yellow ribbons near the Animal-Killing Pavilion. They killed animals in heaven? Leaves line the walkways. There is music and light and there is always the light. The paths are made from marble and granite. People of faith step with conviction onto The Heavenly Centre Stone, weeping and praying for forgiveness or someone to hear their most desperate words of all. Two words on giant concrete slabs are emblazoned across the sky: HEAVEN AND GOD.

There are monuments to the mountains and seas. The Imperial Hall of Heaven has an extravagant triple-eaved roof with blue and yellow tiles symbolising Heaven, Earth and what sounds like the least appealing place of the lot, The Mortal World. Stone steps lead to the slaughterhouse where you can feel and see blood-drops the size of lakes. You can hear the chanting of the ancient world even if you don't know whether they really chanted at all. There are shrines to the gods of cloud, rain, wind and thunder. Memorials to the 4 a.m. marches to the sacrificial altar and 500-year-old trees and the belief that a whisper on Earth is like thunder in heaven.

Across town is The Forbidden City, the fortress with golden bricks and an inscription above an ancient Chinese emperor's throne: 'The way of heaven is profound and mysterious and the way of mankind is difficult.' You like that. The Forbidden City is home to The Palace of Heavenly Purity, the Hall of Preserved Harmony, The Gate of Heavenly Purity, The Gate of Divine Prowess, The Palace of Tranquil Longevity and the Mountain of Accumulated Elegance . . . The Gate of Divine Might, the Lodge of Spiritual Cultivation, The Palace of Earthly Honour, the Pavilion of Prolonging Splendour and what was originally The Hall Of Overwhelming Glory but is now the less stupendously named Hall of Central Harmony. The original name is up for grabs so that is why we have claimed it as our own, hanging the new name across the oak front door of what used to be a spiritually deserted old gym. Another giant tablet flares two more words across the sky: JUSTICE AND HONOUR. The gates to all this magnificence are not The East Gate and The West Gate but The Glorious East

Gate and The Glorious West Gate and all these prodigious buildings and magnificent marble stones of history and enlightenment fill your heart with hope and joy. You think of old friends. A woman stands on The Heavenly Centre Stone and cries, 'Can you hear me, o Lord?' The last sign at the exit of The Temple of Heaven reads 'WISH FOR ACHIEVEMENTS'.

The Brits exude anxiety from the moment they slink out to play the Kiwis. The problem with having such a meticulous and expensive plan is that it has to succeed. GB's confidence seems fragile as if the thread will unravel and snap as soon as things get tight. Their new coach is Tom O'Connor. He's a refined character, the dead opposite of his predecessor, Coach Joe. GB's support staff pile out of the grandstands, filling the court, blowing their whistles, looking at their stopwatches, carrying their clipboards. Any old village idiot can look important if he's carrying a clipboard. *If we stick to the plan, we will win.* More blind faith.

GB skip two points clear. Batt looks bored. Dubberley says, 'Extra time, this.' Benoit Jett craves a GB win. Canada fear their bogey teams, Australia and the Kiwis, but they do not fear the white-skinned Poms. What Benoit Jett would give for a semi-final against GB. The Poms move three goals clear before the difference is pegged back to one. GB flew from the blocks like they were shot haphazardly from a nine-millimetre semi-automatic but if the Kiwis lose, it's never by much. A revival is inevitable. Seriously, GB appear to have as many staff as Australia have players.

The Kiwis grind away but The Poms are more vibrant and red (the most dominant of colours). Union Jacks hang throughout The Hall of Overwhelming Glory. The eyes of The Herculean Jason Roberts flicker and you can see the capillaries, alert. You suspect he has waited a lifetime for these five nights. The English Rose is apprehensive. Dear thing. The Kiwis are dour. Their matches routinely descend into arm wrestles. Veneers of sweat on the top lip. They wait for a flinch and then—bam. Dour can be effective in the right circumstances. They have gold medals from Athens to prove it.

Tom O'Connor rises from his seat. He's as polite as the tea lady. Back in Canada, when there was a rush out the door of people wanting to get to the bus stop, O'Connor asked a flustered woman, 'May I give you a hand with your pram?' You could have sworn he was about to say ma'am. Coach Joe may have been less patient.

Dan Buckingham is the dreadlocked heart and soul of the Kiwis. Alan Ash, who bears a striking resemblance to Rowan Atkinson—not Mr Bean, Rowan Atkinson—is unable to stop him. The gap closes. The English Rose leans back in her chair. She's relaxed enough to be waiting on a martini at TGI Friday's. The GB captain is a tenacious little bulldog called Andrew Barrow. He crashes into the referee, who in turn crashes through an advertising hoarding. The female referee goes arse over tit. Is that offensive? Lighten up, squibs. Live a little.

GB are playing well, but they want it too much. As if they want someone to put them out of their misery and tell them right now where they're going to finish. There's no escaping the first flutterings of panic. Goals cause China-style relief more than unbridled renditions of Ode To Joy. But this is an excruciatingly tight match against the reigning gold medallists so they must be doing something right. Chinese spectators continue to watch with bemusement. As if they've landed in the African wilds just in time for the cheetah to start on the impala. They are curious, apprehensive, and they are not alone.

GB sneak two ahead but then fall one behind. The Kiwis are all sideburns, cold stares and black beer. They are full of *know*. Barrow yaps incessantly, trailing behind his big Rottweiler of a mate, The Herculean Jason Roberts. GB return to one-up with two minutes 24 seconds on the clock. The Kiwi coach turns his back to watch the closing scenes on the big screen. The view from the aerial camera is more revealing but down here on the court, it looks as though he's turned his back on his players. GB score again. O'Connor pumps his fist with typical English reserve. A greater assortment of personalities you have never encountered. The English Rose looks frightened. Be brave, beautiful. Roberts is on the floor, arms everywhere as his chair falls on top of him like a metal octopus.

GB lead by one goal with 30 seconds left. Stage fright brings a turnover. All the Kiwis have to do is run down the clock, score on the bell and keep pressing forward in overtime. They are the masters of set plays with all their *know* but Buckingham, of all people, the sole reason the Kiwis are so close, scores straightaway. No! It's too soon. GB celebrate more than the Kiwis. The scores are tied but Buckingham has given Great Britain 26 seconds to steal the win. Troy Collins seals the deal with 3.8 seconds left and Buckingham is mortified. He's blown it.

The Poms' execution has been precise and the master plan is working. Their celebrations blow the doors open. The English Rose claps politely. She pats Collins on his shoulder. Collins is chuffed. She has spent the evening waiting patiently for an opportunity that never came. Two male members of the GB staff give each other extravagant high-fives in the middle of the court and piss off, the two of you. Haven't you seen The Red Shirts? Do you want to be like *them*? Why can't the support staff from these other countries learn to pipe down? Ellwood never makes a scene. Bless. Benoit Jett is still watching. He's been here all day. He looked exhausted—about five hours ago. China's players hide around the back corridors of The Hall of Overwhelming Glory. It can't be much fun being an underachiever in The Middle Kingdom. GB have one foot in the semi-finals and they look like people on the first day of summer holidays, ahhh, but Buckingham rolls slowly, stops, rolls slowly again, shaking his head, blaming himself, *cursing* himself. He says there's only one thing for it now—annihilate Australia.

'After doing what I just did, I've got to man up. It's my fault we lost. I got the turnover and scored straightaway. I shouldn't have done it. There was a lot of time left. The line was there and I just panicked and scored. I should have taken my time and let the clock run. We should be in overtime right now. Credit to them. They were good. They were that switched on. We started throwing Hail Marys and those won't come off every time. We couldn't go with them like I thought we would. I really didn't think they would make it that hard for us. That Morrison is a big guy. He's got a lot of function for a 2.5.' In other words, Morrison shouldn't be a 2.5.

'We've just got to beat Australia now. We *have* to. We've played them seven times over the last two years. They've beaten us twice. It shows they can beat us on their day, but losing to them twice is two times too often as far as I'm concerned. We beat them convincingly at the Canada Cup but they'll be better for that loss, they'll be more dangerous. We know we can beat them again and I expect us to. I've got some buddies in that team, the players and the coach, but we have a huge rivalry and I expect us to be too good for them. As soon as we hit the pitch, there will be no holding back. It's the toughest pool, this one, and whoever doesn't get through, it's just going to be gut-wrenching for them. It won't be us if everything goes to plan but as you saw tonight, not everything goes to plan all the time. The worry for us is that Australia have the best player in the world right now. Ryley is just a phenomenal player and so hard to stop, but we've got to find a way to stop him. He demands at least two, if not three, players to be on him. When you've only got four on the court, that's a huge amount of attention being taken off their other players. Then at the other end of the court, he's also a huge defensive machine. We've done our homework on him and we've just got to go out tomorrow night and execute those plans. For whoever loses tomorrow night, it is just going to be gutting.'

Is the real China the tiny red love heart stuck to the pavement or the flood of Chinese flags along every congested road? The hagglers shoving passers-by and saying hello-T-shirt-you-want-T-shirt? The wide avenues and towering department stores of Wang Fu Jin Street or the phonebox-sized street stalls selling silk worms for dinner? The shuffling feet outside your room all through the night, the chugging pollution-belching car engines, the neon lights, the microwaves bristling and crackling like broken powerlines. The security cameras hidden in the trees? The wheelchair ramps on Silk Road or the fact they'll be torn down the day the show is over? Is the real China the drinks menu at The Drum and Bell where they say 'be quiet' when you start talking too loudly at one in the morning but gladly fill you with drinks called Orgasm and Sex On The Beach? Is it the polite ladies drawing sketches or the hookers in the lobbies of the five-star hotels? Is it the miniature rockets aimed at the skies to clear the pollution or the cheer-training classes? Is the real China the government instruction to stop spitting because foreigners don't like it, or all the spitting done anyway? Is it the Beijing Beauties Contest or the streets being swept clean of the homeless because they're unsightly? Is it the enforced physical removal of paupers and beggars from Tiananmen Square, or their inevitable return? Is it the 1250 winners of the Beauty Contest being assigned—after they have passed intrusive HIV and pregnancy tests—to walk the streets, looking glamorous, serving as escorts for the Paralympic VIPs, milling around those same high-end hotels and venues as the hookers, the line blurring between the two? Is it the volunteers being told they must be 'Messengers of Love' or the distraught girl kicked out of the Beauty Contest because at five-feet-five and 52 kilograms, she's too fat. Is the real China the luminous grass on The Olympic Green or the sign forbidding you from walking on it?

15

And on the sixth day

The villainous pigs in Orwell's *Animal Farm* are Napolean and Squealer. Before the US play The Assassin's Bullets, Gumbert tells his own versions of Napolean and Squealer, The Red Shirts: 'Every time Japan are on defence, let them hear you.' Hence the courtside histrionics of The Cretinous Red Shirts are proved to be a premeditated tactic from the Americans designed solely to distract the opposition. It has nothing to do with rising excitement levels or encouragement for their own players but everything to do with implementing a plan that goes beyond harmless gamesmanship to take up a position with deplorable sportsmanship.

Zuperman, Cohn and Wilmoth are inseparable. Wilmoth is *kind of* disabled. Good on him for letting it all hang out. He's not pretending to be anything he isn't. Jimmy Crack Corn And He Don't Care. It's not like he's one of those members of Spain's mentally disabled basketball team that won gold at the Special Olympics—with only two players who were mentally disabled. Their players were engineers or the holders of university degrees, fucking outrageous. What possible degree of satisfaction were they planning on getting? Wilmoth isn't cheating. He isn't hiding anything. If anyone has some questions to answer, it's the classifiers. But it just doesn't *look* right having him here. Nothing can change that perception. You imagine Porter, Carr and Batt rolling around together. They'd all be in their chairs—because they'd have to be. That's the difference.

The Assassin's Bullets were woeful against Canada and now they face the US, whose warm-up involves every player taking the ball over the goal line to get a taste of one-point nirvana. Gumbert has stopped being the straitlaced, white-coated professor and become the crazed scientist with his finger on the button of the world's most powerful bomb. The way he hunches over, tilted to the right while looking at everything from the corners of his eyes . . . he's not too flash physically but inside, you just know it, the man is as quick as a whip. America will incinerate Japan if they really are Led Zeppelin but their lead is a paltry three goals at quarter-time. Zuperman furrows his brow and that's a worrying sign because Zuperman would merely furrow his brow two seconds before being sliced in half by a train. The gigantic Sumo Nakazato yells at Zuperman as though he wants to eat him. Reputations can be con jobs. All those you fear, revere, abhor, adore—they're all flesh and blood. Japan keep hanging in; three down at half-time. They've come good. Imagine if they spring the upset to top them all. Kirkland is aggravated. Cohn shakes his head. Seriously, imagine if Japan beat the US tonight. And then if Canada beat the US tomorrow, they can fuck off back home and take The Red Shirts with them. Imagine The Red Shirts leaving The Valley Of The Blind with nothing to show for all their aggressiveness towards disabled athletes from other nations except a report card stamped FAILURE. They are less concerned with ONE WORLD and ONE DREAM than THEIR OWN WORLD and THEIR OWN DREAM.

Wilmoth on. Hammertime. His hands are taped so they arc perfectly across the tops of his wheels. They melt into the rubber as he bashes one Japanese player and then another. Sumo Nakazato is in his way but now Sumo is out of his way. Tropical Cyclone Wilmoth is on the warpath but *still* Japan hang in. Hogsett is all bitter and twisted and starts chewing his bottom lip.

The Japanese bench is becoming excited. They're in this. The Bullet Train Sinichi Shimakawa squints. Imagine, imagine. Nick Springer takes a tumble. The Bullet Train has the decency to inquire about his well-being. Kirkland is covered in so much silver tape he looks bionic. Japan have played countless competitive games this year and lost them all by two or three points. Maybe this will be the one they win. One of the few matches that really count. The Bullet Train slams down a goal like Occo Chino in the NFL. Japan are within two points inside the last quarter! F. Scott Fitzgerald reckons exclamation marks are no good because they're akin to laughing too loud at your own joke. But this ain't no joke. It's just a really surprising fact. Japan are within two! Their bench has a sly grin. Maybe after a year of near-misses, this is when Japan strike. Maybe The Assassin's Bullets have timed it all to perfection and they're peaking in the precise 32-minute timeframe when they're playing the world champions. Perhaps they have been foxing all along. Zuperman remains calm. Japan *still* only trail by two. The United States of America are not an invincible force. They are not. Say it enough and you might start believing it.

Nick Springer's arms are only just long enough to hit his wheels. You really could swear some of these blokes have been designed specifically for this sport. Ravaged by meningococcal, flesh and limbs torn apart and welded back together, important parts missing or messed up, they just fit. Rubbish, of course. But they've found their own niches. That's the key component of all this impossible-is-nothing stuff: the goal must be realistic. Nick Springer will never win Wimbledon, but he's found his own Wimbledon.

Japan maintain nuisance value, but when the pressure is on, the coolest US heads belong to Springer, Zuperman and Kirkland. A Red Shirt is so full of bile and venom that his head is going to explode; his blood and guts all over the court and the body-less head still yabbering on the halfway line. Japan flinch and the bullet whistles past its mark. Their muscles tire and weaken. Sumo needs an ice pack on his shoulder. Kirkland keeps chewing gum with his horse's mouth. The contribution of The Red Shirts has been a constant stream of YEAHs. Kirkland twice taps his chest. Captain Red Shirt moves in next to the players—go away! The value of his input has been nil, but he'll celebrate victory as if he's scored the match-winner with a miracle play in quadruple overtime. Ed Suhr remains a gentle man with silver hair.

Hiroyuki Misaka needs to be replaced. Japan need another Hiro. Too obvious a joke, smartarse? Japan rise again! They're back within two goals. The world champions really are beatable. The Assassin's Bullets fill the air, firing haphazardly, ricocheting off walls, swamping the court with razor-sharp spurts of American blood. Japan are the rats with golden teeth, sly and cunning. Springer becomes America's most invaluable contributor with a decidedly greater impact than Zuperman. Springer's poor excuses for arms can still catch the ball. They can still pass the ball. They can still whip him round the court like he's being delivered by slingshot. He single-handedly rescues the US as Kirkland continues chewing fistfuls of gum like a horse chomping on chaff. The US prevail to reach the semi-finals.

'Very tight game,' Gumbert says. 'You know, you've got the fastest team in the world out there. Shinichi, Shingo—I mean, I've coached Shinichi in my club side. He's one of the fastest guys in wheelchair rugby. You put that kind of speed out there and all you really have to do is get it in his hands. For us, it was a great challenge. We knew going in that a lot of people were already talking about our Canada game, but we knew we were playing a caged animal here. Japan were cornered and they were not going to give up. This was their chance to get to the medal round, and they did not give up on any play.'

To the seemingly innocuous suggestion that America are runaway favourites, Gumbert snaps: 'I disagree with that. There was a time when what you are saying was true. Maybe ten or fifteen years ago, there was a time when the US had a step or two on a few people. But a lot of past American players and coaches have taken a lot of the training tactics overseas with them [Coach Joe!], and those teams have gotten better and started taking this as seriously as we do. They started playing the sport recreationally in other countries, but they're full-time athletes now. The bar has been raised. For anyone to say we're higher up there than somebody else, in my view that's not right any more.'

Gumbert considers the pool of death.

'I'm torn about who will get through,' he says. 'To me, it could be any two of those three teams. Geremy Tinker for the Kiwis, I've coached him in my club side. I know Brad Dubberley and a few of the Australians. I've got players all over this gym who are like brothers and children to me. Any game could go any way in that other group. This next game will burn the barn, it really will. Australia and New Zealand—as a fan of this sport, that is the kind of match I stay back to see. New Zealand are fighting for their lives, the Aussies are fighting to prove they're here and they're ready. They weren't good at the Canada Cup but you have to understand this sport. A bad pass here, somebody gets a first goal or a last goal in a quarter that wasn't expected, it can change the whole dynamics of a tournament. Look at how New Zealand lost to GB last night. One-point games? Gimme a break. We have games where there are only two points in it, we land a couple of body blows and we're seven points ahead and we don't even know how the hell we got there. That can happen for you, or it can happen against you. Those three teams, they really are in a tough pool over there. A lot of people probably would have written off GB, looked at Australia and NZ and said you guys can go on through. But GB is not going to lie down and to have beaten New Zealand, that says it all. They have a lot of quality players who have played for a long time, and they're putting in a lot of resources. They're throwing money and players and staff into it. That's good for them, and it's good for the sport. They have never won a Paralympic medal and they are throwing everything at it, all the resources they can find. I'm going to go back to my bosses and say, "How can Great Britain be getting all this help and we're still amateur hour?"'

GUMBERT ON THE FREAKS: 'As a former player, when I saw my first not-quad, for want of a better word, I was like, wait a minute, what is he doing here? The first guy I saw was a quadruple amputee. He had no arms past his elbows and no legs below his knees. I looked at him and I was a low-pointer but I was like, "I'm going to chew this guy up." He was a lot like Nick Springer, and he came out and just made me look ordinary. I was like, "If that guy can come out here with the limitations he has, and he can do what he does, good on him." I think there's a place in the sport for people who are not quadriplegic. I don't make the rules. I play with what they give us. When they say this player is in, but this player is out, you do sometimes shake your head. You say, "Well, what's the difference?" They tell you one guy has more function than another guy and you have to take their word for it. I'm not a doctor. I trust the decision-makers to do their job and get it right. The good news is that we get to see the high-end of what an athlete is. Not a disabled athlete—an athlete. There will always be people pushing the envelope. I can't tell you how many people have come up to me and said, "I'm a T4 paraplegic and I want to play." They're right on the verge of being able to play but you have to tell them, "Sorry mate, you're not allowed. Your body is too good." They just look at you. "My body is too *what*?" Paraplegics are not allowed in. You break their heart. They look at somebody like a Ryley or our Joel and they're like, "How can this guy play and I can't?" There have been some classified in and classified out again, in and out. They're just on the fringe. I'm glad I don't have to make that decision. I've got enough problems without worrying about who is allowed to play. But I'm glad the sport has people like Ryley and our Joel in it. Ryley's got the experience and as much as that can sound cliched or whatever, it's a big deal. Joel is just nineteen, and so is Ryley, but Joel has only been playing the sport for two years. Ryley has got him on experience and good on him for that. But Joel is a quick learner. He's the perfect individual to have as a coach. If I tell him I need him to run through the wall, he'll run through the wall.' Problem being, of course, that he actually can try.

~

Dubberley compiles a secret document entitled Head On A Plate. It details the strengths and weaknesses of every opposition player in the tournament, revealing when they are likely to bounce the ball, and in which direction, when they will pass the ball, how they are going to do it, which hand they will do it with and to whom they're most likely to do it to. Who is most likely to crash and burn under sustained pressure and who likes to run their mouth. Which of the mouth-runners should be ignored and which can be unsettled if they're verbally engaged. Who can be controlled and who must be kept on a short leash. Dubberley's cheat sheet, distributed to his players in brown paper bags, or a group email, one or the other, highlights one man who must be contained at all costs. Australia's most ruthless and capable individual opponents are listed under headings ascribing the manner in which Dubberley wants them delivered to him at full-time: Head On A Plate. For New Zealand, it's Dan Buckingham.

'Big reacher,' Dubberley writes. 'The man on this team. Carries the ball well. Plays good defence. Gets away with a lot of reaches *and gets a lot of jumps*. Pushes hard and has great control. *We need to limit the amount of time he carries the ball*. Make his teammates do all the work. Bounces: Right is preferred. Best pass: Chest pass and one-handed (right hand). Best side: Either, has really good hands. Prefers to turn: Either side, but after inbounder, always behind. Biggest strength: Reach, good hands and speed.'

Dubberley sits quietly before tip-off. He's alone, and you leave him be. You know what? He doesn't want to be successful half as much as he wants his players to be. He will receive pats on the back from The Learned Gentlemen Of The Australian Paralympic Committee if Australia win a medal, but most of the raving enthusiasm will be reserved for the players. Fair enough, too fucking right. But if Australia bomb out, Dubberley's neck will be on the chopping block. All those times he's crawled across the carpet to point out his hunches on the widescreen television; all those times he's woken late at night with ideas and theories that might (or might not) work; all the time and effort he's poured into helping the eleven players at his feet get themselves a Paralympic medal . . . there's a lot riding on these results. Judgements will be made on Brad Dubberley by the same people in the corridors of power who decided it might be an idea to give him all of 30 minutes to take the job. Perhaps that was a masterstroke. Deny him the time to talk himself out of it. Pounce while he was still flattered by the offer. Perhaps The Learned Gentlemen Of The Australian Paralympic Committee know him better than he knows himself. Or perhaps he was too much of a loose cannon to start with. 'This game is as big as it gets for us,' he says as the Kiwis rumble onto the court like a convoy of trucks. Now they're as sullen and foreboding as the reaper hovering over the boy in Shit Creek.

Dubberley bursts with optimism. He's talking the talk, but the words of a coach can only go so far. Not everything has gone smoothly in camp.

'Part of our lead-up, working with Smithy, was to have these two big fitness sessions,' he says. 'There was no hitting involved. I wanted to put the brakes on that for a couple of days because I didn't want them playing against each other and maybe getting injured. So we had a session where everyone had to do full-on laps around the court for eight minutes, non-stop. One minute off, then another eight minutes the other way. Another minute off, another eight minutes back the other way. It was 24 minutes of flat-out pushing with three minutes' rest. That's hard work. Then we'd have relays. It wasn't just for the fitness. I wanted to see who was willing to fight through the pain barrier now we're here. I wanted to test them. We had some sooks. Seriously, we had some real sooks: "We shouldn't be doing this, we're only a couple of days out from playing, it's too much." But I didn't want us playing every day, hitting each other. I didn't want to risk someone getting hurt like George in Atlanta, or having everyone wrecking their gear. They were furious after that first session. Everyone was pissed off with me. The next day, we were getting a day off. I nearly changed our whole lead-in because of how they reacted to that one session. I nearly changed it so we had early morning training sessions for the rest of the week, just to rip into them. You want to sook? Let's train more. Anyway, we had the day off and the next session, the day after that, I took my chair along.

'It was the exact same training session that had pissed them all off. Twenty-four minutes of pushing, two minutes of rest. The first one had gone down so badly that I said, "Right, everyone is playing for minutes now. If you want to train and not sook and put in, you'll get minutes. If you want to sook about it, see you later, you can sit and watch everyone else play." That fitness session, I was hurting. But I wanted to make a point. I just wanted them to know I wasn't getting them to do this to be a prick. I wanted them to know I was willing to go through whatever pain they went through if it was going to help us succeed. It was the perfect time to do that kind of work. We still had a few days up our sleeves. We just needed one more big session. The only way I could do it was to go through the same routine.

'We were only into about two minutes of the first eight minutes and I was really struggling. But I did the three eight-minute pushes, all the relays. If I was doing it, they should be able to do it. I think they saw that. I hope it was a turning point for us. I was just testing them one last time. You can feel lazy when you have to wait too long to play. I think that's what happened at the Canada Cup and I wanted to snap us out of that. I wanted to give up on those laps—I honestly thought there was no way I was going to finish. But I wanted to stick with them. However much it was hurting, I wanted to make sure they knew that I was with them. That was the whole point. I didn't care if I was slower than them. Scotty and Cam and Ryles were lapping me, but it didn't matter. I just wanted to finish. George went and spewed after the second eight. He spewed his guts up then came back and wanted more. That, to us, was like, "Right, let's go." The team had the coach about to collapse on them, they had one of their really senior blokes putting in so much he was hurling, I think they saw they shouldn't be complaining, that they should be getting into it. I was proud of them. No-one sooked again after that. It was physical, but it was more of a mental thing. Get through this and then we can get out there and play.'

~

China is gazumped by the increasingly cocksure Canada. The Chinese coach with her rawhide face and military past concedes a medal will not be obtained and the immediate, albeit silent, response is, no shit, Sherlock. Erika Schmutz scores a goal. Having a woman score a goal in murderball at the Paralympics would seem a pretty decent way to batter a stereotype. Assuredness has descended upon the Canadians. A belief that was splintered by Batt at the Oceanias in the year his voice broke returned with their victory over the US in the Yellowhammer State, maintained under salmon-pink skies and reinforced here. Benoit Jett is relaxed enough to be wearing a T-shirt and goddamit, he's almost becoming likeable.

'We're definitely in the play-offs and that's a blast,' Willsie says. 'There is a bounce in our step, so to speak. We just can't wait to get out there with America again. We're so familiar. America hold no fears for us, Australia hold no fears. We play America tomorrow. I would say six of our guys play club rugby in the States, so we're teammates with a lot of those guys. When you get out there and play sport in your backyard with the kid from the other side of the fence, you always go harder against the guys you know better. They amp up for us too. I think we all feel that energy. It'll be insane. It'll be the same for the Kiwi–Aussie game. There was a surge in wheelchair rugby after the movie came out because of everything between us and the US, and Australia and NZ are getting that same kind of rivalry going in the Oceania region. All we need is a billion Chinamen to get behind rugby and we can take over the world.'

Round 2: Australia v. New Zealand

NEVER WALK ALONE: 'We struggle against the Kiwis. They've got quality in every points value. They have class players across the board, fantastic coverage. When you've got someone like Gerry Tinker, who's unbelievably fast, and someone like Tim Johnson, who's unbelievably smart, and then you've got someone like Jai White who just sets the best screens around, and then you've got Dan Buckingham, just a fantastically strong player—they're a huge team, filled with talent. There have been guys in Australian teams in the past who have always had this mental block about New Zealand because we knew they used to train a lot harder than us. So when you got in a tough game, we knew they'd done more work and would probably finish stronger than us. Some of our guys really had trouble getting over that but now we know we've done as much work as anyone. It's a mental battle against any team but for us, I think it's an especially big battle against the Kiwis.'

Willsie is in the front row: 'I would not lay one penny on who gets through this. The Kiwis are going to have a rough time because they lost last night. It doesn't matter what you say, coming off a loss like that isn't good. This pool, when we got here this week, I don't know who I would have picked. It's so tight, I still don't know.'

Dubberley is banned from standing up while coaching because the officials behind him cannot see. What an insight to this world that is. Those who want to run wild are chained, those who want to be free are trapped, those who want to speak out are told to shut up, those who should be giving are only prepared to take, someone who conjured up the minor miracle of walking again is told to sit down. How about this for an idea: getting the fucking officials to move. Whose job is more important here? Okay. The officials'. Actually, no. They haven't burned the midnight oil in preparation for this or retired as a player to coach a group of mates in the belief that being their coach is the best way to help them out. Boxall crunches his gloves together. Zipping energy fills The Great Hall.

The Kiwis' haka, their war dance, is intimidatory: facial contortions, the whites of eyes, the poking out of tongues, the thumping of chests, the deafening cries and grunts of tribalism, best referenced as 'a kind of symphony in which the different parts of the body represent many instruments. The hands, arms, legs, feet, voice, eyes, tongue and the body as a whole combine to express courage, annoyance, joy or other feelings relevant to the purpose of the occasion.' The purpose of this occasion is to reach the semi-finals of the Paralympic Games. Old Age and Treachery stares at the floor, not once looking up.

Buckingham, the Head On A Plate, starts for the Kiwis. He will be there at the end. Curtis Palmer can throw a pass cuter than your girlfriend's nose. He hits Batt on the back. *Thump*. Batt draws first blood—the tip-off. Palmer takes the ball off him, that's mine. Batt and Old Age and Treachery crunch him, Batt from the left and his elderly and more treacherous mate from the right. Collider scope. Palmer slumps forward as if he's been hit on either side of his head by the lids of two garbage cans. Batt gives a one-man demonstration of Ginsberg's Howl. He shoulders past Palmer. Turnover to Australia! Batt smiles like he knows everything. Turnover not converted. Batt stops smiling. When you think you know, you don't. The Kiwis triple-team Batt, leaving Old Age and Treachery free. Head On A Plate is so harassed by Batt he throws a panic-strewn pass towards Palmer. It goes bouncing away, head-high and loose. Old Age and Treachery and Palmer are steaming at the ball—and each other—as though they're playing chicken. They're driving head-first towards each other at full speed and the first to turn away is the chook and there can be no more idiotic game in existence than the real one played by hoons in cars. Old Age and Treachery has two hands on the ball. Palmer has half as many. The ball bobbles and stays with Old Age and Treachery. He swings left and chucks a two-handed pass into Batt's bread basket. Batt looks at Dubberley, again grinning. He's enjoying this. Palmer hits the deck. Old Age and Treachery is sprinting around like a hyperactive cattle dog, youth and skill rediscovered, the magic back in his eyes, adrenaline coursing from his big beating heart through radioactive veins like an administered drug, lights all going red to green, as abundant as he's ever been. Hucks bellows 'YEAH!' Yes, the exact same proclamation as The Red Shirts, but Hucks is allowed to. He's a player. Hucks is allowed to be out here in his underpants if he wants to be. This is all so crazed, so haphazard and intoxicatingly mad that it wouldn't come as a surprise.

Australia jump four ahead. It's the greatest possible start to one of the biggest possible matches. Boxall leans back in his chair as if he's found a banana lounge by the pool. Four-up—this'll do. Palmer is trapped in his own half. Dubberley is crowing, throwing his hands in the air in premature celebration. Batt and Head On A Plate are replaced. Hucks corners Palmer, but the Kiwis are inching back. Another arm wrestle. They keep pushing forward, forearms bulging, grimacing, still so full of so much *know*. It's 6–4 to Australia. On the far end of the court, right next to anyone sitting in purgatory, is an oversized Maori man sledging the Australians to within an inch of their remarkable and inspirational lives.

The Oversized Maori is wearing his hat backwards. It says, 'I'm From Earth'. He's yelling at Batt, who tries to ignore him, which only serves to make The Oversized Maori yell at him even more. Back to 6–all and there goes the dream start. The Kiwis have scored four straight goals and they have done so quietly, the murderballing ghouls, devoid of nerves. They rarely celebrate while they move around the court with barely a pulse. Palmer lashes out at Alman and goes to the bin. Batt is rushed back on as the scoreboard starts skewering. He stops Tim Johnson scoring with a wheelie right in front of him; a police car skidding to a sideways halt in front of a runaway stolen vehicle. Tim Johnson appears to be wearing Harry Potter's glasses. Palmer has the ball. Bounces it with his left hand. The Genius Nazim Erdem moseys on over for a look. Not getting into it, not getting out of it. What do we have here? *Click*. The sound of Erdem's chair connecting to a high-pointer is the click of a handgun at the temple of a criminal right before he invokes butchery and bloodshed. Erdem leans forward, staring at the ball all laser-eyed and waiting. Slap—he flicks the ball away. It rebounds off a Kiwi chair and vanishes over the sideline.

Scores stay level. At four-up, there were visions of assured medals and glorious semi-final appearances and maybe even a place in The Big Dance. Now there are stomach-tightening fears of coming third in the group and no big dance, then? The Oversized Maori is a Kiwi version of a Red Shirt. You want to tell him to shut his cake hole. You would like to crush him with your bare hands. The Rebel Scott Vitale cops the wrath of The Oversized Maori and returns fire with a who-the-fuck-are-you-my-patience-is-wearing-very-thin look, a steal and a goal. He turns to The Oversized Maori and offers another. The Oversized Maori continues to slander Vitale, but mainly Batt who does a yapping motion with his hands as if to say come on mate, keep talking.

Batt steams forward. Not fair that his legs *and* hands are poor. Given no legs, he should have been granted hands with every one of the 27 bones he's entitled to, a mechanically faultless carpus, a supple yet strong metacarpus, the appropriate number of digits to fill all the vacancies in his black gloves. He should have been given the hands of a goddamn concert pianist. Tinker Tailor Soldier Spy throws himself at Batt and crashes through the floor. Batt yells in the face of Palmer. Another turnover. Australia steal again and again: 11–8 up! Old Age and Treachery is about to score, but loses the ball. He's human after all. The Oversized Maori is providing a running one-sided commentary.

'Oh Ryley, you losin' it,' he keeps shouting.

'Ryley, what you doin', Ryley? You losing it, man.'

Tinker Tailor Soldier Spy is knocked to the ground for a third time. He recoils as if, using Ohm's Law (voltage = current × resistance), enough volts have been charged into his body to commence electrocution. Vitale has been responsible for flicking the switch. Tinker Tailor Soldier Spy is having an uncomfortable night. Batt calls a time-out one millisecond before he's forced over the sideline by Head On A Plate. He's right in front Gumbert who has started having serious words with The Oversized Maori—in all this noise, it's impossible to tell whose side Gumbert is taking but you have him pegged as a good man with respect and admiration for Batt, even if you also suspect he congratulates the Red Shirts for their high-volume input to each of the US's matches.

Never Walk Alone sneaks a goal when three Kiwis clot around Batt. Just one push, even when you're fucked. The Australian Captain looks relaxed and what a gift that is. Batt receives a favourable call from the referee. It is favourable because Tinker Tailor Soldier Spy has stolen the ball fair and square, but been penalised and sin-binned. The ball comes off Batt's chair and dribbles over the sideline. The referee awards Australia a reprieve. Tinker Tailor Soldier Spy has his arms outstretched; fucking *what*? His head is in his hands and there is so much more where that came from. Now he's looking at Batt as if they're in a confessional and he's waiting for Batt to squeal. What have you got to say for yourself then? Batt gives a look that suggests shit can occasionally happen. Old Age and Treachery keeps popping up where he's needed. Batt traps Head On A Plate and then his wing man, Vitale, chimes in with another hit, another jab to the ribs. They all count.

From The Oversized Maori: 'KEEP IT UP RYLEY! YOU DOIN' REAL GOOD RYLEY, DON'T BLOW IT NOW RYLEY!' You cannot tell if The Oversized Maori is disabled. If this buffoon is an able-bodied thug here for the sole purpose of hounding Batt, most likely under instructions from the Kiwis, shame on him. Three officials are sitting nearby. They say nothing.

The minutes whistle past and there can only be 32. Agonising tension. You want Australia to win with a desperation you have never previously felt at a sporting contest. You want The Oversized Maori to be silenced. You want one of the squeamish officials to turf him out by the ear. One of the officials is biting his nails.

Head On A Plate is sandwiched. Australia are muscling up. They are out-New-Zealanding the New Zealanders. Palmer is taken off. An ice vest goes on. A fan sits on his lap. Not a spectator, nor a groupie, nor an old coot, but an electrical fan attempting to cool the uncoolable quadriplegic. Not sweating, and the resulting high blood pressure, can bring upon a stroke as quickly as boosting. Two goals to Batt, double-clap. Australia lead by two and The Oversized Maori grimaces. He's running out of material. Short ball from Vitale to Batt, who drops it. He thumps the stray ball in anger. He's momentarily filthy but the moment passes. That is also a gift. Harry Potter sprays himself with cool water from a small plastic device you might water your plants with. The Kiwis are so match-hardened and so full of *know* that they score with four seconds left at the end of the first two quarters. That means they get the ball back after both breaks in an invaluable four-goal swing. Batt falls, does a handstand, flicks the chair from under him and sits upright again. It's fair to suggest from the cacophony now filling your ears that the old coots in the crowd are suitably impressed. In all seriousness, if this Maori man is able-bodied you will confront him outside The Hall Of Overwhelming Glory when all this is done and dusted. You will tell him his behaviour is appalling. Australia lead 17–16 at half-time.

The Oversized Maori keeps yelling his veiled insults—then laughing. It's like calling someone a dickhead and then when they take offence you say come on mate, don't be upset, I was only joking! Dickhead. A redheaded official turns around and tut-tuts. It is blatant verbal harassment of the Australian players from a spectator but it goes unchecked. Nice work by the redheaded official. Going tut-tut will do the trick. You're an official. You're supposed to do more than tut-tut then slink back in your chair like a scared child. You are supposed to *officiate*. Calm blue ocean, calm blue ocean. I want to kill him! Gumbert has been animated but as the minutes turn to seconds, even he becomes silent and begins to chew his nails. Batt goes to Sin City. 'YEAH RYLEY, HAVE A REST RYLEY, YOU NEED A REST RYLEY, YOU PUFFIN'.' You lean over to get a good look at The Oversized Maori. He sits in a normal seat as opposed to a wheelchair. A gargantuan man really is sledging a nineteen-year-old kid with virtually no legs and mangled hands and he's laughing about it? Vitale keeps shooting his dagger eyes at The Oversized Maori. The eyes are narrow like knife-slits. The Oversized Maori is starting to enjoy all the attention. The more he says, the more he is noticed. He clearly wants to be noticed. He becomes increasingly loud and obnoxious. Vitale looks at The Oversized Maori like Jesse James took his last glance at The Coward Robert Ford. You shouldn't go on about him like this but you will. You will go out of your way to see

The Oversized Maori after this, you really will. You will sarcastically offer congratulations on his behaviour. Just to see if there's even a flicker of recognition on his powerful face that he may have stepped out of line. You will be as condescending as possible which makes you no better than him, but it's the principle. One display of bone-headed disrespect deserves another.

The seconds are vanishing and the scores remain locked. These all-defining games once every bright blue moon—it's cruel, really. NZ go one-up. The stomach-knot tightens. Back to all-square. A release. The best Australia ever seem to get is all-square. NZ keep inbounding with looping passes for Head On A Plate to take awkwardly at full stretch over his head. These plays are fraught with danger, but Buckingham keeps pulling them off. You're on your feet, you're slouched in your chair, you're rejoicing, you're bemoaning, you're nauseous, delirious. For the first time in your life, you're not even sure you can actually stay and watch. Dubberley and all the Australians are good men. You do not want to see them disappointed. You honestly want to go outside and smoke your first packet of cigarettes since university and come back later tonight to ask the cleaner the score. You hang tight. The Hall Of Overwhelming Glory is noisy and chaotic and wild and confused and fucking magnificent. The beauty of sport. Maybe The Oversized Maori is adding to it.

Vitale is jolted and shunted. Batt doesn't know how to slow down, the kid on a skateboard with no brakes again. He scores and then he sends Old Age and Treachery over in another little trickle of goals. Batt reverses left, does a steeper left, right, a tight circle, hounds Palmer, follows the ball down court, prevents Harry Potter from scoring, hunts down Palmer, who looks up in horror the way people must do the instant before a fatal head-on.

Palmer drops the ball. Batt's mere presence is enough to provoke fear and panic. The recurring theme to all this is *don't panic*. There's a monster climbing through your bedroom window but do not panic. Tinker Tailor Soldier Spy is a Zuperman MK II. He looks like him and plays solid like him. Palmer gets a turnover off Old Age and Treachery and the Kiwis score. Tinker Tailor Soldier Spy appears to never make a mistake. Appearances can be deceiving. Vitale sees Tinker Tailor Soldier Spy hassling Batt and intervenes.

Head On A Plate pinches the ball out of Batt's tray—only to drop it, the ball disappearing like a tyre bounding down a hill until Batt catches it, pulls it against his right wheel and slides it around the turning rim until he has it in his hands. But he drops it again. He keeps chasing it, a two-handed pick-up this time about a millimetre inside the court. He yells time-out. He's shaking his head in self-admonishment but he has just displayed all the skills in the world. One thing Ryley Batt is unlikely to do: panic. He makes 30 centimetres look like an acreage.

Three Kiwis jump on him like the poor bastards working at the Silk Markets on commission with a grand total of five days off a year. The Oversized Maori is still wailing. Batt is on his stomach, sliding across the floor. Dubberley is calm in this maelstrom of anxiety. Back to 25–all. Such a torturous fucking process. Tinker Tailor Soldier Spy flares his nostrils, relishing the fight. For now. The poor bastard cannot see what is coming. The clock is counting down too fast and the Kiwis keep going one-up. One-up is all you need. One-up is as good as 100-up if the final buzzer is sounding. Australia need their last goal to come close enough to full-time to spark the electric chair of extra time and now another Oversized Maori has stuck his head in for a look. The Second Oversized Maori is quiet. He has a green aluminium leg and a brown sandal on the end of it. The Original Oversized Maori talks on a yellow mobile phone. In all deadly seriousness, if he leaves The Great Hall without so much as a limp . . .

It's 27–all. Head On A Plate comes on. So does Palmer. The big guns are wheeling out, the henchmen moving into position. Australia receive the ball with 1 minute 42 seconds remaining. We are into the last minute, the last 50 seconds, the last 40 seconds, and Australia still have the ball but they do not have the goal they need to reach their only hope—overtime. Shit. They run the clock down to 7.3 seconds. Batt is hanging back but then he gets the call from Dubberley: Go! As Batt rockets forward, Dubberley flies down the sideline at the same hectic pace as if they're attached by a rope at their waists. Playing leapfrog, playing leapfrog, they're only playing leapfrog. Batt scores with 7.3 seconds left. This is good and this is bad. Seven-point-three seconds is enough time for the Kiwis to get another goal, the ruthless bastards. Palmer gives the ball to Head On A Plate. Batt is trapped by three men in black. Eyes shoot to the clock. Adrenaline swells the stadium. There are 2.2 seconds remaining. Until three-quarter time. You cannot handle much more of this.

Batt fists the ball so hard it could burst.

The Kiwis lead 29–28.

STEELERS.

PUSH.

In eight minutes, Dubberley will know if Australia are into the medal round. In eight minutes, Australia will know if they've knocked the defending champions out of the Paralympic Games. Batt and Head On A Plate are trading blows like prize heavyweights when the ring is covered in blood and spit and the vampires in the crowd have turned on each other. They're punch-drunk, still throwing 'em because they know nothing else. The Kiwis are always one ahead. It's another frustration dream where you draw level to whatever you most want in this world, unattainable or not, so close you can almost touch and smell and *taste* it, but then you get forced back again. Batt is full throttle at the goal line, Batt stops at the three-man blockade, Batt peers into every nook and cranny and sees there is no way through. He retreats, charges again, retreats, charges. Still no way through. He circles like the murderer trying to find the open window at the side of your house. Head On A Plate insists on breaking free and scoring with Batt-like ease. One down, always one down. In all honesty, you feel doom and gloom. At even-stevens it's looking okay again but nothing more than okay. There is heated debate about the score because the board says 32–31 to Australia. That cannot be right. The Kiwis storm the scorer's table. The wrong is made right. Back to 32–31 to New Zealand. The Oversized Maori falls as quiet as his mate. Can we get another hallelujah? Christine Batt puts her hands to her face. All a bit much, really. She looks like the mother whose son is about to deliver the trickiest line in the school play; the one he's been stuffing up at home. It's exhausting when you care.

Dubberley mouths come on. It's too gripping for words, but they're all we have. Batt scores his umpteenth goal and now it's 32–32. Four minutes left on the clock. Batt is going down the right sideline. Head

On A Plate is trying to tip him over but Batt bumps him off with his hip. Batt goes to the bin again. 'HARD LUCK, RYLEY! GOOD TIMING, RYLEY! YOU'RE *REALLY* BLOWING IT NOW, RYLEY!' The Kiwis won the last Paralympics because they are a group of very fucking tough individuals. They stare straight ahead in those temple-busting moments when others flinch and turn away and make excuses. NZ are forced into a time-out at 35–all. They cannot break through the Australian defence. Defence reflects attitude. The atmosphere really is incredible. 'Great hustle,' Hucks bellows. The Australians are in their poker circle. Their arms are linked. Batt repeats one word, almost to himself: *Everything*. You're on the verge of tears. No idea why, every idea why. They're only playing leapfrog, they're only playing leapfrog, they're only playing leapfrog.

At 1 minute and 57 seconds: Batt is in the bin. Head On A Plate points at him, waving his index finger. Who is he to point?

1min45sec: Head On A Plate scores. NZ lead 36–35.

1min28sec: Batt storms out of the bin like a bull from a gate. He grabs the ball and barges from end to end. He slams home one point like he's slamming his fist on a table. 36–all.

1min16sec: Head On A Plate slams *his* fist on a table. 37–36.

1min2sec: Batt has the ball—and fumbles it. Jesus, sweet Jesus, get the damn ball. It falls straight back into Batt's tray. He sends a long arcing multicoloured rainbow of a pass to Vitale for a goal. 37–all.

50.7sec: The Kiwis are going to have the last play of the game. Harry Potter zips over and the Kiwis are up 38–37 and this is slip-sliding away.

38.2sec: Tinker Tailor Soldier Spy calls for the mechanics. They come on with two spare wheels. They look at his chair and do nothing. It's gamesmanship. Tinker Tailor Soldier Spy is halting Australia's attacking momentum so the Kiwis can reorganise their defence. When a player shouts at the referee that he has a mechanical failure, the referee must stop play immediately. Invariably the call comes from a player whose team is back-pedalling. With his team's defence reorganised, he usually turns around and says, well, can you believe it, I don't need help after all. Maybe this has been fair play from Tinker Tailor Soldier Spy. Or maybe he's due some bad karma. *Everything*. Just that one word from Ryley Batt. *Everything*. The Genius Nazim Erdem has the ball. Australia cannot score yet. It's too soon.

37sec: The Genius having the ball is not ideal. Still 38–37 to the Kiwis. The Great Hall is ablaze.

34sec: Alman has the opportunity to score, but he's brave enough to turn his back. Just one mistake and it's all over. Just one bad pass, one brain snap.

30sec: Alman to Vitale. The Kiwis throw themselves at him, devouring him, *craving* him. They're everywhere, screeching bats.

28sec: Batt is surrounded. The ball goes to Alman, calm, bouncing anxiously three times, calm, thump-thump-thump, calm, a dangerous but necessary pass, calm enough.

18sec: DON'T PANIC.

16sec: Batt.

13sec: He's cornered again. Thirteen seconds! And still one goal down. Palmer is so worried about Batt that he forgets about Vitale going where he's not supposed to be going, doing what he's not supposed to be doing, slipping down the blind side like a ghost, do you see? Every fibre of Dubberley's being tells him to instruct the Australians to score as fast as they fucking can—but it's still too soon. They must exercise the ultimate restraint, waiting, waiting, waiting, then score.

10sec: Batt is surrounded as the clock rips into its LAST TEN SECONDS and it's soon going to be nine and then eight and the grim reaper is standing above Dubberley and why do you always think about the grim reaper and it's about to be over and then Vitale backs up his mate Ryley Batt with a goal that makes your heart burst from your chest and start throbbing right there on the sideline. Every set of bulging eyes in The Hall Of Overwhelming Glory lurches to the clock and it spits out a number: 5.9. There are 5.9 seconds remaining. You are in no fit state. Vitale goal!

5.9sec: Who cares if Vitale wants to wear a cap to dinner? Who fucking cares if he doesn't want to paint his Dunlop Volleys? Vitale goal! 38–all. Harry Potter picks Vitale's chair before the Australian has two wheels back on the court. Vitale lodges the appropriate verbal application for the removal of Harry Potter from his face. *Piss off*.

Vitale had to score when he did. Ideally the goal would have come three seconds later, but that would've been cutting it too fine. The goal might not have come at all. Still, the Kiwis can win. Under normal circumstances, 5.9 seconds is plenty of time. But these are not normal circumstances. Vitale goal! Exclamation mark! F. Scott can get stuffed! That was fucking brilliant. Just 5.9 seconds of defence and Australia are into extra time. Get there, just get to extra time. The Kiwis will wonder why the fight is still going. Australia are bruised and bloodied but they have stayed on their feet. Down, level-pegging. Down again, level-pegging again and two-down would have killed them off, but they've hung in there. There really is everything in the whole wide world to be said for hanging in there. Hold the Paralympic champions for 5.9 seconds and another three minutes will go on the clock and the slate will be wiped clean. Australia could win the tip-off and luxuriate in one-ups, and thanks very much for coming and DEFENCE. DEFENCE. For fuck's sake, defend like fucking ANZACs. Hucks, uncharacteristically quietly, says, 'Hustle.' People are never more serious than when they whisper.

Tinker Tailor Soldier Spy has the inbound.

Batt takes out Harry Potter.

And.

Then.

The.

Fucking.

Ball.

Goes.

Bouncing.

Over.

The.

Fucking.

Sideline.

One bounce, two bounces, three, four, five, six . . . Turnover! Turnover! Turnover! Turnover to Australia! The left side of the clock is paralysed at 5.9 seconds. Tinker Tailor Soldier Spy has managed to throw a pass that evades every other player on the court. The ball hasn't been touched, so the clock hasn't restarted. Turnover! Turnover! Turnover to Australia!

Ryley Batt has the game in his hands. His mother is watching and you think about her, you really do, and the day Ryley turned four and couldn't work out why his legs hadn't grown overnight. Batt and Harry Potter sit back-to-back like they're at the OK Coral and the only resolution to all this can come from a shoot-out at ten pushes. Turn, shoot, kill. Alman passes the ball to Batt, the pass going from one heaving chest to another. The clock restarts. It will stop again in all it takes for anything to happen, the blinking of an eye.

Five . . .

Nazim Erdem has Head On A Plate covered. Genius, that. Just one second of running interference—pure fucking genius.

Four . . .

Batt goes left and then he goes right and where The Damned Hell is he going. He bumps off the newly freed Head On A Plate. It's their last contact for the evening. Goodnight.

Three . . .

Batt arrives in the key like a train powering through a far-flung country station. He puts his head down.

Two . . .

Batt tilts to the left and straightens.

1.8 . . .

He's clear. The mad bastard is clear. He's looped from one side of the court to the other, hurtling along right in front of the grandstand where his mother still sits. The only thing that can stop Batt now is the clock. Two wheels must be over the line for the goal to count. Dubberley leans forward. Batt's head comes up. He sees the red corner post, the key blurring past, and then he sees the goal line. He springs up and into his turn. You imagine him bending his knees. There are nine-hundredths of a second remaining and Batt has still gone no farther than mid-key. With seven-hundredths of a second left, less time than it will take you to read this long-winded sentence, he will still only be halfway through the key. The Genius Nazim Erdem cranes his neck to see over Vitale. You won't remember the goals, Naz? Really? At four-hundredths of a second, Batt is an inch away. Dubberley crouches. Push, mate. Keep pushing. Batt blasts over the line and there are three-hundredths of a second on the clock and Australia have won and it's Ryley Batt and it's game over and it's Ryley Batt looking at the clock and the referee and he bolts to the sideline and the first man to cannon into him is Hucks. They hug like the magnificent bastards they are. Never Walk Alone grabs Batt, The Gentleman Shane Brand joins in, Boxall is going off his head like he's never gone off his head before. The Australians pile in, reaching out for each other, touching fingertips, holding their faces in their hands, ruffling hair while their wheelchairs keep them separated. Batt wraps his arms around Dubberley. He punches the air. His head drops and he exhales. He might need a moment. He applauds the crowd, shakes his head, laughs and thanks The Oversized Maori for his input. He looks as if this is the single greatest moment of his life.

'It is,' he says.

Australia have beaten New Zealand by one goal. Dubberley's men are into the semi-finals. Pardon the language here and elsewhere in this expletive-laden book, but they have fucking won. Australia were 5.9 seconds from oblivion. No matter what happens against GB tomorrow night, their last game will be for a medal. Perhaps it will be for a bronze. Or perhaps it will be for gold. They have reached the last four in the most spectacular possible circumstances under the dome-shaped roof of The Hall Of Overwhelming Glory. Inbound goes askew! Goal to Ryley Batt! They have won. They really have won.

DUBBERLEY: 'I don't know what to say. I'm shaking. Ryley is going to get all the praise and he deserves it but Smithy, Naz, Scotty, the lot of them, they did so many good things. That was an amazing game. I thought we could win in overtime if we got there. The Super Series and a few other places, we've gotten ourselves a good record in overtime matches, and I thought the Kiwis were getting worn out. We had Ryley, we had Scotty out there going great, so at the worst I thought we'd lose by a point and have to beat GB by two tomorrow. I believe we could have done that anyway. Sometimes you need to back yourself and the boys did it. Phenomenal. I knew Ryles was going to get there. Even when there was a second to go, and he had people to beat, I just knew he would get there. He stepped up. This is his moment. He's killed them. I can support him and give him some advice here and there, but he's the one who has to go out and actually do it. Incredible.

'The Kiwis looked after their game, we looked after ours. They wouldn't feel bad about knocking us out so I'm not going to feel bad for them. But at the same time, you think, poor bastards. For two nights straight they've lost by one point. Both of them with the same score, and both of them in the last couple of seconds. A lot of those guys are like brothers to me, so it's hard to see them have to go through it. Dan, Gerry, Curtis, all the boys. Even the coach, you know. It's hard for them to go through this but at the same time, it's a competitive sport and they were here chasing the same thing we are. Ryley is the best player in the game but he can't do it all. Cam stepped up tonight, Scotty played awesome, Bryce played awesome. Scotty has had some injuries and sickness since he's been here, but he's still doing what he has to do. We had to give Ryley a breather in that last quarter. He was worn out but he was coming up to me going, "Let me on, Braddy, let me on, mate. I want another run".'

THE INVALUABLE CAMERON CARR: 'Who made the mistake for them? Tinker? It wasn't Klinkhammer? I don't care. I'm just glad it happened. I don't feel sorry for them. You got a photo of it? I'll put it on my chair the next time we play them. The worst thing in wheelchair sport, maybe every sport, is that once you get a bad result you know the funding is going to be cut off. It's going to be so much harder for them to get back up to the level they were at. They've had this really tight group of seven or eight players who have been around for a while, and they've always seemed to come up with a medal at the Paralympics and the world championships. For them to miss out on the top four, it's a bit of a kick in the arse for them. Two losses by one point. That's what happened to us in Canada. But it happened in Canada, not China, and who cares about Canada now?'

BATT: 'The nerves were ridiculous. Thankfully it came our way at the end. I was hurting that much, I didn't think I could continue that last quarter. It just comes down to heart. The whole team just backed each other up. To get that last goal with zero seconds on the clock—they got too carried away with trying to get that last goal themselves. They normally wouldn't stuff it up like that. It was just the pressure we were putting on them, I think. I feel for them, but

I'm glad it's not us. I saw the ball go out and I was like, "Here we go, we can take this down right now." Any day we get a win over the Kiwis, we'll take it. I was thinking about Athens just then, how it was my first Paralympics and how different it all felt. We came fifth and I was devastated by that, but now we're guaranteed at least fourth. At the worst we'll have improved on what we did before. And we've got a three out of four chance of getting a medal. It's a great feeling as a teenager, I can tell you that.

'What a day. I was really nervous before we started. I had a bit of a headache and stuff, just really nervous, but as soon as I got out on the court the nerves settled. There were a couple of scrappy things by me, but everyone backed me up, the whole team played awesome. It's just great to be in this Australian team. I can't even really remember what happened at the end there, we got the turnover and—you kind of stop thinking. It's weird. It's like something else takes over your body and you just do what you have to do. Incredible game. The best game I've ever played in.'

For now.

'Yeah those two big guys on the sideline,' he says. 'The whole time, one of them was like, "Come on Ryley, come on Ryley, don't muck it up Ryley." I could hear it, and it sort of annoyed me, but it helped me in a way. It fires you up but it does annoy you at the same time—I don't know, you'd rather not have that. I was trying to block it out as much as I could. After the game I was like, "Thanks boys, thanks for coming, thanks for firing me up, hope you enjoyed the game." It got a bit much for a while there but it's over now. I thought the ref was going to say something. I was hoping he would.'

The Ref: 'No comment.'

Why can't you comment?

The Ref: 'I just can't comment.'

No more revealing comment could have been supplied.

OLD AGE AND TREACHERY: 'Their lack of depth hurt them. Look at them—they're shattered. We toughed out a great game. That's a really great result for us. They're a great competitor, New Zealand, so it's a massive achievement. Unreal, unreal. We knew they were going to fight hard and keep coming at us. We just kept saying it was quarter by quarter. I'll tell you what, the pressure is a lot higher in a team sport. In an individual sport, if you lose, you only have to worry about yourself. But I can't just think about myself here. I was getting pretty tired towards the end so I subbed myself off for the last quarter. We had fresh blood ready to go off the bench. The pressure on the sideline is just incredible. When you're out there, moving around and doing stuff, you don't worry too much about what the score is and how much time is left. You're aware it must be getting near the end, then you look up and it's over. But on the bench, five seconds feels like an hour. I was nervous, really nervous, but you just have to trust your teammates. That's been one of the hardest things for me, coming from an individual sport. You have to rely on your teammates and trust them, and I know I can do that now.

'Six seconds left—for them to throw away a ball like that, they will stew on that ball for the next four years. That's the pass that put them out. They've lost two games by one goal and they're gone. That's harsh. But look, they're a team renowned for their control and patience, and the way we pressured them long enough to get a mistake says a lot about us as a team. You've just got to fight it out right till the end, that's the name of the game, and when you've got a guy like Ryley on your team, you can get goals in one or two seconds if you have to. He takes off with amazing pace and he's gone. He's a machine. His work ethic in a game is unsurpassed. The poor bugger, there's always double or triple teams on him. He's got to bust through those and it's exhausting for him. He's our main ball carrier and he's our biggest defender. We know, whenever we can, we've just got to get the ball to Ryley. Just with his speed and strength, he can get guys out of trouble when they're in it. He can screen to get scores for the rest of us; he scores a few himself, and then he gets back to defend in the transition from attack. We just have to keep trying to give him all the cover and support he needs. It's what we did really well back at the Oceanias and it's what we're doing really well here. We're two from two. If we can get a couple more up . . .'

The most regrettable aspect of any meaningful sporting contest is the unavoidable presence of a loser. While the winners swallow their invisible ecstasy pills and look every inch like they could drop dead on the spot and it would no longer matter because they have tasted genuine euphoria at least once in this lifetime, the losers can do nothing except watch with ashen faces and wish it was them. The joy of victory is only so great because defeat feels so rotten. Joy is nothing without despair. Good is meaningless without bad. Wealth-poverty, love-hate, relief-fear, hope-despair, acceptance-abandonment, *acceptance-abandonment,* life-death, suffocation-breath, *suffocation-breath,* truth-deceit, pleasure-pain, justice-injustice, salvation-damnation. Heaven would be nothing without the rancid stench of Hell. One needs the other or both cease to exist. The Australians have taken themselves beyond the point of exhaustion for this moment. You will honestly never forget it for as long as you live and beyond. At times this year you have looked at Dubberley with his mind overflowing with murderball and dreams of The Big Dance and secretly you have thought, mate, why do you bother? This is why he has bothered. Now is why he has bothered. Anything is possible when you can be bothered.

Head On A Plate pushes himself off the court with defeated arms. He looks every bit as gutted as he promised to be. The Kiwis have no interest in play-offs for fifth. The quadriplegic Buckingham was only one twist away from bringing down an Australian megastar whose brain is lucky enough to be on speaking terms with the rest of his sawn-off body. Australia have won and the poor heartbroken Kiwis are quiet and morose and miserable as sin; disbelieving and inconsolable and shot.

'Can't talk tonight,' slurs Head On A Plate. 'There is nothing I can say.'

Dubberley has been true to his word about ordering his players to attack regardless of circumstances. It was easy to be brave with the really small dog at his feet, but it's been another thing to actually do it with too few seconds remaining against the masters of a slow burn. Throughout this epic, Dubberley has told Australia to operate at full ramming speed. To score goals as soon as they became available. Ryley Batt has heeded the call and Australia have made the play-offs with the US, Canada and Great Britain. 'Just took a few gambles,' Dubberley says. He pulls up his shirt and shows the picture on the front of his belt buckle. It's a pair of dice. Double sixes.

~

Halten sie das Telefon. The Mohawked Homunculus, Sali Koeseoglu, is a one-man firestorm and The German Pissheads are leading Great Britain at quarter time. Buckingham and the Kiwis are back in the frame if GB lose. The Mohawked Homunculus has even more stubble and an even more grandiose fuck-you demeanour than last night. He's taunting GB and goading them and annoying them like a hobo with his back up. He's dirty and doesn't care any more. People are never more dangerous than when they've given up. Great Britain lead 22–20 at half-time and The English Rose screeches. Don't raise your voice, dear. It is not becoming. Internet surfing is conducted during the break. A train collision in Los Angeles has left fifteen people dead. But here's what you're really looking for: a memorial web page for Ed Suhr's brother. Each time the page has a visitor, a flower is added to prove someone has remembered him. Flowers abound. Ed Suhr's brother died at the age of 37. One dedication reads: 'Danny, I came across your name in the book *Report from Ground Zero* and your story inspires me. We are about the same age, but I live in a small town in Idaho. I thank you for your sacrifice in protecting our nation and helping our fellow citizens. God will bless you and your family for your heroic part in this devastating event. Until we meet in his heavens, Robert.' Another unsigned tribute states: 'I honour, envy and truly respect you. Rest well, my brother.' No name is attached to the last dedication and you wonder if it has been written by Ed Suhr. England defeat The German Pissheads.

~

The enduring image of a momentous evening isn't of Batt scoring the match-winner. It's very nearly been of a motionless Ryan Scott staring at the luminescent lights across the roof of The Great Hall with an epiphanic oh-my-God expression—an almost blank, disbelieving realisation that such an enchanted moment can actually exist. It's very nearly been of George Hucks travelling at the speed of light to be the first player to ram into his young bull of a mate and congratulate him and thank him and pour rivers of feng shui over him. The most enduring image isn't even the supernova of pleasure that exploded across Dubberley's face when he saw the narrow gap available to Batt and he knew, he just knew, what came next. It isn't even the wonderfully restrained clapping of a tear-filled Christine Batt or the look she was giving Ryley, and he was giving her, when they stared up and down at each other from the court and the grandstand and when for one sweet moment a vacuum sucked away every other person and all the noise and it was just the two of them sharing the kind of cosmic glance two people give when they know exactly what the other is thinking, and why they're thinking it, and for how long they've always thought it, their faces and hearts swelling through their shared connection to some previously untapped source of mutual understanding. It isn't the outbreak of blissfully tremulous joy on the face of Ellwood, good old Kim Ellwood, as she stood back with dignity and humility to let her boys enjoy their revelry without her. No, the everlasting image of a momentous evening comes long after the band has stopped playing.

Bradley Wayne Dubberley and Ryley Douglas Blythman Batt are slowly making their way down a dimly lit corridor deep inside The Hall Of Overwhelming Glory. They are alone and they are quiet as they enter the darkness with Batt in his wheelchair and Dubberley on his sad songs of legs. What a sight this is, what an unforgettable and permanently heart-rending sight this will always be, one man who taught himself to walk when no-one thought he would, and another man who is only so high and mighty in his wheelchair because the first man put him in it. Bradley Wayne Dubberley puts his left hand on the right shoulder of Ryley Douglas Blythman Batt.

'Ryles,' he says.

Batt looks up at him.

'Yes, mate?'

'Ryles,' Dubberley says again. 'Well done, mate.'

These are the moments that make a moment worth living.

16

And on the seventh day

The Great Hall is empty. Soft jazz runs through the bleachers like the beginning of a flood. The cleaner walks across the freshly polished floor and her sandshoes squeak. It will not stay this quiet for long. You close your eyes and you can still see Batt's goal from last night. Australia now play GB, confirmed to be an efficient band churning out results without having an artist drunk on his talent and life like The Rolling Stones when Mick Jagger did 'No Satisfaction' with the Union Jack as his cape and Keith Richards clobbering fans over the head with his guitar. The music becomes the children's choir who lit up the opening ceremony when their voices swam through your skin in opaque and concentric circles. Being inside The Great Hall right now is like watching the most beautiful girl you've ever seen when she's asleep. You're stroking her hair and whispering how you love her but she cannot hear you. You'll be too shy to repeat it when she wakes and so she will never really know. The doors fly open and people pour inside The Great Hall and you lose her to everyone else. Rebel-rousers fill the place like the ever-present Hells Angels overtaking a previously quiet downtown bar. The cleaner says every result is in God's hands so let's not waste our precious time trying to make predictions. She has no interest in small talk or big talk or any kind of talk. It is all in God's hands, she says again, and she gives your desk a light dusting.

Australia versus Great Britain will come after the US tackle Canada in two fixtures of the utmost significance. The Herculean Jason Roberts will approach his modern-day *Voyage to Terra Australis* with the obligatory amount of gusto because up for grabs are the all-important seedings for the semi-finals. The winners of each pool will tackle the second-place team from the opposing pool so if the convicts, with Dubberley hobbling around as if an invisible ball and chain really is holding him back, spear GB and then the US defeat Canada, Australia will be rewarded with a game against a team deep-down they *know* they can beat—Benoit Jett's Canada featuring DJ Curmudgeonly Whitehead—for a place in The Big Dance. Judgement days are coming fast and Gumbert says: 'I'm not going to have to say anything special to get my boys fired up. They'll be ready. The hardest thing in these games is making sure we're not too fired up. We know what we are playing for. If we can't come out and play our high game, we have no business here.'

GB CAPTAIN ANDREW BARROW: 'We're very happy to be in the last four. But the fact remains we've only played two games out of five. I'm not entirely happy with how we played against Germany, and I don't think the team is either. But a win is a win at a Paralympic Games, we won by five, so there's nothing to get too worried about. Everyone says this is the group of death and it is. Ourselves, Australia and New Zealand—any of those teams could have won the tournament. But now New Zealand are out of it, we want to top the pool. With the best respects to Japan, China and Germany, we identified five teams that could definitely win it. Our pool had three of them, so we've dodged the first bullet. We want to consolidate and beat the Aussies and get the favourable draw for the semi-final. There's still a lot at stake. There's still the rivalry you always get between our countries, to start with. If you had to pick a favourite at this point it would be the US and whoever wins tonight, they can avoid the favourites until the gold medal match. That's massive. I saw the States against Japan, and it looked to me like they wobbled. We had our wobble against Germany and maybe they had theirs against Japan. Right now, though, happy days. We're through, but we want to get through on top. There are friendships between these two teams, but once we get on the court, that stops. The Aussies are a nice group of people, but when we step across that line, we want to hurt them.'

BARROW ON BATT: 'Phenomenal player. Trunk kills it in this game. You've got trunk muscles and you're going to be tough. He's got all his abdominal muscles, so he can turn faster and with more control than the rest of us. But I love it. This is international sport. We get a slap off someone like Ryley, we're all big boys and girls in this game and we love it. I love the big hits, the public love the big hits, the superstars deserve their place in the game. They might be superstars because they're superstars functionally, but who cares? They have made their national teams, and they have every right to be out here representing their countries. We believe that when Ryley is on the court, there aren't many other points around him. That's a start for us. That has to put pressure on him. He's only a young lad. He's a big unit as well, but we think we can run him out of steam. He's a big boy for Australia but Jason Roberts is a big boy for us.'

The Herculean Jason Roberts wheels past. 'Here he is,' Barrow says like the fight night promoter with his golden microphone dangling from the roof. 'Jason Roberts, king of the low-pointers right here. That's the man Ryley Batt is not going to enjoy seeing. But he's someone Ryley is going to see a lot of. We believe that Australia are a very good side with one leading light. We are going to shut that light out.'

~

Is the real China when Chairman Mao stood on the Steps of The Forbidden City in 1966 and ordered The Cultural Revolution? All links to the past would be eradicated. All men and women practising ancient traditions would be murdered by the Red Guards. One bow-maker snapped his last creation in half. He hid it in a pile of wood. The Red Guards stormed his house. If they saw his bow, he would die. The Cultural Revolution took a decade to fade. It was another two decades before the man felt safe enough to retrieve his bow, put it back together and ask his father to teach him how to make more. He says there is nothing more joyous than fitting the string to the beautiful, beautiful bow. He says maintaining the tradition of bow-making has little to do with bows because they're irrelevant in the modern world. He says bow-making is devoted to an extension of Chinese history, cultivating a legacy that cannot be allowed to die. Is that the real China?

~

Batt is exhausted. He's quiet, too, as if pondering the universe in the Celestial Gardens. Ed Suhr is having trouble with his bottle of drink. His hands are permanently stiff. He has to put the plastic lid in his mouth and twist it but that doesn't work. Come the end of the game, Ed Suhr's bottle of drink will remain untouched and on the floor. For the ghostly Ed Suhr, just taking a swig from a bottle is in the too-hard basket. All your troubles are light and temporary. Gumbert sits next to him, analysing and scrutinising. He's more fascinating by the minute. Music to make the soul sing. Music is the single greatest thing we have. The Herculean Jason Roberts has gone from looking like The Wild Man of Borneo to someone less formidable. He's shaved his head and looks nothing like the tyrant of days gone by. 'Had to get rid of it,' he says. 'No choice. It's too hot for me in here.' Hucks's undecorated skull looks fearsome but The Herculean Jason Roberts looks smaller and lighter without his Sampson-like locks. He's more of a timid schoolboy than a rough-house murderballer, the chemotherapy patient. Ross Morrison has the temerity to win the tip-off from an initially sluggish Ryley Batt.

The Herculean Jason Roberts is supposed to hound Batt, but the sizeable problem for Roberts is that he's being hounded by Old Age and Treachery. Batt begins in second gear, cruising, not doing much apart from scoring every goal. That's all. Batt can look disinterested early, but in truth he's pacing himself for the mad scramble to come. The Herculean Jason Roberts exhales deeply like a man who has agreed to a task believing it to be a piece of cake—only to stand at the foot of Everest and see the climb is beyond him. Batt wipes Collins along the floor with all the dust and sweat. Springer and Zuperman watch Batt instead of the game. To a degree, despite his protestations, he *is* the game. If Batt has a blinder, Australia can beat anyone. If he has less than a blinder, nothing's guaranteed. Steve Palmer, the poor man's Curtis Palmer, snags Batt as if there's a large meat hook on the end of his chair. Batt lurches around but cannot break free. The Poor Man's Curtis Palmer has the distinct advantage of being a redhead. Feisty souls, redheads. And nearly extinct. A trio of Englishmen jump on Batt. One of them is a redhead. Another is a brunette and another has no hair at all. Batt hurls the ball downtown because *someone* is bound to be free and it's Old Age and Treachery. Australia's goals come quick and automatic while GB's are slow and painstaking. Haunting defence forces GB into the moral defeat of time-outs. Old Age and Treachery grimaces but keeps pushing anyway.

With hair, Samson ripped apart an Asiatic Lion with his bare hands. With hair, he slaughtered the Philistines, smiting them hip and thigh. Without hair he was captured, imprisoned and had his eyes burnt out with a red-hot poker. The Herculean Jason Roberts's powers have been diminished to an identical extent and Australia gouge GB 43–37 to top the pool.

DUBBERLEY: 'It's a bit of a funny feeling. We've been on the rollercoaster ride. Last night was a high but today was very quiet all day. We were happy and confident, and we knew that once we got in the chairs, we'd fire up. We just knew we were going to be fine. They're another great team but for us to come out and perform like that, it's a beautiful thing. We're pretty confident about the semi-final now. It'll be another tough game against another tough team but we can do it. We can do this.'

THE HERCULEAN JASON ROBERTS: 'No sweat, losing. Whatever happened today, we're still in the semis. We're a bit disappointed but believe me, we're ready for the semi-finals. We're going to make the final anyway. That's our job and that's what we're here for. I am totally confident about that. It's our time.'

The US down Canada 37–32 in a match failing to reach any great heights. The four semi-finalists have been in third gear but they're about to roar their engines like a fleet of 747s. Australia have the semi-final they wanted against Lavoie, Willsie and Whitehead.

DUBBERLEY: 'Canada had a full-on hit-out with America, like they normally do, but it was scrappy. A lot of the games at this end of the tournament get scrappy because everyone gets a bit tight. There were a lot of turnovers. We've got a great track record against Canada and that's why we think we can shut them down pretty well. We'll go back and do some more homework on them, and they'll take another look at us, but our game plans are pretty much set. The boys will work on our recovery then come back tomorrow night and try to take them out and hit that gold medal game. I wouldn't write off GB against America. When we were shaking hands with GB we were telling them, "See you in the final." We want the GB guys to get through. Not just because we think we can beat them again, but we get on really well with them, better than we get on with a lot of other countries. They play the game fair, they fight hard. They support us and we support them. But I just felt like we had too much for them tonight. Even Ryley, he's getting better and better. He's in a good mood. He's been telling Scotty, "Aw, your sister kissed me last night." They're stirring each other up. It's a good sign.'

17

And on the eighth day

Semi-final #1: United States v. Great Britain

You look at the bank of people above Ed Suhr and wonder if they're going to fall and kill him like they killed his brother. Why the dark thoughts?

The English players applaud the Americans during the introductions. The favour is not returned. The Americans do not give a rat's arse about perceptions. Nor should they. Springer bounces in his chair as though his wiring has shortcircuited. The Red Shirts have been replaced in the pre-game chant by a heavy-set man in a blue polo shirt. The war cry is thunderous. WHO ARE WE? We know. WHO ARE WE? *We know.* WHO ARE WE? For fuck's sake, we know. You are the USA. The Oversized Maori is back. He's sitting with New Zealand captain Sholto Taylor, which explains a whole lot. The Red Shirts have to stay seated for the same reason that Dubberley has to be in his chair. Heaven forbid the pointy-headed classifiers have their precious unimpeded views obstructed. They're all able-bodied—stand up! Lazy fuckers, stop making Dubberley drag his feet around.

GB's goals are more painful than a skin graft, gruesome work. They barely have time to catch their breath before America snatch the return goal. America, with Springer everywhere. America, with Springer so invaluable for a two-pointer that Gumbert never wants to replace him. America, with Springer the same classification as the unremarkable Cohn, but twice the player. Springer's head is not on a plate, according to Dubberley, but it should be. Kirkland is the dependable world-weary commander standing on the bow of the ship, but Springer is great like Janis Joplin in the 1960s with a bottle of vodka in one hand and companions in the other. Kirkland spews up a turnover, turns it over right back and scores. Sunken faces in red. If God really is moulding the results in his well-worn hands with their long slender fingers, he has no interest in a GB triumph. Barrow throws hopeful glances at O'Connor. The coach looks back at him, mouth agape. No words are spoken.

The Herculean Jason Roberts comes on at 7–6 down in the first quarter. It feels like the US should be leading by more because they are three classes above and blowing seven different kinds of smoke and all that bludgery. The Herculean Jason Roberts parks himself in the key and screams at Kirkland to come and get him. Kirkland comes to get him. The Herculean Jason Roberts glasses him. The ball is jolted from his rigid hands. How important is desire in this world. That's not a question, but a statement of fact. The Herculean Jason Roberts keeps GB competitive through nothing but his sheer willpower. Collins scores for GB. Kirkland fouls. The anger rises inside him. Collins is sprawled on the floor. He starts clapping when the referee decides it might be in everyone's best interests for Kirkland to gather up his possessions and leave for Sin City. He's imprisoned by four white lines. Rat in a cage. Roberts is throwing his elbows around as all four Americans try to prise the ball off him. GB lead 9–8! Tom O'Connor slowly pumps his fist. The English Rose claps politely, but she looks afraid.

Wilmoth's first task is to bludgeon Steve 'The Poor Man's Curtis' Palmer. Nice work, tough guy. We don't mean that in a condescending way. It really is nice work. Springer has to make way when Wilmoth comes on. Dubberley is right: The US are better off with Springer at the bargain basement price of 1.5 points cheaper than a Wilmoth. Morrison keeps holding the ball high and passing over the top. Cohn is piggy in the middle. No-one likes being the piggy in the middle.

For all the earnest discussions about his classification and eligibility, Wilmoth is only a bit-part player.

The US are two goals up. Barrow throws himself at Will Groulx but ends up taking a flesh-burning skid across the floor. Morrison runs him over. The US defence is immovable. Four sentinels. They're the tanks in the photo of the Tiananmen Square Massacre. GB are The Unknown Rebel; brave, outnumbered. They keep chipping away. Another tight one *might* be on the cards. What is being moulded here? The US are not unbeatable, they're not. Say it often enough and you might start believing it. You have never actually seen the US lose. They've been pushed and prodded and tested and stretched but you've only ever seen them succeed. You cannot actually picture them in defeat. You close your eyes and—nothing. Canada's victory at The North America Cup still sounds like an urban myth. The English Rose bites her bottom lip. O'Connor chews on his pen. Madness all around him. The US *might* be beatable. Wilmoth and Groulx are off to the naughty corner. For America, it's unravelling. Barrow nails a long pass for Collins to score. The US sneak to a 15–14 first-quarter scoreline. They're ravelling again. Batt is hounded by autograph hunters, coots young and old, tells them sorry, not now, I have to go and talk to my family.

Porter and Carr arrive like a couple of Joplin's roadies. Come on, sing it. You pray for a final between Australia and the US. There's a difference between The Important Game and The Big Game, you know. GB would be Important. The US would be Big, just as Canada is Big. The semi-final is tonight—tonight! No matter what GB do or say, you just cannot imagine Australia losing to them. And so the satisfaction would be lessened in crushing them. You can picture Australia losing to Canada, as galling as that would be, and you can imagine them losing to the US. But GB? A loss? No. A US victory is desired for the sense of occasion it would bring if Australia get to play them in the final.

Second quarter: You thought The Herculean Jason Roberts was spinning a line when he said GB could topple America. But he is the one guy who really does look like he believes it. At 16–all, Springer lines up Collins. He wants to make a hit and anyone will do. Barrow is antagonistic and combative. They start ignoring the ball in favour of gunning for the man and that's when murderball comes alive. They're in the same classification but Barrow, the only quad of the two, cannot get around the court with the same urgency. Zuperman enters the fray at 19–all. It's close! Roberts is trapped, forced into a time-out, angrily thwacking the ball into the heaving crowd. The US launch one of their hit-and-run missions; a brisk moonlight raid landing a two-goal lead. Collins throws a miracle pass while falling GB score and the US only lead 25–24 at three-quarter time. One goal in it at three-quarter time! If Australia get past Canada, which is clearly no sure thing, could they really receive the ultimate reward by facing candy-from-a-baby GB in the final? Perhaps it wouldn't be such a bad thing.

Cohn's handling switches from okay to poor and occasionally descends into diabolical. For his condition, it's brilliant. His own niche. He fumbles and loses the ball and it's 27–all. GB are going to implement the master plan to such perfection that they will reach the gold medal match and while they appear eminently beatable they are disciplined and professional and confident and so perhaps they can beat Australia but—can they actually do this? Can they actually look at the opportunity being presented to them without becoming fearful? There are times in your life when nothing is as frightening as an open door. They have the chance to defeat the US but it is doubtful whether anyone other than The Herculean Jason Roberts and Andrew Barrow really believe they can finish it off. GB fumble and then they argue and there's your answer. They're scared stupid.

An American flag is taken on a lap of the first tier of the grandstand as if the carrier is Hendrix or God. The man carrying the flag is a lunatic. Or God. Tom O'Connor shifts forward in his seat. Prince Albert has stuck his head in for a look, which everyone seems to get pretty excited about. Why? It's only Prince Albert. The Herculean Jason Roberts throws himself at Cohn so hard he lands flush on top of his bald head. Can you break your neck twice? Hogsett looks nasty. He doesn't give the impression of actually enjoying this. He seems to be hating it and everyone involved. He looks Joe Soares-esque in his manner and that's no compliment. He keeps yapping USA! at the hard-working Collins. The large Englishman's tongue flops out of his mouth. GB are brave but Paralympic medals are not awarded for gallantry. The Americans win 35–32 to enter The Big Dance. The US players develop condescending grins in the final two minutes as if the result was always a lock-in. That is crap and they know it. They have struggled. Zuperman turns and claps the American supporters. His input has amounted to stuff-all. Kirkland appears to go out of his way to be filmed by the TV cameras. He waves one finger in the air but there is something distinctly off-putting about someone trying so hard to get on camera. Springer goes out of his way to *avoid* the networks even though one internet viewer in New York cannot take her eyes off him. Nick Springer is 24 hours away from possibly making good on the promise he made his mother when she was diagnosed with cancer at the beginning of the year. He throws his virtually non-existent arms in the air and the US are into the gold medal match and for Australia that is good (The Big Game) and for Australia that is bad (The Important Game) and while the US are fallible, they are also street-tough and resilient. What we have next in Australia versus Canada is The Big Game and The Important Game all rolled into one.

Semi-final #2: Australia v. Canada

The hour is urgent and the need is great. 'We think Canada might psych themselves out,' Dubberley says. 'We know we're in for a game and a half. I mean, we've played them five or six times the last year or so. There have been all those extra-time games and one-point victories. They beat us one night in Melbourne, we've seen them beat the US at the North America Cup, so we know we're in for a hell of a game. We've been sitting back in the village, knowing Canada are already doing their warm-up. We knew they'd try to fill in time and sure enough when we got here, they were in their chairs, pushing around, having meetings. They go off too early. They're ready to go an hour before they have to be. I think we're better at knowing when to switch on and when to switch off. It's why we don't do a warm-up until 45 minutes before a game. Sitting in the chair is switch-on time. The longer you sit in that game chair, the more you have to wait and it's too draining. It's all playing into our hands. Back in Melbourne, Canada were in their playing chairs an hour and a half before the final, revving each other up. That was fine by us—you can't get hyped up that long before you play. You're exhausted before you even start. We want it to be fresh. We don't do any hitting until just before the game. We want to time it right—build it up, build it up, then hit. We leave it so late that we're almost rushing to get ready in time, we're not sitting around thinking about it too much. We're busy and really energetic when we start. When we're ready, we'll make our noise.'

WILLSIE: 'One of our guys embodies murderball. His name is T-Bone. Number ten for us, Trevor Hirschfield. That kid is off the hook. He'd knock over his mother. Look, we know Australia have a hell of a squad. They were number two on the rankings this year and they earned that ranking. They've knocked us over a couple of times because they play a power game. They're very similar to the US, and to us. They're very smart. You wouldn't know it but we're all smart guys. This is gonna be a blast. Obviously we're not in it for the money or the glory. It's just a blast to play at the highest level against the best players in the world. We've all got so much respect for each other. We'll knock the shit out of each other if we can, but we'll go and have a beer after it. That's the goal. Beat each other up, go get a beer. There's a genuine respect there. There won't be any of that hitting-from-behind crap. We would do anything to win, don't worry about that, but nothing illegal. If you're going to hurt someone, you're going to hurt him fair and square. And then comes the beer. I'm sounding a bit too keen for a beer, aren't I?

'I've been in my chair thirteen years and this is all I've ever wanted to do, play these kind of games. I was a kid playing hockey, what you guys call ice hockey, when I went head-first into the boards and broke my neck. So this is just a natural progression for me. First game I watched, a guy went flying out of his chair and the people who did it to him were laughing at him. They were crazy buggers and I said, "I've got to get into this." It's been a blast ever since. You ask anybody here why they like this sport, and they'll say the aggression. None of us got hurt in a library. We were all crazy bastards to start with. Everybody on our team broke their neck and had a spinal cord injury, most likely doing something at 90 miles an hour.

We all have broken necks, so Ryley does have an advantage—but he's a 3.5 and that's the leveller. In rugby, one man cannot win a game. He's chewing up nearly half their points. The Australians complement him very well in all their line-ups, and they have a few line-ups with Ryley not on the floor that still get the job done for them. Dubberley's done well there, but we're not afraid of Ryley. We respect what he can do as a player, but it's not fear. I love the hitting he does, and I love the power and speed he's got. He gives our sport an extra dimension. He's probably the first to admit he doesn't have great hands, so he's a little susceptible to losing the ball if you can get in there and trap him. But he's a monster out on the court, and I love it. If I wanted an easy time, I wouldn't be here. I'm not afraid of no monster.'

~

Is the real China the green tea or the Coca-Cola? The sandals or the high heels? The sliding bamboo doors or the electronic glass panels? The piss-pot on the floor or the scented ice cubes in the urinal of the six-star? Is it the impatient woman who chews your ear off when you fumble for change at the supermarket or the bilingual angel at the Australian embassy who expedites the replacement for your lost passport so you can get the fuck out of here on time? Is it the twelve-year-old army trainees marching obediently down Fourth Ring Road or the reckless adults ignoring every traffic warning to turn Beijing's roads into a lottery? Is it the police or the heroin smugglers they're chasing? The security guards meticulously checking your pockets or the policeman sleeping in his car while a fist fight takes place about two metres away? Is it the gentle viola playing across the river at night or the punk in wraparound sunglasses playing 'The Devil Went Down to Georgia' on his electric violin?

~

Nerves are jangling. Rummaging black coffee. Electricity illuminates the skin like Galileo's kaleidoscope. All things are working together for good. Beijing feels balmy rather than hot, cosy instead of claustrophobic. The Chinese coots part like the Red Sea when you want to swerve through on your bike. The Big Game, The Big Game. The very real beauty is that absolutely everything is riding on it. It possesses every single ingredient required to make a single sporting contest so fucking magnificent.

Christine Batt slips into her seat. Doug Batt is glued to his TV in Port Macquarie. This is how you see Doug and Christine Batt. They were responsible for giving their son a label that would stick with him for life. He would have looked at them like every kid does and thought, 'What am I? Who am I? Who do *you* think I am?' If they had treated him as being disadvantaged he would have become disadvantaged. They treated him as being great and here he is. You tell Christine Batt that today is your daughter's birthday. Jasmyn is turning six and she is back in Sydney getting all dolled up in her favourite dress for a party that her father will not be attending. She will have presents and candles on her cake and her father will see none of it. You can picture her face and you have never felt so despondent in all your life. All things are working together for bad. Now the coffee tastes like sewage and why won't all these people saying 'Hello-T-shirt' fuck off. Hello-T-shirt-and-get-out-of-my-way. Christine Batt has a beer in her hand. She's inhaled her first cigarette in a decade. Norm Carr says the novelty of Beijing is starting to wear off and he could go a steak. The Australians are on the court, rolling their arms and necks and all things work together for the good again, and with any luck Jasmyn won't even remember that Daddy wasn't there the day she turned six, and The Gentleman Shane Brand is sitting as still as the pillar of society that he is. His *eyes* roll because nothing else can. Canada's marathon warm-up amounts to full-blown pushing and hitting. Dubberley lightly taps the ball, tap-tap-tap just like that, on the floor. He's delivering the good word but for a moment, just a split-second he stares at the floor and becomes lost in his own world. He figures he may as well just sit there.

Batt leaves the huddle and the court and where do you think you're going? Last night dozens of Chinese schoolchildren asked for his autograph with the only possible hitch being that they were asking Hucks for it. Hucks is an obliging chap who said yes, of course, no worries, I'll give you an autograph. He went scribble scribble with his name and the children read it twice and they looked at him and said, 'Not Batt? Batt? Huck? You Huck?' Ryley Batt, King of Kings, Lord of Lords, returns from wherever he has just been and straps himself back in. He looks up and to the right and Christine smiles down at him. Kim Ellwood is hollow with tension. Life-and-death doesn't always have to be a matter of life and death.

Maple leafs are everywhere. Does this feel flat? Perhaps you imagine it. Canada do a 'Whoa Canada!'. But there's still more than a minute to go. Whoa, Canada. Captain Red Shirt is on the sideline applying an ice pack to his right shoulder. He is the only cheerleader in history to have sustained a physical injury. Benoit Jett is standing up in front of the officials in direct contravention of the laws. He wouldn't want to continue with that standing-up shit.

The Big Game begins with Batt tapping Lavoie, *clink*, and here they go again. Whitehead keeps flicking his nose in the manner of a person with a nervous tic that he hopes no-one has noticed. Batt loses the ball to The Curmudgeonly Whitehead and Canada lead 3–1, the bloodsucking freaks at Highgate cemetery and you swear on your dear precious mother's life that the Australians are flat. The Canadians press Australia back like they're shovelling rubbish at the tip. It feels depressingly similar to where the sky is purple perfume and the clouds are salmon-pink and the women are the prettiest little things in creation. Batt ploughs head-long into the photographers and there's your close-up, you intrusive punks. Whitehead shakes his head in admonishment when Batt swats at the ball. One of Batt's swipes finishes higher than anticipated and nearly slaps Whitehead across the face. Pinkhead looks at Batt as if he cannot believe the temerity of his behaviour. It's unclear what he was expecting. Group hug? His expression suggests all this is a bit of a chore. You know those people? Trivialities go wrong and they say 'typical' as if the universe is forever conspiring against them. They say 'welcome to my world' at every inconvenience. Hate those people. Batt nudges him back over halfway. Here we go. Batt steals the ball. Welcome to his world—upbeat and contagious.

The Canadians have the air of those big sturdy types who never lose an argument. If they are losing an argument they just lie so they win it anyway. You bet that at least once in their lives they have woken up and seen the drizzle cascading down their window and thought, 'That'd be right.' Whitehead seems to take Batt's goal as a personal affront. He steals the ball and smirks. Smith thrives on the stifling heat. He makes a break but Whitehead catches him. The Australian Captain slowly rubs his hands in front of the building fire. Old Age and Treachery latches onto one of Canada's high-risk Hail Mary passes. *Holy Mary, Mother of God, pray for us sinners, now and at the hour of our death.* Any goal from Batt that involves the burning of Whitehead and/or Lavoie carries added satisfaction. Batt is in the sin-bin. Daniel Paradis and Patrice Simard stand guard, a couple of slim cigarettes positioned right on the sideline where Batt will have to re-enter the court. They regard him with an uneasy cocktail of apprehension and French–Canadian cool. Batt isn't even on the court and they're still marking him; surely the first time a player has been double-teamed from the wrong end of the sideline, but Batt swats them away and re-enters the fray.

Lavoie grabs hold of his arm. No penalty. Batt protests. Comically, when Batt raises his forearm to show the referee where he's been held, Lavoie *still* has his hand on his arm. And still no penalty. Lavoie laughs at having got away with it. A long ball from Alman fails to hit the mark. Jackie Chan scores and smiles over his shoulder like he's walking off with his arm around the girlfriend of a most bitter enemy. Batt tries to put a hole in Lavoie but misses. He skids across the floor, tailspins, jackknifes, does a backflip to get back up and the crowd goes nutso-bongo. He receives a slap on the shoulder from Old Age and Treachery. Lavoie controls play masterfully, running the clock down to 1.4 seconds until he sends Jackie Chan over. Canada take the first quarter 9–7. Batt shakes his head, perturbed. Canada have already started playing down the clock. They are not here to entertain. They are here to win and if that means putting everyone to sleep, just a pin prick and goodnight, then that is what they will do. A pass from Say (Say What!) Luangkhamdeng is going over the sideline as Whitehead grabs the back of Batt's chair when the referee isn't watching. Who deserves to be admonished here? Whitehead or Benoit Jett? Willsie is a great bloke but as for his 'we would do anything to win, but nothing illegal', please give us a break.

Article 1 of the United Nations Universal Declaration of Human Rights states, 'All human beings are born free and equal in dignity and rights. They are endowed with reason and conscience and should act towards one another in a spirit of brotherhood.' You can throw that in the toilet for the next half-hour because Whitehead is cheating, pure and simple. Good on him if he can get away with it. But let's not pretend it isn't happening. Whitehead is badgering Batt and that is fine but if anyone was grabbing Whitehead's chair, he would be protesting to The National People's Congress. He displays an appalling degree of mock indignation if an Australian so much as thinks about touching his chair, then goes right ahead and grabs their wheels when the referee's attention has been diverted. Batt could look on the bright side and view this special attention as a compliment; an admission that Canada cannot beat him fair and square. It also shows the desperation with which Canada are competing; they are not interested in honourable defeats. It's more of an indictment on Benoit Jett rather than Whitehead because players merely follow their coach's instructions. Finally Batt protests. The referee tells him, 'Okay, I'll watch out for it.' He will do no such thing.

Australia remain three-down. Whitehead throws an extravagant overhead pass and the ball is caught by Chan and Canada score again. Whitehead persists in doing these annoyingly slow fist-pumps accompanied by appallingly smug looks of *yup, uh-huh, sorted.* Batt looks quizzically at Dubberley. How to stop the long balls? Everything is going red and white. There's *another* turnover and the Canadians are about to go four-up. This is going to be a fizzer and Jasmyn would be opening her presents by now. Beating the Kiwis was a miraculous moment but it's all going to end in tears. Whitehead chews gum. He takes a hit from Batt but stays still as if his chair has been concreted to the floor. Canada do lead by four now. Benoit Jett slaps his hands together. For him, this might be a glorious anti-climax. For Dubberley, no big dance, then? Sunken thoughts. Hucks replaces Batt at 15–12 down. You want to be up by three, not down by three, when Batt turns the engine off. Hucks rips in. Little Patrice Simard takes a beating he will not forget. Hucks scores immediately because he must. As well as a disarming fondness for feng shui, he lists his wife as his hero and a successful marriage as his dream.

The Canadians have their tails up. They trap The Australian Captain on his goal line. The Australian Captain looks at the referee and calmly calls a time-out. Chan and Lavoie are irritating him. Lavoie starts yabbering and The Australian Captain nods at him. That's all he does, he just nods at him. Hucks keeps glaring at Lavoie like a Blood to a Crip, daring him to start. *Don't tempt me.* Benoit Jett protests every pro-Australia decision to the officials' bench. Errors creep in but Australia claw back to two-down. They leak again to make it three. A three-point deficit can feel like ten as it does now. Australia need to negotiate their way to all-square. If they can do that before, say, three-quarter time, it'll be on like The Rum Rebellion.

Batt takes the place of Hucks. Old bull has done magnificently. Australia are 17–15 down. Canada yet again start playing the clock down with more than a minute left before half-time. It's not exactly a glowing endorsement of their attacking capabilities. They pass up two clear opportunities to score. Lavoie is strong enough to hold the ball and flick basketball-style passes in any direction. One of The Slim Cigarettes passes it to Whitehead and the big lug drops it. Batt has the ball and scores with Chan trying to shove him into the corner post. Lavoie swings his arms around as if to say, 'No goal! No goal!' He cusses when the referee says: Goal! Goal! Canada lead by one at half-time. It could have been better for Australia, but it could have been diabolically worse. They were nearly gone. Canada's restart just before everyone started sucking their oranges at half-time—do people still suck oranges at half-time?—has been addle-brained and confused. Too late to cost them a goal, but momentum has burst through the front doors of The Hall Of Overwhelming Glory and taken a seat with the Australians.

Vitale's sister slowly waves her national flag from side to side. Zuperman, Cohn and Springer sit together near the sideline. David Willsie goes over and takes them to task. All will be revealed. Cohn ignores him. They all ignore him like the plastic girls at high school being all bee-atchy to someone from outside their bee-atchy little group. Batt sits quietly through the break, building steam, building, building, building steam.

Go.

He hammers Lavoie. Lavoie is up on one wheel. He stares at Ryley Batt like he's seen a corpse. Batt scores, north–south. Batt scores again, more sou'west. Alman's long balls start hitting their mark. Lavoie sneaks away but Batt chases him like police hunt a killer. He's grimacing, head down, refusing to take his eyes off him for a single second. However long it takes, he *will* get him. Australia are coming good. Canada are trapped in their own half past the fifteen-second limit. It's a huge turnover for Australia and Batt converts. Erdem has Lavoie so well hooked that Lavoie has to reach down and attempt unsuccessfully to undo their tangle of metal by hand. Back to all-square. Australia charge with their flags raised. Little Patrice Simard keeps displaying previously unseen levels of skill. The Genius Nazim Erdem and The Rebel Scott Vitale are smothering Lavoie like first girlfriends. Benoit Jett becomes increasingly petulant as if no, no, this cannot be allowed to happen. Lavoie out-sprints Batt in a moral victory. Moral victories will not be enough. Only the miraculous. The wild last-resort Hail Mary passes from Canada keep sticking, but only just. Australia cannot get ahead. THEY ARE SO CLOSE. The Curmudgeonly Whitehead is rigid with tension as opposed to rigid with quadriplegia.

Australia lead! The purple-perfume way they started meant they could be eight-down by now but Batt is getting as close as humanly possible to a state that doesn't really exist: perpetual motion. The Rebel Scott Vitale is a one-man gang and now every time the scores are levelled, Australia receive the ball. They go one-up and spare themselves the anxieties associated with the New Zealand game until all hell broke loose at the end. One-up, all-square, one-up—just so long as it stays one-up. No-one can give you a miracle. You have to position yourself for one. At one-up, Australia are in position. The rest is up to Hendrix. Or God.

Vitale is smashed by Whitehead and the ball squirts free. REGRETS. Vitale's arms flap against the side of his chair like those of a wounded seagull. It's 28–all and Whitehead is celebrating like mad; hitting his chair like an oversized jockey whipping an undersized horse. But Vitale has taken a leaf out of Batt's book by calling a time-out just before hitting the floor. Time-out—*crash*. There's too much happening. Too much activity. Did he call the time-out when he still had the ball? The referee says yes. But Australia lose possession. Vitale is penalised for a foul. He looks at the referee and tells him *No, mate, no*. Dubberley shifts forward. He gives a shit about the Paralympics. All players other than Batt, Jackie Chan and Little Patrice Simard are in gridlock. Batt is single-handedly containing both Canadians. Jackie Chan gets the ball, Batt stops him cold and then scoots over to cover Little Patrice Simard, who scores anyway. Whitehead does another ten-pin fist-pump and it's cruel at three-quarter time: 29–all. A friend is sitting with you. She says, 'Holy Mother of God.'

Vitale is given a breather. He has the exasperated look of wanting to stay on. *Please, mate.* Australia force a turnover. Then turn it over right back. Benoit Jett gets to his feet. Sit. Down. Erdem and Carr are in purgatory. Standing room only. Batt is trapped so efficiently that his wheels are spinning in the air. There's a loose ball—grab it! Carr is pushing down court; Alman slides a pass over his right shoulder. Ball again! Old Age and Treachery rolls it along the floor, scooping it up, calmly giving it to Batt. Australia are 32–31 up. There are five minutes and 25 seconds to go. Those five minutes and 25 seconds will define the last four years and set the tone for the next Paralympic cycle. They will determine whether the appointment of Dubberley has been inspired or idiotic and they will colour Batt's claims to being the greatest player in the world. Dubberley starts rolling back and forth along the sideline at twice the rate. Up and back, rolling stone. Batt keeps pinning The Curmudgeonly Whitehead to the sideline. The Curmudgeonly Whitehead keeps staying in. Lavoie and Whitehead are strong. You keep waiting for one of them to crack but they don't. Someone has to. Parry and thrust. One of the people on this court will crack like Tinker Tailor Soldier Spy and it will haunt them for the term of their natural lives.

Here's a curious thing: Every time Australia score, Zuperman and the Americans celebrate. When Canada score, they become mute. Willsie keeps scowling at them. Batt hits Lavoie so hard he smiles. The thrill of the attempted kill.

Never Walk Alone opens his arms with an uninhibited grin. He's the master of all he surveys again and he loves the fucking lot of it. Action off the ball is as frenetic as the movements on it. Players are trapped and hassled without respite. Wherever Batt is, there's Lavoie. And vice versa. Whitehead commits a foul, lashing out in pure frustration because he's thrown everything at Batt, just about every play he knows and every dirty rotten trick he can think of, but Batt relentlessly powers on. The Curmudgeonly Whitehead can call Ryley Batt every name under the sun and Batt will not leave. He can grab his chair, he can hold his arm, he can provoke him in any way he sees fit. He can keep coming all fucking night if he wants because Ryley Batt is not going away. When the game is there for the taking, he will volunteer for duty. You're unsure if the same can be said for Whitehead. His forearm wipes his brow. Lavoie is the worry. He's crazy enough to think he can get the better of Batt. Which means he probably can.

Christine Batt fidgets with her hair. She stays seated the entire time. Australia can score or The Curmudgeonly Whitehead can face-plant or Batt can slaughter some poor schmuck of a Canadian or Say (Say What!) Luangkhamdeng can give another assist and the entire occupancy of the stadium will get to their feet—except Christine Batt. Too nervous.

Shallow breaths require conscious effort. Attempted deep breaths fall apart and disintegrate into further bouts of panic-strewn panting. This might do you in. Two lousy minutes on the clock. Batt is everywhere, giving everything. Doesn't matter which Canadian has the ball, Batt confronts them. It's 36–all and Batt asks Dubberley for the benefit of his tactical expertise. Take two minutes to score the next goal? Score now? When every other country would have dawdled, Australia charge.

Old Age and Treachery deploys the screen. Full. Steam. Ahead. Australia is 37–36 up and Batt looks as though he might pass out. Old Age and Treachery upends Lavoie like he's emptying the trash on Sunday night. Batt is binned for striking Whitehead, who is carrying on like Batt has committed the crime of the century and needs to be deported without the right to legal counsel. Batt's arm was out and Whitehead was the one making contact. But the sin-bin isn't a bad place for Batt to be. He needs to be *forced* to take a breather. No Batt, though, and anything could happen here. Whitehead has the ball, motionless while the clock starts disappearing. Canada are attempting what Australia pulled off against the Kiwis—a late goal to send it into extra time. Old Age and Treachery is on Whitehead, tiptoeing, shh. Whitehead holds the ball out to his right. It sits in his outstretched palm as if on a platter. Alman sneaks up from behind and—The Curmudgeonly Whitehead pulls the ball close to his chest at the last second. Alman sails by like a shark eyeing off a school of fish. He will be back. Batt tears out of the sin-bin for the final onslaught. Out of the corner of his eye, The Curmudgeonly Whitehead sees Ryley Batt flying at him. Whitehead freezes. *Crash*. Somehow, Whitehead stays upright. Batt turns and hovers, attention alternating between the ball and the clock, the fast-evaporating clock. He nips at the ball, little bites. There's a time-out and then Lavoie gets the goal. It's still 37–all and there are 6.2 seconds on the clock and you cannot breathe.

The clock will restart when Alman's inbound is caught by Batt. The risk is that the ball will be caught by a Canadian intruder. If it's Batt, Golden Balls will have enough time to repeat his Kiwi miracle and score a ticket to The Big Dance for himself and ten especially close mates. Two Canadians are in the key. Batt has the ball! Time on! Six-point-two seconds. The clock starts inverting and soon there will be nothing left. For any of us. Batt swings wide. Pump, push, sing it. But Lavoie nudges Batt over the sideline and overtime it is. Lavoie looks suitably pleased. No-one should ever get too pleased with themselves.

Everything. Batt has already given it, but it hasn't been enough. Now he has to give everything all over again. Overtime. An entire game has come and gone and we're none the wiser about who will be confronting the US in what The Gentleman Shane Brand has so endearingly started calling The Large Dance. Benoit Jett high-fives his assistant and for the next three minutes you will be struck by nerves so savage that during Dubberley's speech, his right arm slowly being raised and lowered as if he's brandishing The Sword Of A Thousand Truths, you are on the verge of being physically ill. STEELERS. PUSH. It's not a wild proclamation. It's not PUSH! It's a grim demand. PUSH. JUST KEEP PUSHING.

You fall to your knees when a ball goes tumbling across the court—for fuck's sake, grab it. You're laughing, crimson-faced, cowering, delirious. You're a grown man, a father of three for Christ's sake, and should know better than to become too emotionally involved in a game of leapfrog—leapfrog, they're only playing leapfrog. But this really is something else. Look at these blokes, all busted and miraculous. You have never been so affected by the knife's edge of competition. Instead of getting up, you crawl under your table because you are so shit-scared of whatever comes next. You are scared of Australia winning and you are scared of them losing. Could they win? Could that really happen? You watch the next three seconds through a small crack underneath the wooden desk that you are supposed to be writing on. Suffice it to say, those three seconds defy description. Then Old Age and Treachery passes the ball to Batt (Youth And Skill). You drag yourself back up off the floor. The noise. The breathtaking noise. You have never experienced anything like it.

Lavoie is outstanding. He only played eight minutes against the US. Now you know why. So he could play virtually every minute against Australia.

Dubberley puts his head in his hands. You know you're really down to your last breath when Brad Dubberley puts his head in his hands.

Australia go one-down from the start of overtime. Is this actually *fun*? The players are required to concentrate on the process of scoring and defending goals but human instinct makes them try to pre-empt the result. When Australia score, all it does is get them back level in that demoralising, energy-sapping, confidence-crushing old chestnut. Australia are forever on the back foot. Canada score again. If Australia go two-down it will be over in an instant because overtime only ever lasts an instant. Canada has won the tip-off and in the majority of overtime games, that's enough. You can run the clock down for two minutes and only a few people will pelt you with tomatoes and suggest you suck. All you have to do is win the tip-off, score, get a turnover at one-up and suck your thumb until the clock tells you to stop. Alman's inbounds keep finding Old Age and Treachery—on the bounce. Every bounce is another cardiac arrest. Again you are not entirely sure this is *enjoyable*. This is invigorating and unforgettable and riveting, but *enjoyable*? Ridiculous tension. You bend in half to put your hands on your trembling knees. It's amazing how an emotion can cause such an unstoppable physical reaction. You know sport probably shouldn't mean so much, but it does. The Curmudgeonly Whitehead finds space and he sees Batt coming for him but what he does not see is the shark coming back for one more look at the plankton.

And then . . .

And then . . .

And then . . .

Turnover to Australia with 40 seconds to go. Keep it calm if you can. TURNOVER OFF THE CURMUDGEONLY WHITEHEAD WITH 40 FUCKING SECONDS TO GO! Batt waves one finger in the air and the atmosphere now, there really is no way of describing it. The expressions and emotions are going off every Richter there ever was. Ellwood smiles and taps her foot. *Please.* Whitehead! Karma, anyone? Hucks is nodding as if he knew it all along. With 40 seconds left, The Curmudgeonly Whitehead has been playing down the clock and waiting for T-minus ten seconds to score at 40–all. He has bounced the ball as per the rules devised by Duncan Campbell, Jerry Terwin, Randy Dueck, Paul LeJeune and Chris Sargent. He has considered all the available options as per his rat-cunning instincts, and then he has wound up for another bounce as per the rules he only occasionally shows such regard for—but he hasn't seen Alman slicing through the cold. With The Curmudgeonly Whitehead resting the ball between his forearm and chin, Alman has shot his hand out and flicked the ball free. TURNOVER! GET THE FUCKING BALL!

Alman has tapped it straight to Batt, who has charged forward before realising he can do what The Curmudgeonly Whitehead was attempting to do by making this a game of next goal wins. TURNOVER! He swings back to halfway, settling, a nineteen-year-old boy more mature than any of the old coots now diving out of their seats in the grandstand. T-minus 30 seconds. Batt loops a pass to Alman as Lavoie and Whitehead sandwich him. The Curmudgeonly Whitehead has half a minute to right his wrong. He will approach the task with due diligence. Father Time says it's T-minus 15 seconds. Batt charges straight ahead. All four Canadians are in front of the goal. Erdem—Erdem!—has immobilised The Curmudgeonly Whitehead. One of these days, you are just going to march up to Nazim Erdem and hug the life out of him. Batt goes hammer and tong for the left corner post. Jared Funk has to reverse to try to cover him. Batt crosses for the goal—Australia lead—at T-minus 7.7 seconds. They are one-up. They have trailed all through overtime until the only time that matters. Now.

Lavoie's inbound goes to The Curmudgeonly Whitehead and Batt is right there. The Curmudgeonly Whitehead passes the ball back to Lavoie at T-minus 5 seconds. Alman parks himself in line with Lavoie and braces for the collision. It hurts, but it's worth it. Alman stops Lavoie from getting through. Brilliant. Lavoie holds the ball high to pass to Funk, who is clear and facing an uninterrupted route to the line. But then Old Age and Treachery shoulders Funk and deters Lavoie from passing. *Even when you're fucked*. Erdem and Batt have everyone else covered. Canada have one last chance to force double overtime. All they need is to find one more goal as easily as they've been peeling them off all night and then we can brace ourselves for another time-out. Canada call for a moment of deep contemplation.

You're upstairs and nearly fall clean off the second tier of the grandstand in your manic rush to see the clock. There they are, the flashing bright lights of the timepiece inside The Hall Of Imminent And Overwhelming Glory: 0.6. The flashing lights: 0.6! 0.6! 0.6! Benoit Jett is motioning at the clock as if he has been dudded one last time. *Welcome to my world. Typical*. It does not matter if you've been dudded, Benoit Jett. Whatever it is, it just is. There are six-hundredths of one second remaining in the second semi-final of the Beijing Paralympic Games and Australia lead by one goal.

Holy Mother of God. Canada has the ball from the right sideline. They're only 5 metres from Australia's goal. Lavoie bolts towards the middle of the key but Batt stops him. Funk has sidled into the key. He positions himself like Kasparov moving his king to check-mate. Funk is one inch from the line. He's close enough to the restart for the ball to reach him on the full. The Curmudgeonly Whitehead will deliver the pass. There is only one possible attempted play coming up. The Curmudgeonly Whitehead will throw the ball to Jared Funk, and then Jared Funk will try to score. Once the ball flies from the fingertips of The Curmudgeonly Whitehead, there is nothing more he can do tonight. The clock will restart the instant Funk gets his touch. If he catches it, he will need to roll one inch even when he's fucked. It is possible. Sitting down? Push your chair back one inch. That took less than six-hundredths of a second. Catch, roll, double overtime, get a dog up ya. Batt, the Genius Nazim Erdem, Alman, and Old Age and Treachery are on the court. The Canadians prepare for The Curmudgeonly Whitehead's throw. Get thousands of people to scream with all the air in their lungs and that is the noise right now.

Funk is clear.

Ball.

The Curmudgeonly Whitehead lobs his pass to Jared Funk. Time, according to the clock and your own gasping heart, has stopped. The ball is in the air so play has resumed, but it hasn't been touched yet so the clock hasn't restarted. Time has literally stopped. In the days, weeks, months and years from now, when you close your eyes and replay this moment so the electrified hairs on the back of your neck can stand upright once more, when at unexpected times and places you find yourself reliving a moment of such warmth and truth and beauty that it will never be erased, the sight of the white volleyball floating through the soft cushions of air inside The Hall Of Overwhelming Glory will become one of those time-in-motion photographs where a sequence of balls are freeze-framed to show the phosphorescent rainbow arc of the one ball used.

The arena falls quiet. The ball leaves the hands of The Curmudgeonly Whitehead and begins its journey towards the outstretched and eager hands of Jared Funk. The ball climbs, peaks and hangs for an instant. A pause, and then it dives towards the ten outstretched fingers of Funk. The Curmudgeonly Whitehead has done well. He has delivered his pass on the right line. He has given it the right depth. Funk will barely have to move a muscle. Catch, score. Dubberley can barely look. The universe melts and stops.

The ball hits Jared Funk on the head, doink, and the clock is zero.

Doink.

The Curmudgeonly Whitehead shakes with fury. No! no! no! And then he collapses. He's protesting as if it's someone else's fault. The referee waves his arms around for game over. The powerful arms of Old Age and Treachery are the first to go up. Batt flies towards the bench. The Rebel Scott Vitale goes straight to Dubberley. Batt's eyes are filled with tears and he tries hard to fend them off. The thought of crying makes him start laughing. Every person with an Australian bent is bear-hugging every other person without a Canadian bent. There are no wheelchairs in this picture and that is God's own truth.

DUBBERLEY: 'I cannot believe this.'

BATT: 'Just so happy. "Thanks, boys." That's what everyone is saying to each other, it's been an awesome year and we feel lucky to be part of it. You just feel like thanking everyone you've done it with. We've got the US, and we've got our medal.'

DUBBERLEY: 'Bloody hell.'

THE INVALUABLE CAMERON CARR: 'How it unfolded, to be on that tightrope and to come away with it like that—everyone is on such a high. We were only a few seconds from the whole thing being over. There's obviously a huge rivalry between us and Canada and yes, that makes it sweeter. We just keep coming away with these really tight wins. A lot of those Canada guys can have a sook and it comes back to bite them. It was the same as the Kiwi game—for the Kiwis and Canada to come up with a mistake when they're so professional, they usually sort of nail those last-minute plays. But I think just the pressure of the Paralympics, the pressure we were putting them under, forced those mistakes. It feels to me like we deserve to be where we are.'

DUBBERLEY: 'What an incredible comeback. To recover the way we did—stuff just wasn't going well at the start but once we got our defence together, we were right. We got up. We got up! Bring on the US. Bring those boys on. We've got nothing to lose now. The pressure is on them, you know? They're number one in the world but we're coming after them. Bring it all on. Unbelievable. We've made it. We've made The Big Dance. That was hard to sit back and watch but we trusted each other and I'll tell you what, we've got a good team here. Anything is possible.'

And maybe it really is. Imagine that, anything being possible, anything you can think of.

'The Big Dance,' Dubberley says, 'get us on the main stage, the last game of the tournament. We've won our medal, let's see if we can do some damage tomorrow night. We've talked about it, we've planned for it, we've trained hard to get to this position—and here we are. We're in the big one. You never know, mate. You just never know what might happen. Here we are playing for the gold. It doesn't feel real, but it is. Just the feeling we have within this team, you know, I wouldn't rule anything out. We're having so much fun, we're so confident and we're so relaxed. When a game gets tight, we pull together. We're doing it for each other. These boys are unbelievable. They deserve a moment like this.'

THE REBEL SCOTT VITALE: 'It's killed me. My arms are gone. It's such a late start for a game, eight o'clock. I lay down during the day but couldn't sleep, I was just thinking about the game the whole day. It's such a long time to wait. I reckon that's why we started so slowly. The nerves—I was shaking. Unbelievable. Unbelievable. Tomorrow is the anniversary of my accident. How's that? Maybe it's destiny—I don't know. It's just good to make it this far. It's good to be here—and we're in with a chance. Only two teams can win a gold medal, and we're one of them.'

'Hotel California' is on the loudspeakers. Such a wonderful place, such a wonderful place. Five minutes after Vitale has looked at the tattoo saying 'REGRETS' with sardonic appreciation, you're still standing behind the court, still staring at it all, staring at nothing and staring at everything, watching these blokes hug each other like few people ever do. You don't want to leave. You do not want this night or this feeling to ever end. Dubberley has watery pink around the rims of his eyes. The big unflappable man has cried. You feel like falling backwards in the crucifix position, staring at the ceiling until the sun comes up. They've won. They really have won a fucking medal.

'Canada played one of the best games I've seen them play in a very long time,' Dubberley says. 'We had to bring everything we had. That's what the Paralympics is about. This is about sport. Forget the wheelchairs. This is sport. They were four-up and the message was,

"Don't worry about the scoreboard. Just keep playing." The one thing we've tried to develop is enough mental toughness so if we're four-down in a game like that, against an unbelievable team like that, we'd be tough enough to stay with them and make it interesting. We pulled back a few goals and it was game on again. The way we started, we were going to lose by ten. But we didn't get too stressed about it. We just had to make sure we scored every opportunity we had, then hit them with big defence. At the end there, when Bryce got his hand on Whitehead's ball and I saw Ryley—it was like, "My God. This could be it." That's all I was thinking: "This could be it".'

Lavoie is dejected and disbelieving. No-one deserves to be treated like this. Dubberley has been unusually lippy. 'More for the team than for myself,' he says. 'I wanted to rally our blokes and give them some confidence. When they brought Whitehead and Fabien out, and had a 1.5 and a 0.5 with them, I was like, "Here we go boys, here we go! This is the line-up we want! It's turnover time here boys!" Two low-pointers was good for us. Our boys started rallying behind that, getting loud as well, and we were all just so pumped, feeding off each other. I was talking it up, but not so much in their face, just trying to give our boys that extra here-we-go. Just the excitement of it all, the adrenaline, it was the biggest game we'll have until 2012. It all just hit me. Then Bryce got his hand to that ball and it was, "For real!" We were hoping all night they would panic if we stayed with them—and they did. We kept telling each other, "We do not lose overtime games." We're pretty tough in that situation. I was just trying to get that point across. We had every reason to be confident. Overtime is when we excel. A lot of teams struggle because they feel like they have to play better than they normally do. They feel like they have to do too much because it's all so rushed. But we can control ourselves. I told them overtime is when we kick arse. We just had to unleash in attack, then hassle them like fucking crazy in defence until they cracked. That last time-out, six-hundredths of a second, I was just standing there—I could not believe my eyes. I couldn't give any messages because the guys had to stay on the court. They were all lined up where they needed to be in the key. If they'd come off to talk to me, it would have opened the key up for Canada. They had to block the key and stay there. I was just sitting there, staring at them. I'm thinking, "We're going to win, six-hundredths of a second, there's not enough time for them." But you still don't really believe it. I'm thinking, "Stop this goal—just stop this one goal and then we can get out of here".'

Dubberley is delirious.

'I can't even think straight,' he says. 'I remember Ryley, when it was evens with about a minute or so to go in overtime, he just goes in this really fast voice, really hyped up, "Braddy, what do you want me to do? Come on Braddy, tell me what you want us to do." I said, "Fuck, mate, I don't know!" And he keeps going, "Come on Braddy, what do you want me to do?" And I'm like, "Shut up, mate, I don't know, just score it!" Great coaching, eh? I had the dice belt on again. It's the lucky charm. Just roll the dice. If he scores it, at worst we go to double overtime. So let's just score it and give ourselves another opportunity in defence. Sure enough, it came off. I just wanted to give ourselves every opportunity to win there and then. If Canada wanted to hold the ball up for 40 seconds to go for one goal, they could go right ahead. I thought let's put them under pressure instead of putting ourselves under all that pressure with the clock running out on us. Running down the clock in that situation isn't anything like you've done before. The seconds just fly past. It really was just slow motion at the end. I thought we'd be okay in double overtime, but we were right in a position to make the final, a few seconds, and you need those little chances to go your way. Sure enough, they didn't score. As soon as I saw the ball go free—it was a truly unbelievable feeling. The ball went bouncing away, you almost can't believe your own eyes. He had to be rolling and catching at the same time if he was going to score. It was phenomenal. We're all stoked. You could say we're all pretty happy about what happened here tonight. We're in the Paralympic final.'

OLD AGE AND TREACHERY: 'I told Brad I was going to do a job for him tonight and I hope I did it.'

DUBBERLEY: 'You were unbelievable.'

OLD AGE AND TREACHERY: 'It's a better feeling than any individual medal I won. They're great but you've only got a select group of people to share it with. You win a team medal, in a close game like this, you've got a wealth of people you can share it with. They're a great bunch of blokes and I love them. It's been a pleasure to change sports and come and do something as fantastic as this with them. I'm new to rugby, but the way Brad has put so much trust and faith in me, the minutes that he's played me—all it can do is build my confidence. Six months ago, two of those balls I took down court, and had to hold up against two massive players like they've got, I would have coughed them up for sure. I'm not ashamed to give the ball to Ryley. He's the bloke who can do the damage. If you end a game with a lot of assists, they're as good as goals. I'm pumped, mate, so pumped, more pumped than I've ever been.'

DUBBERLEY (STILL DELIRIOUS): 'I was trying to get messages out, but I don't think the boys heard anything.'

OLD AGE AND TREACHERY: 'Nope, nothing, couldn't hear a thing. They had the throw-in and we're just lucky it went to a bloke who can't catch. Awesome. Incredible.'

BATT: 'We were terrible at the start. But our comeback and just our heart to get on top in that game, that took a whole lot of effort and guts from all of us. They're a loud team and they'd psyched themselves up but we just dug deep and pulled it out. I have never felt anything like this, just so happy. Getting in the position where you're four goals down, that's a long way to come back in wheelchair rugby. I was very nervous. I did think, you know, "Shit, this might be a bit hard to pull back." They're as good as any team in the world and to give them a four-goal headstart was a disaster. Thank God we got back into it. Fabien gave me a bit of a run for my money tonight. I was pretty buggered, the last quarter or so. He said, "I beat you" after a few of our races and he kept bragging after it. But that's just him, and that's just Canada. They played awesome and so did he. Whitehead—he's just one of those blokes it's hard to like. He grabs your wheels, they all do. Scotty never believes me. We watch a replay and I say, "Watch this, I bet they grab my wheels." He's like, "Are you serious?" Then they do it and Scotty is like, "He does! I'd be punching him in the face".'

DUBBERLEY: 'Four-down, it was still a long game. We just needed to patiently get those goals back. We had little targets for the end of each quarter to get back in range. Those finishes, they're spectacular for the fans, but they're pretty hard for the coaches and the players.

Six seconds left, I was thinking, "Fuck, do we just hold it up and go for one?" But if we lost the ball it's all over and they win. I thought we might as well take a gamble and see where that left us. They played the clock down a lot. They had the lead, so why not? But I'm not a fan of that sort of play. I prefer that if you're in the lead, keep pushing it, you know. You've obviously done something right to get in the lead, so why wouldn't you keep doing it? But it's almost like teams get afraid of big leads. Why hold it up and risk someone getting a piece of it—and then you're screwed. Which is what happened to them. We're back to where we were in Sydney. We're back in the gold medal game. It's all good. It was just, I don't know, the most emotionally charged moment I think I've ever had. I'm so stoked for the boys and their families. That's what this is about for me, the boys and their families. A year ago, we would have lost that game because we wouldn't have been mentally strong enough to come back. We worked on toughening up for those exact situations and we've done it. We've done it! This is big for us, but we're all pretty worn out. Our phones are going off with messages from back home. It's a relief that game is over. It feels like a dream. Is this for real? We got back to the dressing room and when I came through the door, George comes flying across in his chair. We hit each other, hugged each other and just bawled our eyes out.'

18

And on the ninth day

The final: Australia v. the United States of America

Hucks has previously thrown a wild punch at Honky Tonk Bakonkadonk and the Australians still remember the fear of God in Kirkland's eyes and the subsequent withdrawal of the American captain from the fight. Batt is the new Hucks, and so you wish for Batt to kick Kirkland's arse. You wish for him to kick the arse of Cohn and you really wish for him to kick the arses of Wilmoth and Hogsett. You wish for Batt to kick the arse of Zuperman even though you have an unshakeably high regard for a divisive man who called himself the civil engineer, author, friend, athlete, rugby player, mentor, public speaker, asshole and all-round good guy in the best self-description since Bono Vox of O'Connell Street labelled himself 'a scribbling, cigar-smoking, wine-drinking, bible-reading band man; an activist travelling salesman of ideas, chess-player, part-time rock star and opera singer in the loudest folk group in the world.' You are *desperate* for Batt to kick the arses of all those people but you do not especially wish for him to kick the arse of Nick Springer. We wish no ill will towards the man who looks like he's gone through a meat grinder because he knows little about the drama unfolding in a hospital bed in New York. His father has been maintaining a mostly unemotional countenance but the truth of the matter is that their beloved mother and wife might not be long for this world. You want him to play well. Cross your heart and hope to die.

You want Erdem to take every inch. You want him to scrape and claw with his fingernails and rip himself apart just to get one more inch of the court. 'I'm getting tired,' he says. 'I haven't been able to see the sun for the last three days. The first two days, it was beautiful. I could see everything. But now it's started to—I don't know, what is that shit in the air? Smog, or haze, what is it?'

The Kiwi and Canada games have been supernaturally magical and impossibly scripted. In Hungary, on the Tisza River, long-tailed mayflies reproduce—the highest point they can reach—and then they die. Salmon travel 1500 kilometres and climb nearly 2000 metres from the Pacific Ocean to their place of spawning in Canada; their migration takes such an enormous physiological toll that they drop dead on the spot. The Australians have arrived where they wanted to be, this heightened state, and their migration has taken an enormous physical toll, but you don't want them to be killed off just yet. One more night . . .

The Cretinous Red Shirts walk past Erdem. You hope the thing that kicks the arse of The Red Shirts is the most powerful thing of all, karma, and you hope it lasts a lifetime. 'I've seen the American boys around the village,' he says. 'I said hi to a few of them. Ignored a few of them. The Americans, individually, they're not too bad. But collectively, I couldn't be fucked.' The Red Shirts walk past *again*. 'Yeah, there they are,' The Genius says dismissively. 'Look at them. What *are* they?' Three people spit within a fifteen-second period on the way to The Hall of Overwhelming Glory. The first grotesque hack goes in a garden. The second stains the grotty sidewalk. It's rubbed in by a dirty bare foot with black toenails and calluses. The third hack goes up against a wall and slimes down the concrete.

Gumbert offers rumbling laughter about his ill-fated yet profitable trip to Sydney to gain footage of the Oceanias. 'Yep, broke my leg,' he says. 'I love Sydney, it's a beautiful place but my wife has pretty much banned me from ever going back. I was scouting, that's why I went over. On the flight home I was transferring into my seat. They moved an aisle chair on me and it snapped my leg. They had to take me to hospital. I spent five days there. They had to aerovac me back home, and I had another week in hospital in the States. It was quite the ordeal. But I got a lot of good footage over there and it's actually paying off now, so . . .' Gumbert gives the impression of being more than okay with having snapped his leg in trade for good footage. 'Dubberley is a good man,' he says. 'I knew him when he started, when he was sixteen. Brad was captain of a development team against a US team that went over to Australia and played. His first year, we played against one another. He's a good mate. He's done miracles with that team. His whole demeanour—it's not confrontational. He makes it easy for the guys to get along with him. They have respect for him. I can see that.'

Dubberley's finest hour as a player—the Sydney Games. Dubberley's greatest lament—the Sydney Games. He comes clean about his belief that he cost Australia the gold medal. He's convinced his lack of fitness made him run out of puff just as the engraver was preparing to inscribe the names of the Australians on the holiest of holies, the gold medals. Back then he had a cockiness that made him think he could waltz through the Games on the back of a six-week holiday instead of a carefully planned climb to a physical peak that could have held the US at bay for all that was required: two more minutes. Dubberley finds it difficult to express his regrets. He chokes on a few words when he makes his admission eight years after the event to the people he feels the most apologetic towards. 'Yeah, I've told the players,' he says. 'It was pretty hard to do, to be honest. There are only four left from Sydney—Steve, George, Bryce and Naz—plus Kim as manager, and obviously we went through a lot together. It was hard to tell them that I didn't put in any effort before Sydney, but I really wanted the guys who weren't in that team to realise how much I still regret it, and I wanted to stop the newer guys from getting in the same position as me. To tell them I stuffed up, knowing Steve, Bryce, Naz and George had been training while I took it easy, yet I got all the court time—I probably looked like a bit of a dickhead in front of them but I made a mistake back then that I think proved pretty costly. But you learn from it. All the things that go wrong, all the things you regret, you just learn from them all. The best thing I can do as a coach is try to make sure it doesn't happen to anyone else. I know it won't.

'Sydney still feels bittersweet. It always will. We weren't expecting to go that well, we were ranked fifth or sixth going in, so to get a medal was great. But to miss a gold by one goal—I was pissed off with myself. That's why a few of us know what a big opportunity this is. Once every four years—no-one will do anything for months after it. You put such an effort in for so long, then the Paralympics is such a massive thing, then afterwards—what do you do? For a lot of the guys, rugby is all we know.

'Ever since I started coaching, I've told all the guys, especially the younger guys, "You know, you'd want to make sure you train. We lost by one point in Sydney and we haven't had another chance for eight years. If you don't train, you might regret it." But now I've told them the whole story and my plan is—obviously we needed to get in the gold medal game for this—but if we're about to win it, I want to get Steve, George, Bryce and Naz on the floor together at the finish. George, myself and Naz were on the floor at full-time when we lost in Sydney and I'd love nothing more than to be in the position where we're going to win the final here and I can get them on the floor to close it out. That would be my way of paying them back for Sydney. Ever since then we've been on a downward spiral, but we've turned that around and we're back to where we were eight years ago. We're back in the gold medal game. It's taken a while but we're here again. I think the US know we can make a fair bit of noise out there tonight. They know what we've got.'

THE GENIUS NAZIM ERDEM: 'Sydney, I just remember the stadium being chockers. We were on such a high after winning the semi the night before. We were up by four or five at one stage, but started making a few mistakes. We were still up by two or three a long way into the game. We lost it in the last seconds. They scored, and there were less than ten seconds to go. We couldn't score again in time. But it was a top game. You couldn't hear a thing because of the crowd. We could be two feet away and couldn't hear each other. The coach had to wave a towel. If he waved it one way it meant this, another way meant something else. We lost the game but we didn't get done. We played well. They were an unbelievable side and so were we. That's all I remember, just two top sides having a really close game. I don't remember anything about Brad letting us down. I don't agree with him. He got us there.'

THE AUSTRALIAN CAPTAIN: 'It was incredibly disappointing. Silver feels like a loser's reward on that last day. You're happier if you've just won bronze. We just felt devastated, absolutely devastated. In the fullness of time you put it in perspective and it's a great achievement, getting silver. It's a nice medal and it's nice to have at home, it's in the cabinet and all that. But like I say, in a team sport, you don't win silver, you lose gold. Especially when you've got 10 000 people there screaming for you and backing you. There were a couple of turnovers and they just turned the tide. You win your silver medal in the semis. But then you lose—you lose the gold. You go into that last day with the worst-case scenario being a silver. And you end up with the worst-case scenario. As for Brad costing us, that's crap.'

Dubberley's scouting report nominates Honky Tonk Bakonkadonk as Head On A Plate. 'America will have the same attitude they've always had,' he says. 'They will try to intimidate us. My message will be to weather the storm for the first five minutes. Score when the opportunity is there, but don't rush. Don't get rattled. That's when the US thrive, in those first five minutes. They come out charging. They're in your face from the start and they run with that intensity for as long as they can. By the time they run out of steam, they're so far ahead it doesn't matter. But you can keep more of a lid on it the longer the game goes. They intimidate teams from the get-go and try to have it all over by three-quarter time. But they can fall off if you stay with them and show it's not affecting you. They're great front-runners. They get ahead and kick on because their confidence is up. But the longer you stay on their tail, the more nervous they get and that's where our team is better equipped, at the back-end of tight games. Before, if we were ever down, we would find it so hard to come back. If we were winning we'd struggle to hold the lead because we were worried about the other team coming back and beating us. Winning or losing, we struggled to keep our composure. But now it doesn't matter what the score says. We've got that drive and belief. Whether we're in front or behind, we just play.'

BOXALL: 'Ryley is crucial to our success. He's turned from the young ball of fat that he was into this fully grown ball of muscle. There's still a little bit of fat, but he's a muscular boy now. He was relatively quick in Athens but nowhere near as fast as he is now. His game is a lot smarter and he's picked up a lot of tips and tricks from Brad and everybody else. He has a lot of advantages over the other guys and that's great for us. He fits into the freak category. Being born with his disability, he knows exactly how to use his body. A lot of the other guys playing this sport are still getting used to their bodies. A lot of people forget we've got these whole new bodies we're trying to work out. Ryley can use every single muscle he has. They automatically compensate for whatever position he's in. That's got to help him—and us. He's nineteen. Even now, if you want to go by disabled ages, I'm eight and not many other players here are more than ten. Ryley is nineteen in disabled years and that's a massive advantage. He's been outstanding for us. We couldn't have asked for any more from him.'

WILMOTH: 'Not for one second are we taking Australia lightly. Believe me on that. We're going to have to push every minute, all game. They have an incredible player in Ryley. I only met him for the first time in June. I'd heard about him because we've got a similar disability and we play a similar game. He seems like a good guy. I don't know him, really, but he's an awesome player. I will definitely say that, he is an awesome player. He will be an incredible competitor to go up against. Oh man, this is going to be a battle.'

ZUPERMAN: 'We know Australia are a threat. The leaps and bounds they've taken in the last year and a half with Dubberley is wild. He's revolutionised them. He's changed the way they play, the way they view the sport, the way they train and how seriously they take it. Their guys used to be just cutting up and having fun. We knew that and it made it a hell of a lot easier against them. We haven't played them since Athens, so we'll have to see what shape they're in now but to get this far, they're obviously in very good shape. They're a different group.'

Why haven't you played them since Athens? Running scared? Afraid? Give us one of your honest answers. None of that cliched 'we've just never crossed paths' crap. 'Thing is, we've just never crossed paths,' he says. 'The world championships, they lost to Great Britain to miss out on the semi-finals, so we missed them there. Canada Cup, they didn't get through again. We know they're going well, and I know why they are. Ryley is getting older and the players have respect for Dubberley because he knows the game. He's been playing since he was itty-bitty. When you have a coach you respect, when you can really see the qualities you want in a coach and a leader, you start enjoying the game more. And then you start playing better solely because you're having fun. Playing for someone you don't respect is a drudge, man. That is not enjoyable. And if you don't enjoy it, why do it? If it's a drudge, you're not going to win because you don't really give a shit. Part of being a successful player is wanting to play well for your coach. Our team has that, and so does Australia. We're looking forward to this. It's going to be a knock-down drag-out.

'There are a lot of people who want that gold medal, and now there are only two teams left. They'll be playing just as hard as us. We can't just walk up and say, "Yeah, we're going to win this one." We have to play our game. We know how much they want to beat us. They don't have to say it, we can see it in them. There's confidence, and there's cockiness, and I think we're nothing more than confident. We're confident about how we play, but we still have to play the game. It's as simple as that.

'I've got some thinking to do afterwards—this might be my last Paralympics. I really don't know where I'm heading, but I really want to win a gold medal before I go. We've won everything else. To win a gold medal at this level—if that happens, I don't know, that might be the swansong. That might be the time to say, "Okay, that's it." But just having the opportunity is a blessing.'

DUBBERLEY: 'I've gone through our whole team and we've got 54 possible combinations. We'll stick to six. Ryley has energy from the get-go. Naz is just Naz, picks them off and smiles at them for a bit. Our two-pointers, it depends on who we're playing against—this time it'll be Bryce and Greg. We could just as easily go for Scotty and Greg, Scotty and Cam, whatever. I like the look of our twos. They're all interchangeable but because Cam and Smithy are so mentally strong, we're better off having them out there towards the end. Bryce is just Bryce. He can play at any time in any game. Scotty is more of an X-factor, the same as Ryley and Naz. He can do freakish stuff. He's good to throw into the game as soon as we can. Because he's smaller, I think he gets overlooked by the other teams. He can go with America's pace but I doubt they even worry about making too many plans for him. Scotty is different to what he was a year ago. If we're down, Scotty used to find it hard to plough through that. Now he's more switched on. He knows it's not that bad. If we've got Ryley out there, we're always going to be a chance to come back. You can't bank on that, but it's good for blokes like Scotty to have that in their heads. Whatever happens, Ryles can pull something out of his backside for us. George can carry the ship when Ryley's not out there. Even if we play half-a-point down—George and two two-pointers and a point-five—George can carry that. Even if it's just for five minutes, he can keep it at the level we need to be at and then Ryley comes back on with more energy, and we can go up another level again. It's like tightening a chain. I just really, *really* like the look of our team. Ryley *could* play the whole game—but it's too much. He's had four tough games in four days. We could do it as an absolute last resort but it's just so draining and demanding. And with George here, we don't need it. Ryley is better off having a spell—he can do more in 25 minutes fresh than he can by staying out there the whole time.'

DUBBERLEY ON NOT PLAYING THE US SINCE ATHENS: 'To a point, it might work in our favour. They haven't had much court time against our boys. They haven't played Ryley. Or a few of them have, but it was a long time ago. He's a man now. The Ryley they're about to play against isn't the same Ryley they played last time. That game was somewhat thrown because of Scotty and Ryley's classification issues. The last time we had a full-on game against America was six years ago, at the 2002 World Championships. George got stuck into Kirkland, and Kirkland didn't like it. Finally we're getting another shot at them. This is what we wanted. It's what we've waited all year for. We're thinking we can win. If we're turning up thinking we're going to lose, that's exactly what would happen. I'm really confident. I just can't work out a way they can match us if we're at our best. We think we're a shot. I *know* we're a shot.'

HUCKS: 'They're talking about the rugby on TV back home. That's huge for us. When I first started playing, we were the also-rans, no-one had a clue who we were and no-one cared. They had us behind bars. But people back home have started to realise the excitement in the game. A lot of people watching this tonight will want to see another game. People I know back home, the people at work who let me do this, they'd never watched any of it before. But they're buzzing. They're like, "When are you playing at home? When can we come and watch?" It's gone from having no-one knowing about us to everyone being like, "How do we get tickets?" We're in the game now. A few more people are starting to give a shit.'

~

Is the real China the outer Mongolian grasslands and all the beautiful nothingness surrounding the nomads in their tents? Or is it the property developers eyeing off the sacred sites, the burial lands, the temples? Give a Mongolian enough moonshine and he will decry the death of the real China. Is the real China the al fresco dining or the dogs and penis on plates, or the fast food joints popping up like pimples or the McDonald's near Tiananmen Square? Is it the saturation levels of police and army tanks? The death penalty for drug offences or the 12 million Chinese individuals currently addicted to heroin? Is it the 20 million cars on the roads or the 600 more joining them every day? Is the real China the luxurious lounge bar of the luxuriant hotel where the piano man is surrounded by elegant models pouring themselves over the guests while they give everyone their wine? Is it the kid taking a piss on the sidewalk while his father watches or when the father drops his own pants and takes a piss himself? Is it the billions of texts and microwaves and radiations in the air of a city obsessed with all the electronics presently killing the planet? Is the real China the first woman to be on the front line of policing, a job she proudly declares is eliminating the dark side of human society for the good her her country, or the day her family told her she should be ashamed of herself for showing such professional ambition? Is the real China being told that yes, sir, you can go wherever you want—if you have the right permit. Is it the thousands of miles of red lanterns lining the cluttered streets or all the unwalked miles of abject darkness? Is it the taxi driver who winds down his window so he can hurl abuse? Is the real China the dainty little red slippers on the princess' feet or the purple, green and gold Nike pumps? Is it the pretty girl whose job it is to take your rubbish and put it in the bin for you at McDonalds? Is it the peck on the cheek she gives every night? The Pepsi Max? Is it the construction sites and the eight-lane freeways all clogged like a smoker's aorta? When does the building ever end? When does Beijing become happy with what is? Is the real China going a full week without seeing blue sky? Is it the grime and the dirt on your skin and your teeth? Or is it the Chinese gymnast forced to train six hours a day, six days a week, between the ages of nine and twelve because she had been identified as a good jumper at four. The girl was forced in a boarding school and only allowed to see her father for three hours one afternoon a week. He would mark their time together by taking her on a ten-kilometre run. Twleve-year-olds at her academy were told to train with their broken legs still in plaster casts, doing situps with heavy weights on their backs like black Mississippi slaves, taught the virtues of high pain thresholds and mental toughness from the age of nine. 'Daddy, I don't ever want to go back to the academy,' she tells her father in a crimson voice. He tells her that she has to, and then he beats her. She falls during her competition trials and her berating coach tell her, 'You have performed terribly even though we have practised it for years.' The fallen face of that girl after her fall, is that the real China? That feels like the real China.

~

Canada and Great Britain butt heads for the bronze medal. The Hall Of Overwhelming Glory is full of pomp and ceremony. Dawn killings at the sacrificial altar. The bristling and idealistic determination of The Herculean Jason Roberts is slowly replaced by the most profound disappointment. He fights the inevitable as long as he can, as if there must be some cosmic law preventing you from trying this hard but leaving empty-handed. He cannot fathom how GB are going home without a medal. They held their pre-Paralympic training camp in Macau to get used to the heat, they've gone as far as wearing their stupid Great Britain team shirts all day and night to signify their unity, they've employed full-time staff and lined everyone's pockets with silver and now—nothing? Ratshit fourth? Barrow is knocked out. One finger is placed in front of his bloodless face. He's asked how many fingers and replies by going cross-eyed. How many fingers now? One. He stays on. Ellwood sneaks a box of Corona beers into the Australian dressing room. The beer is wrapped in a white towel to avoid offending any lingering Chinese sensibilities about having a good time.

The Herculean Jason Roberts plays in an increasingly gallant but hopeless fashion. O'Connor and Benoit Jett wear impeccable suits. Dubberley does not. The Herculean Jason Roberts is involved in every play in a really valiant attempt to wrestle a medal away from the Canadians, but his big, round hopeful eyes become sad. He's trying to bring someone dear back to life after the doctor has already pronounced her dead. Give it up. The mood is ferocious. The crazy-eyed American guy with his flag around his shoulders runs more laps of the stadium. You think for a second it's Christopher Igoe, but it's not. It's still either Hendrix or God.

Canada prevail 47–41. GB have finished fourth and fourth is the worst place of all. Everyone else gets a medal but you can't have one so go away. The Herculean Jason Roberts keeps looking at the scoreboard and it's over? He's blinking and just staring at the scoreboard like a broken man singing the hollowest blues after a lifetime of mistakes and hurt. You tell him he's a behemoth and try to make him understand that he has been a sight to behold this past week. His head stays low but then these big tear-filled eyes rise from his lap. They're centimetres away from your own and these huge wet orbs are pleading like he wants someone to tell him it's okay, mate, you can still have a medal. These big globes are like the photographs taken of the blue marble planet from outer space and he says, 'I'm really, really sorry, but I can't speak. I just can't do it.' And then a grown man blubbers. It's galling. You can look at a man in a wheelchair without feeling an inch of sympathy, but when you see a grown man cry you feel like falling apart and singing some blues yourself and then Jason Roberts wheels himself away, away, away.

WILLSIE: 'I wouldn't wish that on anyone. I finished fourth in Sydney and I never want-the-fuck to do that again. We've won, we've gotten ourselves a medal, but I'm still bitter about losing to Australia. That was a tough one to walk away from. We didn't hide from that, we used it to help us get up for the bronze. But to lose a semi-final so closely, we thought we deserved that gold or silver medal. We looked so good for so long against Australia. When you go into overtime and lose, even if we know the Aussies are a good team, to lose the way we did was crushing. I'm just cheering like a mad man for the Australians in the final. I've got to tell you, when the Americans were watching our game, they were a bunch of classless fucks. You can write that—classless fucks. It's going to bite them on the ass some day. Hopefully today. The fact that America was cheering for Australia in that game was a slap in the face to the Australians. We're the only team that has ever beaten the Americans. You get that? No other country has ever beaten the Americans in this sport, and we beat them again a month ago. I know they were afraid of us. I know they didn't want to play us in the final. I hope they're taking the Australian team lightly, and I hope you guys stick it down their throats. I'm going to go and grab a cold goddamn beer and cheer some green and yella.'

That's green and gold, champ. But thanks.

THE INVALUABLE CAMERON CARR: 'Willsie was going off after we beat Canada. He was like, "Guys, just go out there and beat those effing pricks." Canada just don't like them. It's very similar to our relationship with the Kiwis, but they've taken it to the next level.'

THE GENIUS NAZIM ERDEM: 'If we put them under pressure, I think it will get to them. They've lost to Canada, and we've beaten Canada, so that makes us pretty confident. America are number one and they deserve to be, but they haven't come up against us yet. I think they're very wary. I think they're not sure what we might do if we get it right. They've been following us around with their little video camera for the last year. They might not have wanted to play us, but they've been pretty keen on having a look at us. They wouldn't have bothered if they weren't worried. They'll be confident they're going to beat us, but we're a dangerous team. I haven't seen them play much and I haven't wanted to. You can overdo it. You can psych yourselves out; if you watch them too much you start seeing things that aren't there. I think the best rugby you can play is on natural ability and instinct. If you're studying and watching them all the time, all you end up thinking about is them. Let them worry about us. That's what Brad has done well—he's always telling us to just worry about us. To play for a gold again—everyone is feeling positive. We think we can do it. It would mean so much to beat them. It would mean that on this day we're the best team in the world and nothing could ever change it. We'd have that for the rest of our lives. It would mean the world to me.'

THE GENIUS ON WILMOTH: 'I haven't really seen him on the floor, but Brad is saying he's not a goer. He's not going to stay in the game long. He's still new, he's still inexperienced, he'll probably turn the ball over a few times. He doesn't get on the court that much. They've got him, we've got Ryley. We'll take Ryley.'

GUMBERT: 'Our ultimate goal was to win five games. We have four under our belt and now it's time to get the last one. What Nick Springer and Joel Wilmoth have given us has been unbelievable. They're the two youngest kids on the team and they've come over here and played like seasoned veterans. Their defensive performances have been phenomenal.'

SPRINGER: 'Our biggest strength is that we're eleven-guys strong. There are eleven different starters on this team and we can confidently play any one of them at any point in the game. We are ready to go.'

ZUPERMAN: 'This is where we wanted to be. Every one of us from the Athens team can remember what the bus ride felt like after we lost in the semi-finals. We don't want to be feeling like that again on the way home tonight. We're playing our butts off and it's showing. But we've only taken small steps to this point. We didn't come here to play in the gold medal game. We came here to win it.'

DUBBERLEY: 'We just have to adjust, accept how big it all is and be excited by it. Whoever gets control of themselves the quickest will win. It's all in the emotions. You just have to adjust to the kind of scene and environment you're not used to. You have to realise it's the biggest event of your life, but you have to find a way to relax in a situation where it's probably not normal to relax. There's that balance being motivated by something that's big—who knows, we might never get another chance in a final like this—but not making it too big in your own head. You've almost got to trick yourself into playing it down—but not too much.'

KIRKLAND: 'Ever since Athens, my motivation has been to make up for the mistakes we made there. We should have been the gold medal winner but we came out playing flat. Over half the team, it was their first time to compete at that level. It was the deer-in-the-headlights look. The pressure got to several guys because they knew the pressure was on us. I just want to get the gold medal back to the USA. We are a dominant force in wheelchair rugby and if we play our game the way we know how, nobody will get in our way. They can't hang with us.'

~

Written on the inside of Hucks's forearm in giant black ink is the word PUSH. Dubberley has the same temporary tattoo. Boxall looks at the US doing their warm-up. Dubberley tells him, 'Concentrate on us. Just us.' Captain Red Shirt rolls up his sleeves as though he is preparing for a physical confrontation. You have no idea. The Australian Captain and Honky Tonk Bakonkadonk receive the referee's instructions. The rest slowly move around the perimeter, sizing each other up and down while retaining an ominous calm. The Australians link arms. They yell who they are—STEELERS. They yell what they want to do—PUSH. Dubberley imparts his final words of wisdom. Batt looks blankly at the glue-pot floor. Dubberley says something in Batt's ear and they laugh. Dubberley slaps his thigh and all the while Nick Springer is watching them.

The players line up. Hucks faces Chance Sumner. Stare-off. Hucks could give a fuck. When he sees someone trying to mess with him, when it finally registers they could be bothered with some doomed attempt at mental disintegration, he laughs. Get out of here. The fuck out of here. Batt and Zuperman are paired up. We're about to learn if Mark Zuperman really is overrated like Ryley Batt said all those months ago in his little slice of God's country. Mark Zupan has 32 minutes plus stoppages to prove otherwise. When all the interruptions, time-outs, heart attacks and pit stops have come and gone, if Zuperman has been the difference, Batt should take the microphone from the gutter-voiced commentators and deliver a formal apology. Hogsett is talking his usual shit. He's like the worst kind of drunk, an angry drunk. Buddhism says the three poisons of the mind are ignorance, craving and hatred. Hogsett is screaming. *You got your A games?* That's what Hogsett is saying. *You're gonna need your A games. You got your A games?* Hogsett should shut up. He's wasting his time even being here. He can bash his gums all he likes because he's unlikely to play a single second. Go away! What a pest. You got *your* A game? And then he comes up with this. He looks up and down the line of Australian players and says in a doomed voice: 'You ready for 32 Minutes of Hell?'

Springer with a mad grin. His father keeps saying that everything is fine back home. The problem with *fine* is that it never really is. Gary Springer has made a concerted effort to shield his son from the fact that his mother is dying right now in her New York hospital bed. She may not last long enough to see the end of the game. You watch Springer and think of a miraculous place inside The Temple Of Heaven called Echo Wall. It's round and perfectly cylindrical, designed for soft and calming conversation. Send the faintest whisper along the wall and you can be heard by a friend 60 metres away. Tell someone on the other side of the world that you love her, and she will hear. Every day from the start of the tournament, Nancy Springer's voice has weakened to the extent that it has now become a hush. Her son makes enough noise for the two of them. *Yeah, got your A games?* His nostrils are flared and his eyes are wild and he's looking for one more dust-up. He's motoring around before the tip-off telling the Australians, 'You ain't seen nothin' like me, you ain't EVER seen nothin' like me.' The reality is that the Australians ain't ever seen someone with so much to play for. His mother is fading from life with a laptop computer on her bed so she can watch them playing leapfrog while the cancer slowly takes her away. She will drift in and out of consciousness while the game, just a game, is played. When she descends into unconsciousness, her friends will bring her back to the land of the living by yelling, 'Nick just stopped the ball! Nick just scored!' She will wake every time the commentator calls her son 'Nick The Tank' for the strength he displays in muscling up to Ryley Batt. The commentator does not know the half of it.

There is so much noise that you don't even hear the whistle that signals the beginning of an end. Australia's starting four: Batt, Old Age and Treachery, Alman, The Genius Nazim Erdem. For the US, we have Springer, Cohn, Groulx, Kirkland. Batt gets the tip-off. Springer jumps on him but Batt scores by running rings around Cohn. Australia lead the final of the Beijing Paralympic Games (Big Dance) by the margin of one goal to nil. Hogsett is still talking but no-one pays him any mind. Springer forces a turnover from Batt and the Australian scratches his head. Springer is going to jump on Batt all night, all night. Gumbert looks like a Wall Street stockbroker. Dubberley does not. Batt gets busy as Kirkland starts quietly. Batt and Springer are all over the court like mosquitoes that no-one else can hit. Gumbert's instructions are issued with the stern pointed finger of a High Court judge. Springer really is giving it to Batt. A loose ball is swooped on by the Americans and they go two-up. Early days yet, so two-up is inconsequential. But still. Batt keeps Cohn covered in his own half. He has him under control while going at half-rat power. Cohn is slowish. His handling of the ball will always be poorish. Batt tries to snatch the ball from Kirkland, but he's used his quota of steals for this lifetime.

The US keep their early lead and Ed Suhr starts shadow boxing. It is difficult to deny Ed Suhr the right to any moments of extreme happiness. Batt juggles the ball and it bounces free but he gets it back. Batt hand-balls it straight to Old Age and Treachery, who swerves past Kirkland to score. Batt chases Cohn at full tilt. It's the kind of mismatch provided by a rhinoceros and a deer. Batt is flying from one side of the court to the other. The ambulance should start its engine. Somebody is going to get hurt. Probably Andy Cohn. It's full throttle. The fastest beginning to any match this year. Cohn escapes assault and battery by a hair's breadth. Hogsett keeps screaming at Batt but does he really think Ryley Batt could give a stuff about his moronic ramblings? Batt's passes start finding their mark. But the fact he has to pass is a worry. Every time he looks up, he sees Springer. *You ain't ever seen nothin' like me.* Groulx grits his teeth and pushes. The veins in his neck expand to bursting point.

He tries to hit Batt but succeeds only in landing in the Australian's lap—with a broken thumb. Australia's defence is so all-encompassing that the US use all their time-outs in the first quarter. There is alarm in the American camp, and Dubberley can smell it. Cohn keeps getting caught. The Americans are being pushed around behind the back shed: *You're not so tough are you?* You swear that every time Cohn gets the ball, he's going to drop it. He appears to be a genuine danger—to the US.

The Rebel Scott Vitale guns down a goal. Alman forces a turnover off Kirkland. All the metallic tape on Kirkland's tall and angular frame makes him resemble Tin Man from the Wizard of Oz. *Oil Can*. It's 8–all. The problem with watching the US from a too-respectable distance for four years is that they have attained some sort of mythical greatness that may or may not be warranted. The Genius Nazim Erdem is right: You run the risk of seeing prowess that isn't necessarily there. You see supposedly great things that need only be classified as very good once they are viewed in the flesh. The Americans are the larger-than-life ensemble cast from the Hollywood movie so they *must* be great, right? But perhaps they are not. Canada beat them because they know them. Playing them so often has stripped away the aura. It's like meeting your hero and being told to fuck off. He's just a man. Discoveries don't have to be a first look at something new. They can be a fresh look at something old. A pass from Erdem to Never Walk Alone goes askew. The US are still two-up. Quick starts are their greatest trick. Christine Batt is wearing face paint. She is a nervous wreck, and for that reason she is not alone. The US lead 12–10 at quarter time.

Hogsett bursts onto the court in a gust of wasted breath, bumping chairs with Cohn. Hogsett—with respect, it doesn't matter if you have your A game. You haven't played a single second yet. Go fetch the coffees, o sluggard. Reiger and McBride come on. Never heard of either of them. Carr does a great pick-up with Tropical Cyclone Wilmoth on his tail. Batt tries his trademark squeezing-just-inside-the-witch's-hat-on-one-wheel trick to score, but Wilmoth shoves him aside in a small but significant moment. The US have the requisite muscle. Batt gives a high one-handed pass to Vitale while Ellwood sits quietly near the spare wheels and a toy kangaroo.

Vitale forces Wilmoth into error. Australia trail 14–13 with possession of the volleyball inflated to within an inch of its life. Wilmoth hurtles towards Batt but a split second before they collide, Batt throws a long ball to Vitale. Batt gladly takes the hit because Vitale is taking the goal. Tropical Cyclone Wilmoth will only be out here for a short time but while he is, he will be a squalling hurricane. His duty is to unleash merry hell in a whirlwind five-minute stint before his blood and thunder and lightning dissipate and the eye of the storm moves off court. The Rebel Scott Vitale's sister finds the full voice of a Renaissance choir. Her brother receives the ball with barely an inch up his sleeve and scores. Dubberley applauds and grins. Australia lead the United States 15–14 in the final of the Paralympic Games and they have more than withstood the opening five minutes and holy crap they could win. After the Oceanias and the Super Series at Aqua-*what*? and the Vancouver debacle (but from where the great avengers were born), they are in The Big Dance and they are winning it. They have a first-quarter lead. You could cry on the spot. Stop it. You watch this game, you just really, really *watch* it. Is this for real?

Hogsett! We liked you in the documentary but what are you *doing*?! He's yelling straight at Batt and Vitale. If he wants to scream, why doesn't he encourage his teammates? Springer strikes Batt with an elbow which, to pay the man his due, is all he can strike him with. Batt is threatening to do it all over again and by that we mean just cast his lengthy and intimidating shadow all over this game and just be the difference between victory and defeat. Athletes do not receive enough credit. None of these players have just lobbed in Beijing and started playing. They have worked tirelessly to build their strength and fitness and skills. Professional golfers talk about how, the more they practise, the luckier they seem to get. Great endeavours are no flukes. Only God-given artistic genius could have created the Statue of David or the ceiling of the Sistine Chapel, but Michelangelo said, 'If people only knew how hard I work to gain my mastery, it wouldn't seem so wonderful at all.' If every person worked at their craft as hard as professional athletes work at theirs—the determination has to be coupled with a passion. A *need* to do it. Hard work without passion is pointless, a blank page. Here's passion:

Michelangelo hitting the knee of his statue of cupid and sobbing, 'Why don't you speak to me?'

Hogsett, shut up! Why are you speaking at all? The Americans are glaring at each other, turning on each other, resentful and confused, looking for someone else to blame. Batt is going less than ballistic, playing with an assured air rather than atomic intensity, rolling around all comfortable effort but still appearing to be at another place that doesn't really exist—terminal velocity. He's picking and choosing his moments to hit the accelerator. Kirkland tries to steal the ball from The Rebel Scott Vitale. The Rebel Scott Vitale laughs in his face. Batt topples over, calling time-out a millisecond before he thuds to the floor. Kirkland fouls The Invaluable Cameron Carr. The Invaluable Cameron Carr mocks him. The high-and-mighty Americans are being cut to size and what a sight to see! Kirkland is ineffective. The demeanour of his players is not entirely attractive. The other six teams are all watching and led by the beer-swilling Willsie, they want nothing more than to see the Americans fail. They can win this, Australia, they really can.

The Invaluable Cameron Carr's handling is outrageously good, but time after time, when Batt gets the ball, Springer traps him with help from Groulx and Cohn. Batt throws an overhead pass for The Invaluable Cameron Carr or The Rebel Scott Vitale to sneak away and score, but it's the hardest yakka and infinitely more desperate than any of their goals against the Kiwis, Canada and GB. Batt sails down the right sideline and the benched Tropical Cyclone Wilmoth, watches the motorcade go by. Update on the court time for Hogsett: nil. The Rebel Scott Vitale opens space for Batt to score again. The US players are yelling at the referee, yelling at each other, they're telling the referee and each other what should be happening and demanding to know why it isn't. They are a bunch of spoilt children who Gumbert is going to struggle to keep under his control if they don't get their way. Australia stay one-up. Mother of God! The Cretinous Red Shirts are angry and agitated and what a beautiful thing it is. A turnover to the US. Captain Red Shirt buries his face in a towel because the US are about to descend into civil war. This says a lot about The Red Shirts. When the US are winning, when it's easy for them to become involved, they are front and centre.

But when the US are in the fight of their lives, when they actually need support, they sit at the back and bury their faces in towels. The US take a 21–20 half-time lead and both teams receive their urgent debriefings and Springer is yet to take his eyes off Ryley Batt. The Australians are in the way of what he wants: the fulfilment of an important and heartflet promise.

This is turning feral. Groulx drops the pig's head. The Rebel Scott Vitale is ruthless enough to grab it, score and scowl. Tropical Cyclone Wilmoth replaces Springer for another search-and-destroy mission. Batt is about to be hit like he's rarely been hit before. The US bench led by those of a cretinous disposition holler, 'De-Fence! De-Fence!' Batt Sc-Ores! Batt Sc-Ores! A wild pass, Old Age and Treachery taps the ball into his lap and registers a goal. HUGE de-fence from Batt, this is the best player in the world by the length of Route 66, but Australia turn it over again. Opportunities to pounce on the shaken Americans are not being taken. Those small moments that decide The Big Game or The Otherworldly Game or The Life Game are not going their way as they did against the muggers and O Canada. Kirkland starts scoring and in no way is it his fault that he looks like the Tin Man. *Oil caaan*. Cohn whinges about a referee's call. Why whinge? A referee has never changed his mind because an athlete started crying, and he's unlikely to start doing so now. Slim Shady keeps complaining and the crowd keep booing him. There's a great deal of entertainment to be had in watching the US go down the gurgler. Slim Shady is only egged on by The Cretinous Red Shirts and you're here to suggest that people who whinge should be bitten by a snake every time they do it. If it happens, if the unthinkable actually occurs and they lose, the Americans are not expected to take defeat especially well. Hogsett, got those coffees yet? Twenty-two flat whites and some manners to go.

Alman's inbound misses the mark. Batt tries to push the ball to Old Age and Treachery but it goes over the sideline. The US still lead by one. But now they have the ball in readiness to extend the lead to two. Kirkland needs his elbow strapped. Egyptian mummies have less wrapping. The US go two-up. *Another* turnover. The US are three-up. No, no, no. Please no. Zuperman flexes a bicep. He has plenty of time to do so because he still hasn't been on the court, either, sullenly sitting with Hogsett like they're the boys at school no-one wants to play with. Batt still looks at ease and he is still hammering away even if the breakthrough isn't immediately forthcoming. He hits Cohn so hard that Cohn snaps forward, lurching as if he's projectile vomiting.

Hucks comes on as Batt departs for his nap. Australia are 31–27 down with three minutes remaining in the third quarter. A rolling ball and The Australian Captain scores. Zuperman is moving up and down the sideline, dropping the hint that he would like to actually play if that is at all fucking possible. Another loose ball and Cohn, of all the uncoordinated people, is the one to latch onto it. And score. Springer is talking incessantly to Hucks. They should call a time-out so the two of them can go outside and sort it out. Springer tries to burn Hucks, but fails. Back in your box, boy. Australia are in the four-down-then-three-down cycle. Not quite a disaster, but very nearly. Hogsett has stopped giving lip. Gumbert is the only man in the joint who can silence him, and he's done just that by refusing to play him. Zuperman and Hogsett keep looking at the clock. Are we going to win? With just as much urgency, are we going to get a game here? Zuperman rolls once more down the sideline. Gumbert doesn't even look at him.

Never Walk Alone sits alone in the sin-bin. He gazes around the stadium to make sure the mental snapshot of this scene and place will never fade, firing off all these internal digital photographs to be framed and hung on the walls of his mind. Batt returns for one last storming of the gates. The Australian Captain veers around Kirkland for a goal. Porter has played a terrific game and never give up, even if it's all so bleeding obvious that you should, just don't ever give up. Hogsett is so smug. Why is he so smug? Gumbert waves him away and he's less smug. Five-down becomes six-down. A second-half charge requires an early goal, not the conceding of one. Tropical Cyclone Wilmoth scores at speed. Now he's sharing a court with Batt, a direct comparison can be made. Batt is light years ahead. Plenty of observations made here and elsewhere are unashamedly drenched in Australian bias, but not that one. Old Age and Treachery keeps shouting encouragement. Australia need five or six turnovers in the next five or six minutes. Sometimes impossible is just plain impossible. Batt keeps toying with Cohn. Dubberley grins broadly. Batt crunches Kirkland. He slices through a Cohn–Kirkland gap like neither of them exist and maybe they really don't. Win, lose or draw, Ryley Batt has been the single most electrifying sight of the Paralympic Games.

In this realm of anything being possible, this magnificent world where a man with no legs can become a bona fide sporting superstar, Australia should be allowed to win. What a joy it would be to scribble-scribble-scribble about Australia overpowering the US in an improbable and stirring victory. What excess bliss there would be in detailing how Ryley Batt flies around Springer and Wilmoth to pluck the gold medal off the top of the China-red witch's hat with another last-minute barn-burner. What an ode to joy it would be if Hogsett's incessant nastiness led to him receiving a technical foul, ejection from the venue and deportation back to the United States without legal counsel. What trembling happiness there would be in placing on the public record the looks of the Australian players when the final whistle sounded to signal the start of their reign as champions of the world, champions of the most important world, *their* world. We want to write a detailed and unashamedly over-the-top depiction of the streams of tears running down everyone's cheeks and why can't we just make it all up? Why can't we write a series of alternate endings and you can take your pick? Yes, yes, yes, let's do that! Old Age and Treachery rips his shirt off and swings it above his head while The Gentleman Shane Brand politely shakes everyone's hand and says how well they did and Ryley Batt hugs his mother and tells her he loves her like Bob Lujano did with his weeping old man in the sweeping ruins. Boxall walks! Fiction, non-fiction, fuck it!

Who.

Cares.

Batt and Cohn have their hands on the ball. Cohn ends up on the floor having one last sook. The Australians attempt to defend their territory in a four-man Great Wall: one of mankind's most staggering achievements, forged 600 years ago to close off the northern border of China and ward off foreign invaders. One million labourers built the defensive fortress across 4000 miles of hostile and mountainous terrain—but America score anyway. The Australian bench are leaning forward in quiet contemplation like seven examples of The Thinker and they're all gazing down into Scott Hogsett's 32 Minutes of Hell.

The US take over. The Red Shirts return to making spectacles (testicles) of themselves. Turnovers overwhelm Australia and these are the true fires and burning pits. Australia are six goals down with three minutes to go. You keep thinking that can't be it. There must more time or the chance to repent or another quarter to go or another game to be played but it's become a physical impossibility and the result will stand for eternity. There are too many points to make up on the red electronic scoreboard and too few minutes remaining and the US are about to win and Hogsett *still* has tormented screams and billowing hatred.

But then! The US throw a maniacal pass. Batt screams 'Ball!' and the deficit is back to four. Get it back to two and, a ball game is on our hands. Wilmoth appears to have lost all interest in the pig's head in favour of crushing any chair with an Australian living in it. He hits The Rebel Scott Vitale so hard that Vitale's stiff frame lurches violently back and forward before taking a few seconds to return to an unsteady equilibrium. Batt scores with gravel in his guts and spit in his eye. Groulx scores two straight goals either side of a turnover from Alman. Springer increases the lead to three after the astonishment of a turnover from Batt. The US lift, Australia lift. Groulx sends Kirkland over for a goal. 'Ball! Batt keeps screaming even when the ball is unavailable. He has seen the odd miracle in his time, and performed a couple of his own, but sometimes belief is unwarranted. You wish you could take it back to the childhood games when, if it was all going wrong, you could tell your mates start again, start again, this one's it.

Australia have just conceded two more turnovers and the score is 36–31. They have gone from one-up and then level-pegging to five-down. The scene becomes as quiet and morose as a military cemetery.

You look at all the corpses and think, what happened here?

Batt barges over for two goals in seventeen seconds. There's a hopeful five-to-six goal merry-go-round for a short while and then—and then!—Cohn loses the ball like you knew he would to make it

43–39 to the US and then—and then!—Batt scores and the Australians (Batt, Alman, The Genius Nazim Erdem and The Rebel Scott Vitale) are reinvigorated and the Americans can make no progress and the Australians are piling into them with fists and feet and then Cohn loses control once more. Australia has the ball and then—and then!—for a fleeting second here comes another impossibility and of course it is because such a miraculous week *had* to have one more astonishing twist. The ball goes in the air and the coin is spinning and Australia call heads—but it comes down tails. Springer scores for 44–40. And then—and then—Groulx scores for 45–40. And then—and then—Groulx goes over for 46–40. Batt finishes with 22 goals, 13 assists and a drink of water on the sideline with 39 seconds remaining. Water will always be life. The US score three goals in the last minute to Kirkland, Cohn and Groulx. The score finishes an unjust and misrepresentative 53–44.

Here's your take. Australia entered the largest of all the dances thinking they would win, but human nature took over and they became inquisitive. The final became an exploratory mission to see if their extreme self-belief was warranted and then at half-time, up to their necks in it, not only matching the US but appearing to be the better team, they sat back for a split second and basked in the knowledge of *we really are as good as them*. But in the time it took for that enlightening thought to come and go, the US had pounced. By the time Australia fired up again, it was too late.

Gumbert, Suhr and Springer are all class. A few of their countrymen do not. Dubberley slumps in his chair but then straightens. He slaps The Australian Captain on the shoulder. They have arrived at the Great Hall without guarantees and will be leaving with silver medals. The Red Shirts hug like a couple of humping rhinoceros, slapping Batt on the shoulder and slap him a bit hard, to be honest. Previous descriptions of The Cretinous Red Shirts have been less than complimentary based on nothing more than a negative vibe. With America having won, you've been prepared to forgive and forget because at the very least they have contributed to the dramatic theatre. They've undoubtedly worked hard behind the scenes to prepare the American players for their five triumphant matches so hallelujah for them, but then Batt comes forth with his revelation and The Cretinous Red Shirts are revealed for what they truly are. Disgusting.

'One of their guys came off the court and said to me, "Move", Batt says. 'I was just sitting there, where I was allowed to be, where I was *supposed* to be, and I said, "No, you can go around me." This was during the game. He didn't say anything back—but elbowed me in the face. The big guy. He got me straight in the face. I looked at the ref. He saw it but he just went like that [arms spread] like there was nothing he could do. I was like, "Are you kidding me?" It was a big elbow straight in my face. Nothing happened from the ref so I was like, "Whatever". There was nothing I could do about it. You don't see it in the footage, that's what I'm spewing about. You see me after it, when I'm looking at the referee going, "What about that?" I was really pissed off. It gave me a bit more fire in the belly. It was the second half, early in the third quarter, so it was a shame I couldn't use that to get us home. I'm not too annoyed it happened, who cares, but I am annoyed you don't see it in the footage because it would have showed what an absolute wanker he is. I was a bit dirty, but it happens with people like that, I suppose.'

The guilty party should be banned for life. Or get on the telephone and apologise.

As for Hogsett, Batt says: 'He's just a full-on talker. I could hear him in the background all night but I wasn't going to focus on it. If they want to do that, if they think the only way they can beat us is to start doing that, they can keep doing it because I just don't think it affects any of our players. It would have done in the past but it doesn't now. We're past all that. It's a compliment. It shows how worried they are. We'll get them next time.'

Tomorrow, tomorrow, there will always be tomorrow.

Zuperman is running a gear below the rest of the Americans in their breathtaking revelry. Australian players console each other and it's a sad scene, really, but one journey ends so you just go start another. Carr looks angry. Dubberley hugs him. And then Dubberley does the most bizarre thing—he orders a warm-down. His players hesitate. A warm-down? In preparation for . . . what? The Australian players do as they are told and start rolling back and forth inside The Hall Of Overwhelming Glory. From the baseline to the centre circle they go, back and forth to Dubberley despite their next match being fuck-knows-when. The older players might never play again but here they are, warming down, and what a beautiful and big-hearted thing it is, Dubberley standing in the middle of the court wanting to do everything right till the bitter end. He's watching his players come at him then retreat, looking at his own reflection in the floorboards and then watching even that retreat.

~

The red carpet comes out and you think about Brad Dubberley watching the waves roll in at Palm Beach when the self-confessed cripple first turned up in your life. *Sorry mate, they just had to do some panel-beating on my head*. You think of him crawling across the cream carpet at his cul-de-sac home to pause the video and point out all the intricacies that still make no sense. You think of all the times he's said everything is cool mate, sweet, and you think of Dead Man's Hole in Texas where the green mineral pool is carved into the steep limestone cliff.

'Mark,' Carr says. 'Congratulations.'

Zuperman acknowledges the words but there's no joy. His contribution has been as inconsequential as that of his mate Hogsett: neither of them has played. At least Zuperman hasn't carried on like a halfwit. At least he has retained his dignity. Grace, pride, dignity, those things are king. Zuperman accepts his first and probably last Paralympic gold medal, raising it to the crowd with a wry grin like you do when you're pretending one emotion but those who know you best can see another. Zuperman is royally pissed off and everyone knows it.

'I saw Zuperman after the game,' Carr says. 'I was dirty that we lost, I was throwing my tape in the bin when he came out grumbling. I told him congratulations and he had a bit of a whinge that he never got on. He probably had his publicist there typing up his story, all ready to go, but they had to delete it all because he didn't get to play. He probably had his own TV crew here but they had nothing to film.' Told that Captain Red Shirt elbowed Batt in the face, a deplorable act which in the real world would earn him an assault charge, The Invaluable Cameron Carr laughs: 'Ryles should have jumped on him and bitten him. He should have grabbed hold of him and said, "Ever heard about drop bears, mate? We've got drop bears in Australia—and I'm one of them".'

The largest podium in history is erected to fit the 33 medallists and their 32 wheelchairs. It stinks to the highest heaven that Dubberley, Gumbert and Benoit Jett are denied medals. Their contributions have been immense. Hogsett gets a gold to hang up in the pool room but Dubberley, Gumbert and Jett get nothing for their toil? Ten grand is a joke for the work done by Bradley Wayne Dubberley this year. Acne-covered pre-pubescents dishing up the slop at McDonalds are on more coin. Loaded? Throw some cash at this lot. They don't have a single sponsor. Hogsett *should* get a medal of course. He's part of the winning squad and hurrah for that but when Dubberley is 80 and bald with no teeth, whittling sticks on his back porch, he deserves to have received *something* tangible to remind him of the glory days.

The ceremony begins. Wilmoth stands in the middle of the Americans tall and proud with his hands behind his back like a naval officer ready for inspection. Good on him. Springer looks to the sky all happy-sad, sad-happy, numb more like it. He has played with fire and brimstone and will be the first US player to receive his gold. He has been tremendous. The next time Dubberley sits at his laptop and considers the identity of the American Head On A Plate, it will be Springer. The US anthem is played and that's when Dubberley cannot help imagining his players belting out *Advance Australia Fair* with their faces all unbelievable and kablooey instead of listening to the opening refrain of *O say can you see* . . . Would that not be stupendous right now? To be rejoicing in a rumbling version of *Australians all* . . . But perhaps this is more fitting. Perhaps this is more real. Fairytales are allowed to be bullshit.

'I've never seen anyone dominate a Paralympics like Ryley has dominated here, but he keeps telling everyone he's sorry,' Dubberley says. *Tomorrow, tomorrow, the recurring theme is tomorrow.*

'The world championships are what we have our sights set on now. We'll just start all over again. If he's feeling that bad already—he's only nineteen and in a way, he's only just beginning. It's been a huge year for him. We all had a learning curve at the Canada Cup, Ryley included. He didn't play his best, the team didn't play its best and I didn't coach my best. But I think that played into our favour once we got here. Teams had heard about him but they hadn't really seen him. They know about him now. There is not one person here who could argue against him being the best player in the world. Not after this. He's just been the man of these Paralympics, phenomenal. So many other blokes stepped up. Smithy will end up being my assistant coach. He's put his name in and I'm sure he'll get it. The same deal as me, he wants to do what is best for the team and if he isn't playing again after this, he feels like with his experience, all his expertise with the fitness and everything else, the best way he can help everyone out is to be one of the coaches.'

But what happened here?

During those 32 Minutes In Scott Hogsett's Hell, what happened?

'You have to give America a lot of praise,' Dubberley says. 'They were better on the night but don't worry, we'll get them, I've got no doubt about that. Our boys played really well, but we just didn't keep it up the whole game. That first half was high-quality rugby. The second half wasn't so good. Maybe the Canada game took more out of us than we thought. We pegged them back once but the second time, they got away and we just couldn't go with them. I'm proud of our boys. They played phenomenally all week. It's not quite what we wanted—I'd love to be out here now watching the boys get gold medals, but we could have lost to New Zealand, or Great Britain, or Canada, and not been here at all. We were tough enough to get past those two awesome teams in our group, phenomenal teams, and then we got past Canada on top of it. The boys are getting to take some hardware home and it was a great run to the final. We're disappointed not to have won, but the US played unbelievably. Defensively, both teams were strong in the first half. It's rare in a game of this calibre for both teams to be out of time-outs by half-time, but that's how tough it was. It was close, but the US kicked on. We'll be back. We'll find another big dance.'

Batt is swamped by interviewers and knee-high autograph hunters who have belatedly begun to recognise the subtle differences between a Batt and a George Hucks. 'We were on top of them for a while there, great defence both teams, but there were a couple of little slip-ups and they're a good enough team to make the most of those,' Batt says. 'That second half wasn't our best. We tried to play catch-up, we were a couple down, and the risk in playing catch-up is that it can lead to even more turnovers and you get even more behind. We're a bit upset about it but such is life, I suppose. Great game by the US. They're tough competitors and hopefully we can get them next time. I'm not too disappointed. I'm more disappointed for the guys who might be retiring after this. I wanted to get them a gold medal before they go. Unfortunately it didn't happen today. We knew it was going to be a war when we came in here, and it was. It was the most intense first half I've ever played. I'm actually pretty stoked with silver. Coming here, I was going to be happy having any medal to take home. It's a great feeling and it hasn't sunk in yet. Silver is a better colour than gold, anyway.'

Those are Batt's words straight after the final. Months later, resting his elbows against a pool table in western Sydney, he admits: 'At the time, I *thought* silver was great—it's a better colour, all that garbage. But now, I'm not so sure. I *was* happy enough. I said to myself before we went to Beijing, I'll be happy with any colour medal. And I *was* over the moon. But now, looking back, we had a real chance of getting that gold. We really could have snapped it up. That's what sort of annoys me now. I was stoked, I was like, "I don't care, I don't want the gold anyway", but now I'm like, "We could have had it, we could all have gold medals right now instead of silver." It's put the fire in my belly to do it in 2012. Now I know what the boys have all been through. When Steve and George were saying before the trial "It's not over yet, we've still got to get that gold", I get that now. It's just a weird feeling, saying to yourself, "God, I could have gotten that gold." You sort of feel like an ungrateful person, wanting more than you've got. I'm still happy with silver, of course, but gold would have been so much sweeter.

'Myself, Scotty and a couple of other players hadn't played the US properly before. We played them in Athens, but I was fifteen years old and pretty much can't even remember it. The US definitely know what they're doing out there but I think I put them on a bit of a pedestal and I regret that now. I think a few of us did. Once you're out there on a court with them, they're nothing special. We just didn't play the game we normally play. We saw we could beat them and that kind of put us off, if anything. When we got our turnovers, we threw it straight back. We hadn't done that in any of our other matches. That wasn't us. We'd normally get a turnover and score. I wish we could replay that game right now because I think we'd come out on top. I think if we got one or two goals up on them, they'd fold.'

The greatest competitive surfer in history is American Kelly Slater. He has all the mystique and aura that any professional athlete has ever had. He goes out of his way to avoid free-surfing with his rivals because he knows they hold him in such high regard. He ensures that being in a heat with him, just being in the same stretch of water, is enough to mess with their heads. He knows he is placed on a pedestal and carries an unbeatable air in their eyes, not his, and goes to great lengths to nurture it, rarely if ever surfing with them outside of competition. Asked if he thinks Gumbert employed the same sleight of hand with all of his rejections of Australian match-ups for the previous four years, Batt replies: 'For sure. And because they've got great depth, they can have really strong training hit-outs within their own team so they don't need to play a lot of matches. There's no way they're unbeatable. I can just see us getting after them. It will probably be another couple of years until we get the chance, but I just want another crack at them. One of these days we won't just beat them. We will smash them.'

Gumbert and Springer say what they must.

GUMBERT: 'Congratulations to Australia and Brad Dubberley. They were an incredible opponent with an incredible player on their team. It was a battle, as we knew it would be. We knew it would take us all four quarters. They lived up to the hype. We threw everything at them, everything we had. It was a great match and . . .' Yada, yada.

Springer is distracted. 'That was hard-fought,' he says. 'I'd never played them before, and we went in not knowing what to expect. I think both teams were kind of feeling like that. We knew they had one of the best players in the world but we just played as a team and fought.' *One* of the best players? 'They're a young team and we look forward to seeing what they're going to bring in the future.'

These quiet and respectful words do not even touch the surface of what Nick Springer is thinking and feeling. He's not even in the room, not really.

The Australian dressing room repeats that silver is great, silver is great, but there's a downside to silver. It's not gold. 'Ryley is feeling sorry for himself,' Dubberley says. 'Not that he should be. In no way should he be. He did everything he possibly could have. He reckons he let everyone down. Because he's the main guy, he feels like it's his fault we lost. It's not anyone's fault. They played better in the second half. That's it. We gave everything we could, but it was their night. We're all pretty shattered because we thought we could have won, but we let it slip. When we got into the huddle after the game, I told them we should be proud of ourselves. We set ourselves a pretty daunting goal this year and we nearly pulled it off. We know we can beat them and we will get it done next time. We don't have to harp on with all the sentimental stuff. We all know what we're thinking without having to say it. It's been a great year and that first half of the final, it was anyone's ball game. That second half—you know what that was? It was just sport.'

DUBBERLEY ON THE WARM-DOWN: 'As much as it sucks tonight, we can get America. The game was over but I wanted to finish it off the right way. It might have looked a bit stupid, but I wanted to soak up the support from the families and everyone up in the stands. The Americans could still see us. I wanted to leave a lasting memory. This was our court. I think the most memorable games and the most amazing finishes all had us in them. The best player in the tournament was ours. This was our court and these other teams, the US, Canada, Japan, they were all watching us warm down. We were on our court with no-one else out there. These Paralympics are over, but we've got years ahead of us. I wanted the US and everyone else to know we're not done yet. Who cares what it looked like. I'm glad we did it.'

The US flag goes up. Groulx's chest heaves. He was based in Virginia with the navy when he had his back-breaker of a motorcycle accident. Countless members of the US Paralympic team are war veterans. 'It meant a lot to me to see the flag raised,' Groulx says. 'One of the things that drove me as a competitor was to have that moment; to be able to hear the national anthem played.' Groulx went from being active enough to serve the US Navy to learning how to drive a car with hand controls. The first time he attempted to turn right, he fell in his passenger's lap. Hogsett clutches his medal as if he thinks he's about to be mugged. Dubberley is in the crowd and Australia's players keep looking at him, holding up their medals and pointing at him. That's his moment. That's his reward. In Melbourne and Canada, nobody gave a stuff about him or any of his players. That is still the case but all these blokes genuinely care about each other so nothing else matters. When you know yourself, *really* know yourself, everyone else's opinion becomes irrelevant. ABC has shown every one of Australia's matches in prime time. When the *Sydney Morning Herald*'s chief rugby writer decides on his player of the year, he will overlook the able-bodied Wallabies and give his award to Ryley Batt. When a leading sports magazine lists the toughest sportsmen in the country, they will place Batt above a world champion boxer. They've had just one look.

Captain Red Shirt walks out with a handheld video camera. How you want someone to elbow *him* in the head. He looks pretty pleased with himself. The camera pans the crowd. You tell the camera that its owner is a disgrace. You sincerely hope he hears it when he gets back home and crawls back under his rock.

Eleven Australians are lined up on the medal podium. Their names are Greg Smith, Steve Porter, Ryan Scott, Bryce Alman, Grant Boxall, Scott Vitale, Shane Brand, Cameron Carr, Ryley Batt, Nazim Erdem and George Hucks. They roll forward to receive their Paralympic medals. Dubberley becomes emotional and you could hug him like you would a brother. Chinese princesses in creaseless dresses carry pink flowers. The heavenly angels sing and the Canadians have their bronze medals and they look pleased enough. The Australians are *starting* to understand the enormity of their achievement. Silver is fucking magnificent. Too right. Great Britain have to watch from afar. The Herculean Jason Roberts again fights back tears. He is a man among men. Hogsett sits on his hands while the rest of the stadium applaud the Australians. The stadium erupts when Batt receives his medal. He has burned the house down these last five days. You cannot see Christine Batt in this sea of people but you imagine her dam-busting pride. The ovation for Batt goes on. He looks more and more embarrassed. George, shucks. In his perfect world, Ryley Batt would play, win, duck off home. And *still* Hogsett is motionless while every other player and spectator is applauding Batt. Wilmoth has brushed his hair for the cameras. The Australian Captain blows kisses to the crowd. Somewhere in Beijing, down near Hou Hai Lake, there's a karaoke bar with his name on it. Cigarettes may or may not be involved.

'Coaches should definitely, definitely get medals,' Batt says. 'They're pretty much the heart and soul of their teams. They don't get enough credit. It pisses me off that the staff can't even stand out on the stage with us. It's ridiculous. It doesn't give Brad—or any of the coaches—enough credit.'

DUBBERLEY: 'The whole ride, from go to whoa, has been huge,' he says. 'I'll never forget that medal ceremony. It's the best one I've had and I wasn't even in it. Obviously we wanted the gold but to see the guys get their medals, pointing and looking over our way, yeah, that was a bit of a tear-jerker for me. I did tear up. We're like family. We're brothers. The actual medal—it's just a thing. Doesn't mean anything. That ceremony, when the guys looked over our way, that was *the* moment of the Games for me. We've done something pretty good together. Beating the Canadians, beating the Kiwis, they were really, really special nights. Just that rush to your head in those moments, it's overwhelming and something I'll never forget. A few of the Americans looked at Gumby with their medals—he was in front of us—but only a few did it. I don't know if they've got the same spirit we have. I was looking at our blokes with their medals and thinking, "Yep, that's awesome. Check it out. Bloody awesome."

'But then the American flag went up and that was as gutted as I felt for the whole Paralympics. That was really hard to watch. It could have been our flag. It was so close and so far. The US deserved it, but we deserved it too. They just got us on the day, just a couple of turnovers. It could have been so different. Ultimately, I think we lost because of inexperience and maybe we fatigued too much towards the end. They played awesome in the second half, but we gave them a few soft goals. They're used to playing the really big games whereas a lot of our guys, it was their first final of a major international tournament. Even Oceanias, the Super Series—they're not massively big tournaments. World championships and the Paralympics, they're the big ones. It was live on TV in Australia, the whole bit, it was such a big occasion and not all of our boys are used to that. Next time, we will be.'

TOMORROW. Dubberley relinquished the glory of playing for the back-room satisfaction of being a mentor. But who has mentored him? No-one. He has done this virtually alone. The silver medal he received in Sydney was for himself. The silver he doesn't receive in Beijing is for everybody else. The greatest satisfaction resides in the latter. By the time Dubberley wakes, his phone will have been immobilised by congratulatory text messages. The Gentleman Shane Brand is beaming but then Dubberley is poleaxed by a thought, just a thought. He hasn't played The Gentleman Shane Brand in the final. Brand is the only Australian to have missed out. He doesn't even mention it, so no-one has realised—except Dubberley when it's all too late. His face falls to the floor. Brand could have gone on in those final minutes when Australia were in the seventh layer of Scott Hogsett's Hell. 'I'm shattered about that,' Dubberley says. 'I feel really, really bad.' There's a stark contrast between the reactions of Zuperman and The Gentleman Shane Brand to being denied involvement in the decider. This is not a criticism of Zuperman because he had every right to be disappointed, but it's an irrefutable insight into the incorruptible character of The Gentleman Shane Brand. He wouldn't even think to bemoan his fate. 'Yeah, that's Shane,' Dubberley says. 'Someone else might have asked to go on, but Shane wouldn't do that. He just sat there. I suppose they're at different stages of their careers. Zuperman can be about himself, but our guys have been about the team. Shane is part of our team no matter what.' Batt is *still* aplogising to everyone. 'We're like, "Dude, we don't want to hear you apologise any more", Dubbberley says. 'We wouldn't be where we are right now without you, so shut up about it. The same for Ryan, the same for Naz, we wouldn't be where we are without any of them. We all did everything we could so there's nothing to be sorry for. We put a show on. We gave ourselves an opportunity to win. We've won a medal at the Paralympic Games and that's pretty huge.'

BATT: 'I went up to Steve and George after the game and I did say sorry, I couldn't get them a gold. I shouldn't have said that, but I just really wanted to get them the gold they didn't have. It would have been an awesome way to send them off if they do retire. Hopefully silver is still good enough for them.' Why are you sorry? You've said all year it's not a one-man team so why, individually, are you sorry? 'I feel like I stuffed that game up, in a way,' he says. 'I dropped a lot of balls I shouldn't have. There was a lot of pressure from the US but—we'd get a turnover and I'd throw it back. Stuff like that, I just shouldn't have done. I'm not usually doing that. I still think we deserved to be number one, but we just didn't play as well as the US. The rest of the tournament, I think we probably played better than them. The saddest thing for me is how the blokes from New Zealand are all talking about retiring. I just don't think they can handle what happened to them. It was pretty cruel, those two games they lost. It's difficult for them because they're used to having so much success—it'd be a shame to see them break up because they're such a strong team. I know some of them are getting a bit older and have been playing for a while, but some of them are still new players and they can still have a decent team. It wouldn't be good if New Zealand stopped being a force, but it might be about to happen. I do feel sorry for them.'

THE INVALUABLE CAMERON CARR: 'We've just got to take the next step up and start knocking the US off. It shouldn't be this lopsided with the US and the rest of the world. It's hard to get to play them, that's the thing. They're Yanks and don't like going outside their own little universe. They think everyone should come to them. I was pissed off after the game but I'm alright now. The amount of trash talking they were doing just before we were introduced—it was ridiculous. Hogsett started talking and I felt like saying to the guy across from me, I think it was Kirkland, "Does your mate always go on like this?" I wanted to punch him. They're always loud but you know any time they start to lose, they're going to pipe down. That's where I want to get with them. They'll go quiet and we'll know we've got 'em.

'But it's shattering to lose because I really thought we could beat them. Aussie Rules, they always say the third quarter is the premiership quarter. The breaks could have gone either way, and they went their way. You only need one or two turnovers, the other team drops their head a bit and all of a sudden the difference is four or five and, shit, that's it. At half-time we were like, "These guys aren't all they're made out to be." We won silver, but lost gold. I was devastated and went into the room a bit cranky and Smithy had to go, "Come on mate, we still won silver." And then you reflect on it and that's a pretty good medal to have in the cupboard at home. Shoved in the wardrobe somewhere. And it gives you another four years to get everything right. We've still got a lot of improvement in us, and that's the really exciting thing. It doesn't have to end here. It's just the beginning.'

CARR ON SPRINGER: 'He was unbelievable for them. He wants to come over to Australia and play and I hope he does. I was listening to his trash talk and thinking, "Well, listen to this bloke." There were obviously a few emotions running around there for him. I heard him say, with his flowers, that he was going to give them to his mum. He was the difference. He was getting tired, but they could take him off and still be okay and then he'd come back and fire up again. For us, Ryley was getting more and more tired but he had to keep playing. He'd already played all those minutes during the week and he does so much on the court—if there's one thing he can do, it's probably just trust other people a little bit more so he doesn't have to run around doing everything. It's hard for him to keep up. He's that good he does it anyway, but we've got to help him out a bit more. Credit to America, thought they're very professional and get the job done the big wankers.'

Dubberley keeps saying with absolute certainty that Australia will beat the US at their next meeting. Given the US are so determined to stay 15 000 kilometres away, the world championships in the maples leafs in 2010 are likely to be the next meeting unless some cashed-up entrepreneur steps in and organises what someone really should get going: five matches between Australia and the US over five nights in five different Australian cities. Can we respectfully suggest that kind of series would go off its tits? Failing that, there's every chance two long years will come and go before Australia have the chance to exact revenge.

'We don't have to look up to them at all,' Dubberley says. 'We can just keep trusting what we've got. We can make other teams look up to us from now on. That's what was happening here. By the time we get to London, I think we'll already be number one. Bring that shit on. I think it'll happen. I want to try to poach some athletes from different sports. We need the newly injured—but we also need people who are already elite athletes. Why can't they come over to us? If they see our sport and like it better than whatever they're doing now, why not see if they're interested? The other sports might not like it, but we're not forcing anyone to come. There might be a few out there who want to be involved. Smithy has shown it can work. He's only been playing rugby for two years and look how far he's come. They've already got that athlete's mentality to training and putting in and succeeding. We'll look for some quad amps, some females with the point-five discounts they're going to get, maybe people who are on the track or playing basketball. They could all offer the team a fair bit. We'll throw the net out and see what we can catch.'

Batt becomes a cult figure of Zuperman-esque proportions. 'It's unbelievable, what he's done,' The Invaluable Cameron Carr says. 'I keep thinking about what his parents must be feeling. I mean, I suppose, it would have been so hard having him as a kid and thinking, "What is life going to be like for him?" To have him so welcomed and loved by everyone now—that must be amazing for them to see. He's switched on and nothing goes to his head. There's still that shy side to him that you probably don't see. Sometimes a few of us will go out to dinner. He'll hang back and say, "You go first." Or he'll sort of shy away from groups. There's still that side to him where he might find it a bit harder than he's letting on, but it's incredible what he's doing with himself.'

Hundreds of people mob Batt at Port Macquarie Airport in unprecedented scenes for a Paralympian. 'I still don't like attention that much, I get a bit uncomfortable,' he says. 'But I want to get to the stage where wheelchair rugby is seen as a big sport in Australia. I want it to be the biggest of all the Paralympic sports. I think it should be. It's definitely the most exciting. I'll do anything now with the media. I'll go to schools and talk to them, just to get the sport's name out there, try to get some money in the sport. Hopefully we've started putting wheelchair rugby and the Paralympics on the map. It feels like a lot of people have watched it. I'll go down the street—I was in Brisbane with my mates and people were like, "You're that murder-baller, Ryley." It's pretty cool to hear that. If people know about the sport—unreal. Every town you go to, you get the same thing. I was cruising around Sydney—"Ryley! Ryley Batt!" Sometimes I tell them, "Nah, I'm not Ryley Batt, I don't know who you're talking about." It doesn't always work. Probably not too many people look like me. Little kids are the best—they do school assignments on you, that sort of stuff. It's bizarre to think someone has heard about me and wants to write about me. To have one kid want to do a project on you—it's a bit of an honour for that to happen. To be able to motivate people like that is amazing, but most people still look at you and they're like, "You're in a wheelchair, you can't do much." You go to an airport and go to get your bag—you lean forward and they go to catch you because they think you're going to fall over. You're like, "What?! I'm okay!" They're trying to be nice and you just have to tell them, "I'm sweet, don't worry about me." It takes a while for people to realise what people in wheelchairs can and cannot do. Hopefully that is changing. I just want to keep trying as much stuff as I can. I can't run or walk but there's a way around everything. Or as Steve says, "You can get through anything with a big enough run-up." That's the funniest thing I've ever heard. How are we going to take a run-up? But it's true. Anyone can do pretty much whatever they want.'

A large tattoo is sprawled down Batt's left arm. 'You've got the trees, you've got the mountains, the moon—I'm going to get Shangri-La written around it,' he says. Shangri-La is the Himalayan utopia, the embodiment of the exoticism of the Orient, the permanently happy land. 'Shangri-La to me means Valley of Peace, where I grew up,' he says. 'My farm was Shangri-La. I'll get the other arm done too. It'll be the bad side. Good and evil. One tattoo for each. There's a bit of good and evil in all of us.'

Some kid.

Nancy Springer's heart rate dropped at full-time but spiked again during the medal presentation when her son received his gold medal and looked to where she now resides. HEAVEN AND GOD. 'I was standing there in China, and I was watching him, and I was so hoarse when they put the medal on him,' Gary Springer says. 'I was so proud. It was one of the greatest moments. But I was also thinking that the Games are over and now I have to tell him that we have to leave in the morning because his mother is in a coma.' Nancy Springer passes away the following day. 'She wanted it so much for Nick,' Gary says. 'She wanted it more than anything. She waited for the gold medal game and then she let herself go.'

Nick says: 'This is my mother's medal. It's how I'm going to remember her.'

Nick's parents coined the phrase 'the new normal' to help cope with their changed circumstances when he lost his chunks of arms and legs at the age of fourteen. Nancy's role in the new normal included her mission to raise awareness about Springer's disease and ensure he retained his independence and drive when both could have been lost to the wolves. She succeeded with both before she went to the grave. When Nancy was diagnosed with cancer at the start of the year, Nick's first reaction had been an offer to quit the American team and withdraw from the sport altogether so he could be constantly by her side. She told him to go to the Paralympics and win her a gold medal and now there's a new normal because Nancy is no longer here. Doctors say that in the last 48 hours of her life, her heart rate peaked during the murderball final in Beijing. Nick is last seen under the scorching lights of The Hall of Overwhelming Glory when his fearsome glazed look of the last five days is finally allowed to vanish. He looks so young, scared and innocent. He's asked how he's feeling.

'You know,' he says. 'I cannot feel a thing.'

19

The end

SHIT CREEK, 1 DECEMBER 2008. I am standing in Shit Creek where Brad Dubberley lay with his life in the hands of the skeletal reaper. Freezing water across my ankles. Big old ugly rock is hidden beneath hundred-foot gum trees leaning forward as if they're keeping secrets. I hate big old ugly rock for being so fucking clueless as to what it did in the black and white photograph. I can understand Dubberley's cousin Kelly weeping and threatening to blow the fucking thing up because here's what I want to do: blow the fucking thing up. If there are people in this world abhorrent enough to sell drugs in the shape of teddy bears in the hope they will sucker children into buying them, people prepared to cheat, steal, rape and kill without regard for the consequences, there must be someone out there prepared to hand over enough explosives to turn big old ugly rock and the rest of Shit Creek to rubble. Fucking rock. I want to kick it and punch it and abuse it and get rid of it, but I do not have the right. This is Brad Dubberley's rock and he says it must stay.

'It's not a bad place for me,' he says.

'It doesn't scare me and it doesn't frighten me. It's not even like I think, This is where something really bad happened. It's just like, "Oh, yeah, this changed my life, this place. This is where I had my accident." No-one wants to be injured but time goes on and you get to the point where you're thinking about it all. The first couple of months, I probably did go through the whole, "Why me? Why me? What did I do to deserve this?" But things can go wrong in anyone's life. Money, deaths in the family, I don't know, anything. You keep going. What else can you do? You just have to tell yourself to keep going. It doesn't mean everyone can do it. Some quads will never walk, no matter how hard they try. And it just might not be in someone's makeup to fight. But I wanted to. They told me I wouldn't see the night through, so I wanted to be around in the morning. They said I wouldn't see out the week, so I wanted to get that far. Then they were like, "You're never going to walk again." They thought I was going to die, but they were wrong. I just wanted to do all the stuff I wasn't supposed to be doing.'

One thing has bothered me all year. The moral to the story. Surround yourself with the good people and tell the rest to piss off? One more push, even when you're fucked? Is that it? A dog-eared notebook was kept all through these travels and now the pages are filled with the scribble-scribble of a twelve-month journey that proved I know nothing. I have struggled to understand the reasons for these burdens being handed to such good people. Why isn't quadriplegia delivered to the pedophiles, the drug fiends? *For I will restore faith unto you, and I will heal you of your wounds*, said the Lord. Well, didn't He mean it? Where are His miracle cures? If you are willing. Isn't He willing? Why doesn't He make these people whole?

Big old ugly rock. Pull up a pew. What to think? There's all this scribble-scribble. 'Think big! Think really fucking big! Live large! Live really fucking large! Be full of praise. People require oxygen, appreciation and enthusiasm to survive. No-one will forget what you said. Live with courage, live with integrity and above all, live with passion for nothing is gained without it. Now, now, now. Just live for now. Say yes. Don't doubt, don't fear, don't worry, just say yes. Love everyone and everything but don't just pretend to love them, really love them. Forgive everyone their sins. Half the world's shortcomings would vanish in an instant. Forget all your vendettas and grudges. They are a waste of time. Replace them with grace, mercy and dignity. Be compassionate and generous. Give more than you ever thought you could.' The scribble-scribble is never-ending from these pages about to be left in the creek. 'Wake up! Wake up! Surrender every cell. Thirst for knowledge. Do not ever fucking dare give up. Reach out to your partner, reach out to your friends, reach out to your children. Avoid blame and guilt. Be free! Be free! Go barefoot. Your instincts are strong. You are fearless and committed. Tell yourself from now on. Sing! Sing! Be generous with your finances, generous with your praise, generous with all you have. Disregard all your Plan Bs. Make a Plan A and nail it. Delete your worst memory and your deepest regret. Look your demons in the eye and tell them all to fuck off. Hope, dream, believe. *Thou shalt live*. Fight the good fight. Weep, laugh, hug, plummet, soar. Bruise, bleed, lose a few teeth. Scar and heal because at the end of the day, we're all broken.' All of which is exactly the kind of over-emotional and hyperbolic crap that Dubberley hates.

'We were going after something we wanted, that's all,' he says. 'It doesn't matter what the prize is and it doesn't even really matter if you get it. You can still go after it. For us, it was about sport and trying to succeed. It had nothing to do with disability. We've all moved on from our accidents and the disabled side of it. We don't wake up every morning and spend the day thinking about the past. I don't even see our guys as being disabled, to be honest. They're injured. Even Ryan and Naz, the most affected, they're doing more with their lives than a lot of able-bodied people. I honestly don't see any of us as being disabled. It's not the right word. We're living our lives a bit differently, but we're living as well as anyone. We've just adapted. I've been "disabled" for fifteen years and I don't even see it as being hard. I can walk a little bit but most of the time I have to use my chair, so I just do it. There's no real difference to my life and yours. I can't run around playing footy, but I can still work, drive, have fun, hang out with my mates, do all the same stuff as everyone else. Even for the guys who do use their wheelchairs every second of every day, they've got the fullest lives. They do whatever they want with a few adjustments. Something has happened to us all, but that's just been one part of our lives. Everyone has something happen to them. Deaths, divorces, your finances—it's just the way it is and whatever your situation is, you just have to try to adapt. Don't you?'

A disabled man cannot sleep. He stares at the ceiling and starts matching each of his physical ailments to a letter of the alphabet. A is easy—he's asthmatic. B—he's bald. C—he has cataracts. D—he's a diabetic. The man makes it all the way to Q before he has to stop. Next morning, he tells his wife that he couldn't think of a damn thing wrong with him that started with the letter Q. 'You dear thing,' she says. 'You're quadriplegic.' Among the great mysteries of life: why people with no hardships invent them.

If disabled isn't the word, what is?

'It's not disabled, it's not handicapped—for me, and I can say this and get away with it because it applies to me—crippled is a better word. At least you can have a laugh about it. I'd call myself a cripple. But even that's wrong. A crippled bird can't live like every other bird, and that's not us. We still live in the same world and even if we can't get around in the same way as everyone else, we can still get around. Crippled isn't the word, paralysed isn't the world, handicapped isn't the word. I've racked my brain over this. It's not even physically challenged. I don't know what the right word is, I really don't. Disabled sounds like you're completely broken. You get your phone disconnected and it doesn't work at all. Disabled—it's not a bad word, but it's not good. It's a different way of life, for sure, but plenty of people have different lives to what people might think is normal.'

Fucking rock. A crow stares at me from the top of a gum tree. *You have no business here.* The bushland around Shit Creek is quiet. This is the black and white photograph of where the twelve-year-old boy broke his neck. The woods are thick and full of hissing. I walk along a dirt track. Dark clouds and rain squalls. Fists-full of cloud who are angry enough to swallow me whole. The crow follows me all through the woods. *No business.* The trees are dead with rotting bark. I really can see the twelve-year-old smart-arse gallivanting through this maze of paths and trees. *Snap.* It's so silent and still. *Snap.* I keep looking back. I'm scared by a noise, a broken branch, the hurried marching footsteps, the rat-a-tat- machine-gun talk of his frazzled mates, but no-one is there. The path is thick with stones and weeds. Watch your step. Hate to fall. Deeper into the jungle I go, heart thrumming. The hundred-foot gum trees are blacking out the sky. The sticks are the human snakes. Iron gates to secluded homes are padlocked. A tree has collapsed face-first across the narrow track. *Snap*. The rotting bark is trampled into the earth with everyone else. A bearded man in overalls is carrying a gun. *No business*. Grubs and insects are on the path and the sticks slither back through the gorse. The hill is steep.

'Things can be cut short,' Dubberley says.

'It's one thing to say that, but when you've actually lived it, when everything really does change from one day to the next, you start believing it. I've had it happen to me. A lot of people have. Everything isn't necessarily as permanent as we think. You have an accident, it makes you really think about what you want to do with your life, and how you want to be. A lot of people get to 40 or 50 and they haven't done any of the things they used to really want to do. An accident makes you realise there might not be much time left. People get so busy they don't have time to step back and look at the bigger picture. It doesn't matter if you achieve or not. If you do everything the way you know you should, you can't fail. You're going to focus on different things at different times of your life and if you have a fair dig at all of them, what else can you do? How can you regret anything? You'll look back on it and feel good because you went about it in the right way.

'In sport, you might lose, but does that mean you've failed? Shit no. I think about GB in Beijing, and I don't think of them as having failed. They put up a really good fight. You can get unlucky in sport and lose. You can do everything absolutely perfectly right and execute it all just the way you want, but something happens that you can't control and you get beaten. There's nothing wrong with that. You're going to be pissed off you lost but in 50 years you'll be like, shit, "Look what I did with my life. Look how far I pushed myself." Who cares whether you actually won or not? You might think you have it all sorted, but you don't. Some things are out of your control. You just do not know what could happen next. It's a great thing when you realise that. You kind of get freed up. You stop trying to control everything. You can make all the plans you want, but you have to know they might change. That's not bad. It's good. You might only have one more day to go. Probably not, but you can't know that for sure. What if you did? What would you do then? People need challenges, I think. People need to go find them.'

I'd never felt so cold as when I arrived in Shit Creek. Now I am warm. I'd never been so full of hate as when I first laid eyes on the rock. Now I am calm. I contemplate the rock and what it tried to do. I contemplate the victim and what he has become. No-one can ever be forsaken. Big old ugly rock starts shining like a diamond. Brad Dubberley is alive and kicking like a mule and nothing can be done to stop him.

In the background of the black and white photograph, a blanket has been thrown against the embankment where I now sit. Look at that photograph. The blanket has folded into the shape of a pair of angel's wings. If that is not possible, why is it not possible? Believe in the supernatural. We are here, something from nothing. Is that not supernatural enough? It's the first day of summer and here comes the sun. If you think your problems are insurmountable, think again. If you think your life is a complete fucking disaster, don't give up. If you're totally and utterly convinced it's simply not possible to achieve whatever you want in this lifetime, don't be so sure. You know what? Let's not get pithy. Not everything can be a fairytale. Maybe your life really is up the chute, you damn fool. Maybe you'll never achieve your heart's desire. But you know what else? You just might.

Printed in Great Britain
by Amazon